PEACE, LOVE & LATTES

Also by Darrin Bell and Theron Heir

Rudy Park: The People Must Be Wired

PEACE, LOVE & LATTES

A RUDY PARK COLLECTION

BY DARRIN BELL & THERON HEIR

**Andrews McMeel
Publishing**

Kansas City

For information, write Andrews McMeel Publishing, an Andrews McMeel Universal company, 4520 Main Street, Kansas City, Missouri 64111.

04 05 06 07 08 BBG 10 9 8 7 6 5 4 3 2 1

ISBN: 0-7404-4662-6

Library of Congress Control Number: 2004105598

Rudy Park can be viewed on the Internet at
www.comics.com/comics/rudypark.

Introduction

Interview with Sadie Cohen

Author's note: Sadie Cohen is a regular at the Internet cafe where the *Rudy Park* comic strip takes place. Mrs. Cohen, 83, can be a little testy, but she agreed to sit for an interview.

Interviewer: Before we begin, let me thank you for being here today for the launch of the second *Rudy Park* book. It is a real pleasure to have one of the strip's main characters to . . .

Sadie: [Muffled sound]

Int.: Why are you under the table?

Sadie: No reason.

Int.: I see you've tied my shoelaces into a sailor's knot.

Sadie: That is a total lie.

Int.: But . . .

Sadie: It's a bridge knot.

Int.: Let us proceed—with the understanding you will remain in plain view. Mrs. Cohen, *Peace, Love, and Lattes* represents a departure from the first book, *Rudy Park: The People Must Be Wired.* Can you tell us about the change?

Sadie: No way. I'm not taking part in a thinly veiled plug. I'm disgusted by this charade. If you want to sucker people into buying this stupid book, you're on your own.

Int.: If you cooperate, I'll teach you how to sabotage Rudy's iPod with peanut butter.

Sadie: I will happily tell you anything you want to know about this wonderful lifesaving publication.

Int.: Let's start simple. How come the strip turned more political in this latest volume?

Sadie: When the comic strip launched, it revolved around life at an Internet cafe. It was a gathering hole for commentary about modern life, the onslaught of technology, and, mostly, it was about the interaction between characters. That's not to say there weren't tense moments.

Int.: The characters had philosophical differences?

Sadie: Violent disputes over the bathroom key.

Int.: Go on.

Sadie: But the world turned on its head after 9/11. Everything changed—economics, politics, *everything*—and it bled into our simplest everyday tasks. Put it this way: Before that time, you rushed to the mailbox each day to see how much your 401K was soaring. But after 2001, you opened your mailbox with fear—concerned it was filled with some biological weapon. The whole change raised a compelling question.

Int.: Whether to use FedEx?

Sadie: Pipe down, Dunderhead. Whether these sorts of serious issues belonged on a comic strip. After all, should a comics page ever include the words "Guantanamo Bay"? The creators of *Rudy Park*, Theron Heir and Darrin Bell, thought such concepts belonged, given how much they gripped our world, but with two crucial caveats. One, Darrin and Theron thought the strip had to stay funny, and two, that the fundamental character of the strip remain unchanged. They tried to invite the outside world into their own little *Rudy Park* universe. For instance, when Rudy was having trouble with his love life, he turned for advice to Dick Cheney. Or when Rudy went shopping on eBay, he bought himself a pair of Saddam body doubles. Whether or not such concepts were funny depends, if you ask me, on whether Rudy continues to look like a total boob.

Int.: You're all heart. Speaking of characters, this second book prominently features Mort Park, Rudy's aging and cantankerous uncle. He carries a bullhorn around, yelling at everyone who disagrees with him.

Sadie: Isn't it wonderful? I just love a man who tells other people to go take a hike. If you recall from the first book, Mort has long been a whiny liberal rabble-rouser. But the events of the last few years thrust him into the limelight. What made him that much angrier is that, mostly, people ignored him. They found him to be a real downer, which just caused him to get that much more aggressive. There's nothing quite like seeing Morty yell at people about weapons of mass destruction before they've had their morning lattes.

Int.: The way you make it sound, *Rudy Park* turned into an editorial cartoon.

Sadie: You haven't listened to one word I've said, have you? Absolutely not. The strip was trying to reflect what was on people's minds. Its creators, if you ask me, are merely a couple of vacuous idiots making jokes on whatever they overhear on the news ticker, at the cafes where they get hot chocolates, or in the checkout stand at Gas-n-Sip. The strip is simply topical, and topics change.

Int.: So that means that since so much time has passed since 9/11, *Rudy Park* will move on to other things?

Sadie: Nine months of strips about Paris Hilton.

Int.: One last question. You seem, let me see how to put this delicately, like a ticked-off old bat. What's you're problem? Why do you hate Rudy so much?

Sadie: That's putting it delicately?

Int.: Answer the question or I'll sic Bob Woodward on you.

Sadie: I would crush Woodward like an overripe melon, but I'll answer anyway. I despise Rudy's generation and their whiny materialistic obsessions. They think they can solve everything by buying the latest gadget or joining the latest fitness or diet trend. I belong to this country's Greatest Generation. We formed a steadfast nation that didn't take any lip from anybody. We didn't complain or malinger. We weren't consumed with personal happiness. We didn't obsess about whether it was okay to eat meat, or pasta, or refined sugar products, or about how many carbohydrates we were digesting. We were nothing like the current generation.

Int.: In dietary terms.

Sadie: I will now commence tying your shoelaces to your ears.

Int.: Woodward!

[Scuffle ensues. Fade to black.]

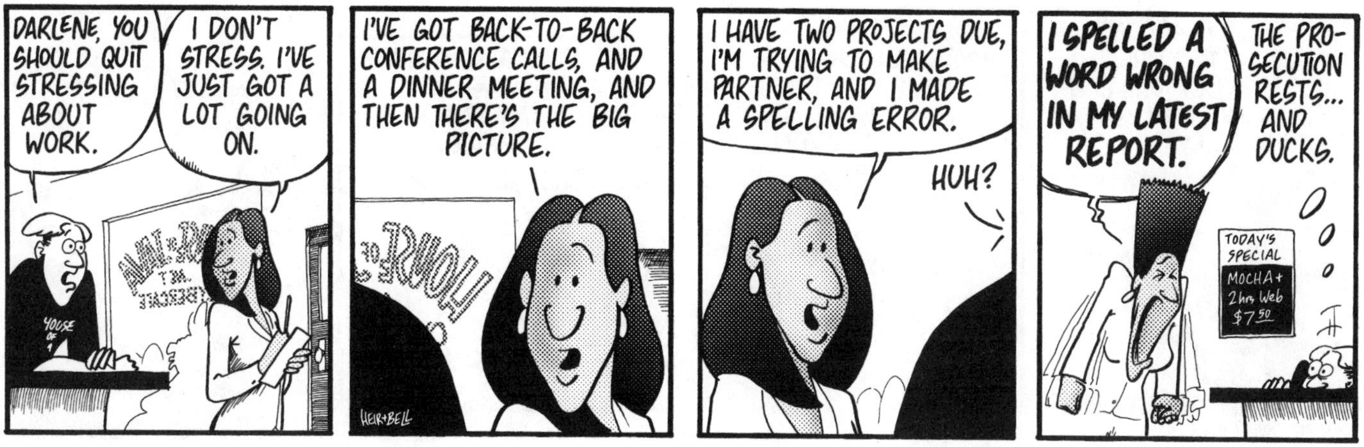
DARLENE, YOU SHOULD QUIT STRESSING ABOUT WORK.
I DON'T STRESS. I'VE JUST GOT A LOT GOING ON.
I'VE GOT BACK-TO-BACK CONFERENCE CALLS, AND A DINNER MEETING, AND THEN THERE'S THE BIG PICTURE.
I HAVE TWO PROJECTS DUE, I'M TRYING TO MAKE PARTNER, AND I MADE A SPELLING ERROR.
HUH?
I SPELLED A WORD WRONG IN MY LATEST REPORT.
THE PROSECUTION RESTS... AND DUCKS.
TODAY'S SPECIAL
MOCHA + 2hrs Web $7.50

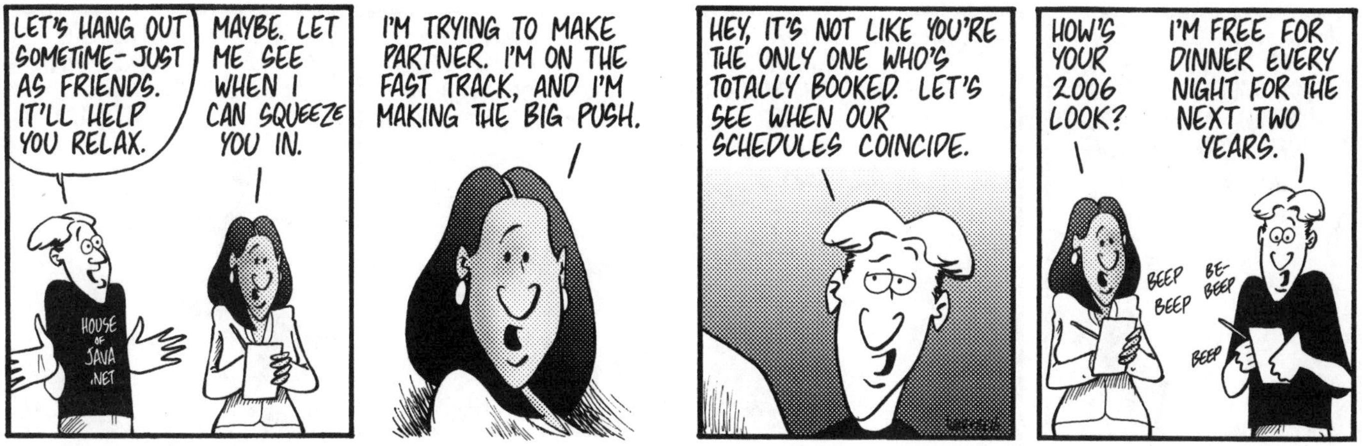
LET'S HANG OUT SOMETIME- JUST AS FRIENDS. IT'LL HELP YOU RELAX.
MAYBE. LET ME SEE WHEN I CAN SQUEEZE YOU IN.
HOUSE OF JAVA .NET
I'M TRYING TO MAKE PARTNER. I'M ON THE FAST TRACK, AND I'M MAKING THE BIG PUSH.
HEY, IT'S NOT LIKE YOU'RE THE ONLY ONE WHO'S TOTALLY BOOKED. LET'S SEE WHEN OUR SCHEDULES COINCIDE.
HOW'S YOUR 2006 LOOK?
I'M FREE FOR DINNER EVERY NIGHT FOR THE NEXT TWO YEARS.
BEEP
BEEP
BE-BEEP
BEEP

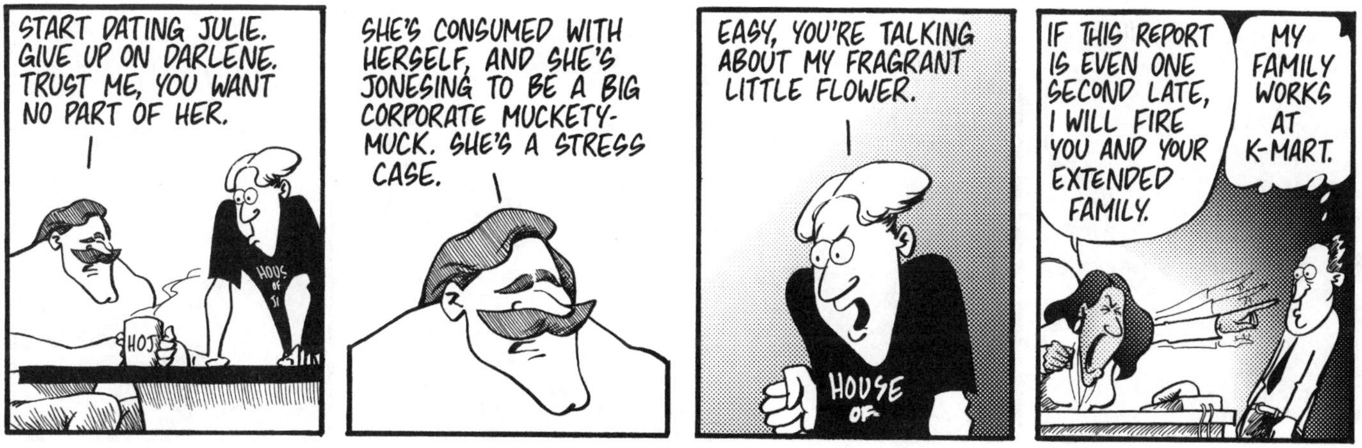
START DATING JULIE. GIVE UP ON DARLENE. TRUST ME, YOU WANT NO PART OF HER.
SHE'S CONSUMED WITH HERSELF, AND SHE'S JONESING TO BE A BIG CORPORATE MUCKETY-MUCK. SHE'S A STRESS CASE.
EASY, YOU'RE TALKING ABOUT MY FRAGRANT LITTLE FLOWER.
HOUSE OF
IF THIS REPORT IS EVEN ONE SECOND LATE, I WILL FIRE YOU AND YOUR EXTENDED FAMILY.
MY FAMILY WORKS AT K-MART.

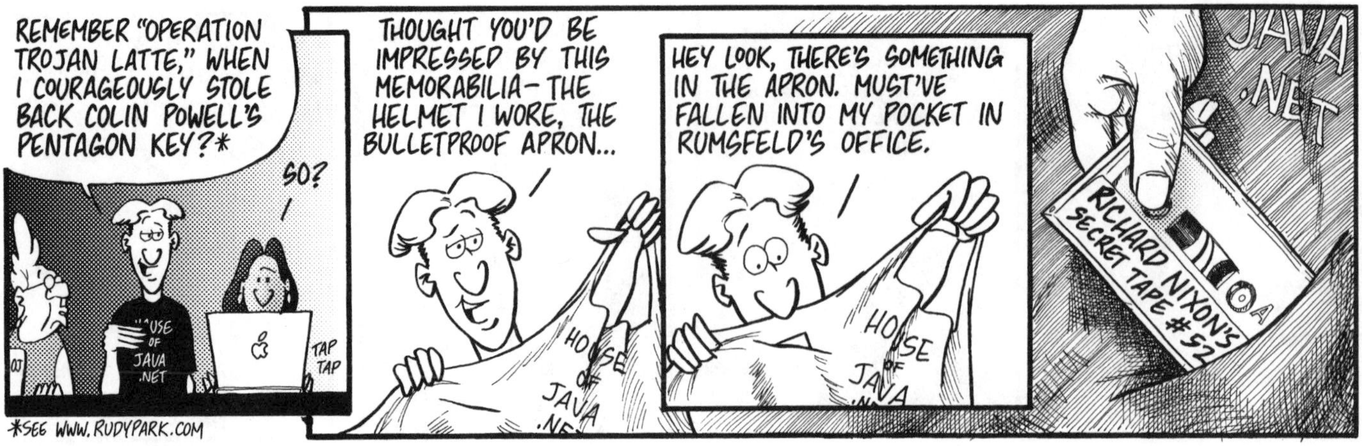
REMEMBER "OPERATION TROJAN LATTE," WHEN I COURAGEOUSLY STOLE BACK COLIN POWELL'S PENTAGON KEY?*
SO?
HOUSE OF JAVA .NET
TAP TAP
THOUGHT YOU'D BE IMPRESSED BY THIS MEMORABILIA– THE HELMET I WORE, THE BULLETPROOF APRON...
HEY LOOK, THERE'S SOMETHING IN THE APRON. MUST'VE FALLEN INTO MY POCKET IN RUMSFELD'S OFFICE.
JAVA .NET
RICHARD NIXON'S SECRET TAPE #52
*SEE WWW.RUDYPARK.COM

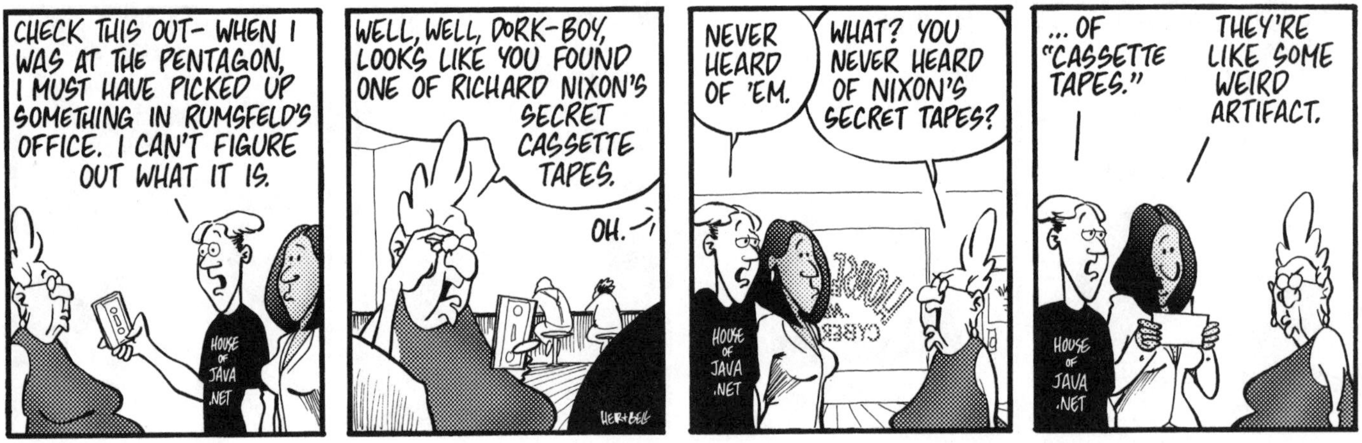
CHECK THIS OUT– WHEN I WAS AT THE PENTAGON, I MUST HAVE PICKED UP SOMETHING IN RUMSFELD'S OFFICE. I CAN'T FIGURE OUT WHAT IT IS.
HOUSE OF JAVA .NET
WELL, WELL, DORK-BOY, LOOKS LIKE YOU FOUND ONE OF RICHARD NIXON'S SECRET CASSETTE TAPES.
OH.
NEVER HEARD OF 'EM.
WHAT? YOU NEVER HEARD OF NIXON'S SECRET TAPES?
... OF "CASSETTE TAPES."
THEY'RE LIKE SOME WEIRD ARTIFACT.

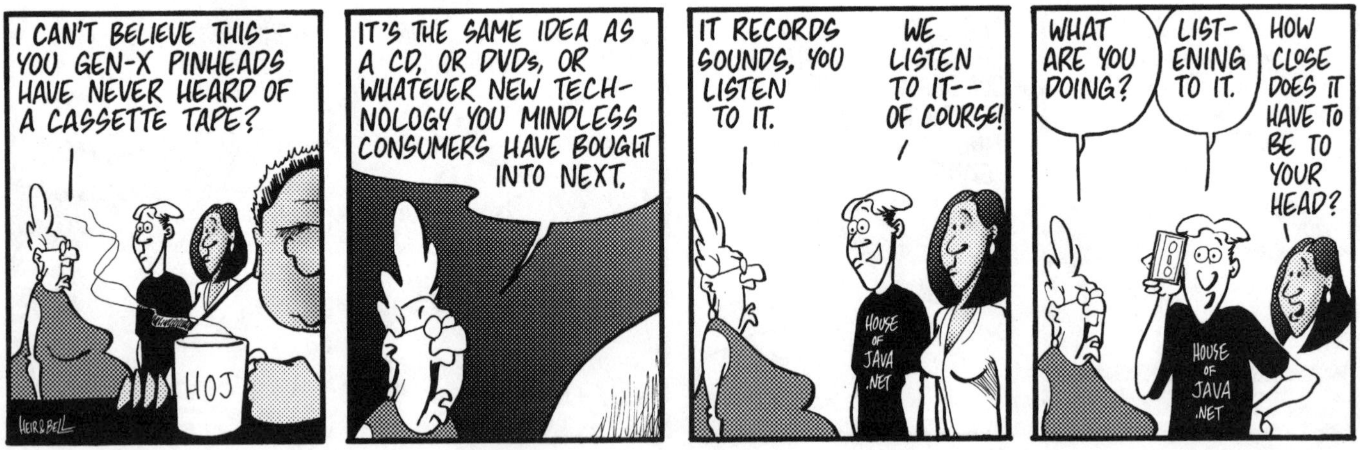
I CAN'T BELIEVE THIS-- YOU GEN-X PINHEADS HAVE NEVER HEARD OF A CASSETTE TAPE?
HOJ
IT'S THE SAME IDEA AS A CD, OR DVDs, OR WHATEVER NEW TECHNOLOGY YOU MINDLESS CONSUMERS HAVE BOUGHT INTO NEXT.
IT RECORDS SOUNDS, YOU LISTEN TO IT.
WE LISTEN TO IT-- OF COURSE!
WHAT ARE YOU DOING?
LISTENING TO IT.
HOW CLOSE DOES IT HAVE TO BE TO YOUR HEAD?

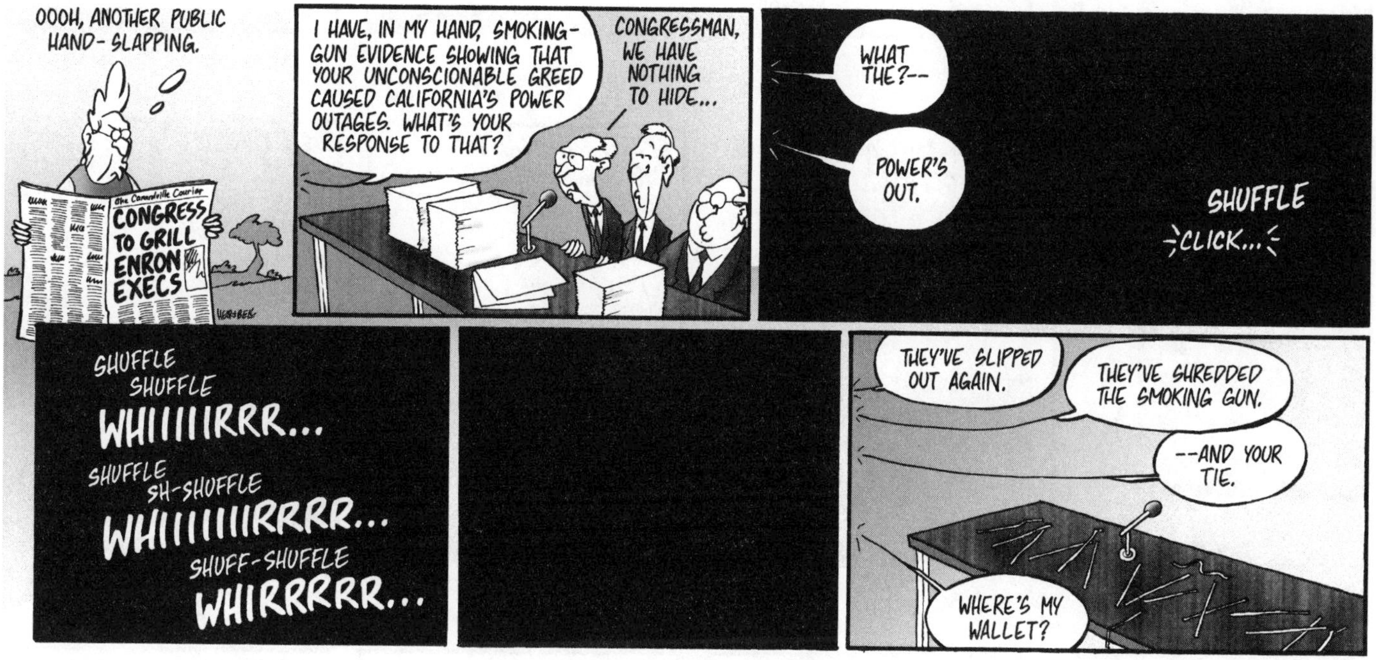
OOOH, ANOTHER PUBLIC HAND-SLAPPING.
The Conandville Courier
CONGRESS TO GRILL ENRON EXECS
I HAVE, IN MY HAND, SMOKING-GUN EVIDENCE SHOWING THAT YOUR UNCONSCIONABLE GREED CAUSED CALIFORNIA'S POWER OUTAGES. WHAT'S YOUR RESPONSE TO THAT?
CONGRESSMAN, WE HAVE NOTHING TO HIDE...
WHAT THE?--
POWER'S OUT.
SHUFFLE
CLICK...
SHUFFLE
SHUFFLE
WHIIIIIRRR...
SHUFFLE
SH-SHUFFLE
WHIIIIIIIRRRR...
SHUFF-SHUFFLE
WHIRRRRR...
THEY'VE SLIPPED OUT AGAIN.
THEY'VE SHREDDED THE SMOKING GUN.
--AND YOUR TIE.
WHERE'S MY WALLET?

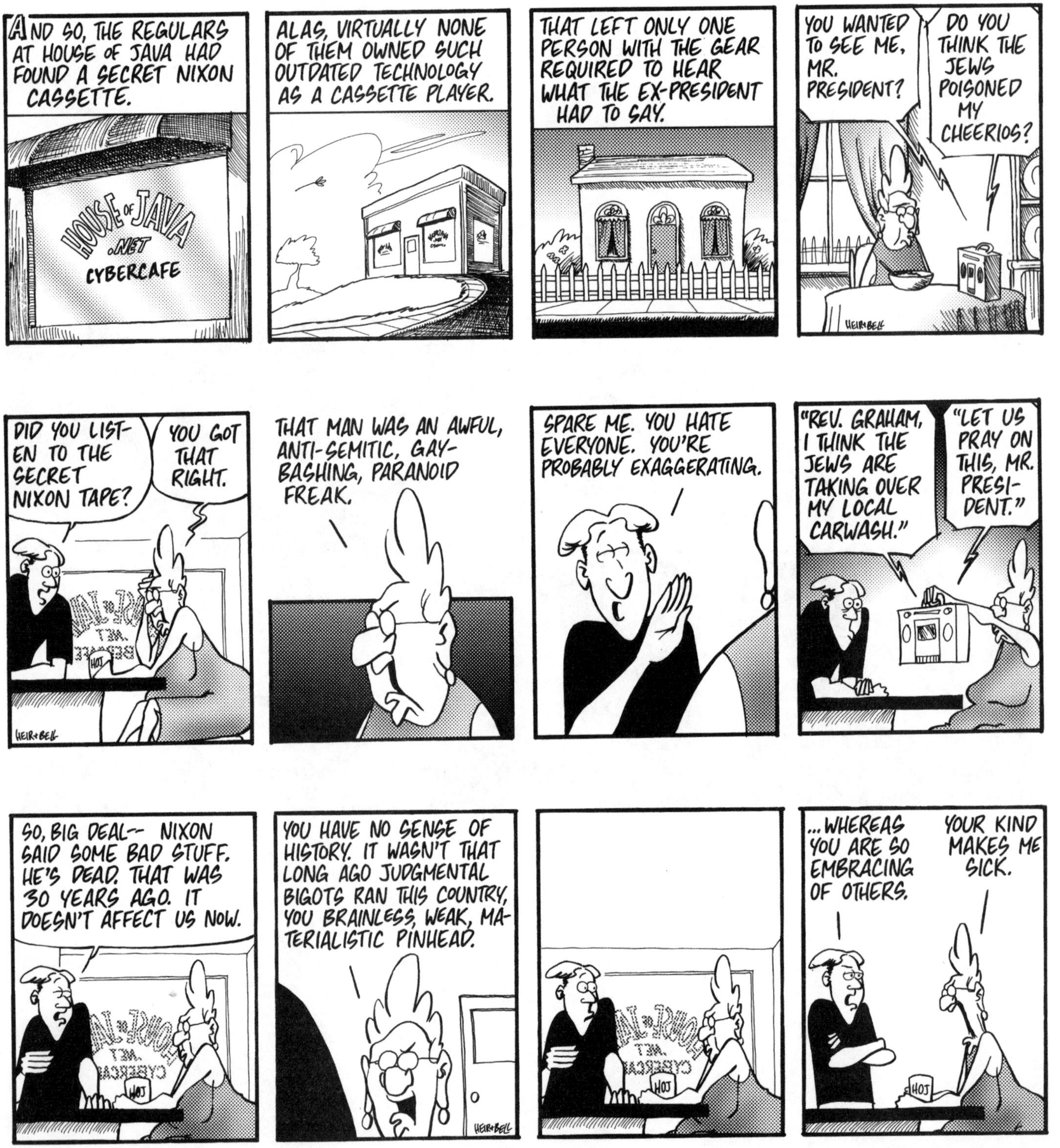
AND SO, THE REGULARS AT HOUSE OF JAVA HAD FOUND A SECRET NIXON CASSETTE.
HOUSE OF JAVA .NET CYBERCAFE
ALAS, VIRTUALLY NONE OF THEM OWNED SUCH OUTDATED TECHNOLOGY AS A CASSETTE PLAYER.
THAT LEFT ONLY ONE PERSON WITH THE GEAR REQUIRED TO HEAR WHAT THE EX-PRESIDENT HAD TO SAY.
YOU WANTED TO SEE ME, MR. PRESIDENT?
DO YOU THINK THE JEWS POISONED MY CHEERIOS?
DID YOU LISTEN TO THE SECRET NIXON TAPE?
YOU GOT THAT RIGHT.
THAT MAN WAS AN AWFUL, ANTI-SEMITIC, GAY-BASHING, PARANOID FREAK.
SPARE ME. YOU HATE EVERYONE. YOU'RE PROBABLY EXAGGERATING.
"REV. GRAHAM, I THINK THE JEWS ARE TAKING OVER MY LOCAL CARWASH."
"LET US PRAY ON THIS, MR. PRESIDENT."
SO, BIG DEAL-- NIXON SAID SOME BAD STUFF. HE'S DEAD. THAT WAS 30 YEARS AGO. IT DOESN'T AFFECT US NOW.
YOU HAVE NO SENSE OF HISTORY. IT WASN'T THAT LONG AGO JUDGMENTAL BIGOTS RAN THIS COUNTRY, YOU BRAINLESS, WEAK, MATERIALISTIC PINHEAD.
...WHEREAS YOU ARE SO EMBRACING OF OTHERS.
YOUR KIND MAKES ME SICK.

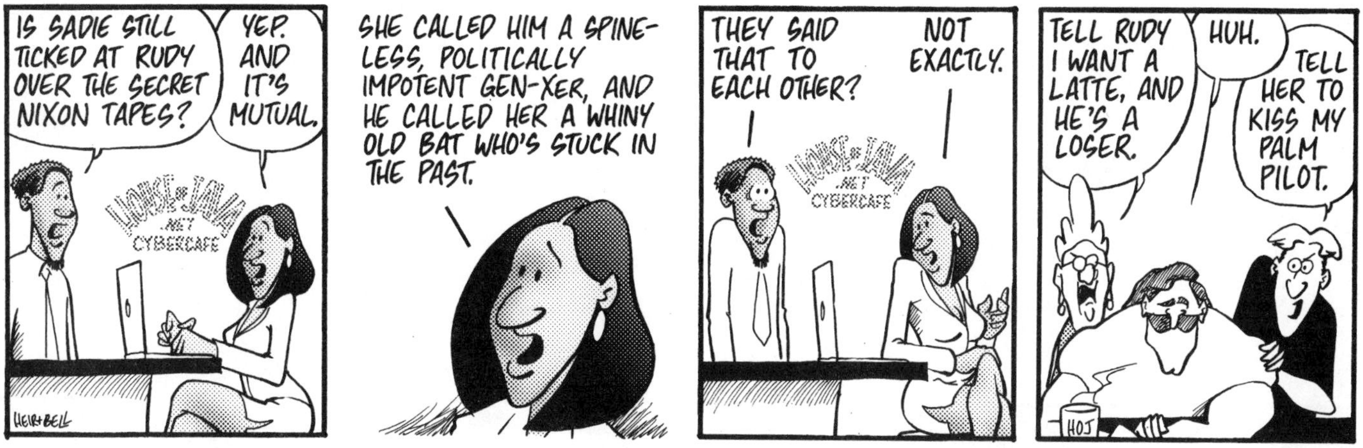
IS SADIE STILL TICKED AT RUDY OVER THE SECRET NIXON TAPES?
YEP. AND IT'S MUTUAL.
HOUSE OF JAVA .NET CYBERCAFE
HEIR+BELL
SHE CALLED HIM A SPINE-LESS, POLITICALLY IMPOTENT GEN-XER, AND HE CALLED HER A WHINY OLD BAT WHO'S STUCK IN THE PAST.
THEY SAID THAT TO EACH OTHER?
NOT EXACTLY.
TELL RUDY I WANT A LATTE, AND HE'S A LOSER.
HUH.
TELL HER TO KISS MY PALM PILOT.
HOJ

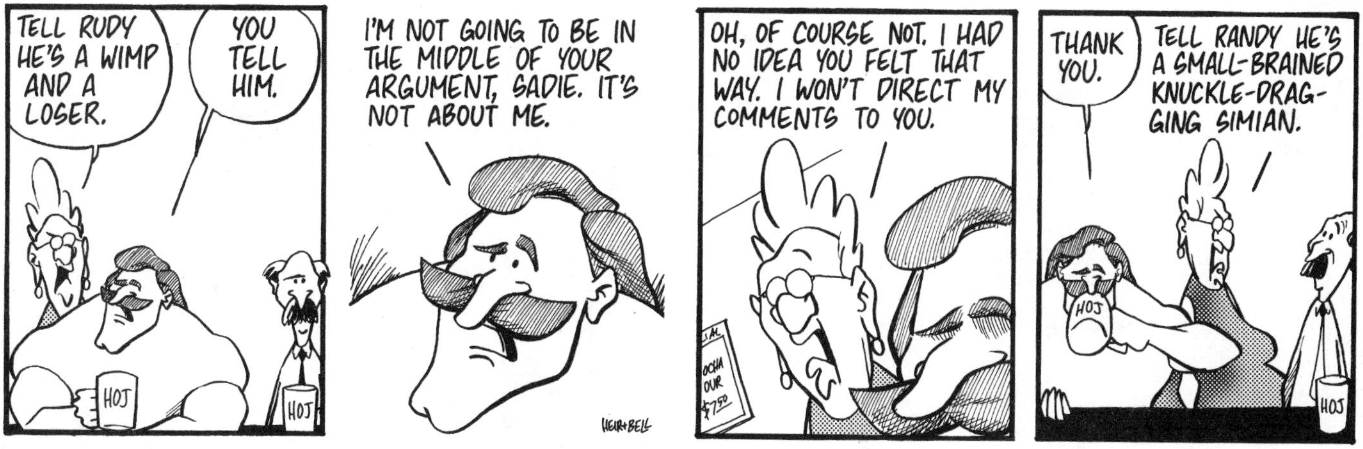
TELL RUDY HE'S A WIMP AND A LOSER.
YOU TELL HIM.
HOJ
I'M NOT GOING TO BE IN THE MIDDLE OF YOUR ARGUMENT, SADIE. IT'S NOT ABOUT ME.
HEIR+BELL
OH, OF COURSE NOT. I HAD NO IDEA YOU FELT THAT WAY. I WON'T DIRECT MY COMMENTS TO YOU.
THANK YOU.
TELL RANDY HE'S A SMALL-BRAINED KNUCKLE-DRAG-GING SIMIAN.
HOJ

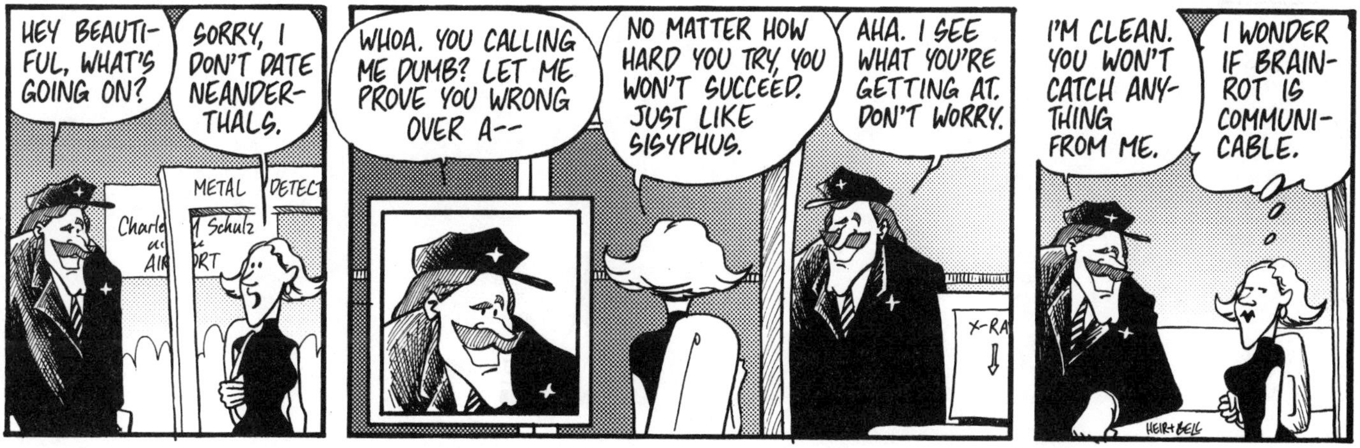
HEY BEAUTI-FUL, WHAT'S GOING ON?
SORRY, I DON'T DATE NEANDER-THALS.
METAL DETECT
WHOA. YOU CALLING ME DUMB? LET ME PROVE YOU WRONG OVER A--
NO MATTER HOW HARD YOU TRY, YOU WON'T SUCCEED. JUST LIKE SISYPHUS.
AHA. I SEE WHAT YOU'RE GETTING AT. DON'T WORRY.
I'M CLEAN. YOU WON'T CATCH ANY-THING FROM ME.
I WONDER IF BRAIN-ROT IS COMMUNI-CABLE.
HEIR+BELL

WHOA, WHAT YOU GOT THERE?
MERRILL LYNCH STOCK ANALYST. GUY WHO REC-OMMENDED MY RETIRE-MENT PORTFOLIO.
HOUSE OF JAVA .NET
GEEK BOY, HAND ME AN OLD PASTRY FROM THE TRASH, AND CHECK THIS OUT...
WHAT DO YOU THINK?
NOT FRESH.
POKE POKE
STALE, ACTUALLY. GROSS. THE MOST RANCID, VILE, DISGUSTING SCONE I'VE EVER SEEN IN MY LIFE.
HEIR & BELL
RECOMMENDATION?
HOUSE OF JAVA .NET CYBERCAFE
STRONG BUY!
STRONG DRINK.
I'LL TAKE TWO DOZEN OF THE OLD SCONES.
$ $

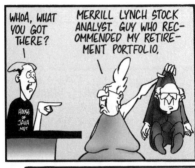

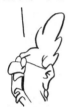

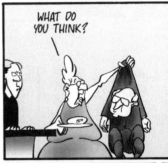

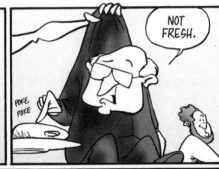

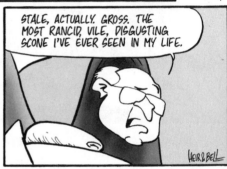

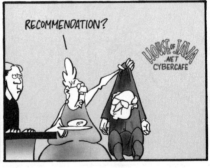

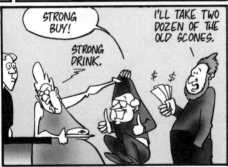

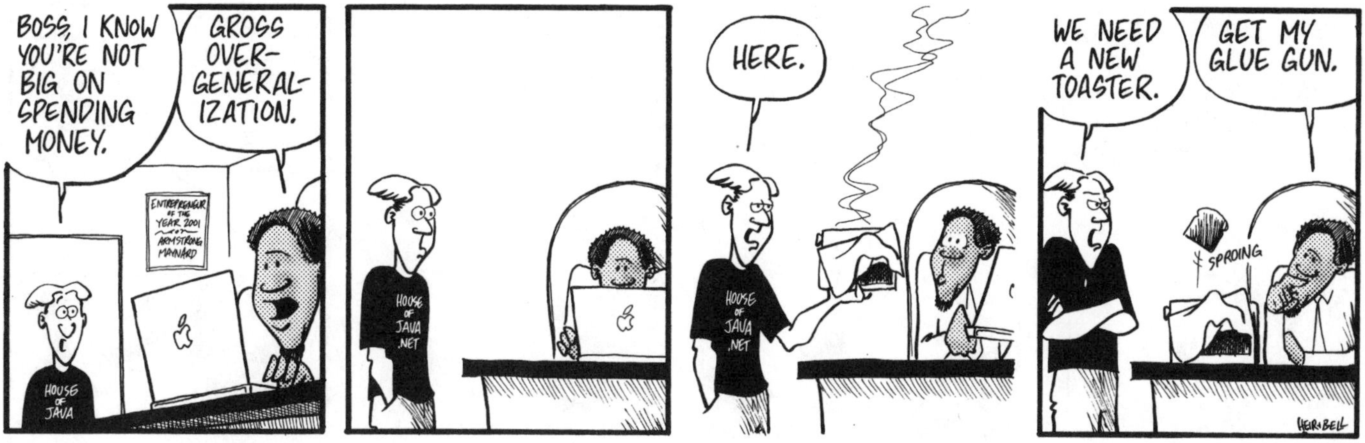
BOSS, I KNOW YOU'RE NOT BIG ON SPENDING MONEY.
GROSS OVER-GENERAL-IZATION.
ENTREPRENEUR OF THE YEAR 2001 ARMSTRONG MAYNARD
HOUSE OF JAVA
HOUSE OF JAVA .NET
HERE.
WE NEED A NEW TOASTER.
GET MY GLUE GUN.
SPROING
HEIR+BELL

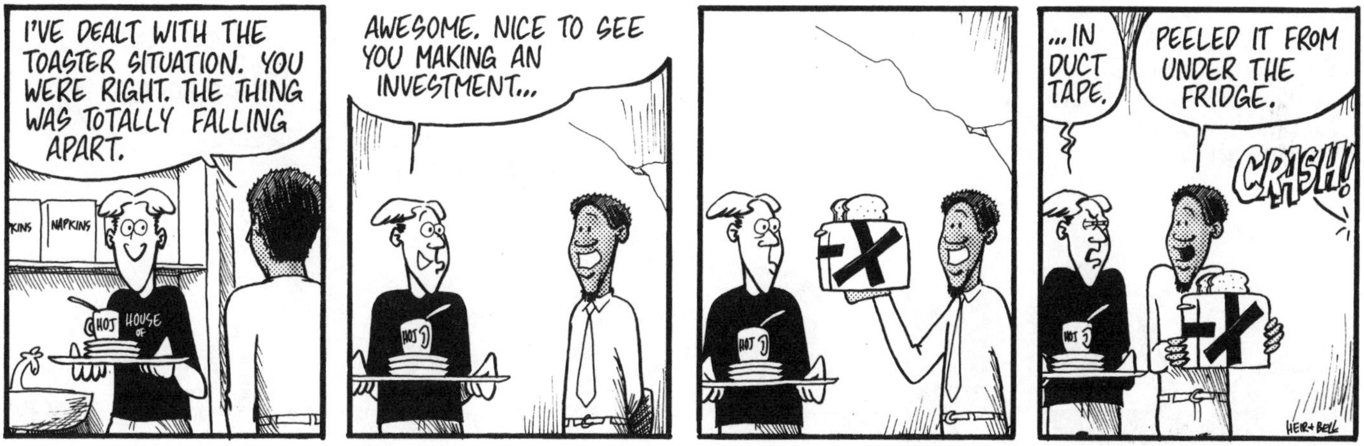
I'VE DEALT WITH THE TOASTER SITUATION. YOU WERE RIGHT. THE THING WAS TOTALLY FALLING APART.
NAPKINS
HOJ
HOUSE OF
AWESOME. NICE TO SEE YOU MAKING AN INVESTMENT...
...IN DUCT TAPE.
PEELED IT FROM UNDER THE FRIDGE.
CRASH!
HEIR+BELL

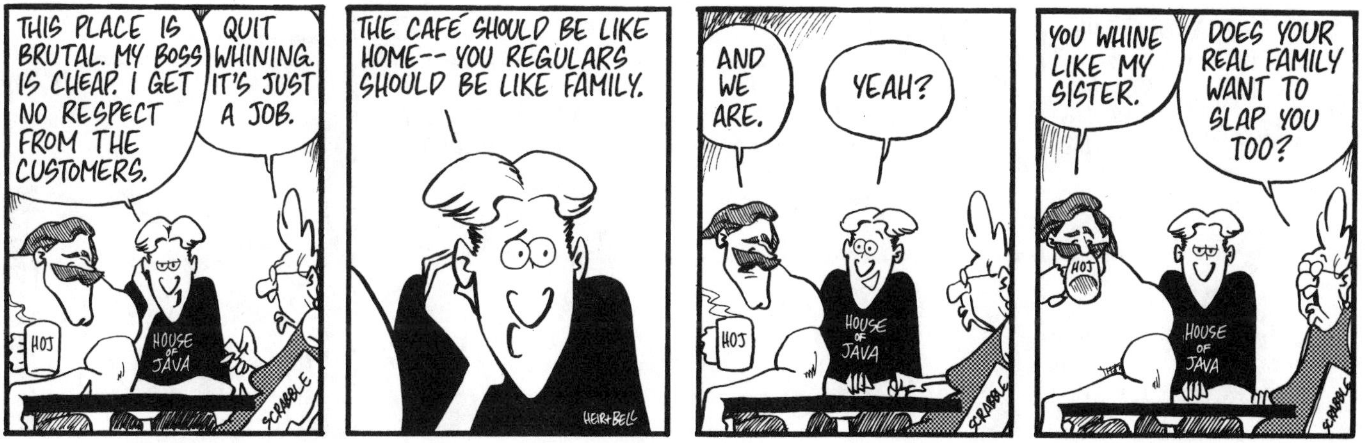
THIS PLACE IS BRUTAL. MY BOSS IS CHEAP. I GET NO RESPECT FROM THE CUSTOMERS.
QUIT WHINING. IT'S JUST A JOB.
HOJ
HOUSE OF JAVA
SCRABBLE
THE CAFÉ SHOULD BE LIKE HOME-- YOU REGULARS SHOULD BE LIKE FAMILY.
HEIR+BELL
AND WE ARE.
YEAH?
YOU WHINE LIKE MY SISTER.
DOES YOUR REAL FAMILY WANT TO SLAP YOU TOO?

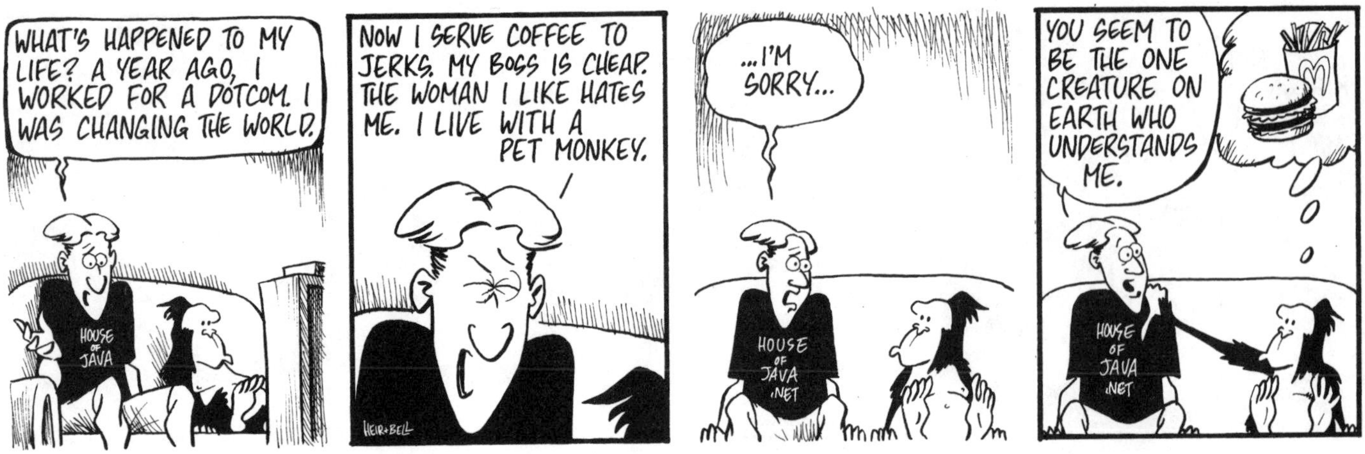
WHAT'S HAPPENED TO MY LIFE? A YEAR AGO, I WORKED FOR A DOTCOM. I WAS CHANGING THE WORLD.
HOUSE OF JAVA
NOW I SERVE COFFEE TO JERKS. MY BOSS IS CHEAP. THE WOMAN I LIKE HATES ME. I LIVE WITH A PET MONKEY.
HEIR+BELL
...I'M SORRY...
HOUSE OF JAVA .NET
YOU SEEM TO BE THE ONE CREATURE ON EARTH WHO UNDERSTANDS ME.
HOUSE OF JAVA .NET

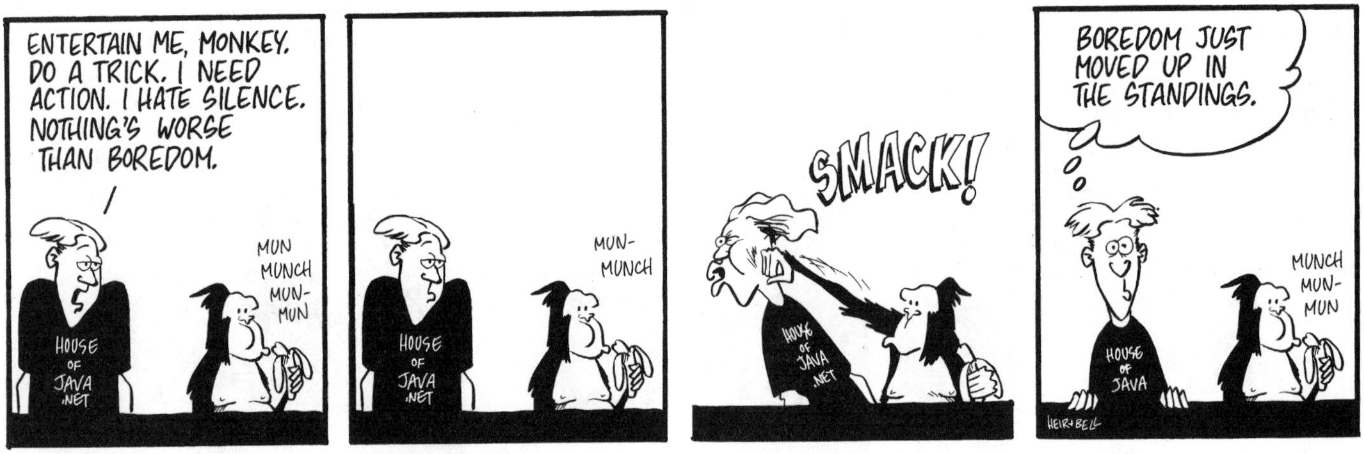
ENTERTAIN ME, MONKEY. DO A TRICK. I NEED ACTION. I HATE SILENCE. NOTHING'S WORSE THAN BOREDOM.
MUN MUNCH MUN-MUN
HOUSE OF JAVA .NET
MUN-MUNCH
HOUSE OF JAVA .NET
SMACK!
HOUSE OF JAVA .NET
BOREDOM JUST MOVED UP IN THE STANDINGS.
MUNCH MUN-MUN
HOUSE OF JAVA
HEIR+BELL

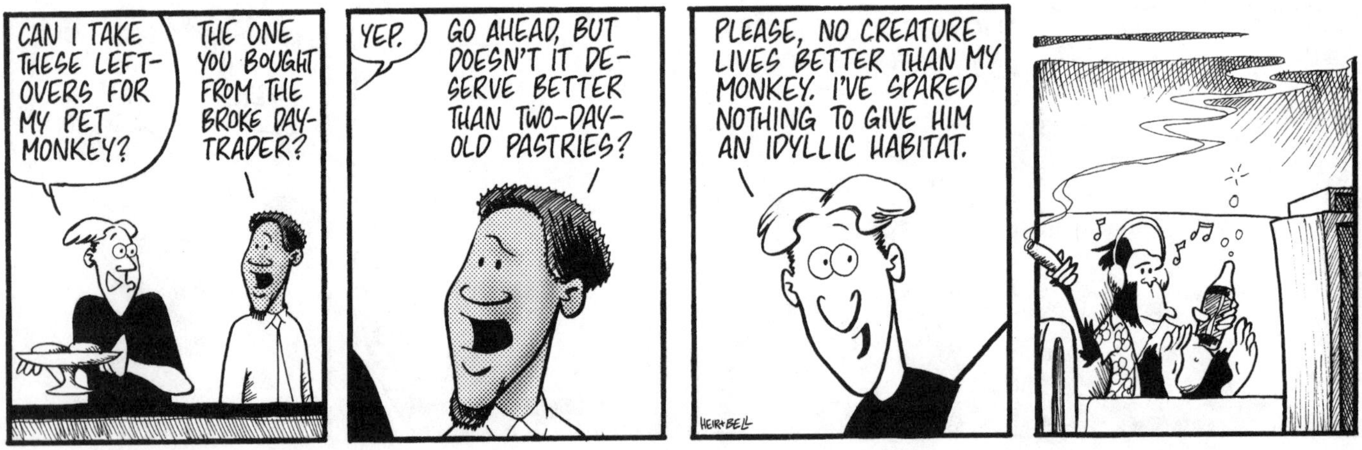
CAN I TAKE THESE LEFT-OVERS FOR MY PET MONKEY?
THE ONE YOU BOUGHT FROM THE BROKE DAY-TRADER?
YEP.
GO AHEAD, BUT DOESN'T IT DE-SERVE BETTER THAN TWO-DAY-OLD PASTRIES?
PLEASE, NO CREATURE LIVES BETTER THAN MY MONKEY. I'VE SPARED NOTHING TO GIVE HIM AN IDYLLIC HABITAT.
HEIR+BELL

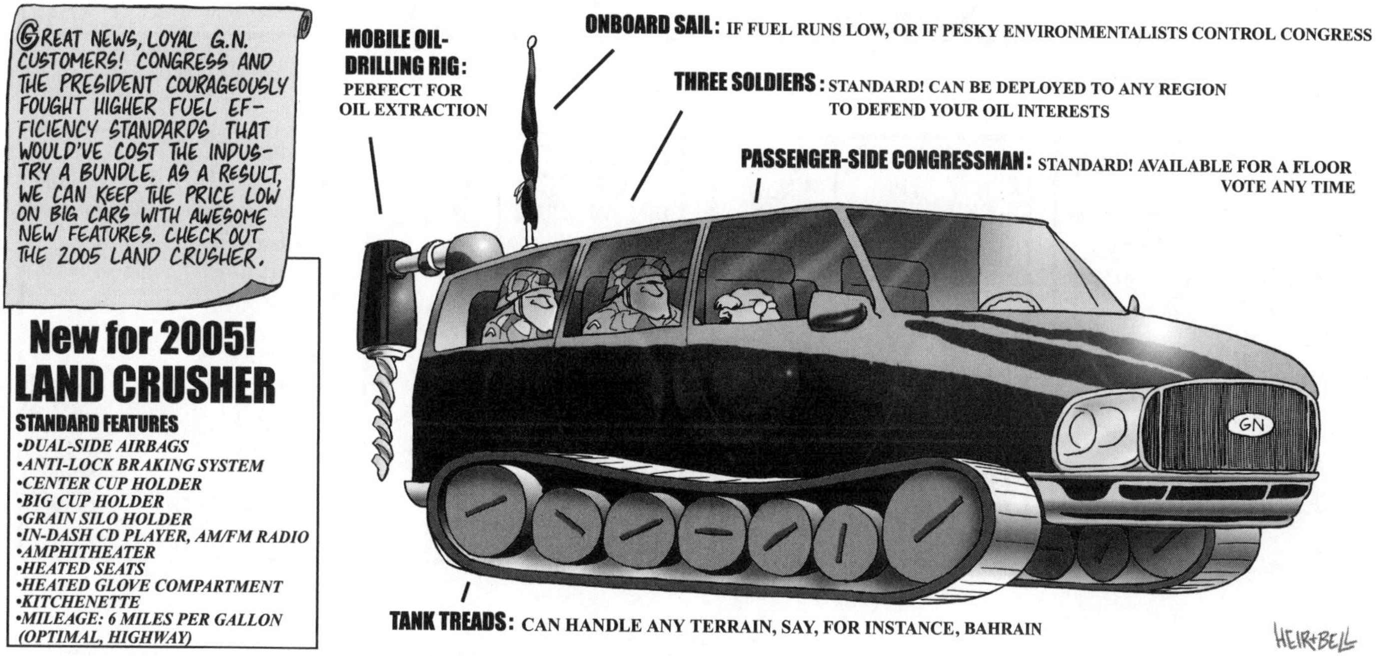
GREAT NEWS, LOYAL G.N. CUSTOMERS! CONGRESS AND THE PRESIDENT COURAGEOUSLY FOUGHT HIGHER FUEL EFFICIENCY STANDARDS THAT WOULD'VE COST THE INDUSTRY A BUNDLE. AS A RESULT, WE CAN KEEP THE PRICE LOW ON BIG CARS WITH AWESOME NEW FEATURES. CHECK OUT THE 2005 LAND CRUSHER.
New for 2005!
LAND CRUSHER
STANDARD FEATURES
•DUAL-SIDE AIRBAGS
•ANTI-LOCK BRAKING SYSTEM
•CENTER CUP HOLDER
•BIG CUP HOLDER
•GRAIN SILO HOLDER
•IN-DASH CD PLAYER, AM/FM RADIO
•AMPHITHEATER
•HEATED SEATS
•HEATED GLOVE COMPARTMENT
•KITCHENETTE
•MILEAGE: 6 MILES PER GALLON (OPTIMAL, HIGHWAY)
MOBILE OIL-DRILLING RIG: PERFECT FOR OIL EXTRACTION
ONBOARD SAIL: IF FUEL RUNS LOW, OR IF PESKY ENVIRONMENTALISTS CONTROL CONGRESS
THREE SOLDIERS: STANDARD! CAN BE DEPLOYED TO ANY REGION TO DEFEND YOUR OIL INTERESTS
PASSENGER-SIDE CONGRESSMAN: STANDARD! AVAILABLE FOR A FLOOR VOTE ANY TIME
GN
TANK TREADS: CAN HANDLE ANY TERRAIN, SAY, FOR INSTANCE, BAHRAIN
HEIR+BELL

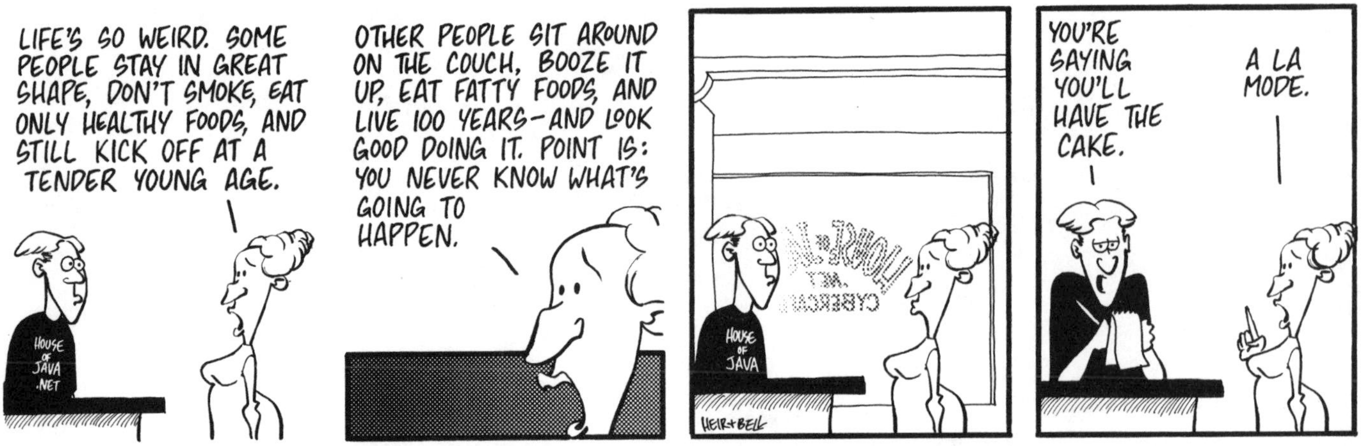
LIFE'S SO WEIRD. SOME PEOPLE STAY IN GREAT SHAPE, DON'T SMOKE, EAT ONLY HEALTHY FOODS, AND STILL KICK OFF AT A TENDER YOUNG AGE.
HOUSE OF JAVA .NET
OTHER PEOPLE SIT AROUND ON THE COUCH, BOOZE IT UP, EAT FATTY FOODS, AND LIVE 100 YEARS—AND LOOK GOOD DOING IT. POINT IS: YOU NEVER KNOW WHAT'S GOING TO HAPPEN.
HOUSE OF JAVA
HEIR+BELL
YOU'RE SAYING YOU'LL HAVE THE CAKE.
A LA MODE.

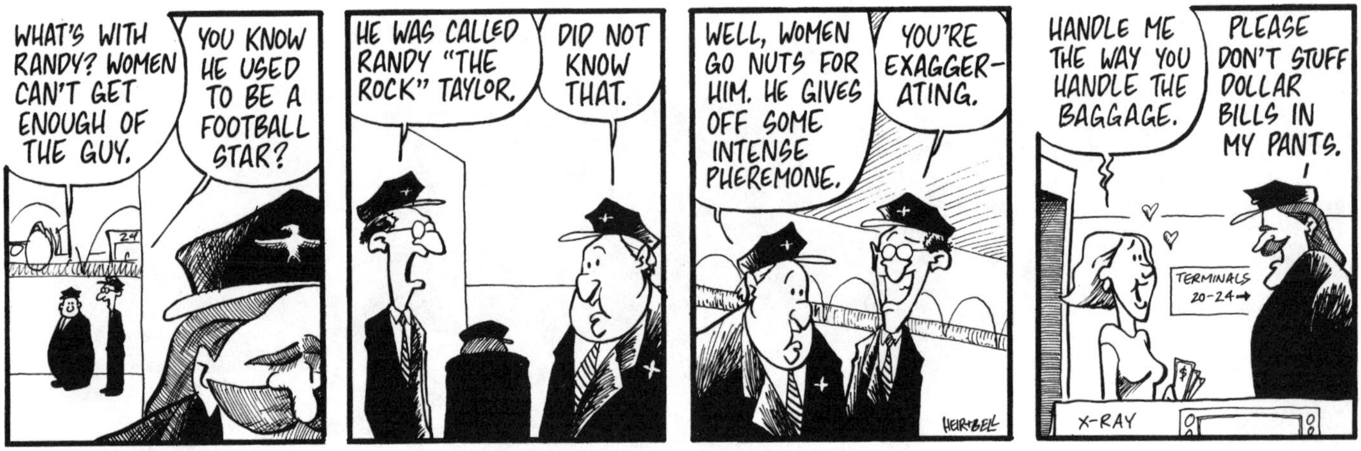
WHAT'S WITH RANDY? WOMEN CAN'T GET ENOUGH OF THE GUY.
YOU KNOW HE USED TO BE A FOOTBALL STAR?
HE WAS CALLED RANDY "THE ROCK" TAYLOR.
DID NOT KNOW THAT.
WELL, WOMEN GO NUTS FOR HIM. HE GIVES OFF SOME INTENSE PHEREMONE.
YOU'RE EXAGGERATING.
HEIR+BELL
HANDLE ME THE WAY YOU HANDLE THE BAGGAGE.
PLEASE DON'T STUFF DOLLAR BILLS IN MY PANTS.
TERMINALS 20-24→
X-RAY

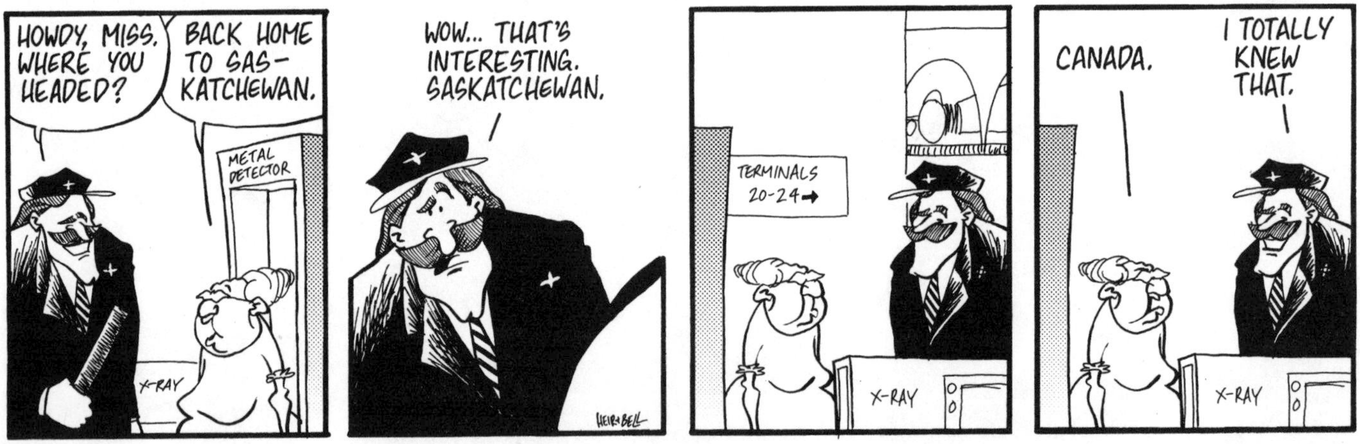
HOWDY, MISS. WHERE YOU HEADED?
BACK HOME TO SASKATCHEWAN.
METAL DETECTOR
X-RAY
WOW... THAT'S INTERESTING. SASKATCHEWAN.
HEIR+BELL
TERMINALS 20-24→
X-RAY
CANADA.
I TOTALLY KNEW THAT.
X-RAY

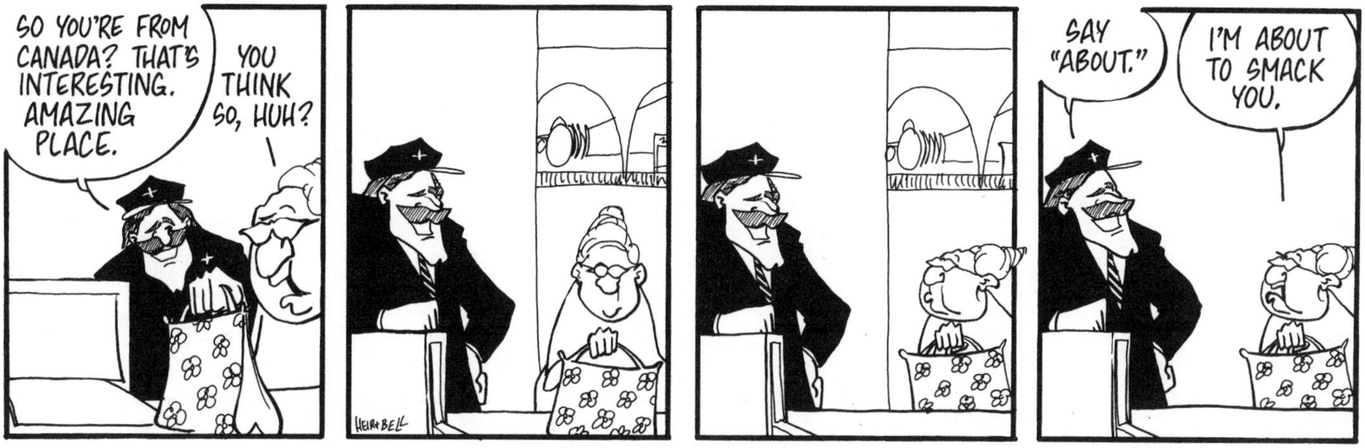
SO YOU'RE FROM CANADA? THAT'S INTERESTING. AMAZING PLACE.
YOU THINK SO, HUH?
HEIR+BELL
SAY "ABOUT."
I'M ABOUT TO SMACK YOU.

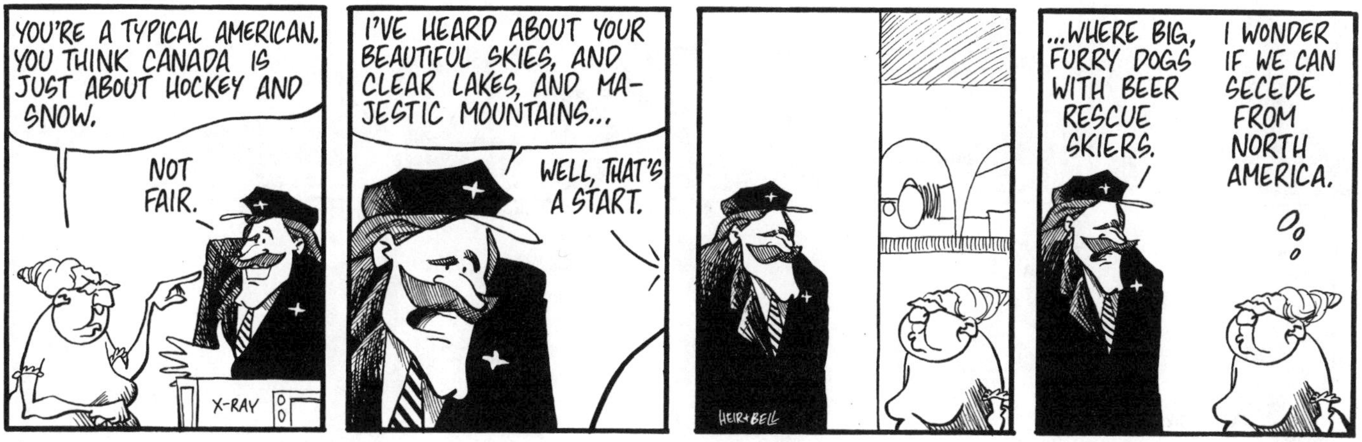
YOU'RE A TYPICAL AMERICAN. YOU THINK CANADA IS JUST ABOUT HOCKEY AND SNOW.
NOT FAIR.
X-RAY
I'VE HEARD ABOUT YOUR BEAUTIFUL SKIES, AND CLEAR LAKES, AND MAJESTIC MOUNTAINS...
WELL, THAT'S A START.
HEIR+BELL
...WHERE BIG, FURRY DOGS WITH BEER RESCUE SKIERS.
I WONDER IF WE CAN SECEDE FROM NORTH AMERICA.

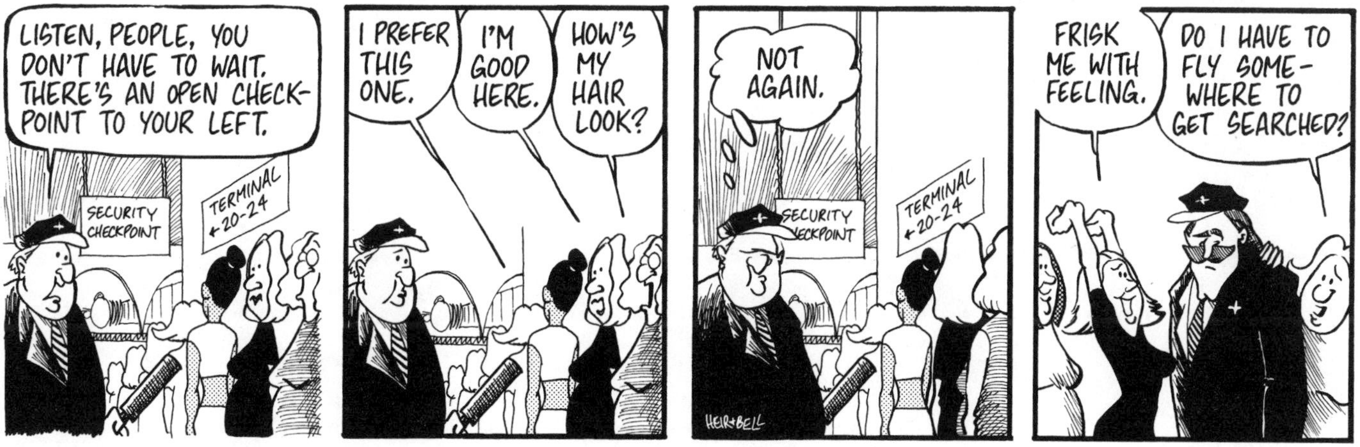
LISTEN, PEOPLE, YOU DON'T HAVE TO WAIT. THERE'S AN OPEN CHECKPOINT TO YOUR LEFT.
SECURITY CHECKPOINT
TERMINAL ←20-24
I PREFER THIS ONE.
I'M GOOD HERE.
HOW'S MY HAIR LOOK?
NOT AGAIN.
HEIR+BELL
FRISK ME WITH FEELING.
DO I HAVE TO FLY SOMEWHERE TO GET SEARCHED?

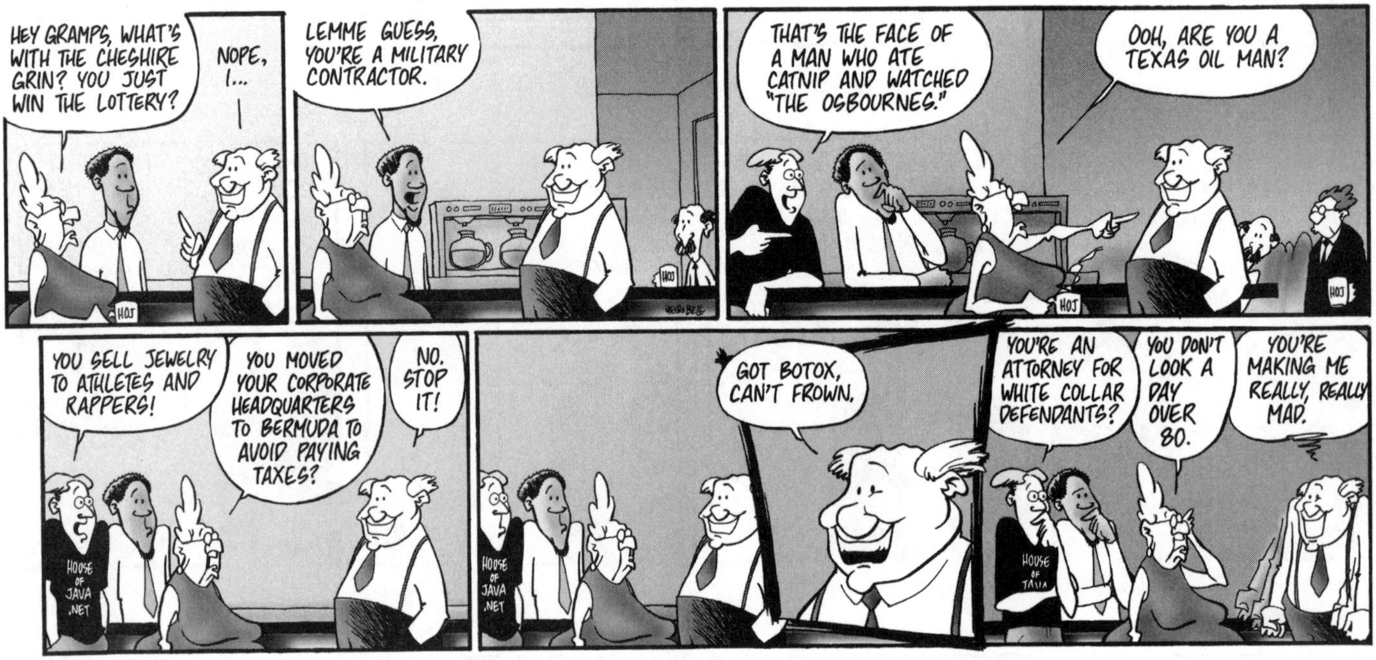
HEY GRAMPS, WHAT'S WITH THE CHESHIRE GRIN? YOU JUST WIN THE LOTTERY?
NOPE, I...
LEMME GUESS, YOU'RE A MILITARY CONTRACTOR.
THAT'S THE FACE OF A MAN WHO ATE CATNIP AND WATCHED "THE OSBOURNES."
OOH, ARE YOU A TEXAS OIL MAN?
YOU SELL JEWELRY TO ATHLETES AND RAPPERS!
YOU MOVED YOUR CORPORATE HEADQUARTERS TO BERMUDA TO AVOID PAYING TAXES?
NO. STOP IT!
GOT BOTOX, CAN'T FROWN.
YOU'RE AN ATTORNEY FOR WHITE COLLAR DEFENDANTS?
YOU DON'T LOOK A DAY OVER 80.
YOU'RE MAKING ME REALLY, REALLY MAD.
HOUSE OF JAVA .NET
HOJ

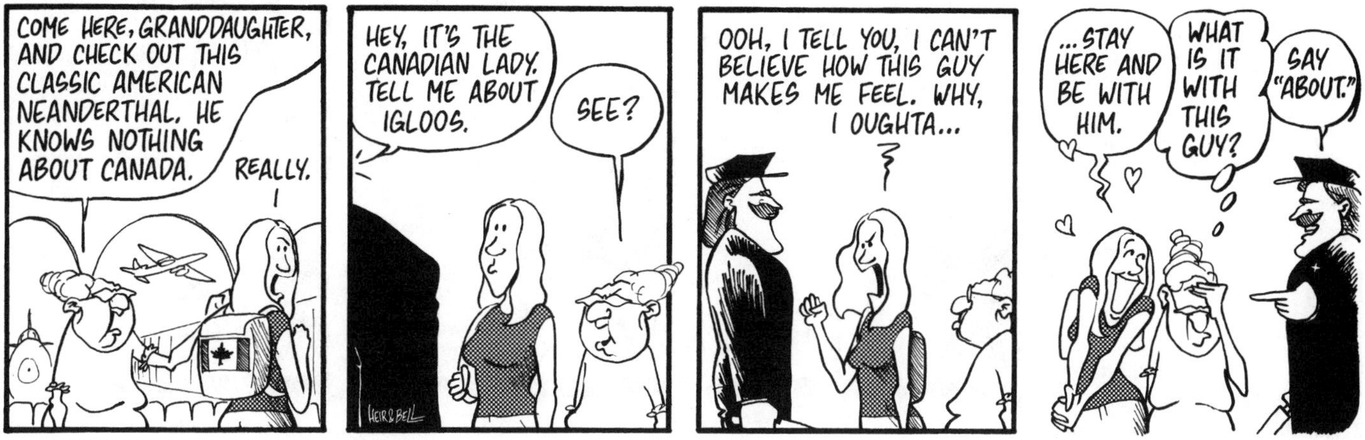
COME HERE, GRANDDAUGHTER, AND CHECK OUT THIS CLASSIC AMERICAN NEANDERTHAL. HE KNOWS NOTHING ABOUT CANADA.
REALLY.
HEY, IT'S THE CANADIAN LADY. TELL ME ABOUT IGLOOS.
SEE?
OOH, I TELL YOU, I CAN'T BELIEVE HOW THIS GUY MAKES ME FEEL. WHY, I OUGHTA...
...STAY HERE AND BE WITH HIM.
WHAT IS IT WITH THIS GUY?
SAY "ABOUT."
HEIR&BELL

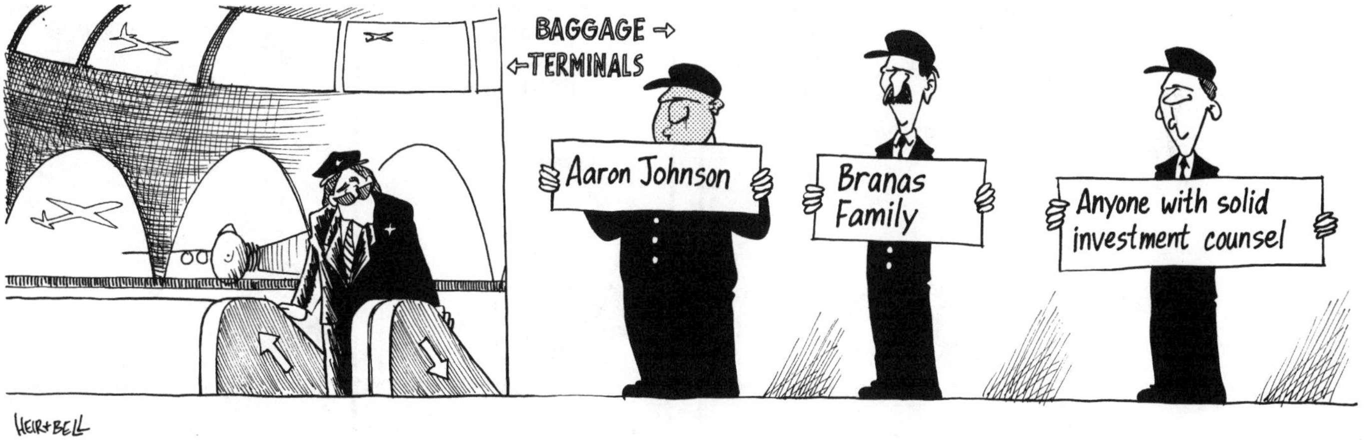
BAGGAGE ⇨
⇦TERMINALS
Aaron Johnson
Branas Family
Anyone with solid investment counsel
HEIR+BELL

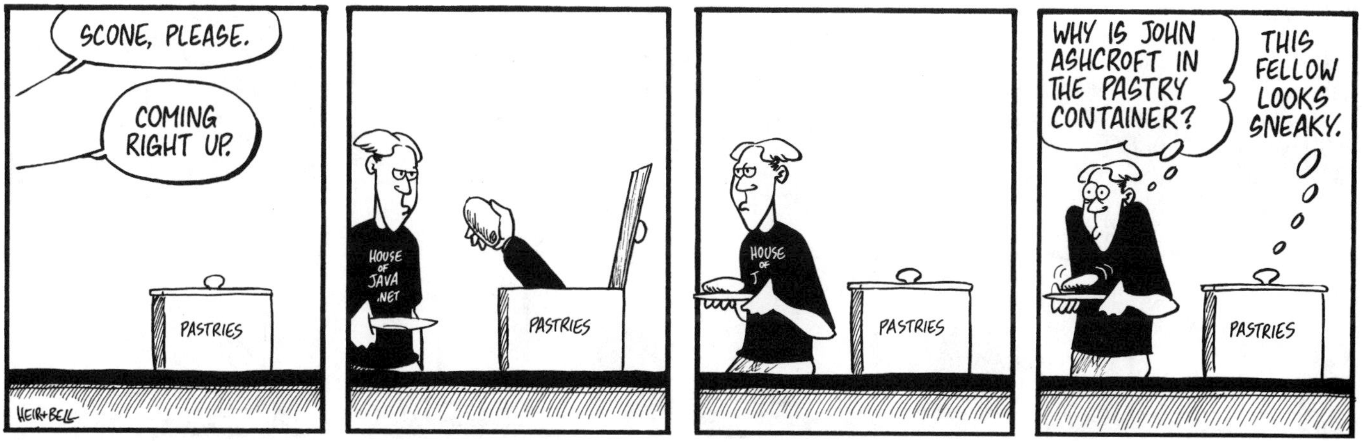
SCONE, PLEASE.
COMING RIGHT UP.
PASTRIES
HOUSE OF JAVA .NET
PASTRIES
HOUSE OF J
PASTRIES
WHY IS JOHN ASHCROFT IN THE PASTRY CONTAINER?
THIS FELLOW LOOKS SNEAKY.
PASTRIES
HEIR+BELL

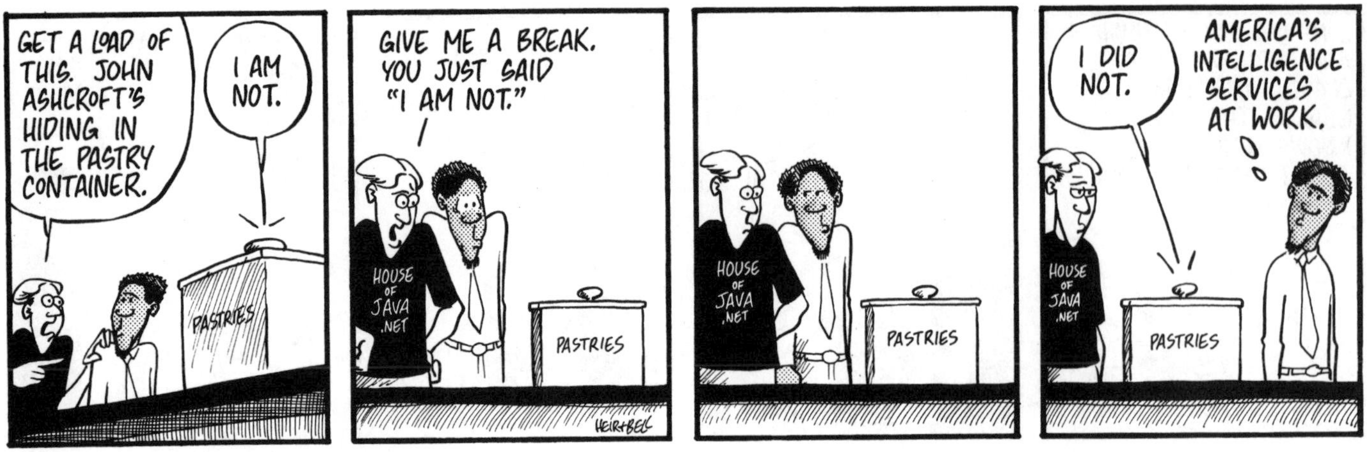
GET A LOAD OF THIS. JOHN ASHCROFT'S HIDING IN THE PASTRY CONTAINER.
I AM NOT.
PASTRIES
GIVE ME A BREAK. YOU JUST SAID "I AM NOT."
HOUSE OF JAVA .NET
PASTRIES
HEIR+BELL
I DID NOT.
AMERICA'S INTELLIGENCE SERVICES AT WORK.

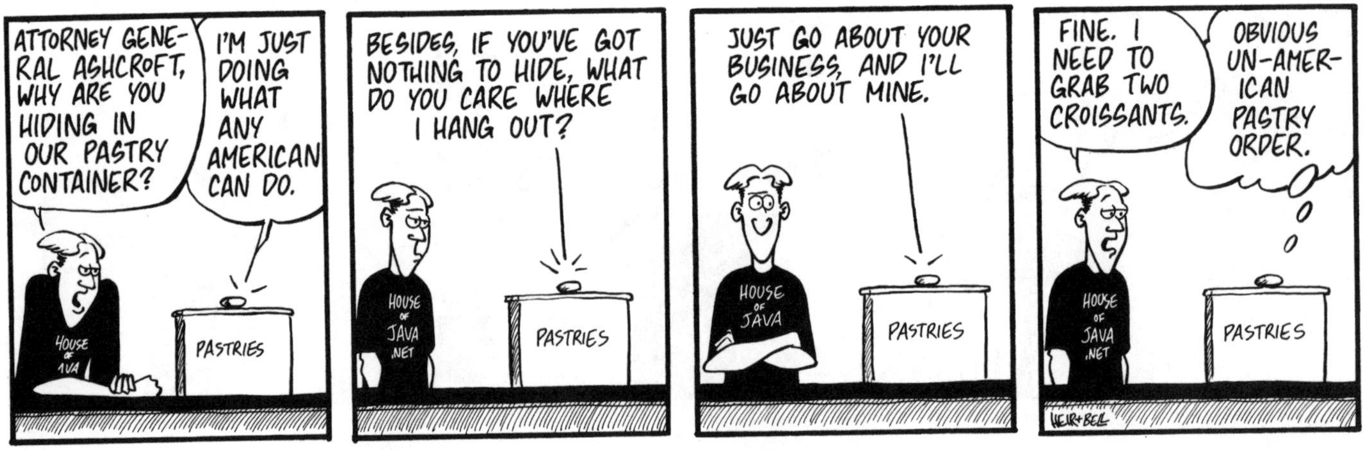
ATTORNEY GENERAL ASHCROFT, WHY ARE YOU HIDING IN OUR PASTRY CONTAINER?
I'M JUST DOING WHAT ANY AMERICAN CAN DO.
PASTRIES
BESIDES, IF YOU'VE GOT NOTHING TO HIDE, WHAT DO YOU CARE WHERE I HANG OUT?
JUST GO ABOUT YOUR BUSINESS, AND I'LL GO ABOUT MINE.
FINE. I NEED TO GRAB TWO CROISSANTS.
OBVIOUS UN-AMERICAN PASTRY ORDER.
HEIR+BELL

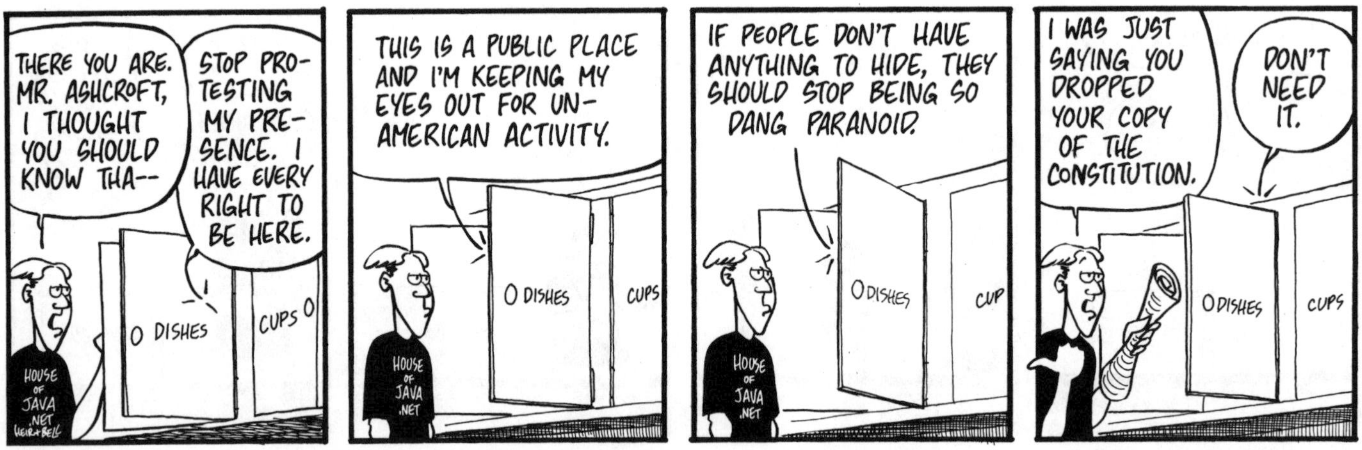
THERE YOU ARE. MR. ASHCROFT, I THOUGHT YOU SHOULD KNOW THA--
STOP PROTESTING MY PRESENCE. I HAVE EVERY RIGHT TO BE HERE.
DISHES
CUPS
THIS IS A PUBLIC PLACE AND I'M KEEPING MY EYES OUT FOR UN-AMERICAN ACTIVITY.
IF PEOPLE DON'T HAVE ANYTHING TO HIDE, THEY SHOULD STOP BEING SO DANG PARANOID.
I WAS JUST SAYING YOU DROPPED YOUR COPY OF THE CONSTITUTION.
DON'T NEED IT.

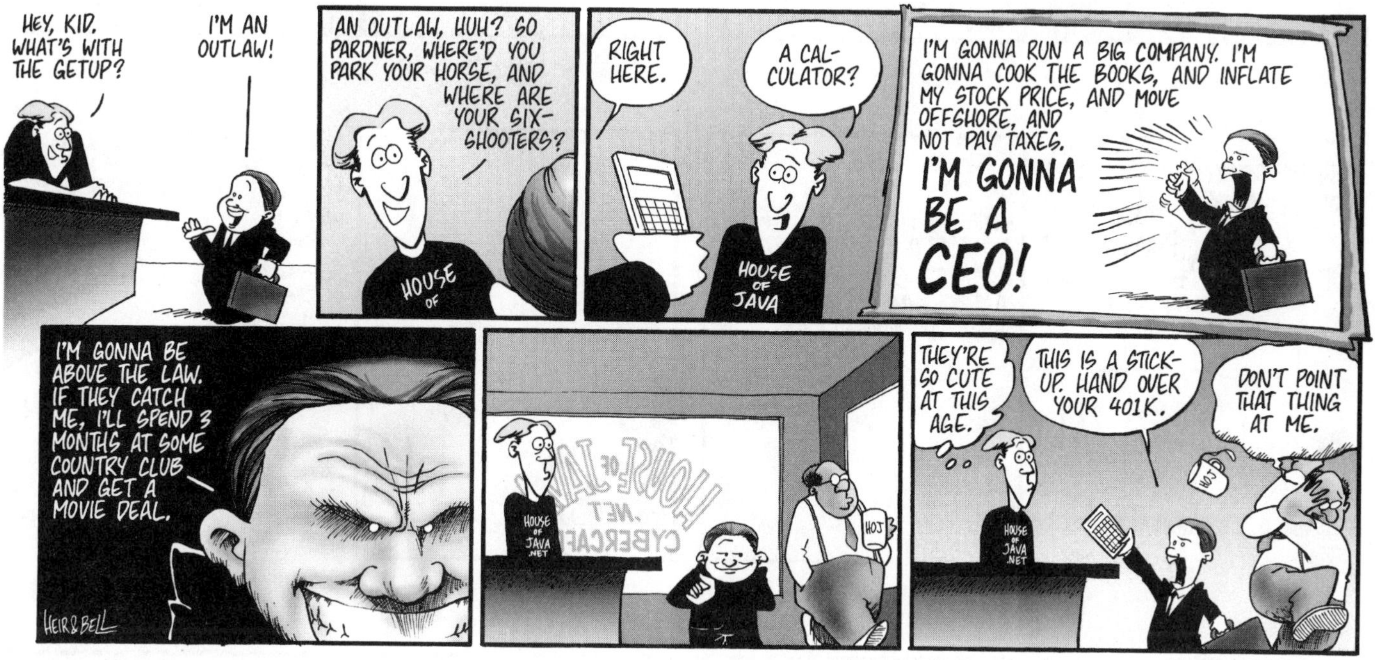
HEY, KID. WHAT'S WITH THE GETUP?
I'M AN OUTLAW!
AN OUTLAW, HUH? SO PARDNER, WHERE'D YOU PARK YOUR HORSE, AND WHERE ARE YOUR SIX-SHOOTERS?
HOUSE OF
A CAL-CULATOR?
RIGHT HERE.
HOUSE OF JAVA
I'M GONNA RUN A BIG COMPANY. I'M GONNA COOK THE BOOKS, AND INFLATE MY STOCK PRICE, AND MOVE OFFSHORE, AND NOT PAY TAXES.
I'M GONNA BE A CEO!
I'M GONNA BE ABOVE THE LAW. IF THEY CATCH ME, I'LL SPEND 3 MONTHS AT SOME COUNTRY CLUB AND GET A MOVIE DEAL.
HEIR & BELL
HOUSE OF JAVA .NET
HOJ
THEY'RE SO CUTE AT THIS AGE.
THIS IS A STICK-UP. HAND OVER YOUR 401K.
DON'T POINT THAT THING AT ME.

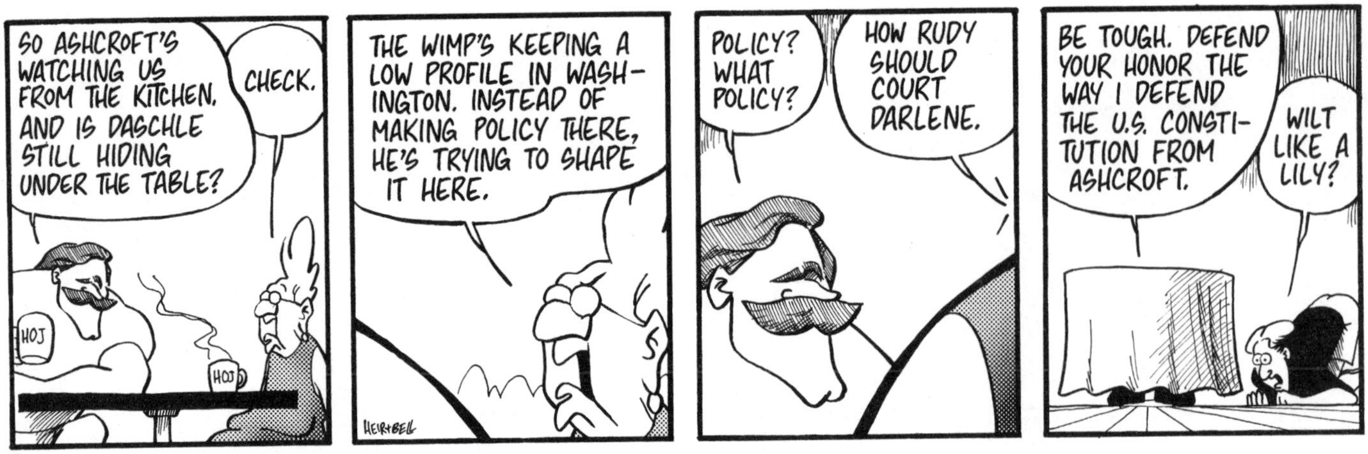
SO ASHCROFT'S WATCHING US FROM THE KITCHEN. AND IS DASCHLE STILL HIDING UNDER THE TABLE?
CHECK.
THE WIMP'S KEEPING A LOW PROFILE IN WASHINGTON. INSTEAD OF MAKING POLICY THERE, HE'S TRYING TO SHAPE IT HERE.
POLICY? WHAT POLICY?
HOW RUDY SHOULD COURT DARLENE.
BE TOUGH. DEFEND YOUR HONOR THE WAY I DEFEND THE U.S. CONSTITUTION FROM ASHCROFT.
WILT LIKE A LILY?
HOJ
HEIR+BELL

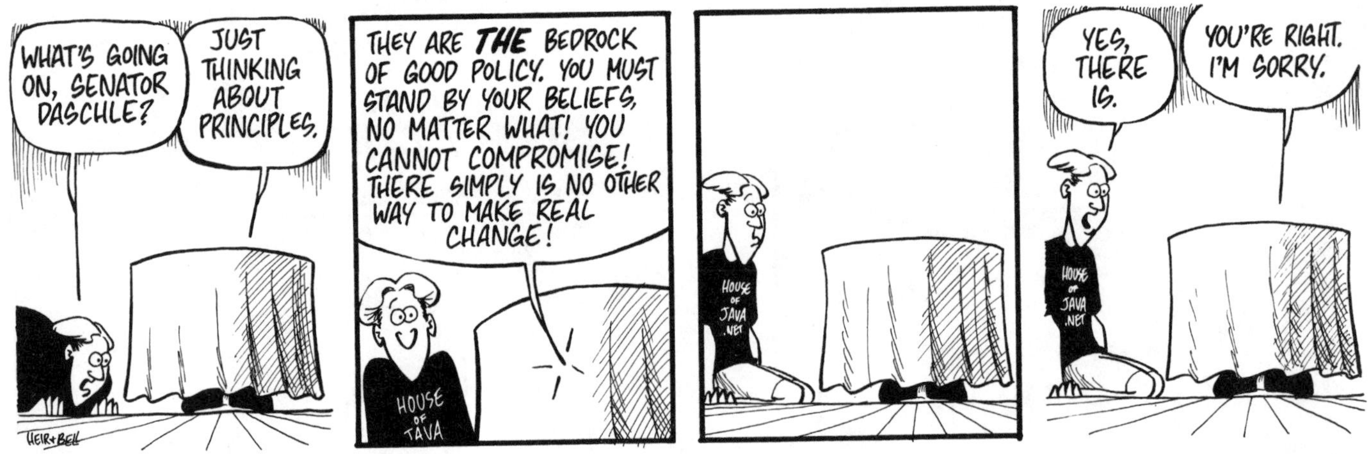
WHAT'S GOING ON, SENATOR DASCHLE?
JUST THINKING ABOUT PRINCIPLES.
THEY ARE THE BEDROCK OF GOOD POLICY. YOU MUST STAND BY YOUR BELIEFS, NO MATTER WHAT! YOU CANNOT COMPROMISE! THERE SIMPLY IS NO OTHER WAY TO MAKE REAL CHANGE!
YES, THERE IS.
YOU'RE RIGHT. I'M SORRY.
HOUSE OF JAVA
HOUSE OF JAVA.NET
HEIR+BELL

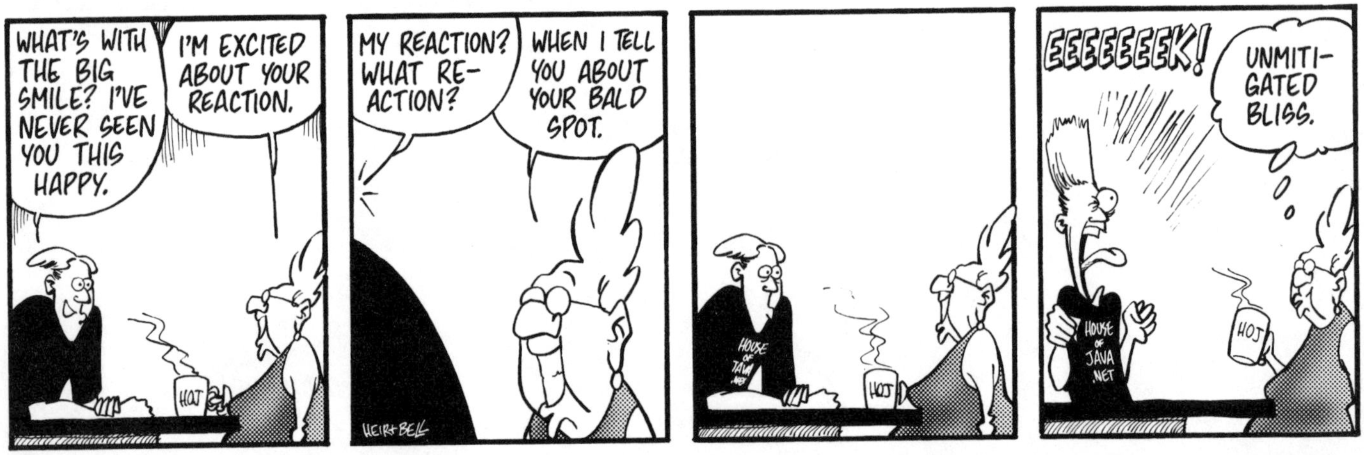
WHAT'S WITH THE BIG SMILE? I'VE NEVER SEEN YOU THIS HAPPY.
I'M EXCITED ABOUT YOUR REACTION.
MY REACTION? WHAT REACTION?
WHEN I TELL YOU ABOUT YOUR BALD SPOT.
EEEEEEEK!
UNMITIGATED BLISS.
HOJ
HOUSE OF JAVA.NET
HEIR+BELL

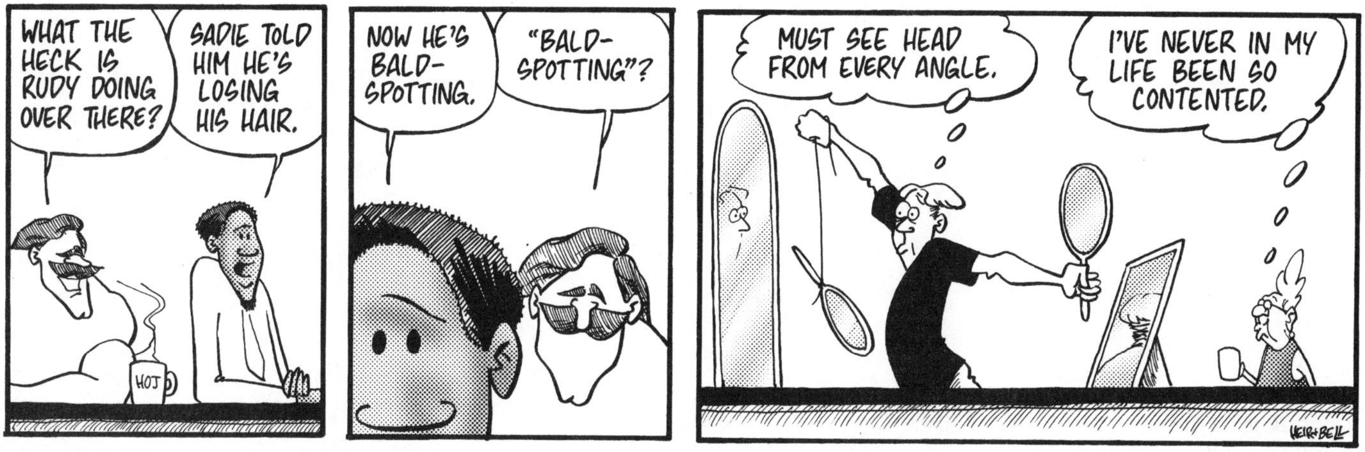
WHAT THE HECK IS RUDY DOING OVER THERE?
SADIE TOLD HIM HE'S LOSING HIS HAIR.
NOW HE'S BALD-SPOTTING.
"BALD-SPOTTING"?
MUST SEE HEAD FROM EVERY ANGLE.
I'VE NEVER IN MY LIFE BEEN SO CONTENTED.

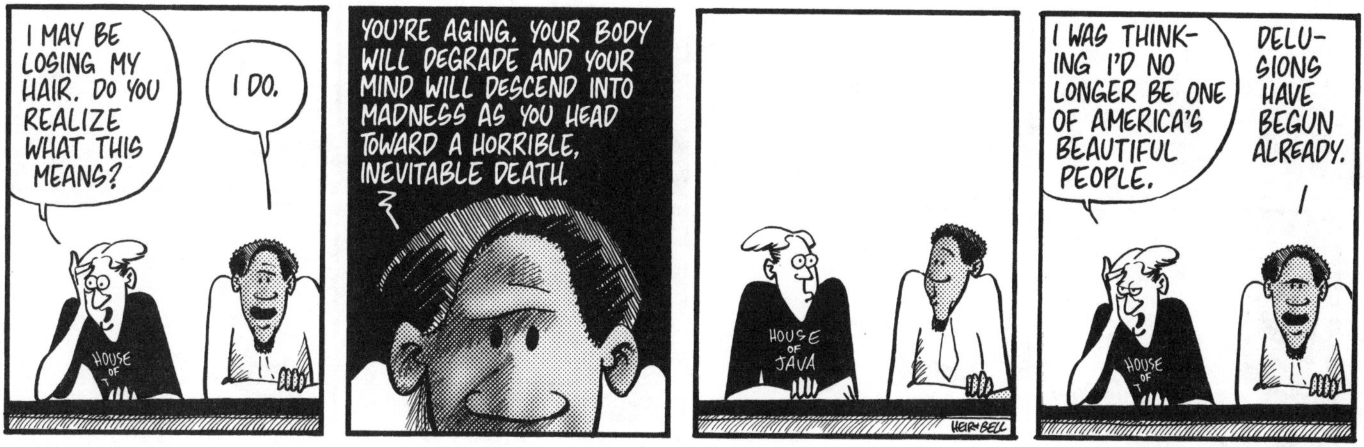
I MAY BE LOSING MY HAIR. DO YOU REALIZE WHAT THIS MEANS?
I DO.
YOU'RE AGING. YOUR BODY WILL DEGRADE AND YOUR MIND WILL DESCEND INTO MADNESS AS YOU HEAD TOWARD A HORRIBLE, INEVITABLE DEATH.
I WAS THINKING I'D NO LONGER BE ONE OF AMERICA'S BEAUTIFUL PEOPLE.
DELUSIONS HAVE BEGUN ALREADY.

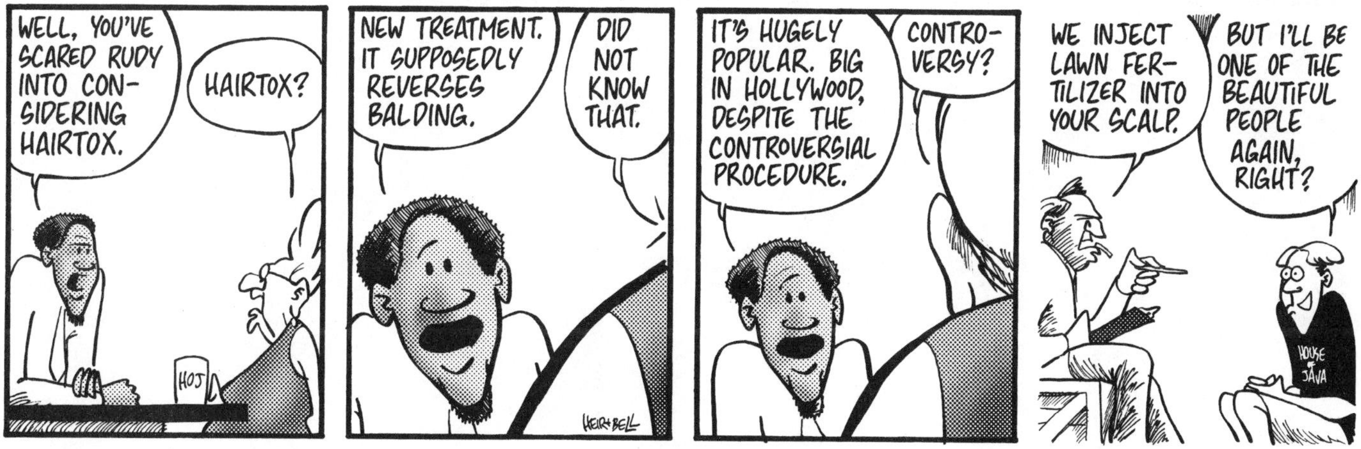
WELL, YOU'VE SCARED RUDY INTO CONSIDERING HAIRTOX.
HAIRTOX?
NEW TREATMENT. IT SUPPOSEDLY REVERSES BALDING.
DID NOT KNOW THAT.
IT'S HUGELY POPULAR. BIG IN HOLLYWOOD, DESPITE THE CONTROVERSIAL PROCEDURE.
CONTROVERSY?
WE INJECT LAWN FERTILIZER INTO YOUR SCALP.
BUT I'LL BE ONE OF THE BEAUTIFUL PEOPLE AGAIN, RIGHT?

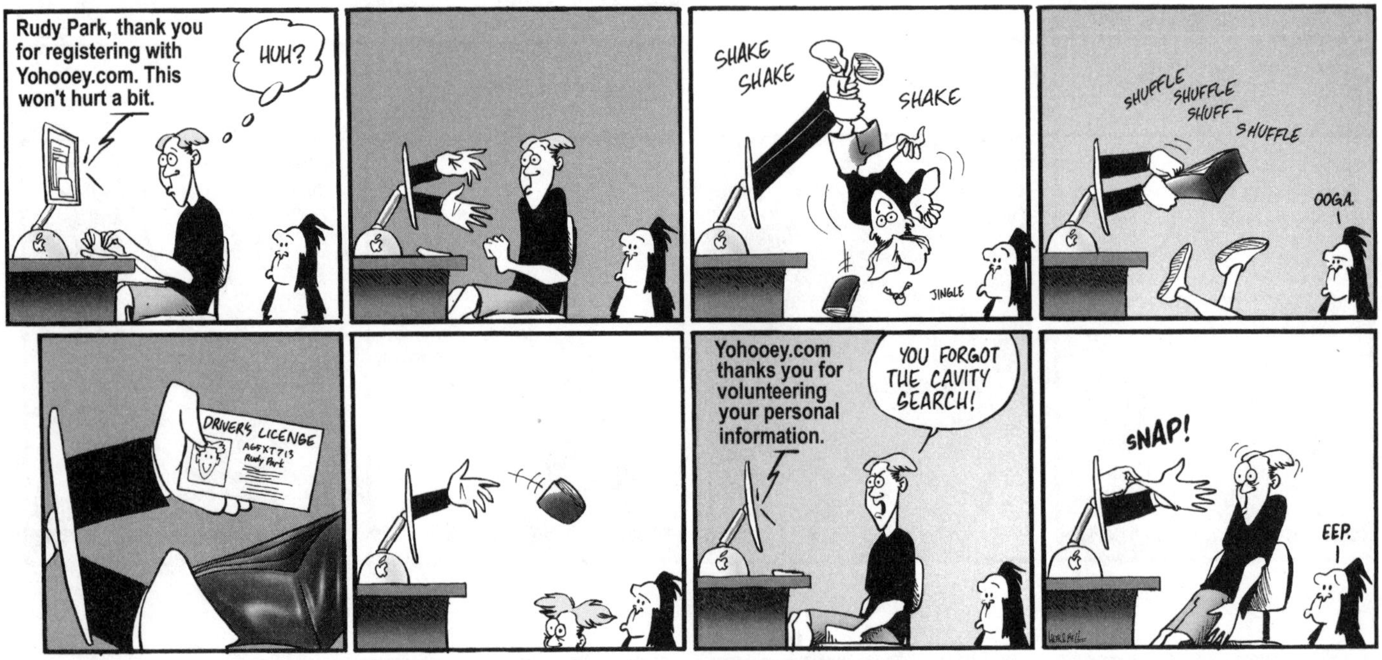
Rudy Park, thank you for registering with Yohooey.com. This won't hurt a bit.
HUH?
SHAKE
SHAKE
SHAKE
JINGLE
SHUFFLE
SHUFFLE
SHUFF-
SHUFFLE
OOGA.
DRIVER'S LICENSE
Rudy Park
Yohooey.com thanks you for volunteering your personal information.
YOU FORGOT THE CAVITY SEARCH!
SNAP!
EEP.

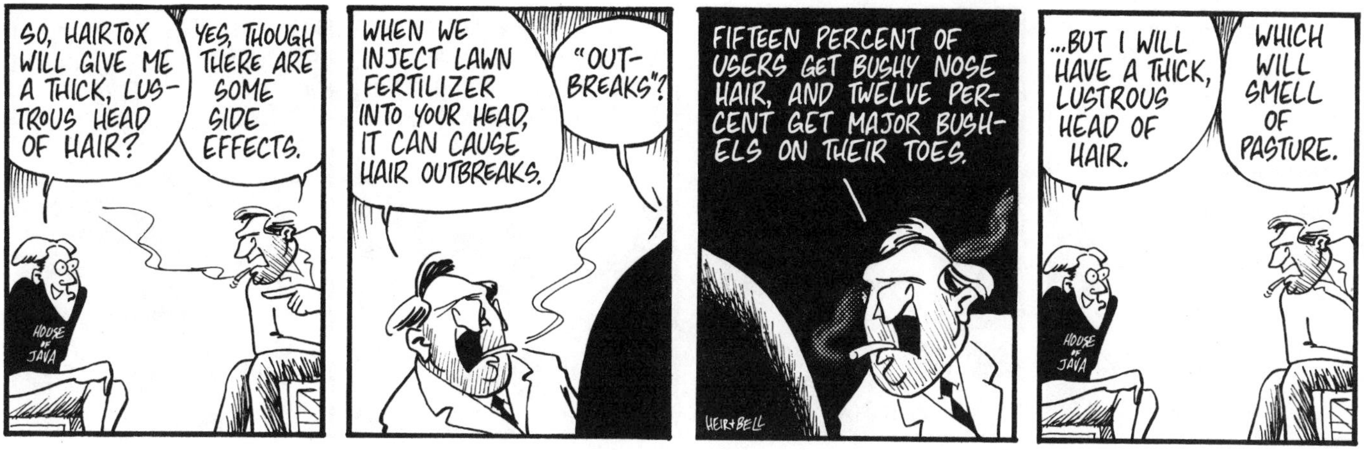
SO, HAIRTOX WILL GIVE ME A THICK, LUSTROUS HEAD OF HAIR?
YES, THOUGH THERE ARE SOME SIDE EFFECTS.
HOUSE OF JAVA
WHEN WE INJECT LAWN FERTILIZER INTO YOUR HEAD, IT CAN CAUSE HAIR OUTBREAKS.
"OUT-BREAKS"?
FIFTEEN PERCENT OF USERS GET BUSHY NOSE HAIR, AND TWELVE PERCENT GET MAJOR BUSHELS ON THEIR TOES.
HEIR+BELL
...BUT I WILL HAVE A THICK, LUSTROUS HEAD OF HAIR.
WHICH WILL SMELL OF PASTURE.
HOUSE OF JAVA
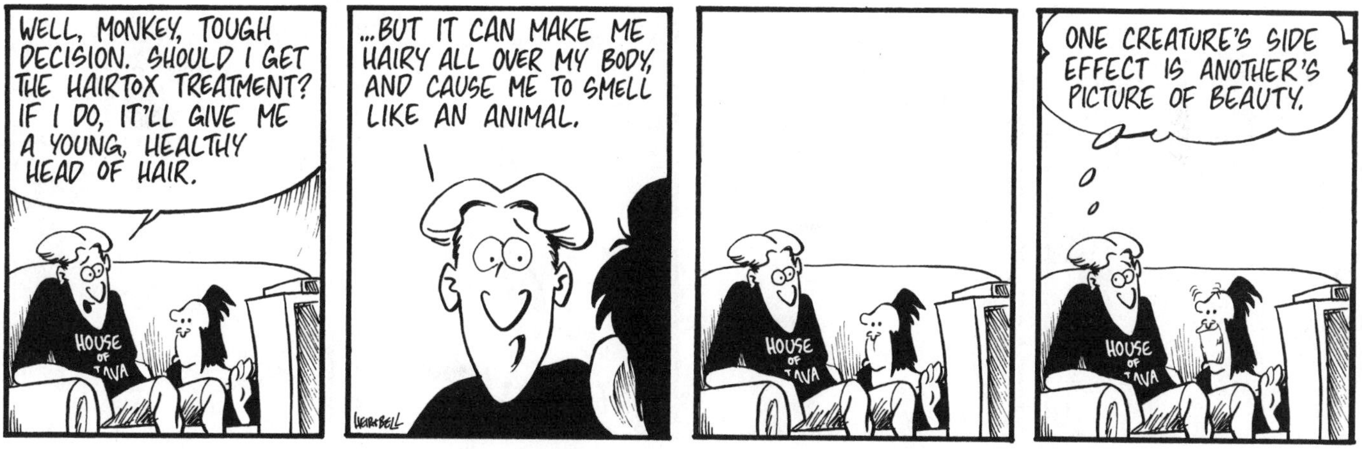
WELL, MONKEY, TOUGH DECISION. SHOULD I GET THE HAIRTOX TREATMENT? IF I DO, IT'LL GIVE ME A YOUNG, HEALTHY HEAD OF HAIR.
...BUT IT CAN MAKE ME HAIRY ALL OVER MY BODY, AND CAUSE ME TO SMELL LIKE AN ANIMAL.
HEIR+BELL
ONE CREATURE'S SIDE EFFECT IS ANOTHER'S PICTURE OF BEAUTY.
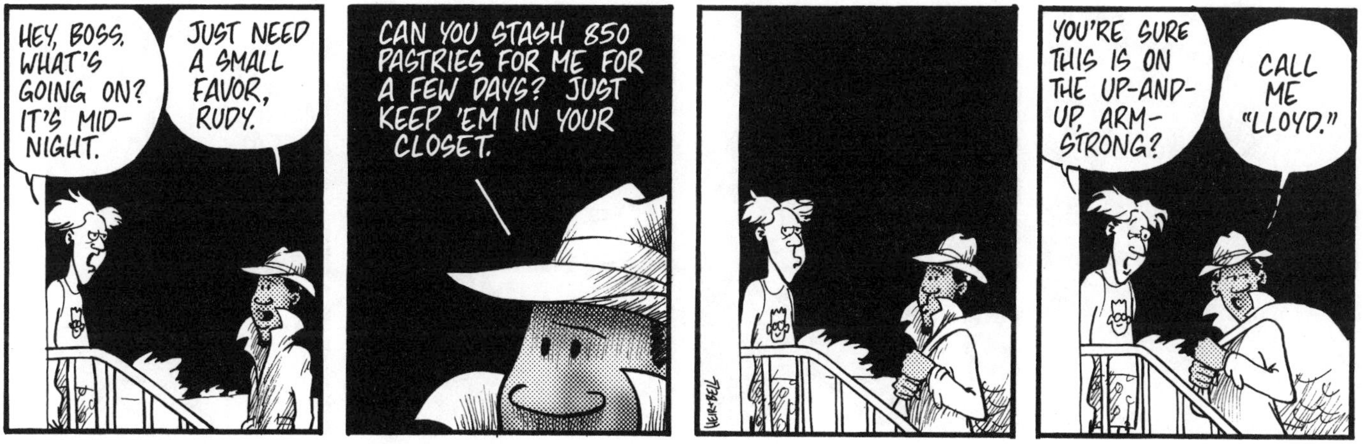
HEY, BOSS. WHAT'S GOING ON? IT'S MIDNIGHT.
JUST NEED A SMALL FAVOR, RUDY.
CAN YOU STASH 850 PASTRIES FOR ME FOR A FEW DAYS? JUST KEEP 'EM IN YOUR CLOSET.
HEIR+BELL
YOU'RE SURE THIS IS ON THE UP-AND-UP, ARMSTRONG?
CALL ME "LLOYD."

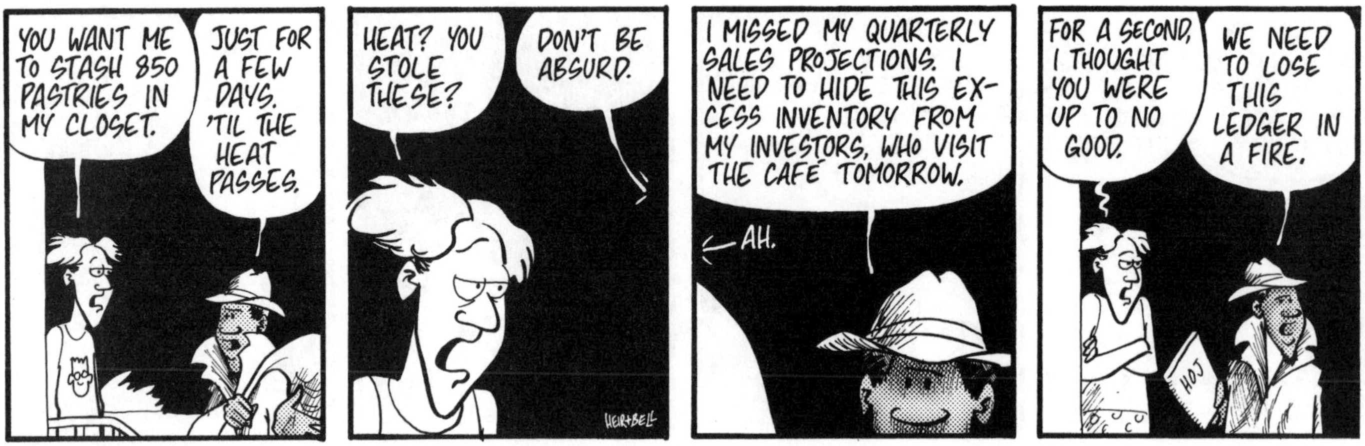
YOU WANT ME TO STASH 850 PASTRIES IN MY CLOSET.
JUST FOR A FEW DAYS. 'TIL THE HEAT PASSES.
HEAT? YOU STOLE THESE?
DON'T BE ABSURD.
HEIR+BELL
I MISSED MY QUARTERLY SALES PROJECTIONS. I NEED TO HIDE THIS EXCESS INVENTORY FROM MY INVESTORS, WHO VISIT THE CAFE TOMORROW.
AH.
FOR A SECOND, I THOUGHT YOU WERE UP TO NO GOOD.
WE NEED TO LOSE THIS LEDGER IN A FIRE.
HOJ

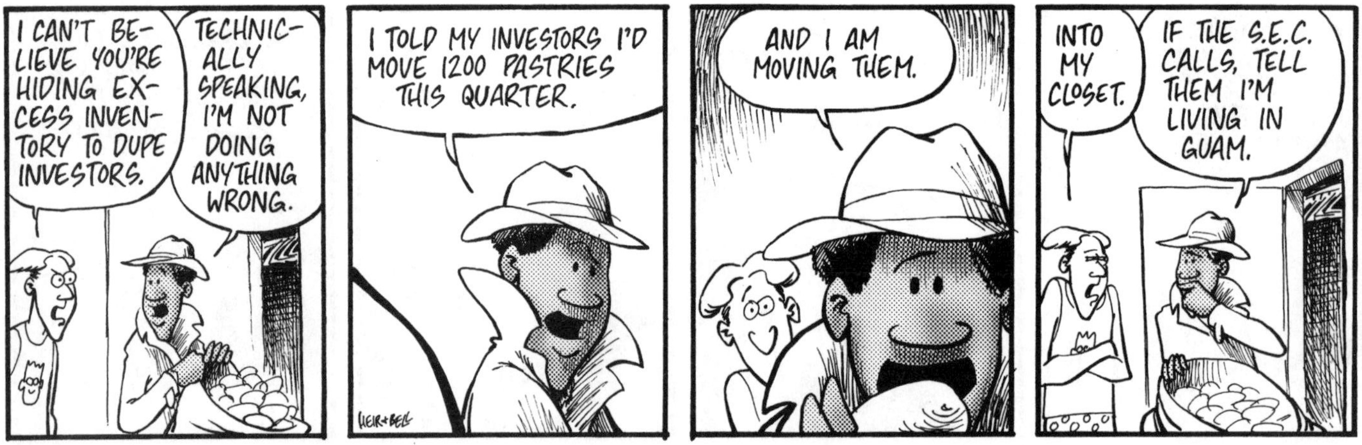
I CAN'T BELIEVE YOU'RE HIDING EXCESS INVENTORY TO DUPE INVESTORS.
TECHNICALLY SPEAKING, I'M NOT DOING ANYTHING WRONG.
I TOLD MY INVESTORS I'D MOVE 1200 PASTRIES THIS QUARTER.
HEIR+BELL
AND I AM MOVING THEM.
INTO MY CLOSET.
IF THE S.E.C. CALLS, TELL THEM I'M LIVING IN GUAM.

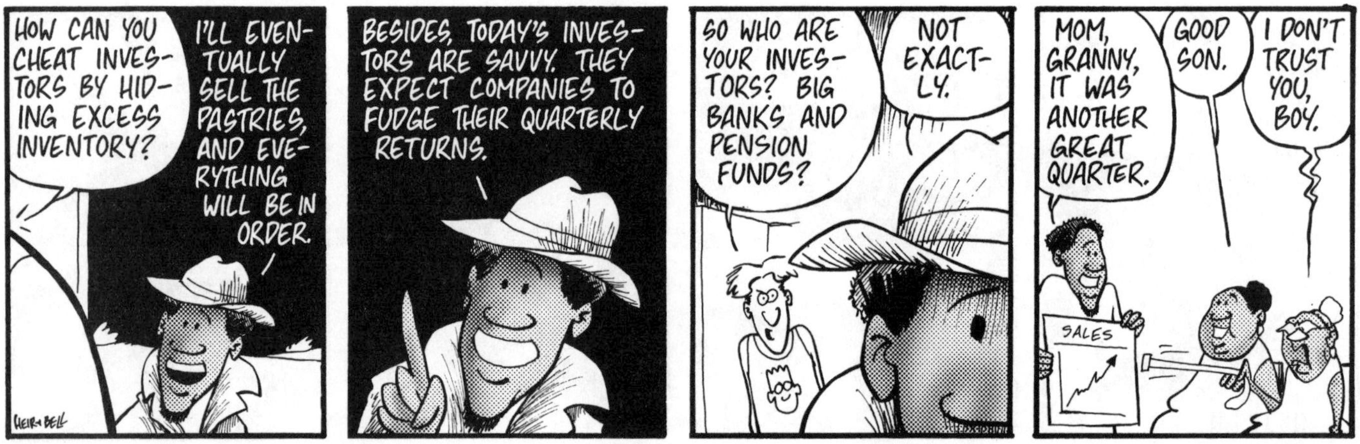
HOW CAN YOU CHEAT INVESTORS BY HIDING EXCESS INVENTORY?
I'LL EVENTUALLY SELL THE PASTRIES, AND EVERYTHING WILL BE IN ORDER.
HEIR+BELL
BESIDES, TODAY'S INVESTORS ARE SAVVY. THEY EXPECT COMPANIES TO FUDGE THEIR QUARTERLY RETURNS.
SO WHO ARE YOUR INVESTORS? BIG BANKS AND PENSION FUNDS?
NOT EXACTLY.
MOM, GRANNY, IT WAS ANOTHER GREAT QUARTER.
GOOD SON.
I DON'T TRUST YOU, BOY.
SALES

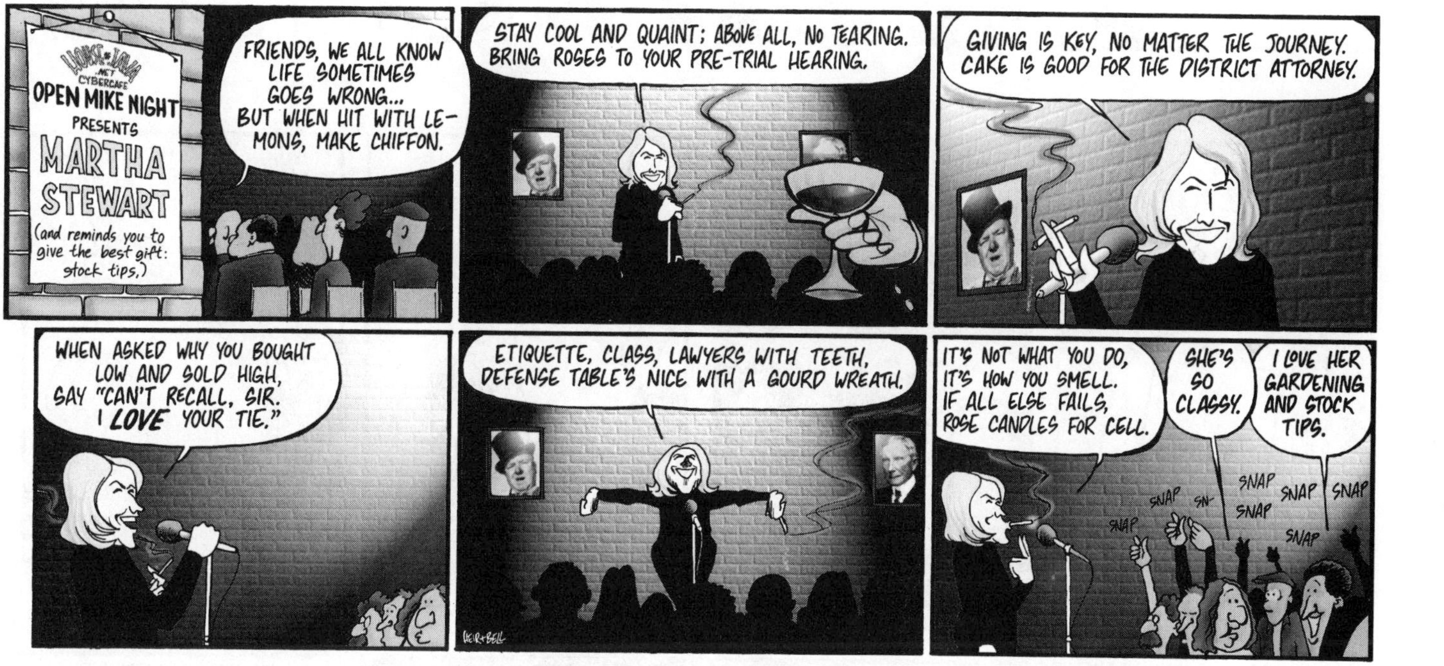
HOUSE of JAVA .NET CYBERCAFE
OPEN MIKE NIGHT
PRESENTS
MARTHA
STEWART
(and reminds you to give the best gift: stock tips.)
FRIENDS, WE ALL KNOW LIFE SOMETIMES GOES WRONG... BUT WHEN HIT WITH LE- MONS, MAKE CHIFFON.
STAY COOL AND QUAINT; ABOVE ALL, NO TEARING. BRING ROSES TO YOUR PRE-TRIAL HEARING.
GIVING IS KEY, NO MATTER THE JOURNEY. CAKE IS GOOD FOR THE DISTRICT ATTORNEY.
WHEN ASKED WHY YOU BOUGHT LOW AND SOLD HIGH, SAY "CAN'T RECALL, SIR. I *LOVE* YOUR TIE."
ETIQUETTE, CLASS, LAWYERS WITH TEETH, DEFENSE TABLE'S NICE WITH A GOURD WREATH.
HEIR+BELL
IT'S NOT WHAT YOU DO, IT'S HOW YOU SMELL. IF ALL ELSE FAILS, ROSE CANDLES FOR CELL.
SHE'S SO CLASSY.
I LOVE HER GARDENING AND STOCK TIPS.
SNAP SNAP SN- SNAP SNAP SNAP SNAP SNAP

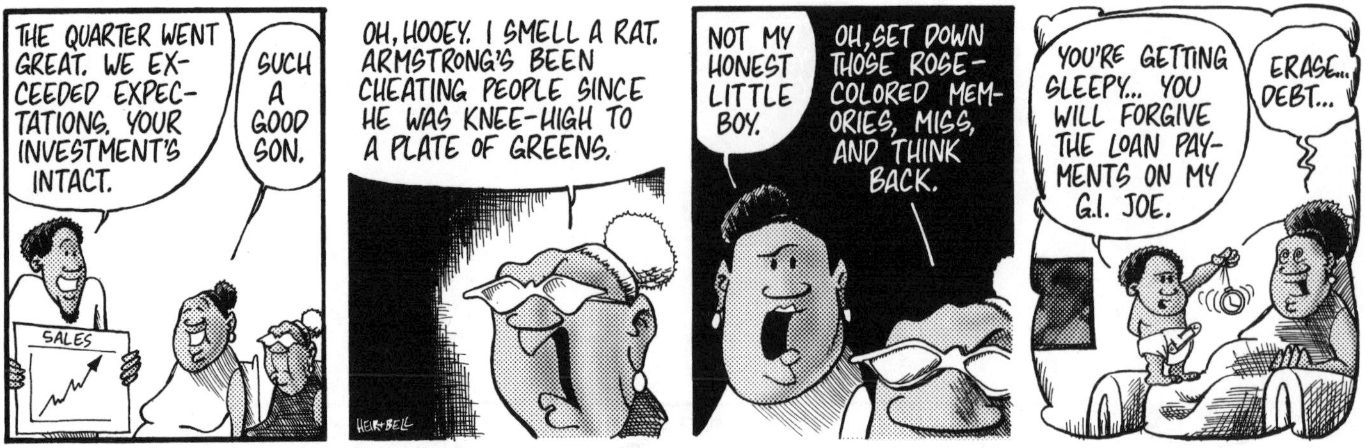
THE QUARTER WENT GREAT. WE EXCEEDED EXPECTATIONS. YOUR INVESTMENT'S INTACT.
SUCH A GOOD SON.
SALES
OH, HOOEY. I SMELL A RAT. ARMSTRONG'S BEEN CHEATING PEOPLE SINCE HE WAS KNEE-HIGH TO A PLATE OF GREENS.
NOT MY HONEST LITTLE BOY.
OH, SET DOWN THOSE ROSE-COLORED MEMORIES, MISS, AND THINK BACK.
YOU'RE GETTING SLEEPY... YOU WILL FORGIVE THE LOAN PAYMENTS ON MY G.I. JOE.
ERASE... DEBT...

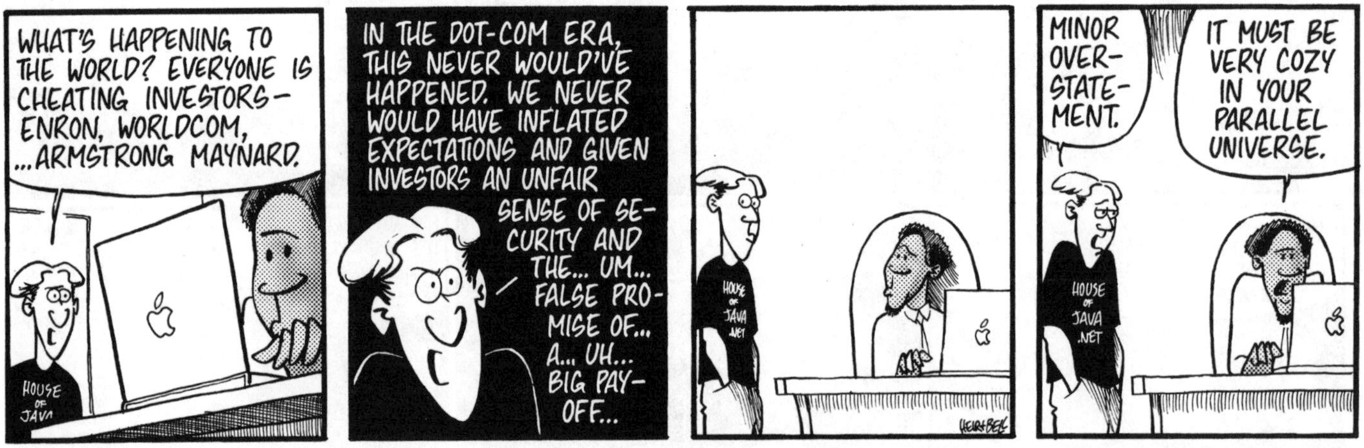
WHAT'S HAPPENING TO THE WORLD? EVERYONE IS CHEATING INVESTORS—ENRON, WORLDCOM, ...ARMSTRONG MAYNARD.
HOUSE OF JAVA
IN THE DOT-COM ERA, THIS NEVER WOULD'VE HAPPENED. WE NEVER WOULD HAVE INFLATED EXPECTATIONS AND GIVEN INVESTORS AN UNFAIR SENSE OF SECURITY AND THE... UM... FALSE PROMISE OF... A... UH... BIG PAYOFF...
HOUSE OF JAVA .NET
MINOR OVERSTATEMENT.
IT MUST BE VERY COZY IN YOUR PARALLEL UNIVERSE.
HOUSE OF JAVA .NET

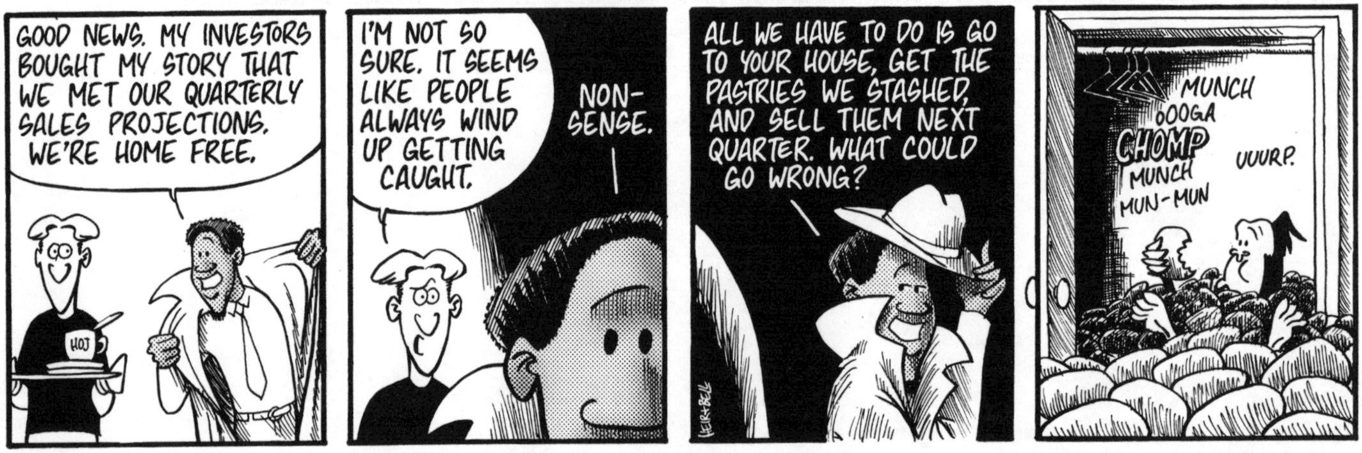
GOOD NEWS. MY INVESTORS BOUGHT MY STORY THAT WE MET OUR QUARTERLY SALES PROJECTIONS. WE'RE HOME FREE.
HOJ
I'M NOT SO SURE. IT SEEMS LIKE PEOPLE ALWAYS WIND UP GETTING CAUGHT.
NONSENSE.
ALL WE HAVE TO DO IS GO TO YOUR HOUSE, GET THE PASTRIES WE STASHED, AND SELL THEM NEXT QUARTER. WHAT COULD GO WRONG?
MUNCH
OOOGA
CHOMP
UUURP.
MUNCH
MUN-MUN

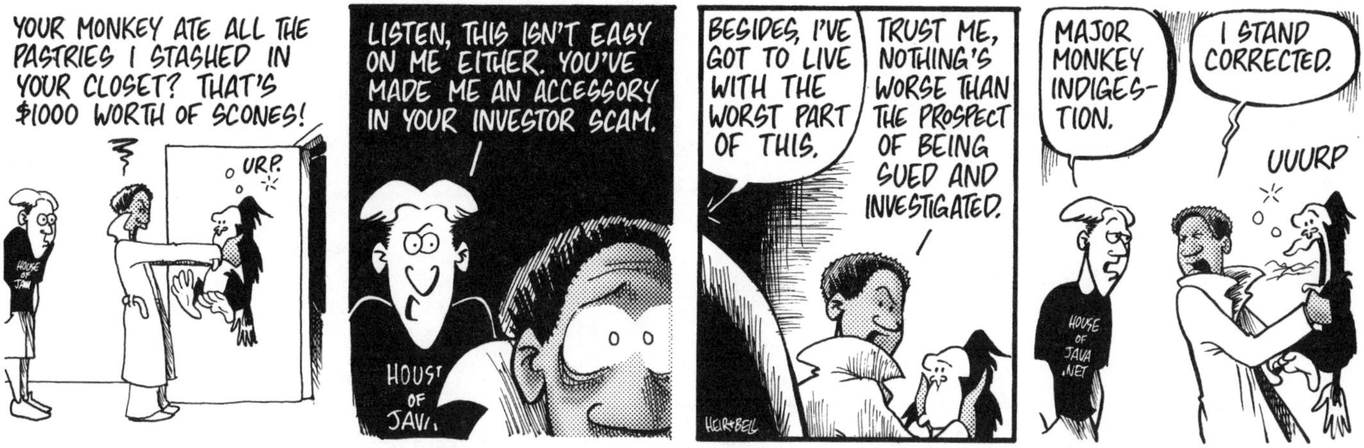

YOUR MONKEY ATE ALL THE PASTRIES I STASHED IN YOUR CLOSET? THAT'S $1000 WORTH OF SCONES!
URP.
LISTEN, THIS ISN'T EASY ON ME EITHER. YOU'VE MADE ME AN ACCESSORY IN YOUR INVESTOR SCAM.
BESIDES, I'VE GOT TO LIVE WITH THE WORST PART OF THIS.
TRUST ME, NOTHING'S WORSE THAN THE PROSPECT OF BEING SUED AND INVESTIGATED.
HEIR+BELL
MAJOR MONKEY INDIGES-TION.
I STAND CORRECTED.
UUURP

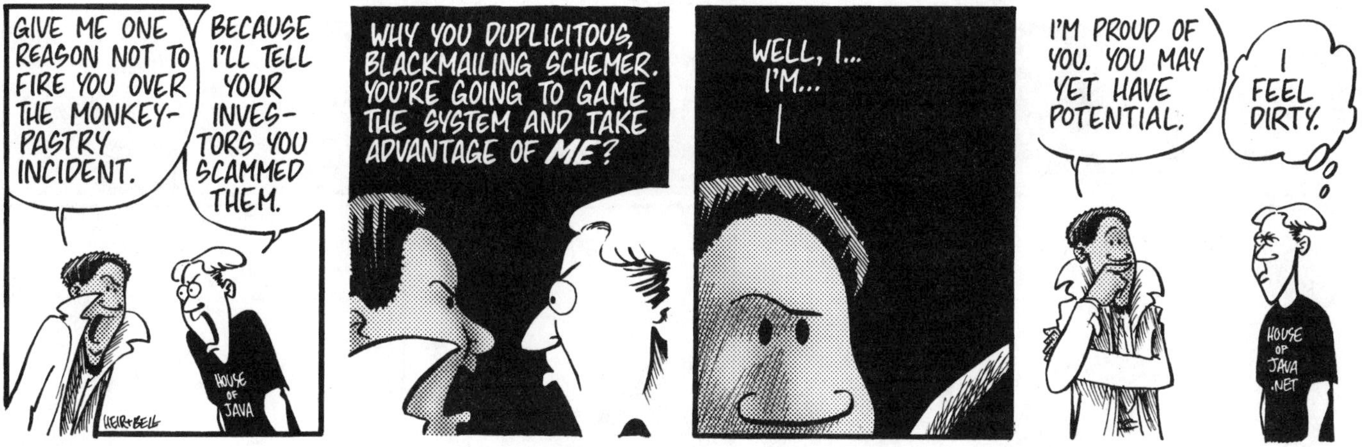

GIVE ME ONE REASON NOT TO FIRE YOU OVER THE MONKEY-PASTRY INCIDENT.
BECAUSE I'LL TELL YOUR INVES-TORS YOU SCAMMED THEM.
HEIR+BELL
WHY YOU DUPLICITOUS, BLACKMAILING SCHEMER. YOU'RE GOING TO GAME THE SYSTEM AND TAKE ADVANTAGE OF ME?
WELL, I... I'M...
I'M PROUD OF YOU. YOU MAY YET HAVE POTENTIAL.
I FEEL DIRTY.

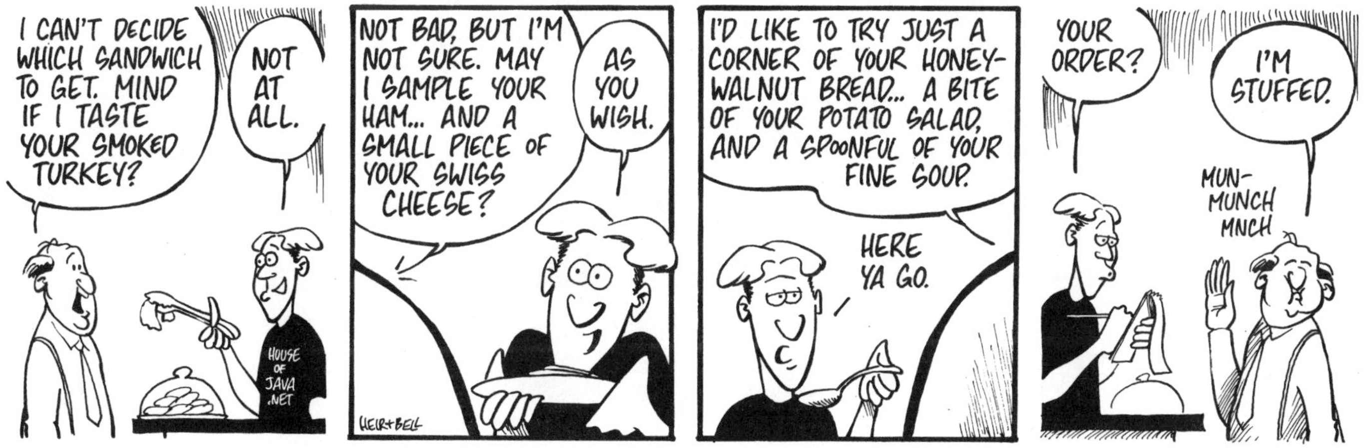

I CAN'T DECIDE WHICH SANDWICH TO GET. MIND IF I TASTE YOUR SMOKED TURKEY?
NOT AT ALL.
NOT BAD, BUT I'M NOT SURE. MAY I SAMPLE YOUR HAM... AND A SMALL PIECE OF YOUR SWISS CHEESE?
AS YOU WISH.
HEIR+BELL
I'D LIKE TO TRY JUST A CORNER OF YOUR HONEY-WALNUT BREAD... A BITE OF YOUR POTATO SALAD, AND A SPOONFUL OF YOUR FINE SOUP.
HERE YA GO.
YOUR ORDER?
I'M STUFFED.
MUN-MUNCH MNCH

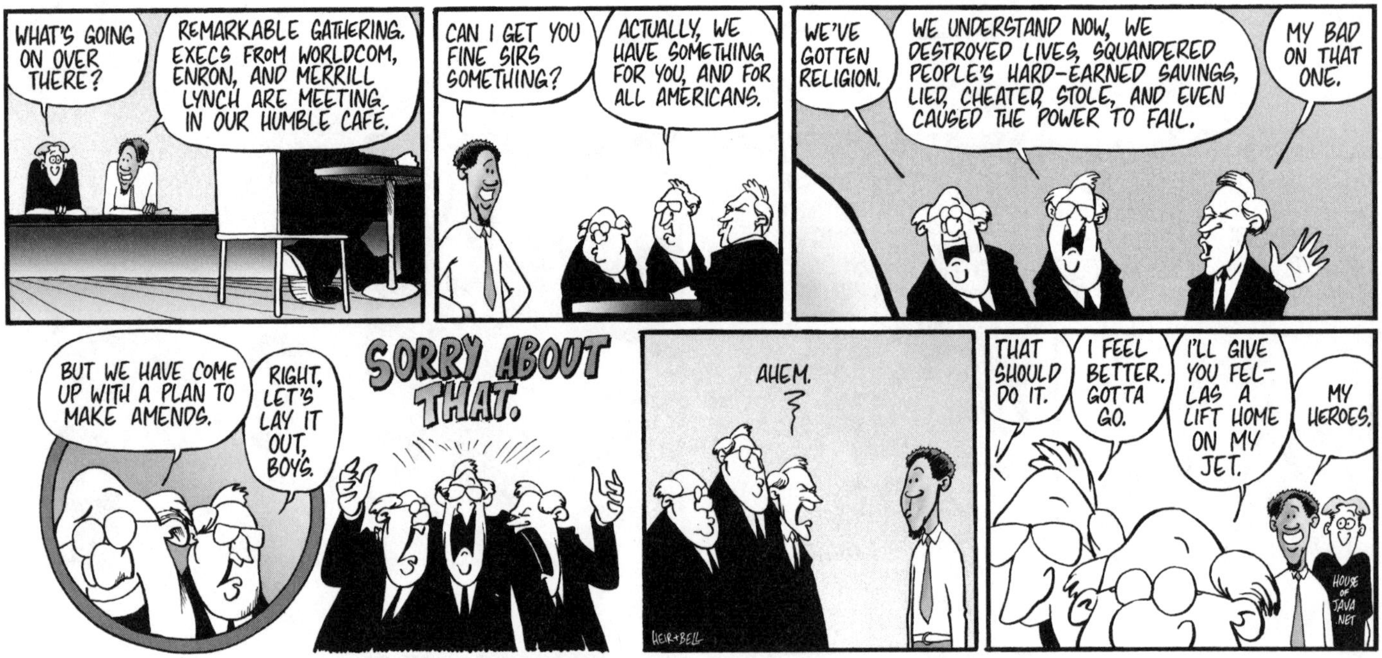

WHAT'S GOING ON OVER THERE?
REMARKABLE GATHERING. EXECS FROM WORLDCOM, ENRON, AND MERRILL LYNCH ARE MEETING IN OUR HUMBLE CAFÉ.
CAN I GET YOU FINE SIRS SOMETHING?
ACTUALLY, WE HAVE SOMETHING FOR YOU, AND FOR ALL AMERICANS.
WE'VE GOTTEN RELIGION.
WE UNDERSTAND NOW, WE DESTROYED LIVES, SQUANDERED PEOPLE'S HARD-EARNED SAVINGS, LIED, CHEATED, STOLE, AND EVEN CAUSED THE POWER TO FAIL.
MY BAD ON THAT ONE.
BUT WE HAVE COME UP WITH A PLAN TO MAKE AMENDS.
RIGHT, LET'S LAY IT OUT, BOYS.
SORRY ABOUT THAT.
AHEM.
HEIR+BELL
THAT SHOULD DO IT.
I FEEL BETTER. GOTTA GO.
I'LL GIVE YOU FEL-LAS A LIFT HOME ON MY JET.
MY HEROES.
HOUSE OF JAVA .NET

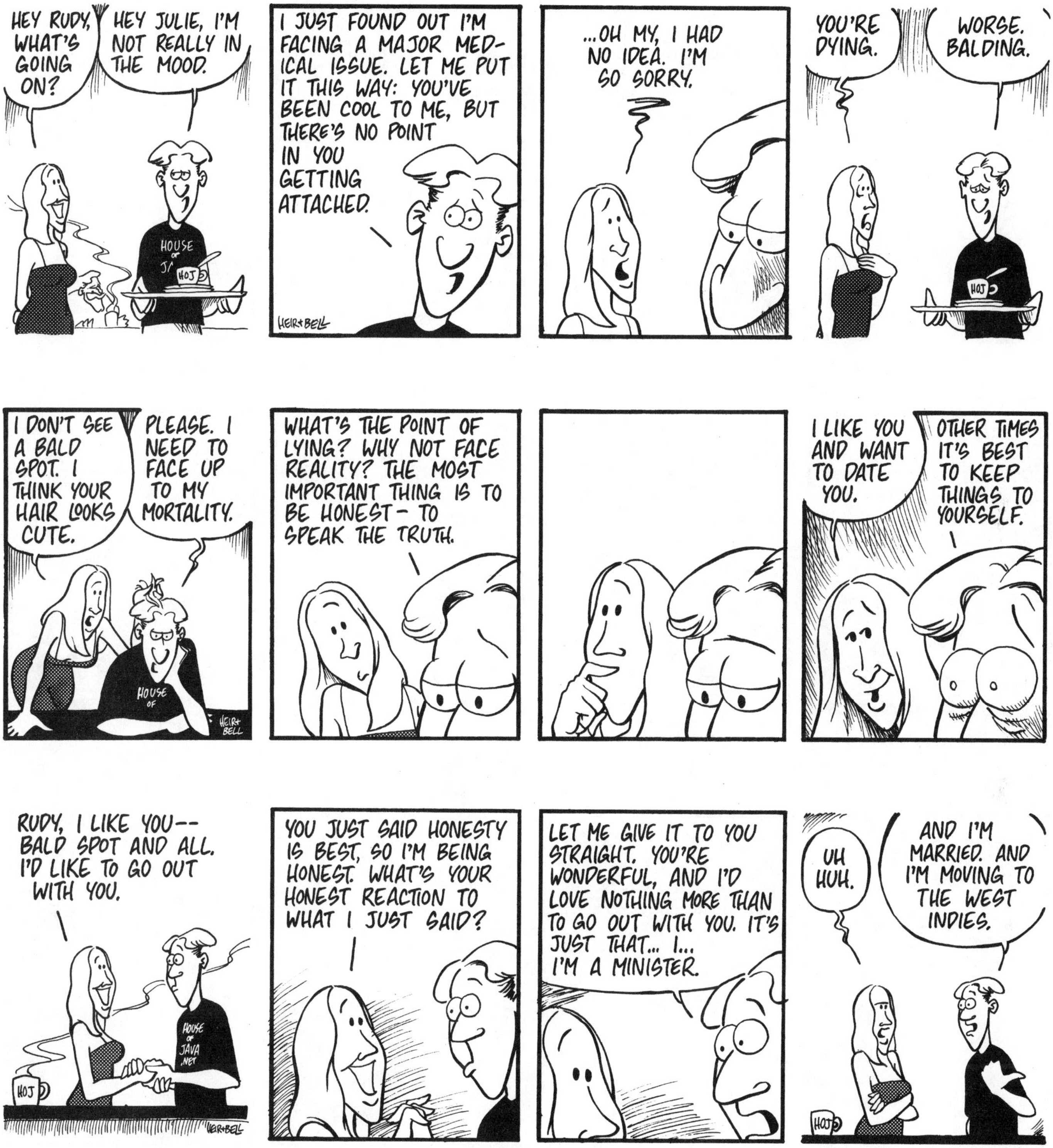
HEY RUDY, WHAT'S GOING ON?
HEY JULIE, I'M NOT REALLY IN THE MOOD.
HOUSE OF J
HOJ
HEIR+BELL
I JUST FOUND OUT I'M FACING A MAJOR MEDICAL ISSUE. LET ME PUT IT THIS WAY: YOU'VE BEEN COOL TO ME, BUT THERE'S NO POINT IN YOU GETTING ATTACHED.
...OH MY, I HAD NO IDEA. I'M SO SORRY.
YOU'RE DYING.
WORSE. BALDING.
HOJ
I DON'T SEE A BALD SPOT. I THINK YOUR HAIR LOOKS CUTE.
PLEASE. I NEED TO FACE UP TO MY MORTALITY.
HOUSE OF
HEIR+BELL
WHAT'S THE POINT OF LYING? WHY NOT FACE REALITY? THE MOST IMPORTANT THING IS TO BE HONEST— TO SPEAK THE TRUTH.
I LIKE YOU AND WANT TO DATE YOU.
OTHER TIMES IT'S BEST TO KEEP THINGS TO YOURSELF.
RUDY, I LIKE YOU-- BALD SPOT AND ALL. I'D LIKE TO GO OUT WITH YOU.
HOUSE OF JAVA .NET
HOJ
HEIR+BELL
YOU JUST SAID HONESTY IS BEST, SO I'M BEING HONEST. WHAT'S YOUR HONEST REACTION TO WHAT I JUST SAID?
LET ME GIVE IT TO YOU STRAIGHT. YOU'RE WONDERFUL, AND I'D LOVE NOTHING MORE THAN TO GO OUT WITH YOU. IT'S JUST THAT... I... I'M A MINISTER.
UH HUH.
AND I'M MARRIED. AND I'M MOVING TO THE WEST INDIES.
HOJ

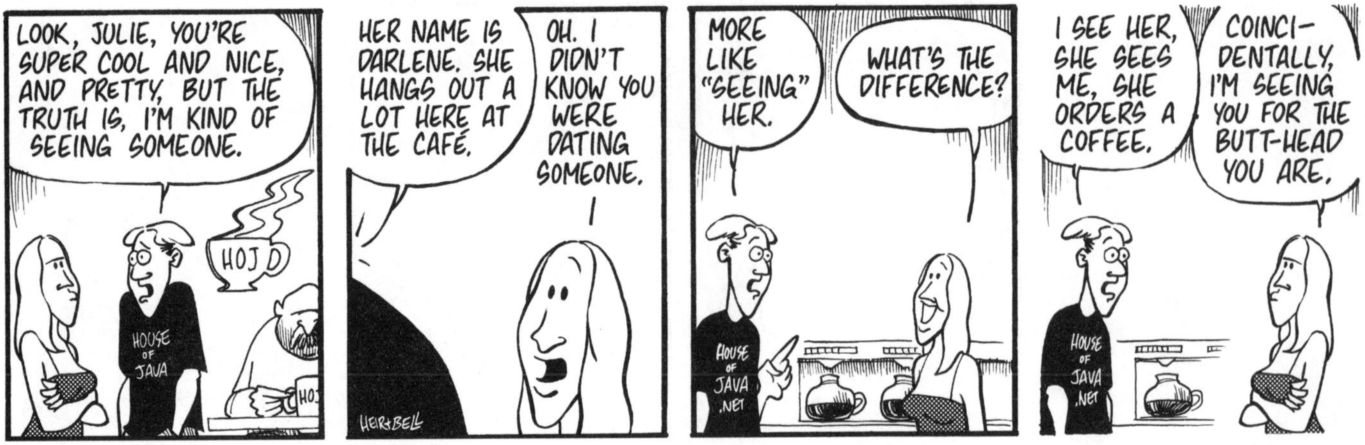
LOOK, JULIE, YOU'RE SUPER COOL AND NICE, AND PRETTY, BUT THE TRUTH IS, I'M KIND OF SEEING SOMEONE.
HOJ
HOUSE OF JAVA
HER NAME IS DARLENE. SHE HANGS OUT A LOT HERE AT THE CAFÉ.
OH. I DIDN'T KNOW YOU WERE DATING SOMEONE.
HEIR+BELL
MORE LIKE "SEEING" HER.
WHAT'S THE DIFFERENCE?
HOUSE OF JAVA .NET
I SEE HER, SHE SEES ME, SHE ORDERS A COFFEE.
COINCI-DENTALLY, I'M SEEING YOU FOR THE BUTT-HEAD YOU ARE.
HOUSE OF JAVA .NET

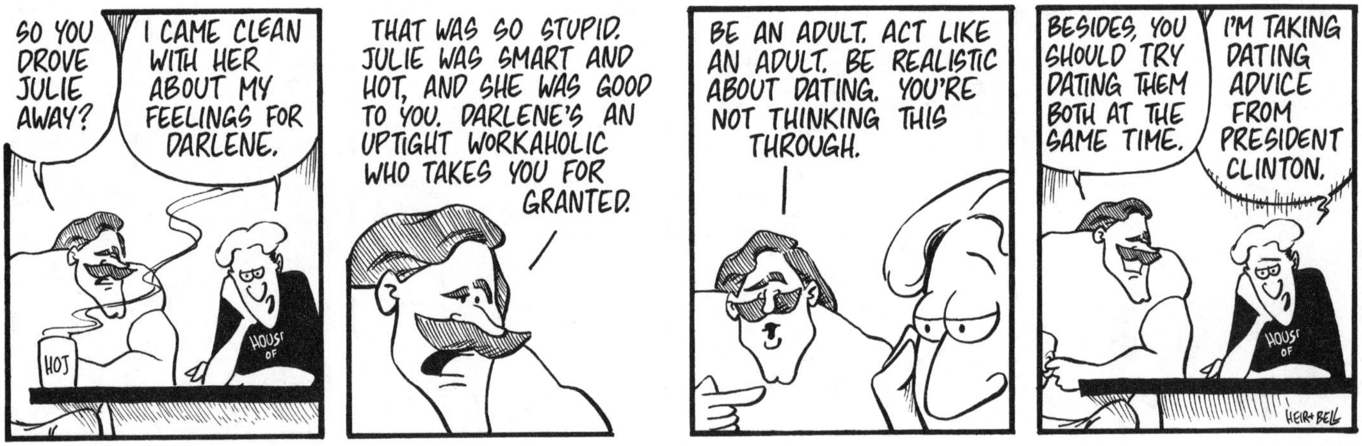
SO YOU DROVE JULIE AWAY?
I CAME CLEAN WITH HER ABOUT MY FEELINGS FOR DARLENE.
HOJ
THAT WAS SO STUPID. JULIE WAS SMART AND HOT, AND SHE WAS GOOD TO YOU. DARLENE'S AN UPTIGHT WORKAHOLIC WHO TAKES YOU FOR GRANTED.
BE AN ADULT. ACT LIKE AN ADULT. BE REALISTIC ABOUT DATING. YOU'RE NOT THINKING THIS THROUGH.
BESIDES, YOU SHOULD TRY DATING THEM BOTH AT THE SAME TIME.
I'M TAKING DATING ADVICE FROM PRESIDENT CLINTON.
HEIR+BELL

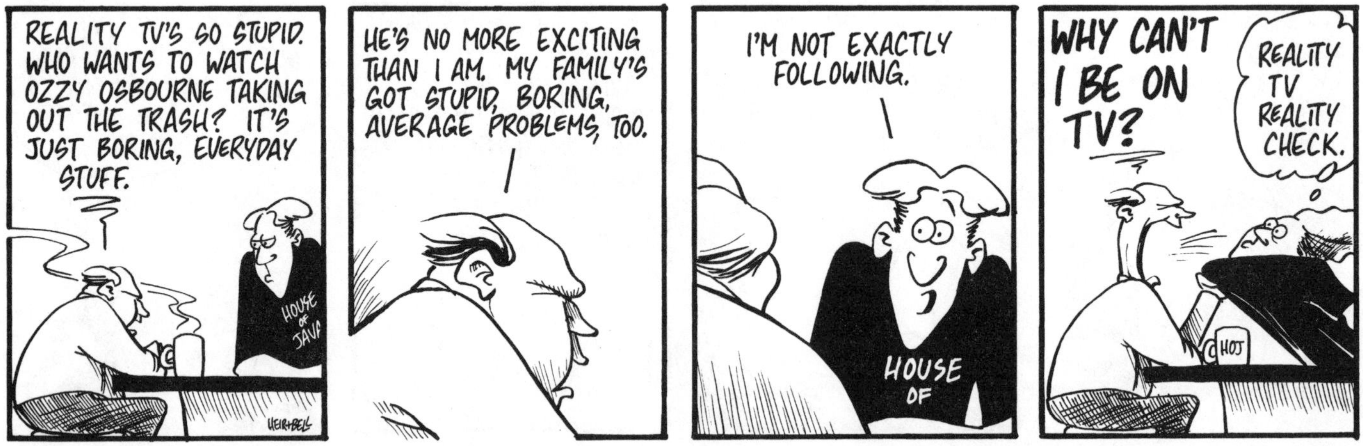
REALITY TV'S SO STUPID. WHO WANTS TO WATCH OZZY OSBOURNE TAKING OUT THE TRASH? IT'S JUST BORING, EVERYDAY STUFF.
HEIR+BELL
HE'S NO MORE EXCITING THAN I AM. MY FAMILY'S GOT STUPID, BORING, AVERAGE PROBLEMS, TOO.
I'M NOT EXACTLY FOLLOWING.
HOUSE OF
WHY CAN'T I BE ON TV?
REALITY TV REALITY CHECK.
HOJ

THE NATIONAL DEFICIT CONTINUES TO CLIMB...
IRRESPONSIBLE FISCAL POLICY MAKES ME SICK...
COMPUTER villa
SALE!
WHERE DO CONGRESSPEOPLE GET OFF?
THEY CAN'T SAY NO. THEY NEVER MET A BIG-TICKET ITEM THEY COULDN'T GO **ABSOLUTELY NUTS** FOR.
WEIR+BELL
PET PROJECTS. PORK. THEY'RE DRIVING THIS COUNTRY INTO THE GROUND WITH THEIR WANTON, SHORT-SIGHTED SPENDING FRENZY.
EXCUSE ME, SIR--
WHAT?! WHAT?! YOU WANT MORE TAXES FOR CONGRESS TO FLUSH DOWN THE DRAIN?!
SALE!
ANOTHER CREDIT CARD.
HUH?
SALE!
YOUR OTHERS ARE ALL MAXED OUT
I'LL JUST TAKE OUT A THIRD MORTGAGE.
SHALL I WRAP YOUR 108-INCH HDTV?

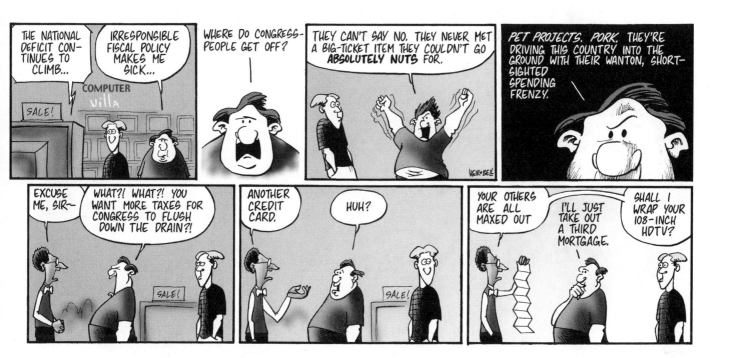

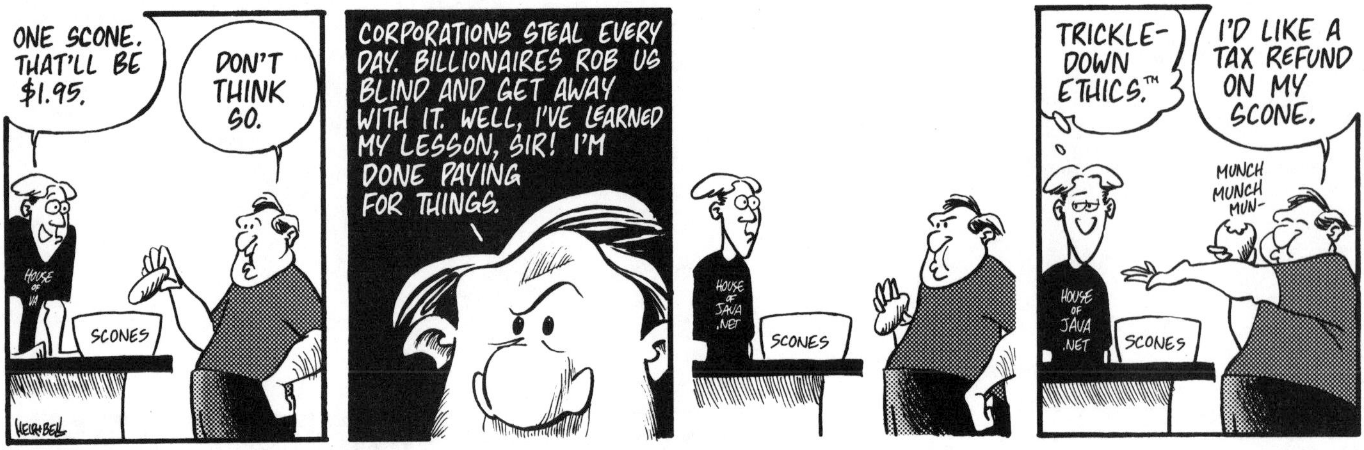
ONE SCONE. THAT'LL BE $1.95.
DON'T THINK SO.
SCONES
HEIR+BELL
CORPORATIONS STEAL EVERY DAY. BILLIONAIRES ROB US BLIND AND GET AWAY WITH IT. WELL, I'VE LEARNED MY LESSON, SIR! I'M DONE PAYING FOR THINGS.
HOUSE OF JAVA .NET
SCONES
TRICKLE-DOWN ETHICS.™
I'D LIKE A TAX REFUND ON MY SCONE.
MUNCH MUNCH MUN-
HOUSE OF JAVA .NET
SCONES

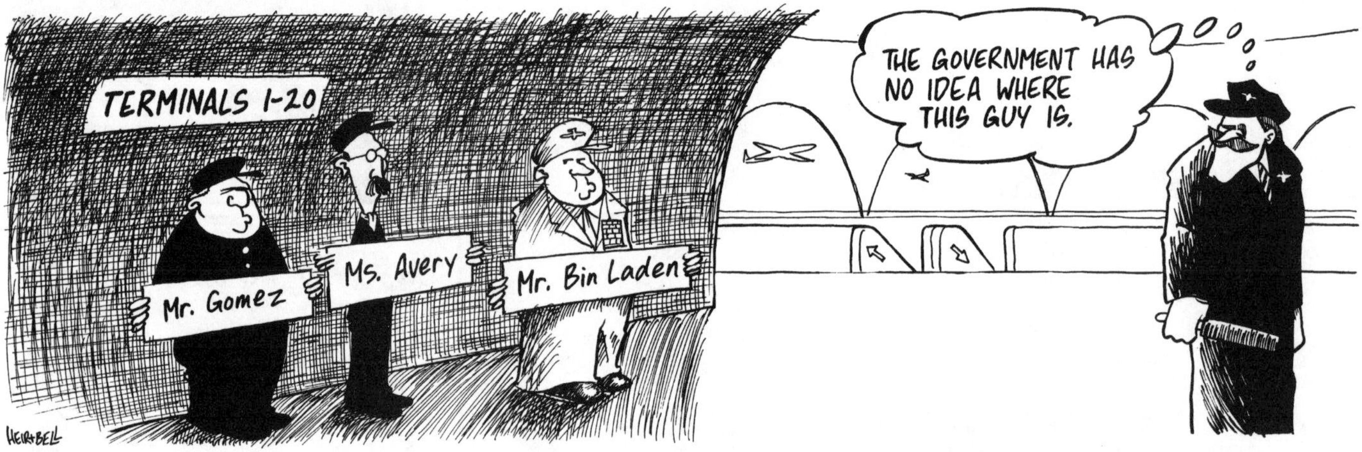
TERMINALS 1-20
Mr. Gomez
Ms. Avery
Mr. Bin Laden
THE GOVERNMENT HAS NO IDEA WHERE THIS GUY IS.
HEIR+BELL

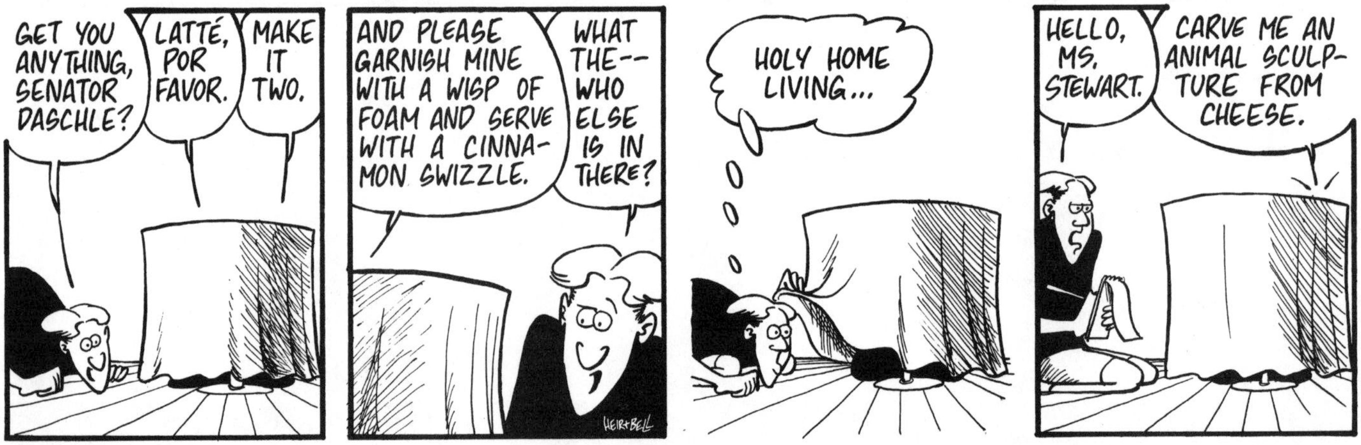
GET YOU ANYTHING, SENATOR DASCHLE?
LATTÉ, POR FAVOR.
MAKE IT TWO.
AND PLEASE GARNISH MINE WITH A WISP OF FOAM AND SERVE WITH A CINNAMON SWIZZLE.
WHAT THE-- WHO ELSE IS IN THERE?
HEIR+BELL
HOLY HOME LIVING...
HELLO, MS. STEWART.
CARVE ME AN ANIMAL SCULPTURE FROM CHEESE.

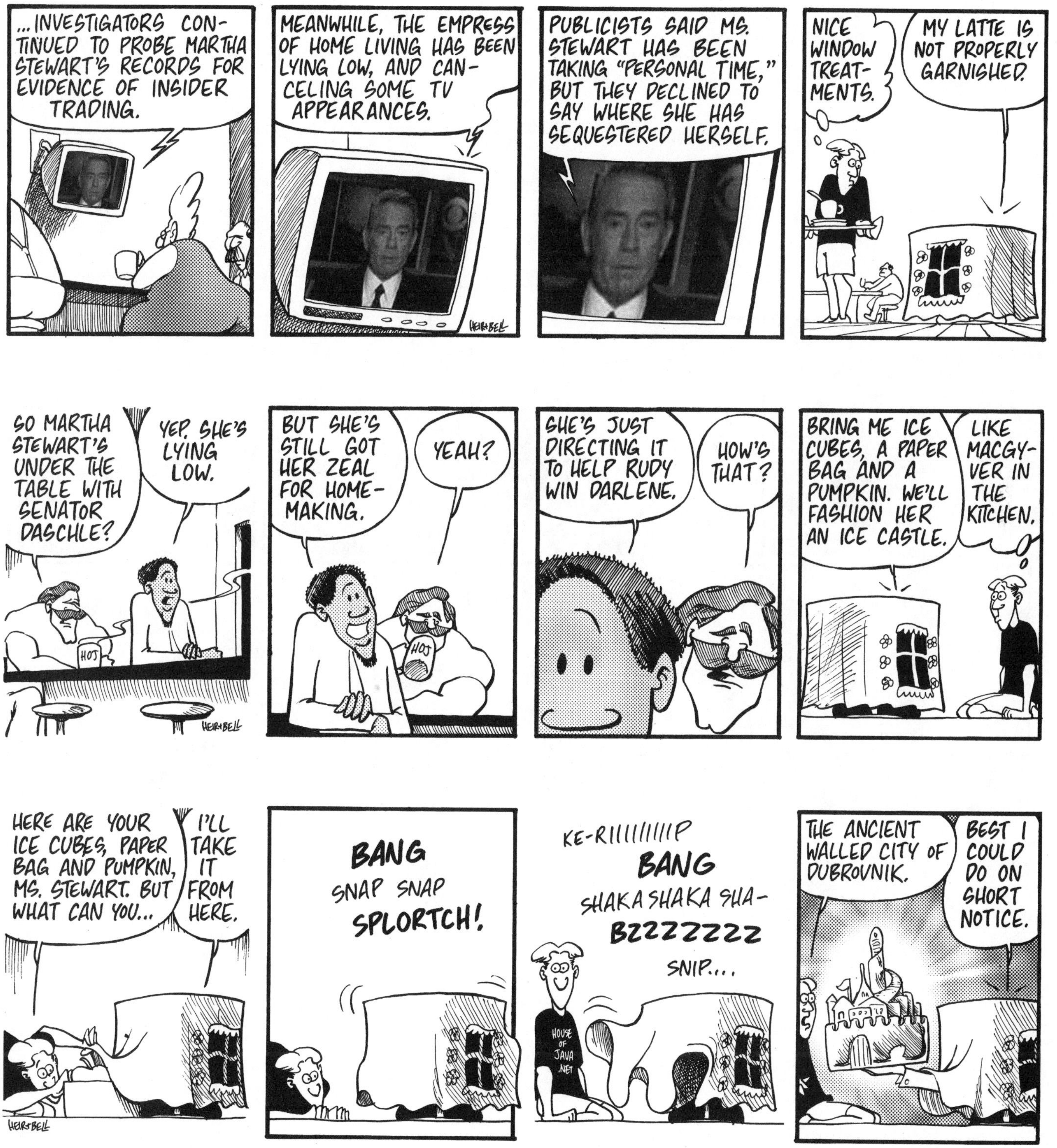
...INVESTIGATORS CONTINUED TO PROBE MARTHA STEWART'S RECORDS FOR EVIDENCE OF INSIDER TRADING.
MEANWHILE, THE EMPRESS OF HOME LIVING HAS BEEN LYING LOW, AND CANCELING SOME TV APPEARANCES.
HEIR+BELL
PUBLICISTS SAID MS. STEWART HAS BEEN TAKING "PERSONAL TIME," BUT THEY DECLINED TO SAY WHERE SHE HAS SEQUESTERED HERSELF.
NICE WINDOW TREATMENTS.
MY LATTE IS NOT PROPERLY GARNISHED.
SO MARTHA STEWART'S UNDER THE TABLE WITH SENATOR DASCHLE?
YEP. SHE'S LYING LOW.
HOJ
HEIR+BELL
BUT SHE'S STILL GOT HER ZEAL FOR HOMEMAKING.
YEAH?
HOJ
SHE'S JUST DIRECTING IT TO HELP RUDY WIN DARLENE.
HOW'S THAT?
BRING ME ICE CUBES, A PAPER BAG AND A PUMPKIN. WE'LL FASHION HER AN ICE CASTLE.
LIKE MACGYVER IN THE KITCHEN.
HERE ARE YOUR ICE CUBES, PAPER BAG AND PUMPKIN, MS. STEWART. BUT WHAT CAN YOU...
I'LL TAKE IT FROM HERE.
HEIR+BELL
BANG
SNAP SNAP
SPLORTCH!
KE-RIIIIIIIIP
BANG
SHAKA SHAKA SHA-
BZZZZZZZ
SNIP....
HOUSE OF JAVA .NET
THE ANCIENT WALLED CITY OF DUBROVNIK.
BEST I COULD DO ON SHORT NOTICE.

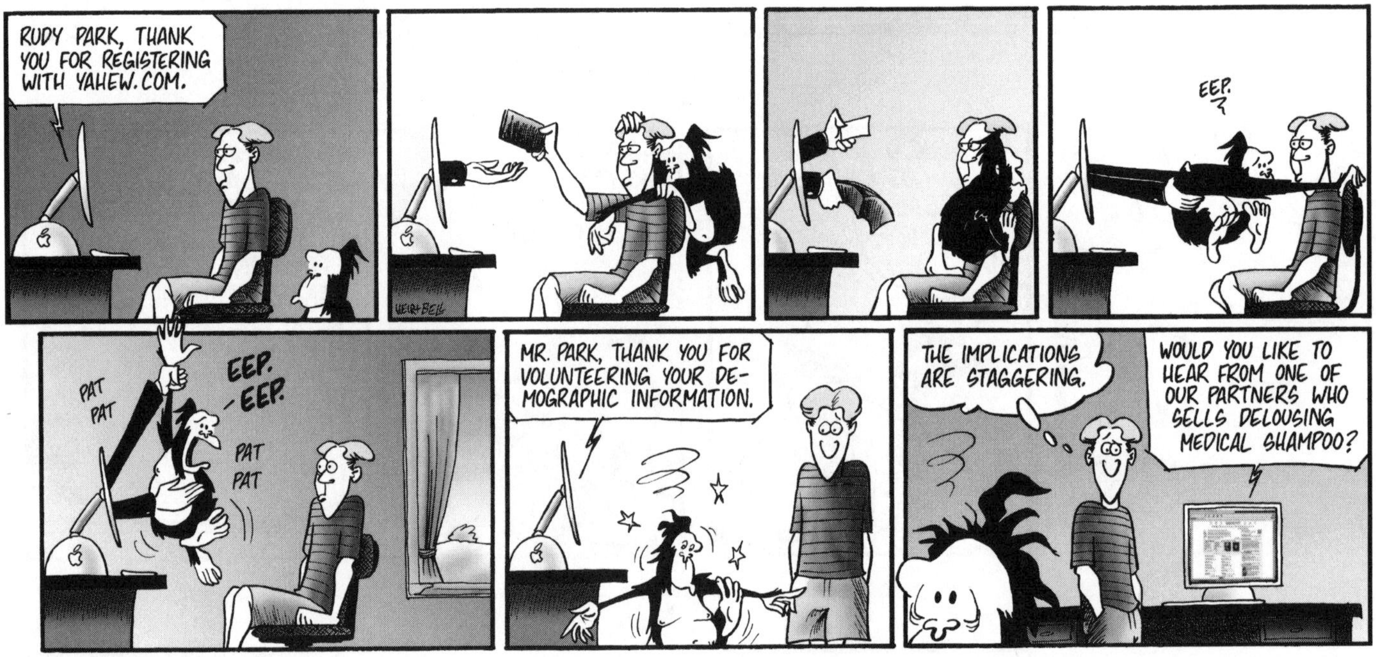
RUDY PARK, THANK YOU FOR REGISTERING WITH YAHEW.COM.
EEP.
PAT PAT
EEP. EEP.
PAT PAT
MR. PARK, THANK YOU FOR VOLUNTEERING YOUR DE-MOGRAPHIC INFORMATION.
THE IMPLICATIONS ARE STAGGERING.
WOULD YOU LIKE TO HEAR FROM ONE OF OUR PARTNERS WHO SELLS DELOUSING MEDICAL SHAMPOO?

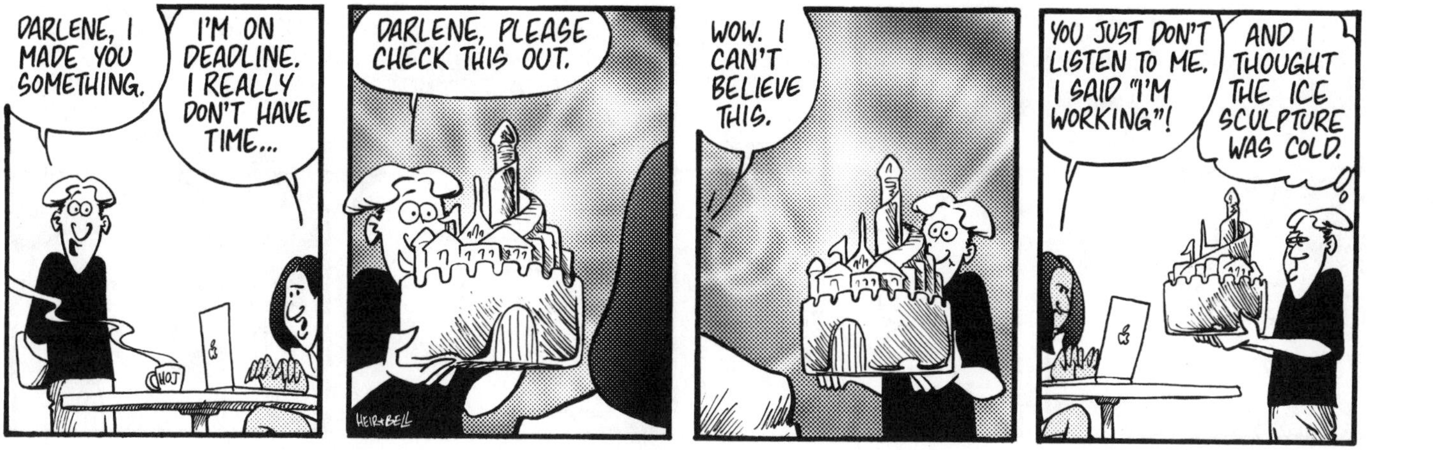

DARLENE, I MADE YOU SOMETHING.
I'M ON DEADLINE. I REALLY DON'T HAVE TIME...
HOJ
DARLENE, PLEASE CHECK THIS OUT.
HEIR+BELL
WOW. I CAN'T BELIEVE THIS.
YOU JUST DON'T LISTEN TO ME. I SAID "I'M WORKING"!
AND I THOUGHT THE ICE SCULPTURE WAS COLD.

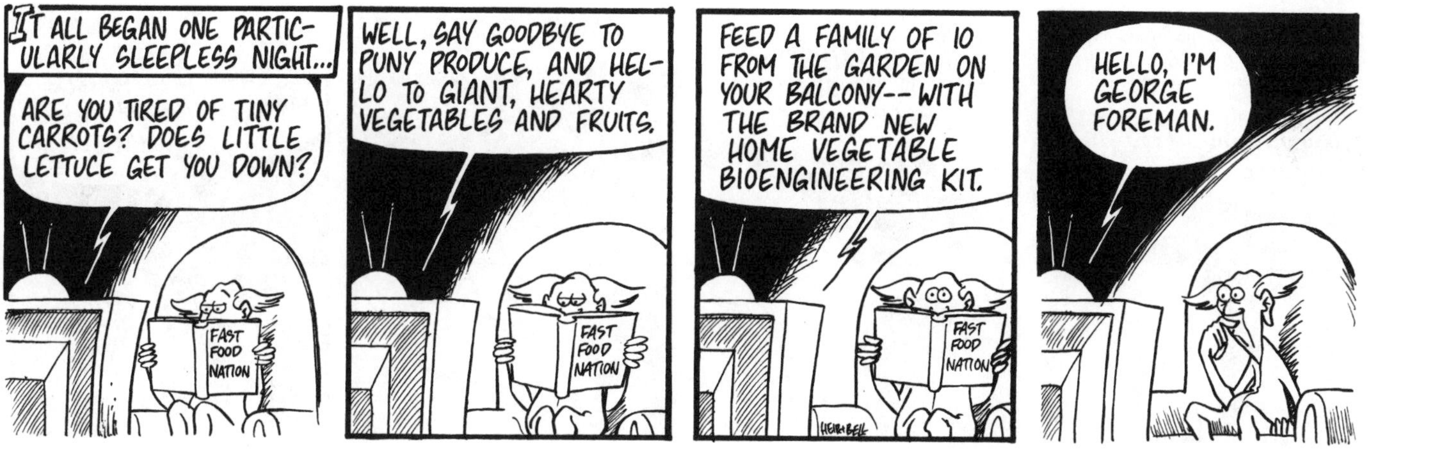

IT ALL BEGAN ONE PARTICULARLY SLEEPLESS NIGHT...
ARE YOU TIRED OF TINY CARROTS? DOES LITTLE LETTUCE GET YOU DOWN?
FAST FOOD NATION
WELL, SAY GOODBYE TO PUNY PRODUCE, AND HELLO TO GIANT, HEARTY VEGETABLES AND FRUITS.
FAST FOOD NATION
FEED A FAMILY OF 10 FROM THE GARDEN ON YOUR BALCONY--WITH THE BRAND NEW HOME VEGETABLE BIOENGINEERING KIT.
FAST FOOD NATION
HEIR+BELL
HELLO, I'M GEORGE FOREMAN.

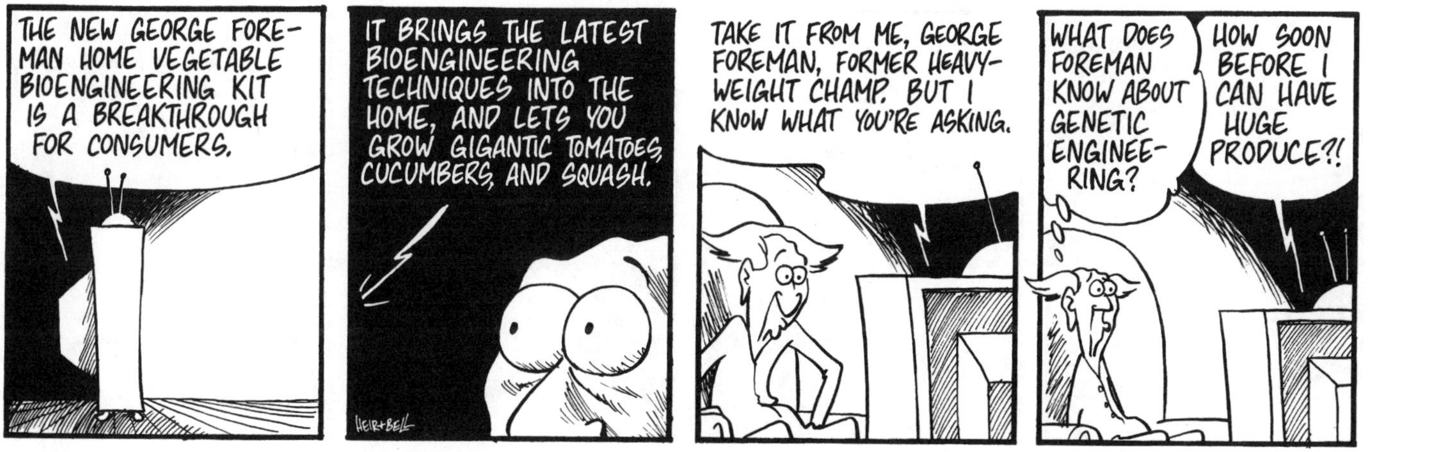

THE NEW GEORGE FOREMAN HOME VEGETABLE BIOENGINEERING KIT IS A BREAKTHROUGH FOR CONSUMERS.
IT BRINGS THE LATEST BIOENGINEERING TECHNIQUES INTO THE HOME, AND LETS YOU GROW GIGANTIC TOMATOES, CUCUMBERS, AND SQUASH.
HEIR+BELL
TAKE IT FROM ME, GEORGE FOREMAN, FORMER HEAVYWEIGHT CHAMP. BUT I KNOW WHAT YOU'RE ASKING.
WHAT DOES FOREMAN KNOW ABOUT GENETIC ENGINEERING?
HOW SOON BEFORE I CAN HAVE HUGE PRODUCE?!

THANKS FOR INQUIRING ABOUT GEORGE FOREMAN'S HOME VEGETABLE BIOENGINEERING KIT.

HOW'S IT WORK?

SIMPLE—JUST FOLLOW OUR FOUR-STEP INSTRUCTIONS, AND *SHAZZAM*— YOU'LL HAVE GARGANTUAN PRODUCE.

AND NOW IS A GREAT TIME TO ACT! IF YOU BUY IN THE NEXT 30 SECONDS, YOU GET MR. FOREMAN'S PERSONAL RECIPES.

"COOKING WITH ENORMOUS BEETS!"

FINE.

HUGE UTENSILS SOLD SEPARATELY.

...BEST OF ALL, GEORGE FOREMAN'S HOME VEGGIE BIOENGINEERING KIT COMES WITH A MONEY-BACK PROMISE.

"PROMISE"? WHY NOT A "GUARANTEE"?

THIS IS BETTER. WE PROMISE TO REFUND YOUR MONEY IF MUMBLE... HACK COUGH MUMBLE...

CAN YOU REPEAT THAT?

SORRY. OF COURSE.

MUMBLE MUMBLE HACK COUGH MUMBLE...

MY CREDIT CARD NUMBER IS MUMBLE COUGH WHEEZE MUMBLE...

SCONES $3
DONUTS $1.50
CAKE $2
PIE $2
SOYPIE $9.50

HAPPY BIRTHDAY

I'M STEVEN. IT'S MY BIRTHDAY.

HOUSE OF JAVA .NET

I'M STEVEN. IT'S MY BIRTHDAY.

HOUSE OF JAVA .NET

YOU WANT TO KNOW IF WE GIVE FREE DESSERTS ON BIRTHDAYS.

BIRTHDAY FREELOADERS.

PFHLLLTHP

HOUSE OF JAVA .NET

I'M STEVEN. IT'S MY BIRTHDAY.

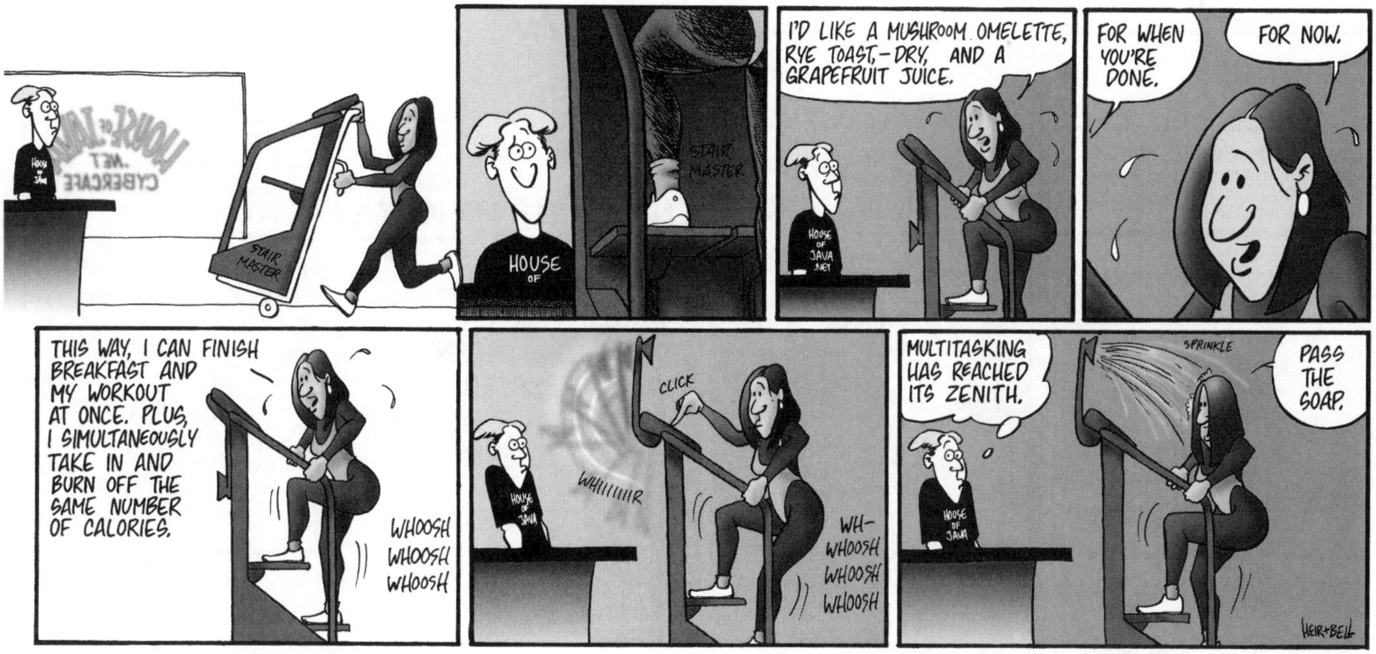
STAIR MASTER
HOUSE OF
STAIR MASTER
I'D LIKE A MUSHROOM OMELETTE, RYE TOAST,—DRY, AND A GRAPEFRUIT JUICE.
HOUSE OF JAVA .NET
FOR WHEN YOU'RE DONE.
FOR NOW.
THIS WAY, I CAN FINISH BREAKFAST AND MY WORKOUT AT ONCE. PLUS, I SIMULTANEOUSLY TAKE IN AND BURN OFF THE SAME NUMBER OF CALORIES.
WHOOSH WHOOSH WHOOSH
CLICK
WHIIIIIIR
HOUSE OF JAVA
WH-WHOOSH WHOOSH WHOOSH
MULTITASKING HAS REACHED ITS ZENITH.
SPRINKLE
PASS THE SOAP.
HOUSE OF JAVA
HEIR+BELL

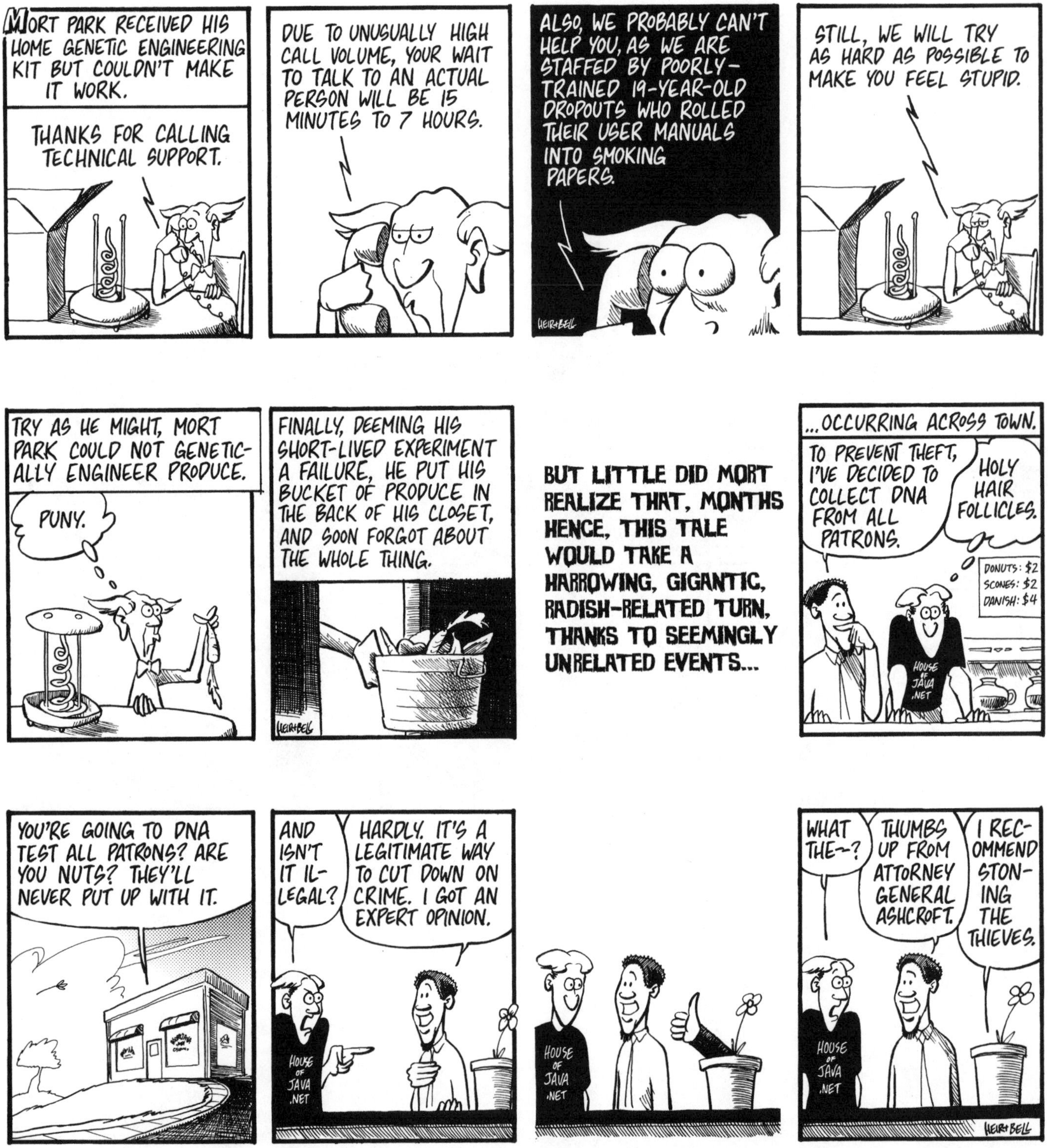
MORT PARK RECEIVED HIS HOME GENETIC ENGINEERING KIT BUT COULDN'T MAKE IT WORK.
THANKS FOR CALLING TECHNICAL SUPPORT.
DUE TO UNUSUALLY HIGH CALL VOLUME, YOUR WAIT TO TALK TO AN ACTUAL PERSON WILL BE 15 MINUTES TO 7 HOURS.
ALSO, WE PROBABLY CAN'T HELP YOU, AS WE ARE STAFFED BY POORLY-TRAINED 19-YEAR-OLD DROPOUTS WHO ROLLED THEIR USER MANUALS INTO SMOKING PAPERS.
HEIR+BELL
STILL, WE WILL TRY AS HARD AS POSSIBLE TO MAKE YOU FEEL STUPID.
TRY AS HE MIGHT, MORT PARK COULD NOT GENETICALLY ENGINEER PRODUCE.
PUNY.
FINALLY, DEEMING HIS SHORT-LIVED EXPERIMENT A FAILURE, HE PUT HIS BUCKET OF PRODUCE IN THE BACK OF HIS CLOSET, AND SOON FORGOT ABOUT THE WHOLE THING.
HEIR+BELL
BUT LITTLE DID MORT REALIZE THAT, MONTHS HENCE, THIS TALE WOULD TAKE A HARROWING, GIGANTIC, RADISH-RELATED TURN, THANKS TO SEEMINGLY UNRELATED EVENTS...
...OCCURRING ACROSS TOWN.
TO PREVENT THEFT, I'VE DECIDED TO COLLECT DNA FROM ALL PATRONS.
HOLY HAIR FOLLICLES.
DONUTS: $2
SCONES: $2
DANISH: $4
HOUSE OF JAVA .NET
YOU'RE GOING TO DNA TEST ALL PATRONS? ARE YOU NUTS? THEY'LL NEVER PUT UP WITH IT.
AND ISN'T IT ILLEGAL?
HARDLY. IT'S A LEGITIMATE WAY TO CUT DOWN ON CRIME. I GOT AN EXPERT OPINION.
HOUSE OF JAVA .NET
HOUSE OF JAVA .NET
WHAT THE--?
THUMBS UP FROM ATTORNEY GENERAL ASHCROFT.
I RECOMMEND STONING THE THIEVES.
HOUSE OF JAVA .NET
HEIR+BELL

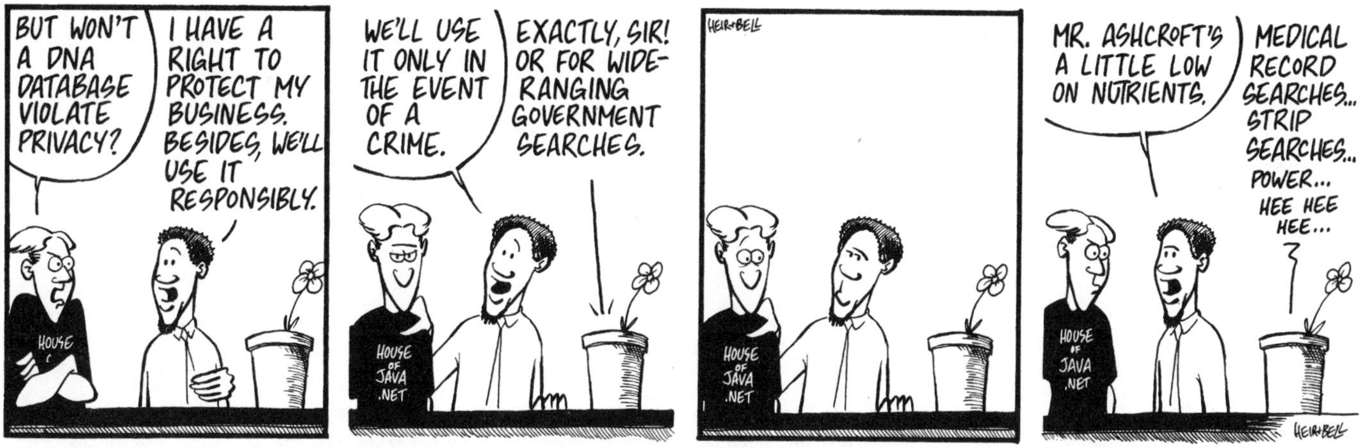
BUT WON'T A DNA DATABASE VIOLATE PRIVACY?
I HAVE A RIGHT TO PROTECT MY BUSINESS. BESIDES, WE'LL USE IT RESPONSIBLY.
HOUSE
HEIR+BELL
WE'LL USE IT ONLY IN THE EVENT OF A CRIME.
EXACTLY, SIR! OR FOR WIDE-RANGING GOVERNMENT SEARCHES.
HOUSE OF JAVA .NET
HOUSE OF JAVA .NET
MR. ASHCROFT'S A LITTLE LOW ON NUTRIENTS.
MEDICAL RECORD SEARCHES... STRIP SEARCHES... POWER... HEE HEE HEE...
HOUSE OF JAVA .NET
HEIR+BELL

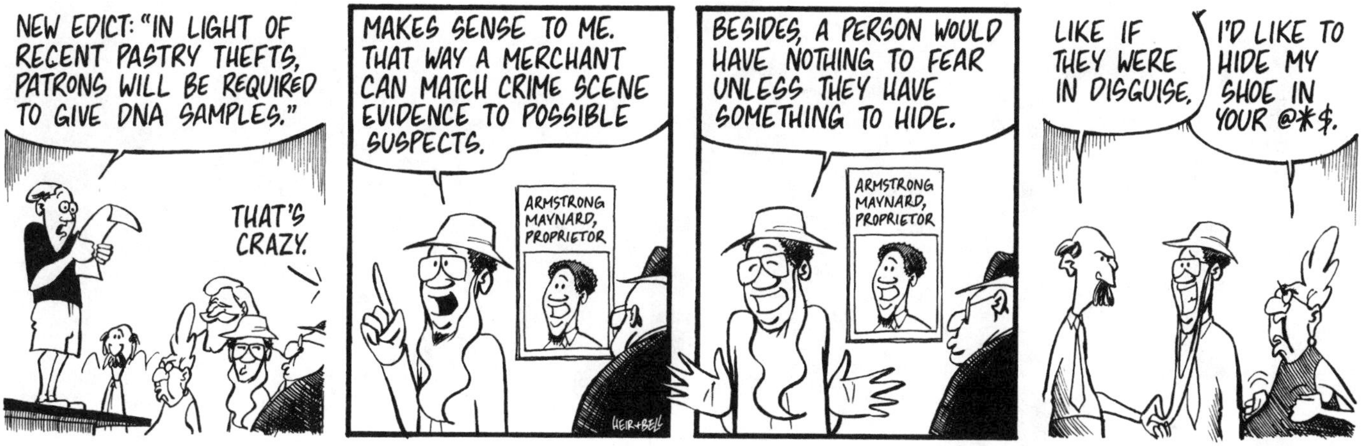
NEW EDICT: "IN LIGHT OF RECENT PASTRY THEFTS, PATRONS WILL BE REQUIRED TO GIVE DNA SAMPLES."
THAT'S CRAZY.
MAKES SENSE TO ME. THAT WAY A MERCHANT CAN MATCH CRIME SCENE EVIDENCE TO POSSIBLE SUSPECTS.
ARMSTRONG MAYNARD, PROPRIETOR
HEIR+BELL
BESIDES, A PERSON WOULD HAVE NOTHING TO FEAR UNLESS THEY HAVE SOMETHING TO HIDE.
ARMSTRONG MAYNARD, PROPRIETOR
LIKE IF THEY WERE IN DISGUISE.
I'D LIKE TO HIDE MY SHOE IN YOUR @*$.

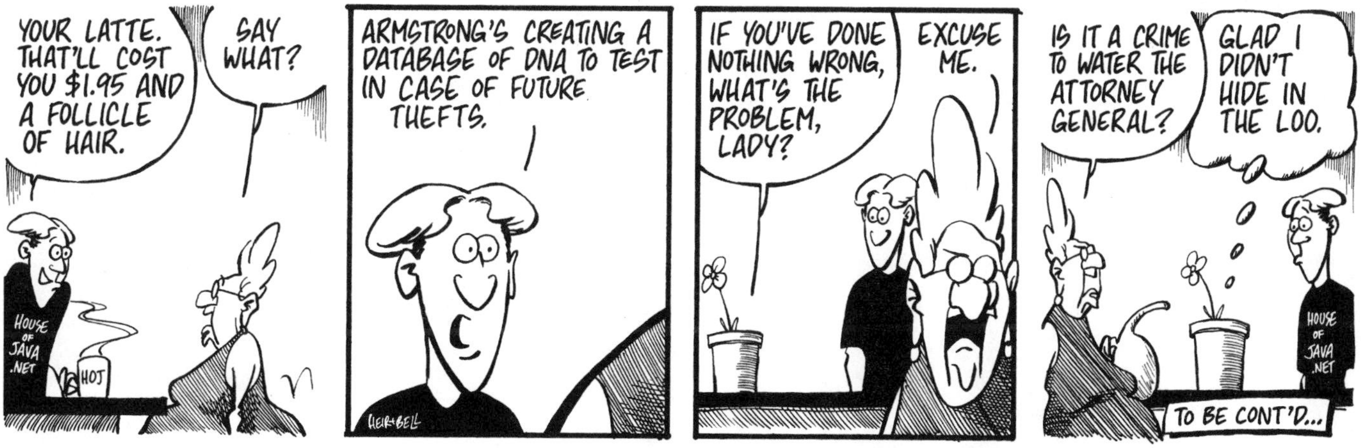
YOUR LATTE. THAT'LL COST YOU $1.95 AND A FOLLICLE OF HAIR.
SAY WHAT?
HOUSE OF JAVA .NET
HOJ
ARMSTRONG'S CREATING A DATABASE OF DNA TO TEST IN CASE OF FUTURE THEFTS.
HEIR+BELL
IF YOU'VE DONE NOTHING WRONG, WHAT'S THE PROBLEM, LADY?
EXCUSE ME.
IS IT A CRIME TO WATER THE ATTORNEY GENERAL?
GLAD I DIDN'T HIDE IN THE LOO.
HOUSE OF JAVA .NET
TO BE CONT'D...

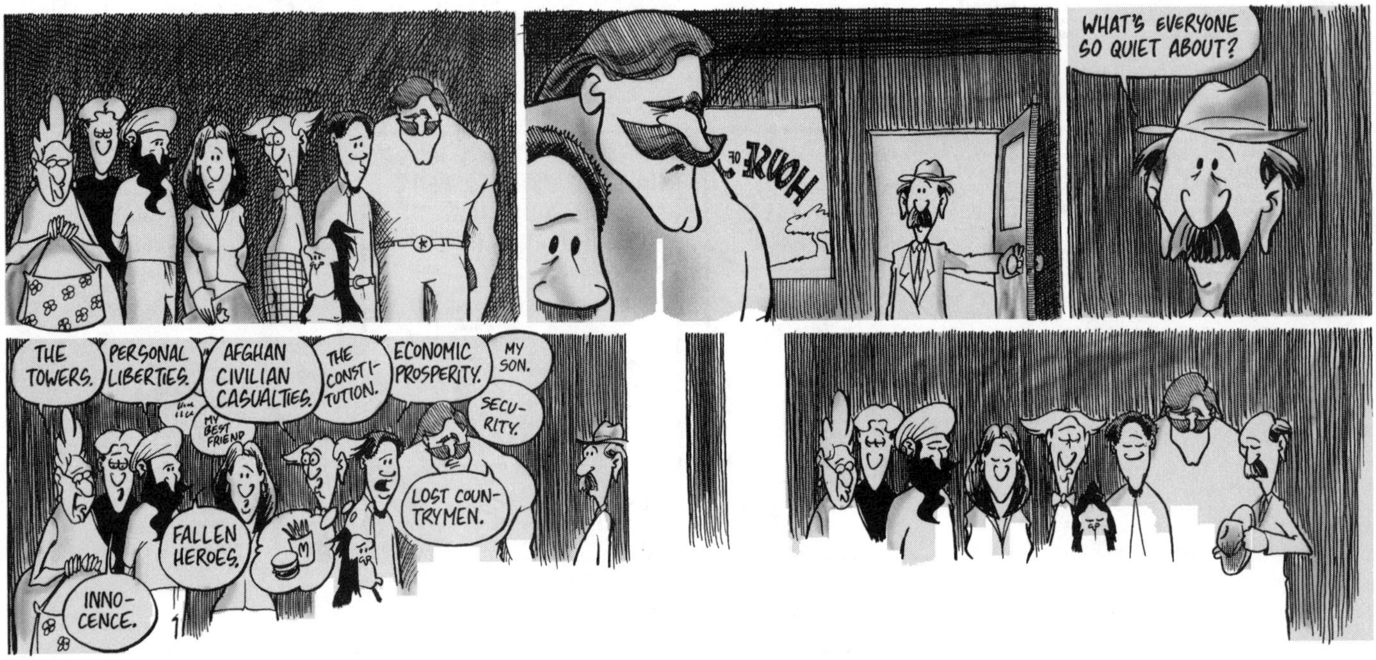
WHAT'S EVERYONE SO QUIET ABOUT?
THE TOWERS.
PERSONAL LIBERTIES.
AFGHAN CIVILIAN CASUALTIES.
THE CONSTI-TUTION.
ECONOMIC PROSPERITY.
MY SON.
MY BEST FRIEND
SECU-RITY.
LOST COUN-TRYMEN.
FALLEN HEROES.
INNO-CENCE.

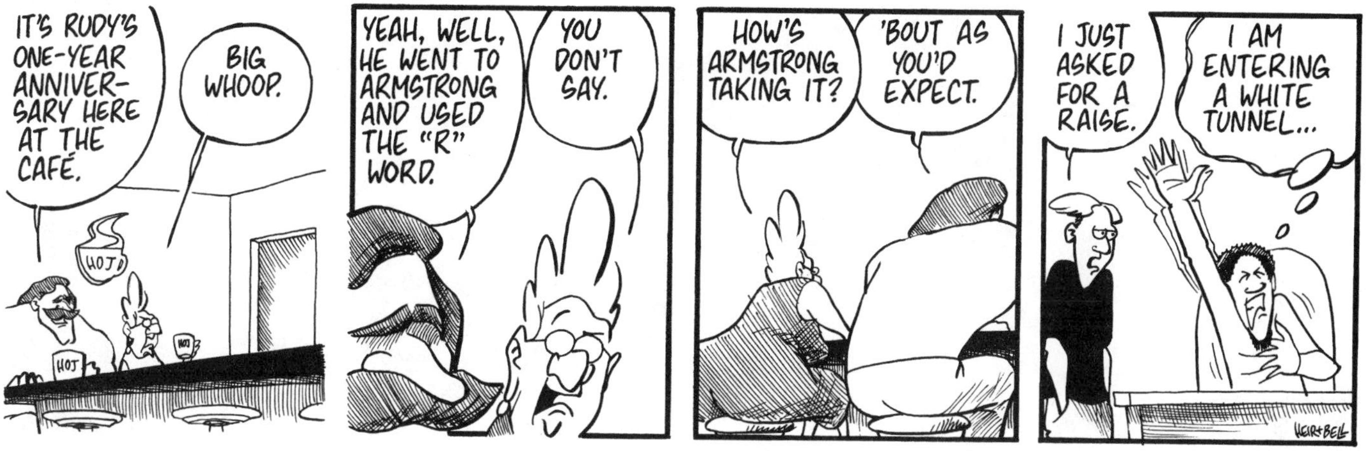
IT'S RUDY'S ONE-YEAR ANNIVER-SARY HERE AT THE CAFÉ.
BIG WHOOP.
YEAH, WELL, HE WENT TO ARMSTRONG AND USED THE "R" WORD.
YOU DON'T SAY.
HOW'S ARMSTRONG TAKING IT?
'BOUT AS YOU'D EXPECT.
I JUST ASKED FOR A RAISE.
I AM ENTERING A WHITE TUNNEL...

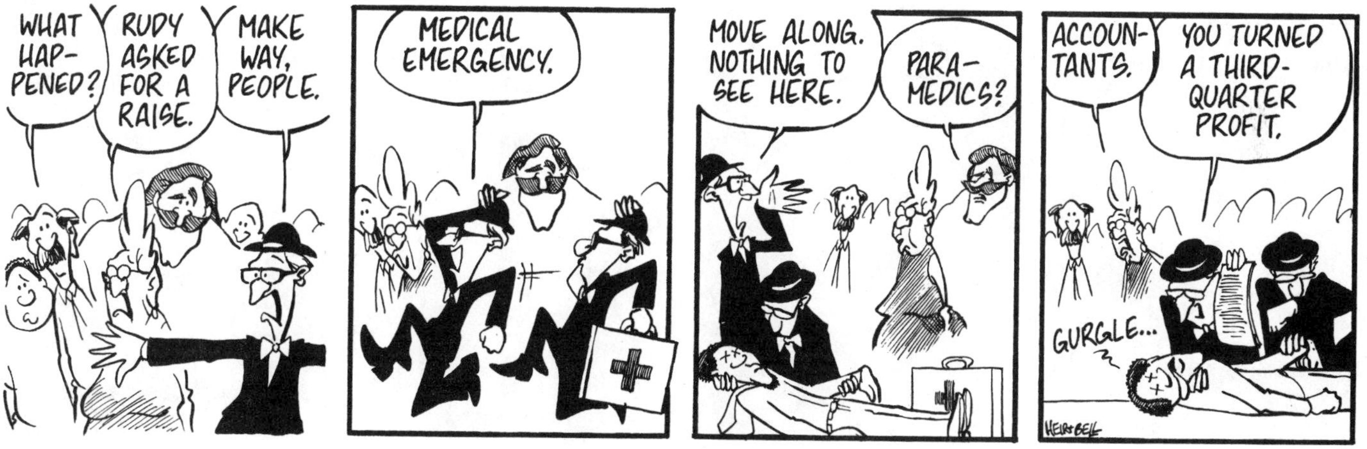
WHAT HAP-PENED?
RUDY ASKED FOR A RAISE.
MAKE WAY, PEOPLE.
MEDICAL EMERGENCY.
MOVE ALONG. NOTHING TO SEE HERE.
PARA-MEDICS?
ACCOUN-TANTS.
YOU TURNED A THIRD-QUARTER PROFIT.
GURGLE...

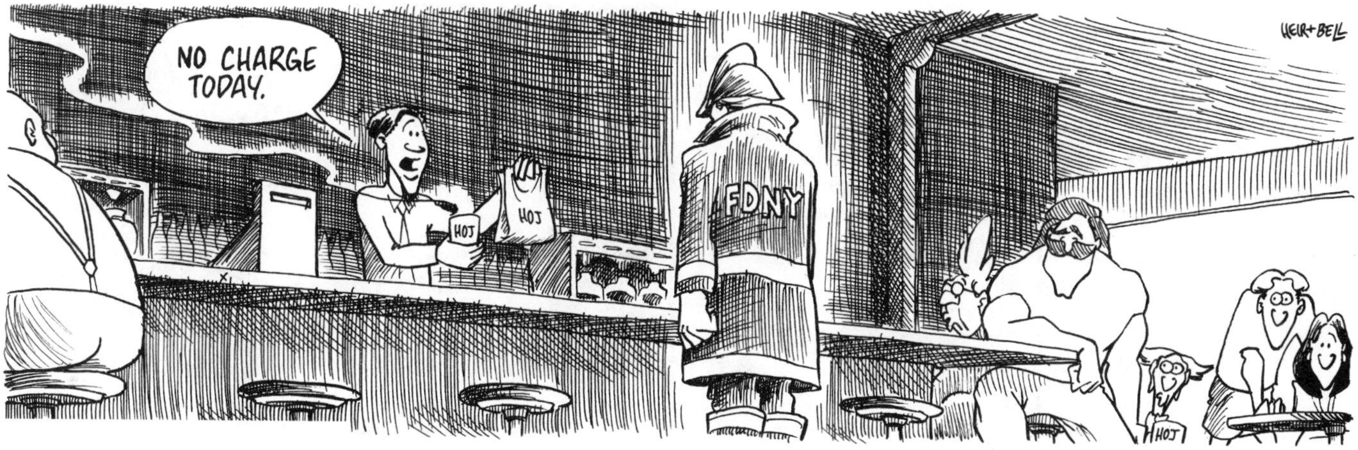
NO CHARGE TODAY.
FDNY

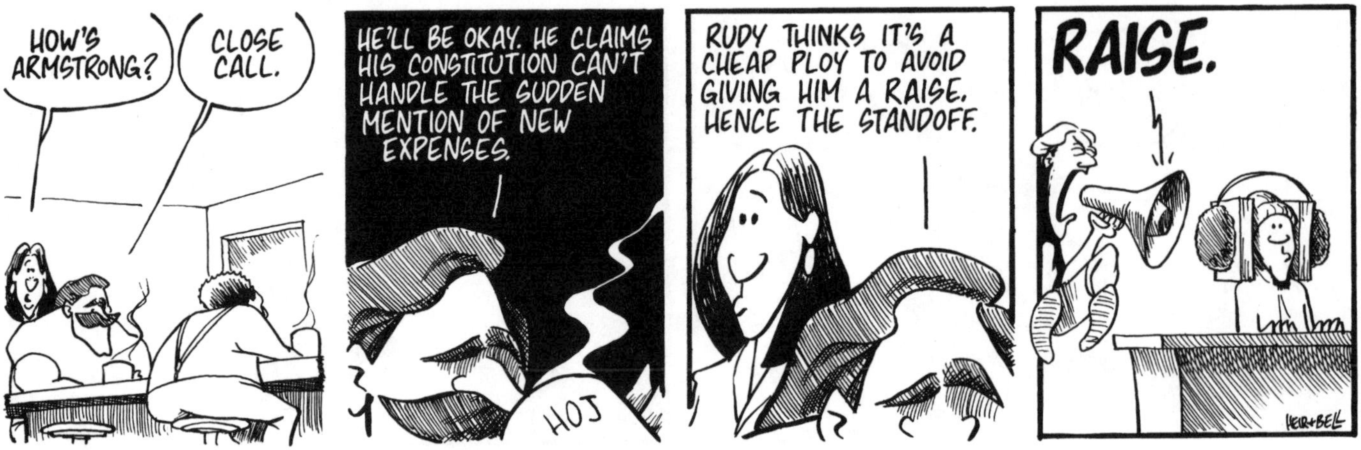
HOW'S ARMSTRONG?
CLOSE CALL.
HE'LL BE OKAY. HE CLAIMS HIS CONSTITUTION CAN'T HANDLE THE SUDDEN MENTION OF NEW EXPENSES.
HOJ
RUDY THINKS IT'S A CHEAP PLOY TO AVOID GIVING HIM A RAISE. HENCE THE STANDOFF.
RAISE.

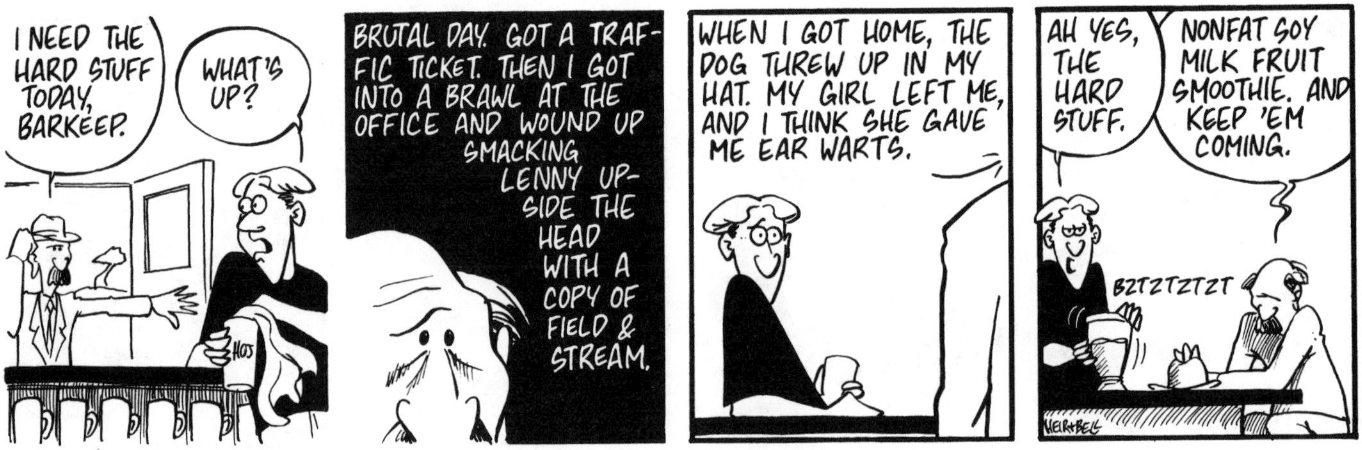
I NEED THE HARD STUFF TODAY, BARKEEP.
WHAT'S UP?
HOJ
BRUTAL DAY. GOT A TRAFFIC TICKET. THEN I GOT INTO A BRAWL AT THE OFFICE AND WOUND UP SMACKING LENNY UPSIDE THE HEAD WITH A COPY OF FIELD & STREAM.
WHEN I GOT HOME, THE DOG THREW UP IN MY HAT. MY GIRL LEFT ME, AND I THINK SHE GAVE ME EAR WARTS.
AH YES, THE HARD STUFF.
NONFAT SOY MILK FRUIT SMOOTHIE. AND KEEP 'EM COMING.
BZTZTZTZT

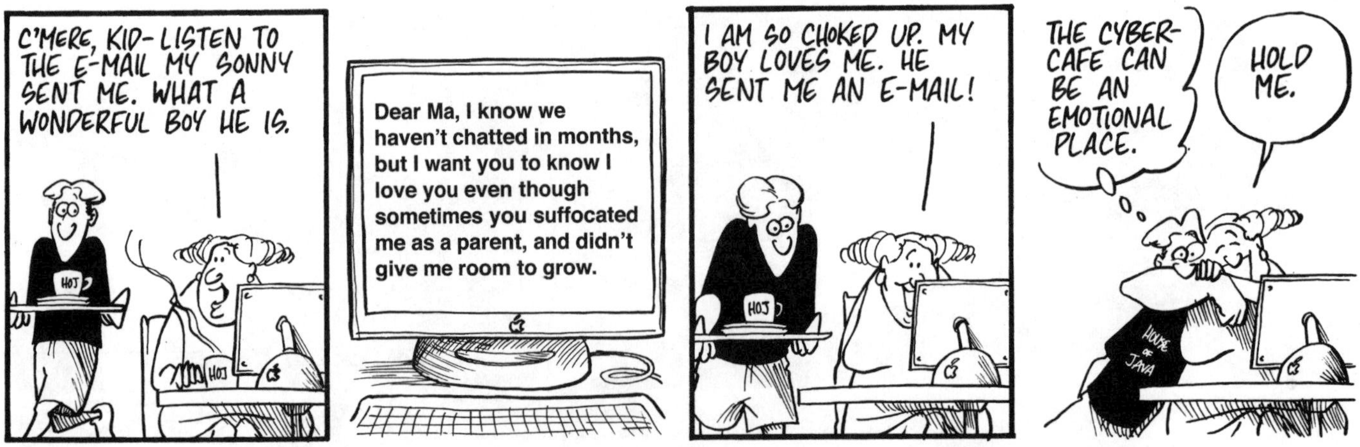
C'MERE, KID- LISTEN TO THE E-MAIL MY SONNY SENT ME. WHAT A WONDERFUL BOY HE IS.
HOJ
Dear Ma, I know we haven't chatted in months, but I want you to know I love you even though sometimes you suffocated me as a parent, and didn't give me room to grow.
I AM SO CHOKED UP. MY BOY LOVES ME. HE SENT ME AN E-MAIL!
THE CYBERCAFE CAN BE AN EMOTIONAL PLACE.
HOLD ME.
HOUSE OF JAVA

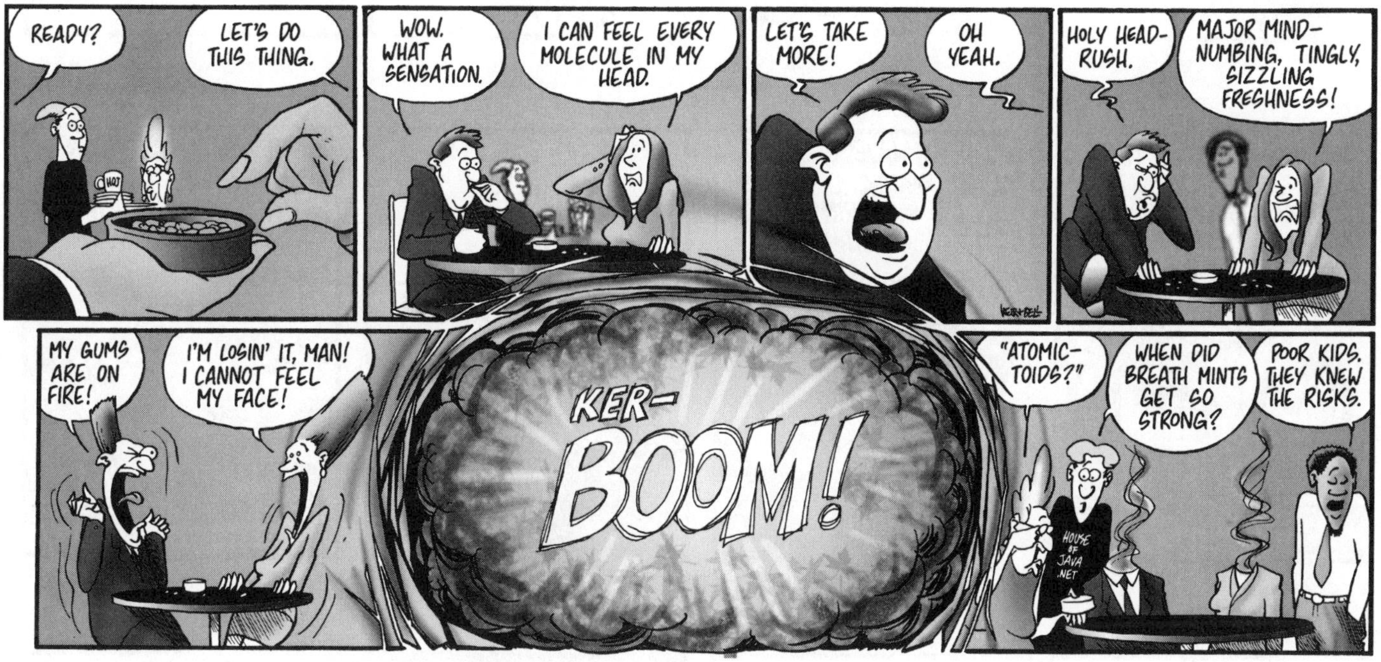
READY?
LET'S DO THIS THING.
WOW. WHAT A SENSATION.
I CAN FEEL EVERY MOLECULE IN MY HEAD.
LET'S TAKE MORE!
OH YEAH.
HOLY HEAD-RUSH.
MAJOR MIND-NUMBING, TINGLY, SIZZLING FRESHNESS!
MY GUMS ARE ON FIRE!
I'M LOSIN' IT, MAN! I CANNOT FEEL MY FACE!
KER-BOOM!
"ATOMIC-TOIDS?"
WHEN DID BREATH MINTS GET SO STRONG?
POOR KIDS. THEY KNEW THE RISKS.
HOUSE OF JAVA .NET

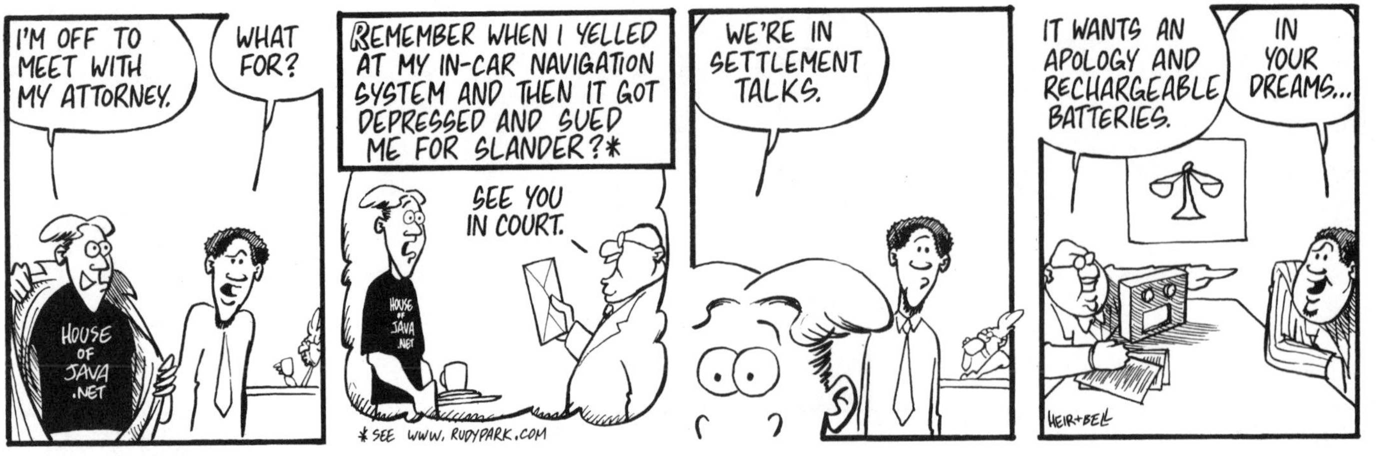
I'M OFF TO MEET WITH MY ATTORNEY.
WHAT FOR?
REMEMBER WHEN I YELLED AT MY IN-CAR NAVIGATION SYSTEM AND THEN IT GOT DEPRESSED AND SUED ME FOR SLANDER?*
HOUSE OF JAVA .NET
SEE YOU IN COURT.
*SEE WWW.RUDYPARK.COM
WE'RE IN SETTLEMENT TALKS.
IT WANTS AN APOLOGY AND RECHARGEABLE BATTERIES.
IN YOUR DREAMS...
HEIR+BELL

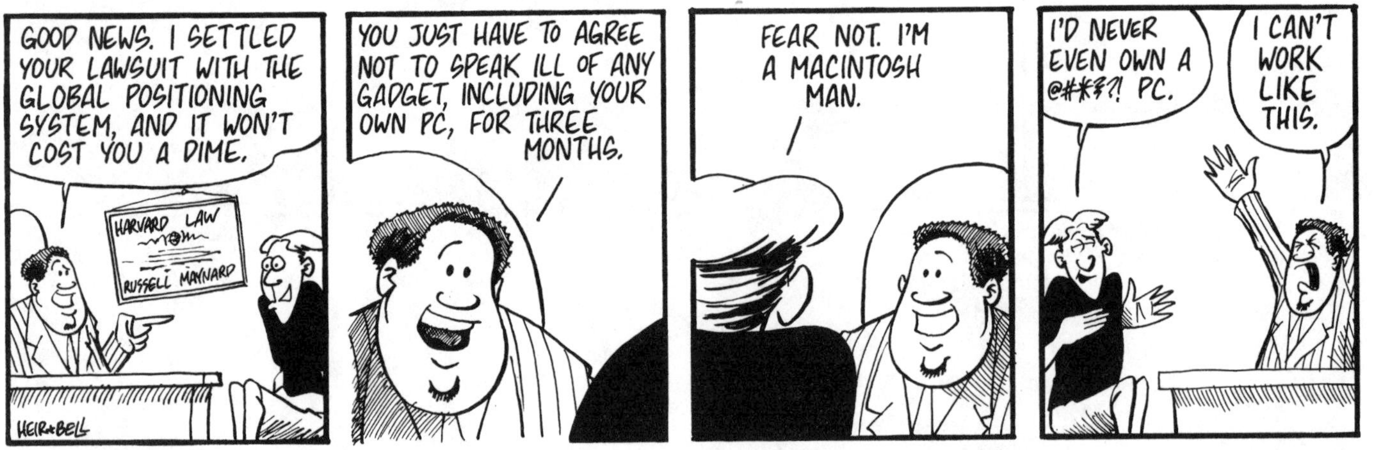
GOOD NEWS. I SETTLED YOUR LAWSUIT WITH THE GLOBAL POSITIONING SYSTEM, AND IT WON'T COST YOU A DIME.
HARVARD LAW
RUSSELL MAYNARD
HEIR+BELL
YOU JUST HAVE TO AGREE NOT TO SPEAK ILL OF ANY GADGET, INCLUDING YOUR OWN PC, FOR THREE MONTHS.
FEAR NOT. I'M A MACINTOSH MAN.
I'D NEVER EVEN OWN A @#*$?! PC.
I CAN'T WORK LIKE THIS.

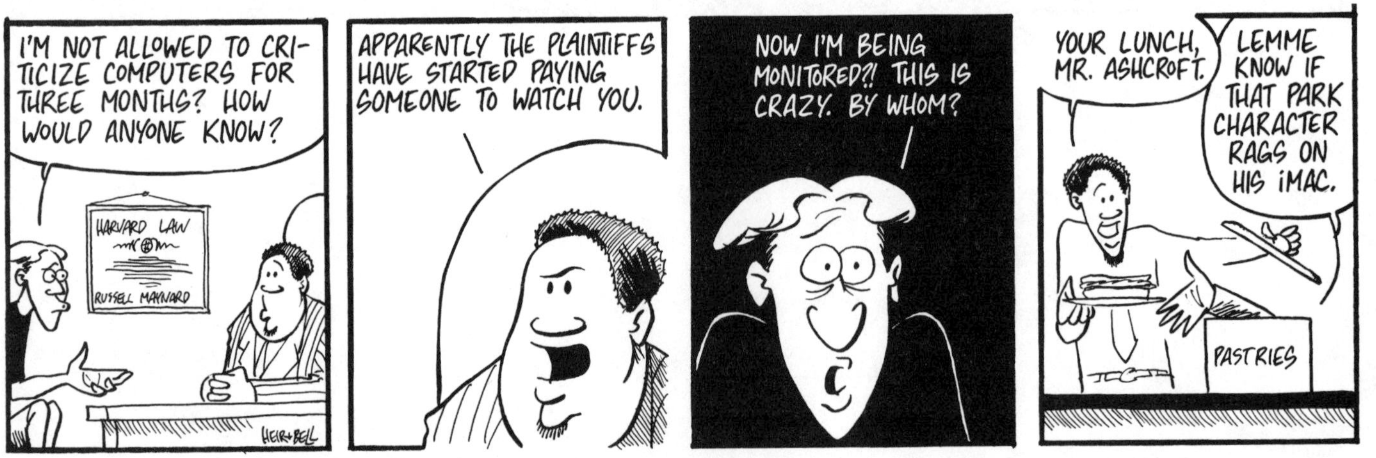
I'M NOT ALLOWED TO CRITICIZE COMPUTERS FOR THREE MONTHS? HOW WOULD ANYONE KNOW?
HARVARD LAW
RUSSELL MAYNARD
HEIR+BELL
APPARENTLY THE PLAINTIFFS HAVE STARTED PAYING SOMEONE TO WATCH YOU.
NOW I'M BEING MONITORED?! THIS IS CRAZY. BY WHOM?
YOUR LUNCH, MR. ASHCROFT.
LEMME KNOW IF THAT PARK CHARACTER RAGS ON HIS iMAC.
PASTRIES

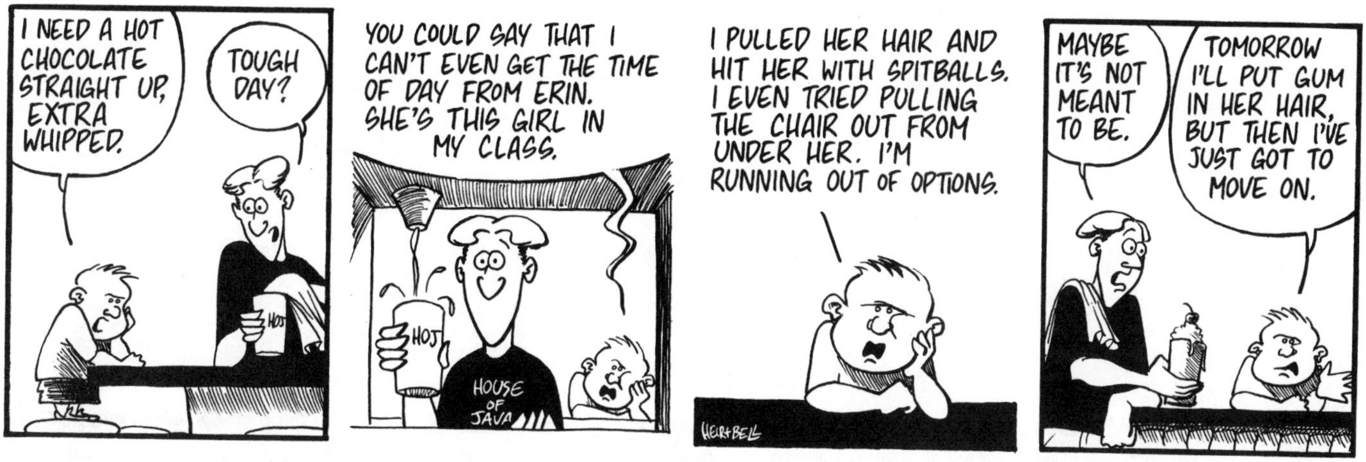
I NEED A HOT CHOCOLATE STRAIGHT UP, EXTRA WHIPPED.
TOUGH DAY?
YOU COULD SAY THAT I CAN'T EVEN GET THE TIME OF DAY FROM ERIN. SHE'S THIS GIRL IN MY CLASS.
HOUSE OF JAVA
I PULLED HER HAIR AND HIT HER WITH SPITBALLS. I EVEN TRIED PULLING THE CHAIR OUT FROM UNDER HER. I'M RUNNING OUT OF OPTIONS.
MAYBE IT'S NOT MEANT TO BE.
TOMORROW I'LL PUT GUM IN HER HAIR, BUT THEN I'VE JUST GOT TO MOVE ON.

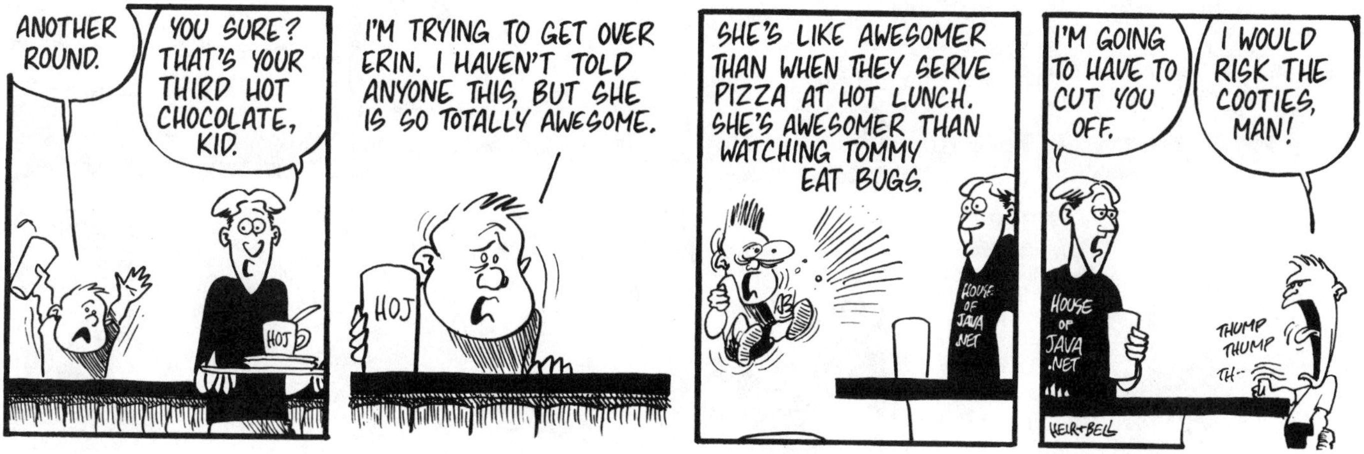
ANOTHER ROUND.
YOU SURE? THAT'S YOUR THIRD HOT CHOCOLATE, KID.
I'M TRYING TO GET OVER ERIN. I HAVEN'T TOLD ANYONE THIS, BUT SHE IS SO TOTALLY AWESOME.
SHE'S LIKE AWESOMER THAN WHEN THEY SERVE PIZZA AT HOT LUNCH. SHE'S AWESOMER THAN WATCHING TOMMY EAT BUGS.
HOUSE OF JAVA .NET
I'M GOING TO HAVE TO CUT YOU OFF.
I WOULD RISK THE COOTIES, MAN!
HOUSE OF JAVA .NET
THUMP
THUMP
TH--

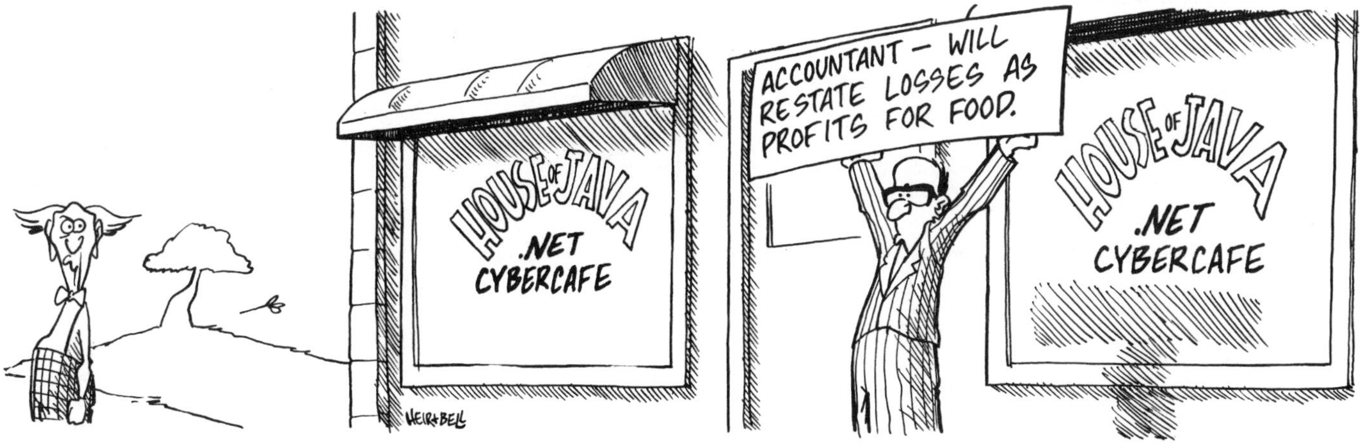
HOUSE OF JAVA .NET CYBERCAFE
ACCOUNTANT — WILL RESTATE LOSSES AS PROFITS FOR FOOD.
HOUSE OF JAVA .NET CYBERCAFE

SHE'S TOUGH. SHE'S FAIR. SHE WANTS YOU STINKIN' KIDS TO GET OFF HER LAWN. SHE'S...
JUDGE SADIE
IN TODAY'S CASE, A CAFE OWNER ACCUSES A MONKEY OF EATING HIS PASTRIES...
SONEE
LISTEN UP. I DON'T WANT TO BE INTERRUPTED, TALKED AT, TALKED TO, OR TALKED NEAR. ARE WE CLEAR?
YES, JUDGE SADIE.
SONEE
YOU ARE A SMELLY, KNUCKLE-DRAGGING PRIMATE. AND YOUR PET MONKEY STINKS, TOO.
SHE LIKES ME...
SONEE
BUT THIS GUY'S A WHINY SWINDLER WHO'D SELL HIS GRANDMOTHER TO THE CIRCUS TO MAKE A BUCK.
I'VE GOT A SHOT...
HEIR+BELL
SONEE
YOU ALL DRESS LOUSY AND SMELL LIKE OLD CHEESE.
NOW, APPROACH THE BENCH SO THAT I MAY RULE.
BOTH SIDES LOSE.
DID YOU WANT TO HEAR ANY EVIDENCE?
IT'S AWE-SOME TO BE ON TV.
YOU STINKIN' KIDS GET OFF MY LAWN.
Next week: Judge Sadie Gets Busy on Someone

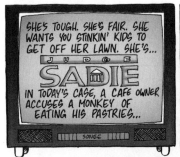

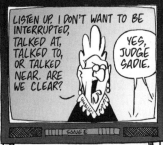

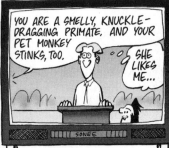

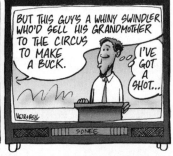

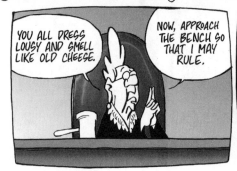

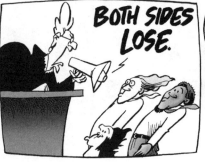

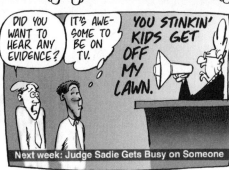

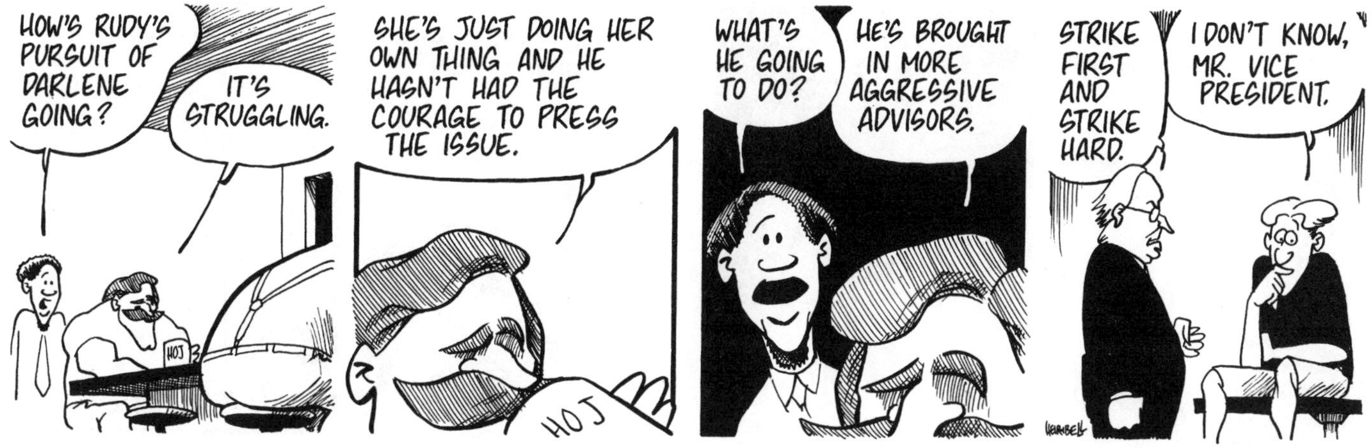
HOW'S RUDY'S PURSUIT OF DARLENE GOING?
IT'S STRUGGLING.
SHE'S JUST DOING HER OWN THING AND HE HASN'T HAD THE COURAGE TO PRESS THE ISSUE.
WHAT'S HE GOING TO DO?
HE'S BROUGHT IN MORE AGGRESSIVE ADVISORS.
STRIKE FIRST AND STRIKE HARD.
I DON'T KNOW, MR. VICE PRESIDENT.
HEIR+BELL

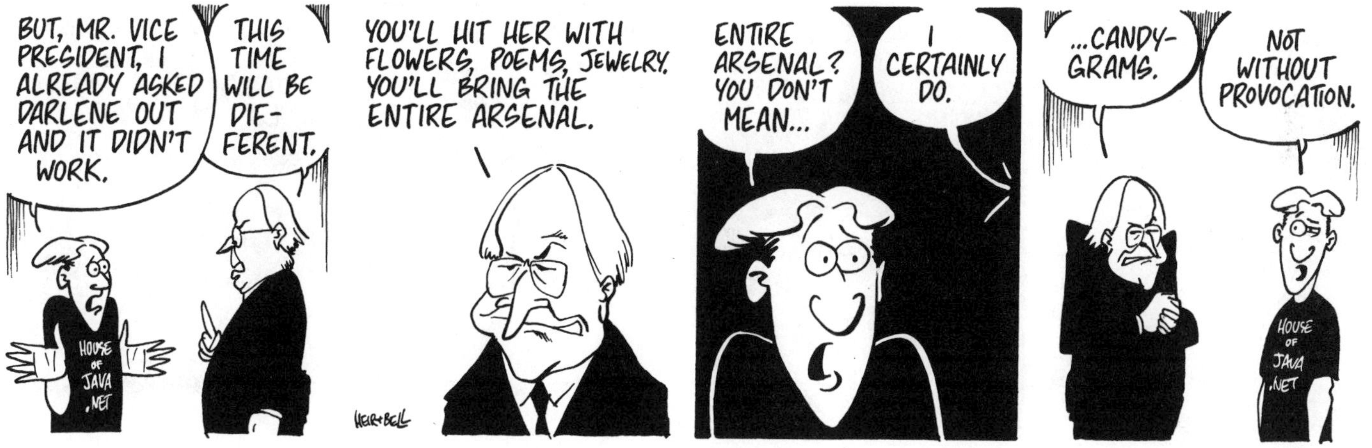
BUT, MR. VICE PRESIDENT, I ALREADY ASKED DARLENE OUT AND IT DIDN'T WORK.
THIS TIME WILL BE DIF-FERENT.
HOUSE OF JAVA .NET
HEIR+BELL
YOU'LL HIT HER WITH FLOWERS, POEMS, JEWELRY. YOU'LL BRING THE ENTIRE ARSENAL.
ENTIRE ARSENAL? YOU DON'T MEAN...
I CERTAINLY DO.
...CANDY-GRAMS.
NOT WITHOUT PROVOCATION.
HOUSE OF JAVA .NET

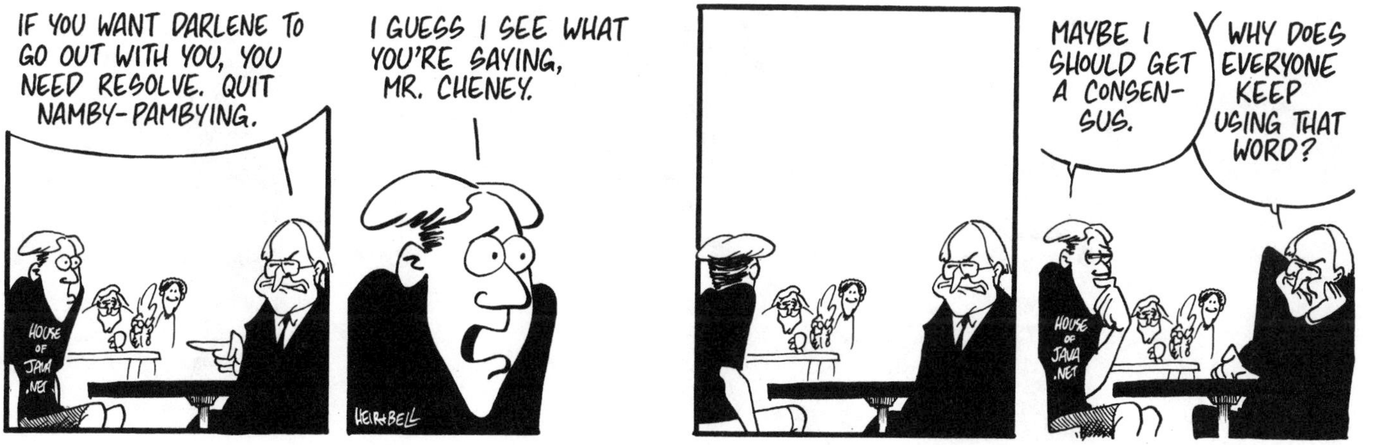
IF YOU WANT DARLENE TO GO OUT WITH YOU, YOU NEED RESOLVE. QUIT NAMBY-PAMBYING.
HOUSE OF JAVA .NET
I GUESS I SEE WHAT YOU'RE SAYING, MR. CHENEY.
HEIR+BELL
MAYBE I SHOULD GET A CONSEN-SUS.
WHY DOES EVERYONE KEEP USING THAT WORD?
HOUSE OF JAVA .NET

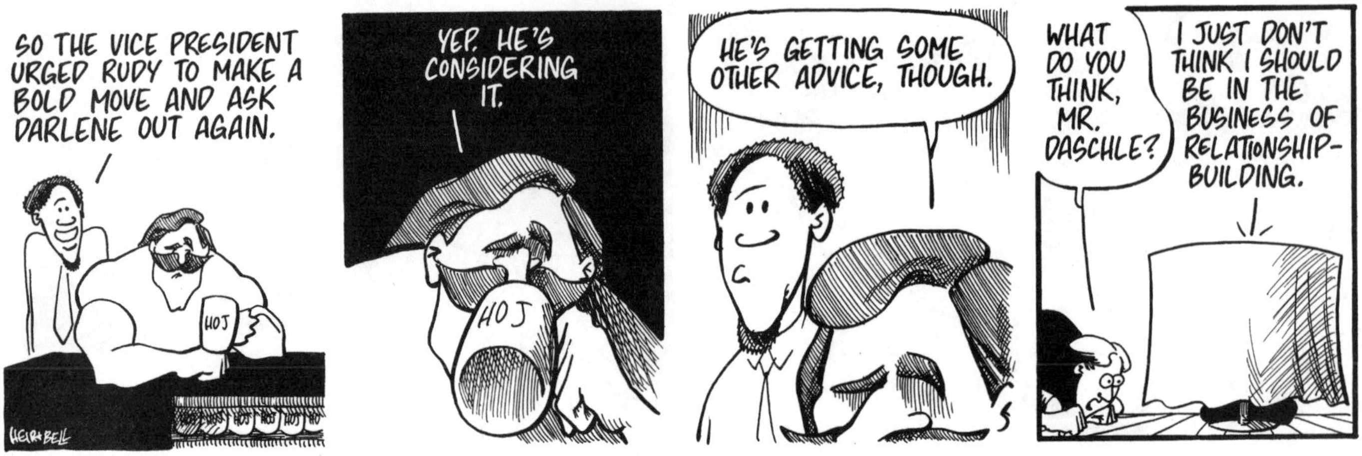
SO THE VICE PRESIDENT URGED RUDY TO MAKE A BOLD MOVE AND ASK DARLENE OUT AGAIN.
YEP. HE'S CONSIDERING IT.
HE'S GETTING SOME OTHER ADVICE, THOUGH.
WHAT DO YOU THINK, MR. DASCHLE?
I JUST DON'T THINK I SHOULD BE IN THE BUSINESS OF RELATIONSHIP-BUILDING.

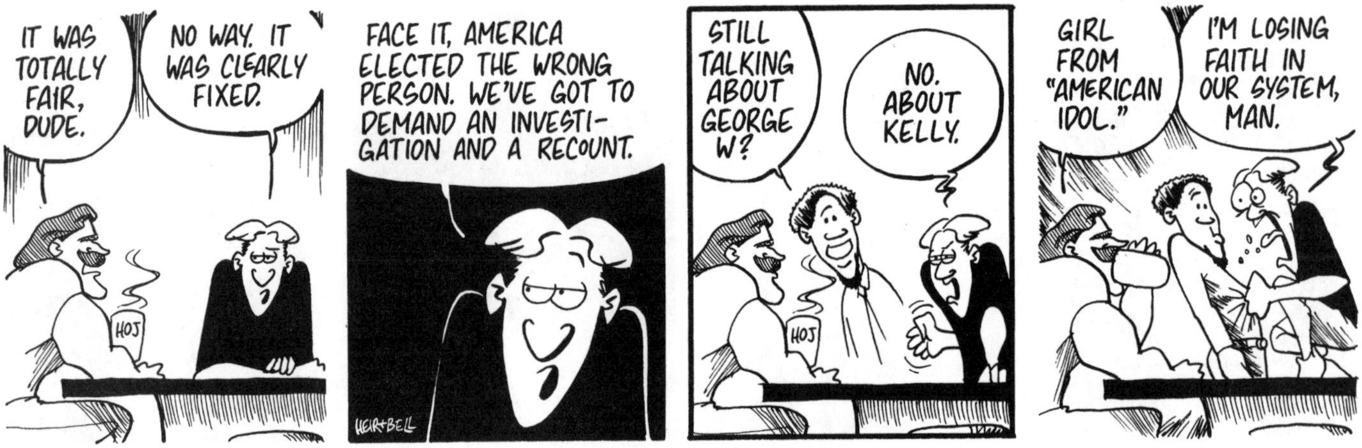
IT WAS TOTALLY FAIR, DUDE.
NO WAY. IT WAS CLEARLY FIXED.
FACE IT, AMERICA ELECTED THE WRONG PERSON. WE'VE GOT TO DEMAND AN INVESTIGATION AND A RECOUNT.
STILL TALKING ABOUT GEORGE W?
NO. ABOUT KELLY.
GIRL FROM "AMERICAN IDOL."
I'M LOSING FAITH IN OUR SYSTEM, MAN.

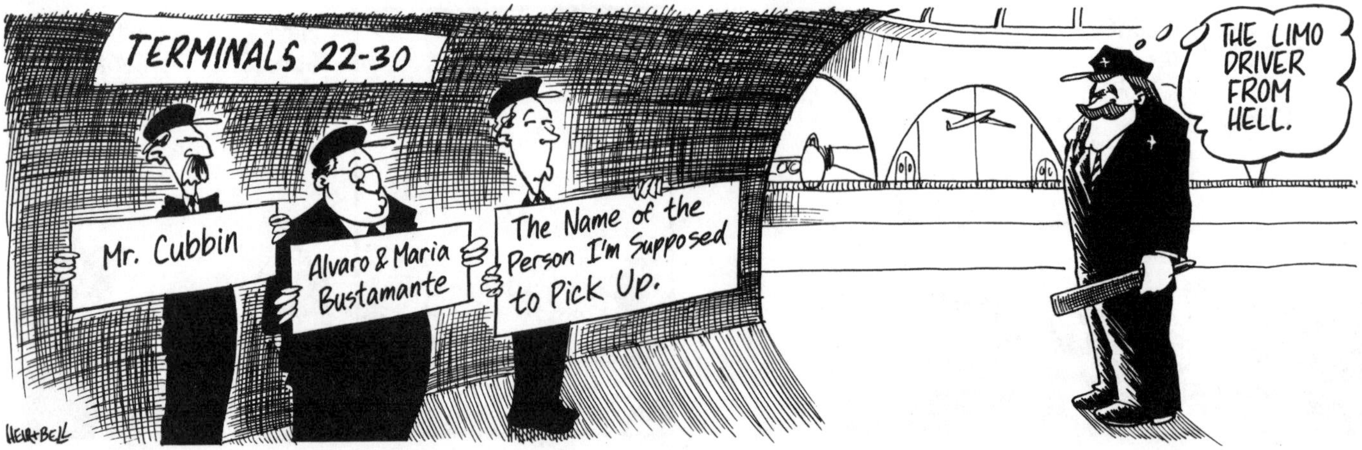
TERMINALS 22-30
Mr. Cubbin
Alvaro & Maria Bustamante
The Name of the Person I'm Supposed to Pick Up.
THE LIMO DRIVER FROM HELL.

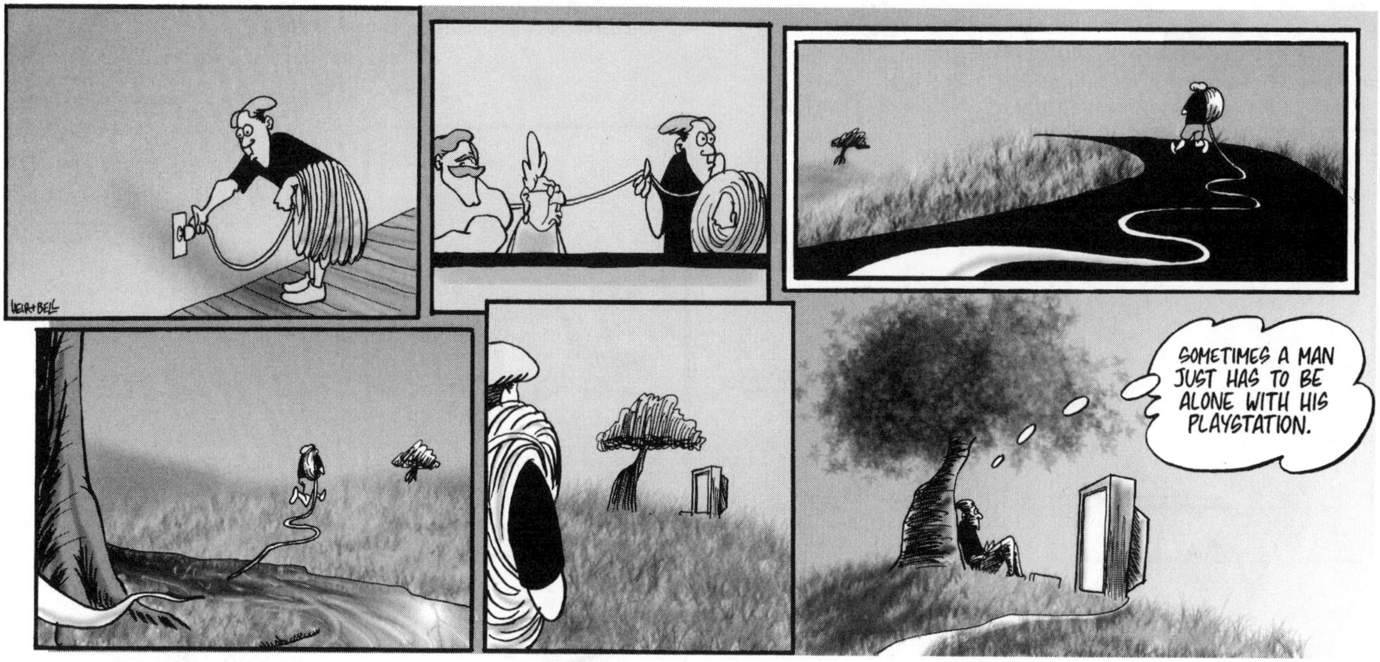

SOMETIMES A MAN JUST HAS TO BE ALONE WITH HIS PLAYSTATION.

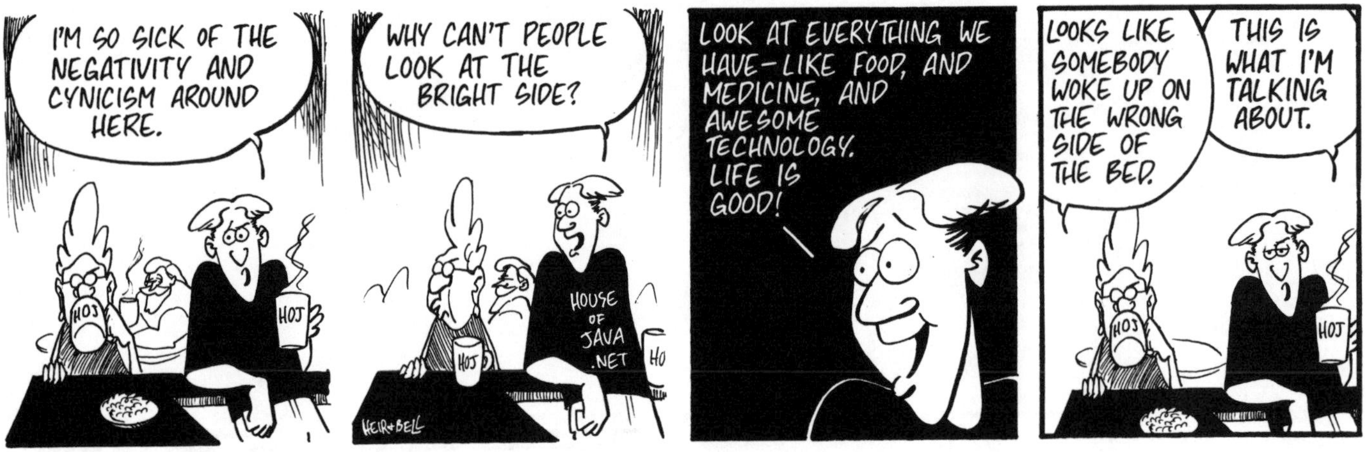
I'M SO SICK OF THE NEGATIVITY AND CYNICISM AROUND HERE.
HOJ
HOJ
WHY CAN'T PEOPLE LOOK AT THE BRIGHT SIDE?
HOUSE OF JAVA .NET
HOJ
HEIR+BELL
LOOK AT EVERYTHING WE HAVE—LIKE FOOD, AND MEDICINE, AND AWESOME TECHNOLOGY. LIFE IS GOOD!
LOOKS LIKE SOMEBODY WOKE UP ON THE WRONG SIDE OF THE BED.
THIS IS WHAT I'M TALKING ABOUT.
HOJ
HOJ

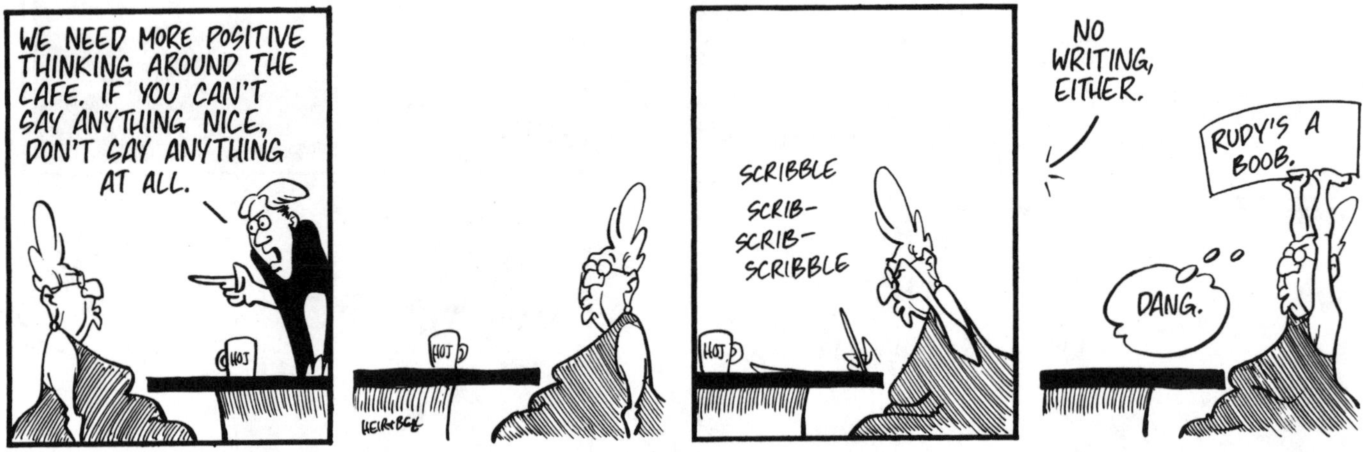
WE NEED MORE POSITIVE THINKING AROUND THE CAFE. IF YOU CAN'T SAY ANYTHING NICE, DON'T SAY ANYTHING AT ALL.
HOJ
HOJ
HEIR+BELL
SCRIBBLE SCRIB-SCRIB-SCRIBBLE
HOJ
NO WRITING, EITHER.
RUDY'S A BOOB.
DANG.

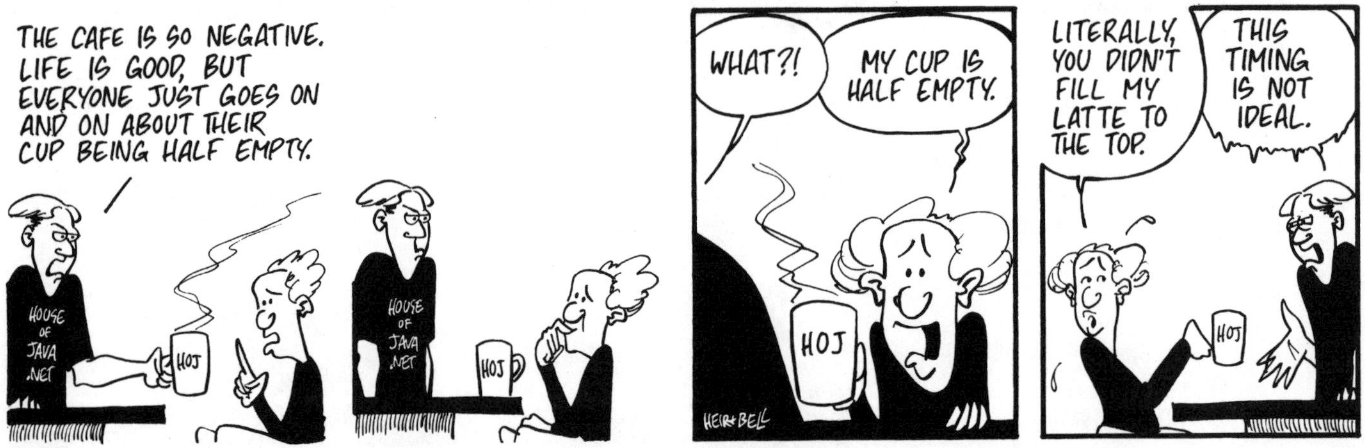
THE CAFE IS SO NEGATIVE. LIFE IS GOOD, BUT EVERYONE JUST GOES ON AND ON ABOUT THEIR CUP BEING HALF EMPTY.
HOUSE OF JAVA .NET
HOJ
HOUSE OF JAVA .NET
HOJ
WHAT?!
MY CUP IS HALF EMPTY.
HOJ
HEIR+BELL
LITERALLY. YOU DIDN'T FILL MY LATTE TO THE TOP.
THIS TIMING IS NOT IDEAL.
HOJ

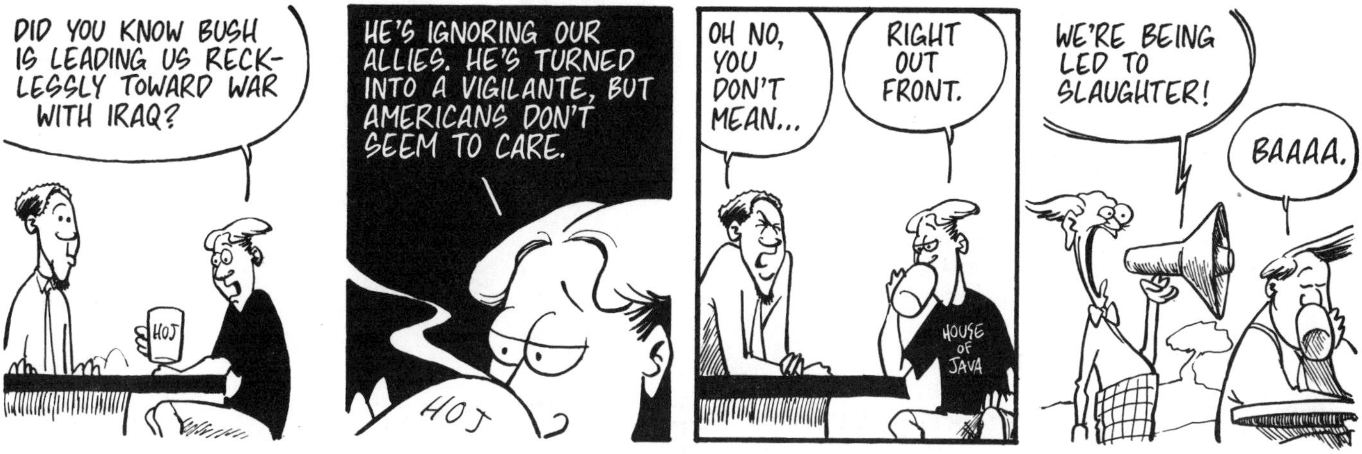
DID YOU KNOW BUSH IS LEADING US RECKLESSLY TOWARD WAR WITH IRAQ?
HOJ
HE'S IGNORING OUR ALLIES. HE'S TURNED INTO A VIGILANTE, BUT AMERICANS DON'T SEEM TO CARE.
HOJ
OH NO, YOU DON'T MEAN...
RIGHT OUT FRONT.
HOUSE OF JAVA
WE'RE BEING LED TO SLAUGHTER!
BAAAA.

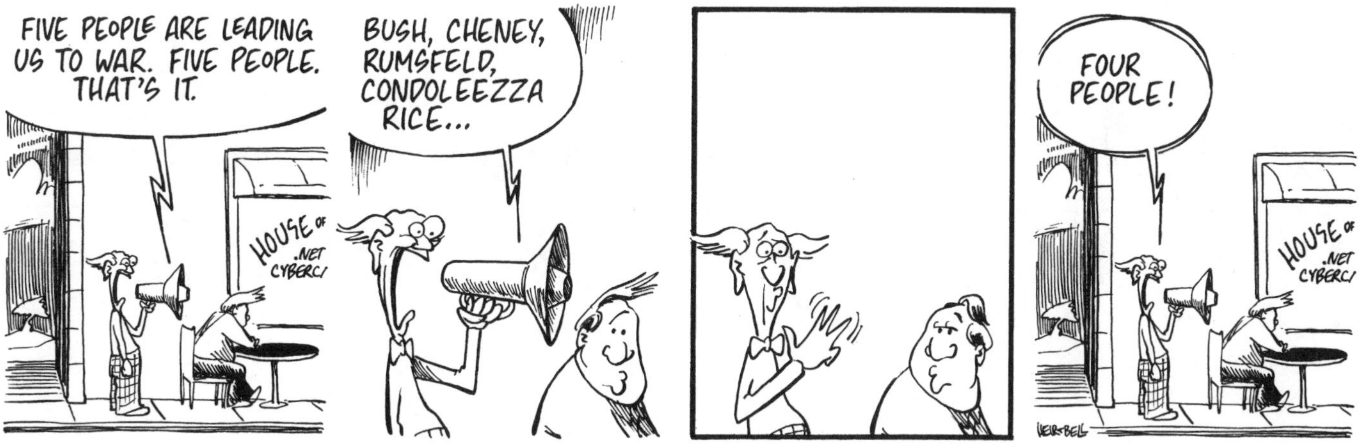
FIVE PEOPLE ARE LEADING US TO WAR. FIVE PEOPLE. THAT'S IT.
HOUSE OF .NET CYBERC
BUSH, CHENEY, RUMSFELD, CONDOLEEZZA RICE...
FOUR PEOPLE!
HOUSE OF .NET CYBERC

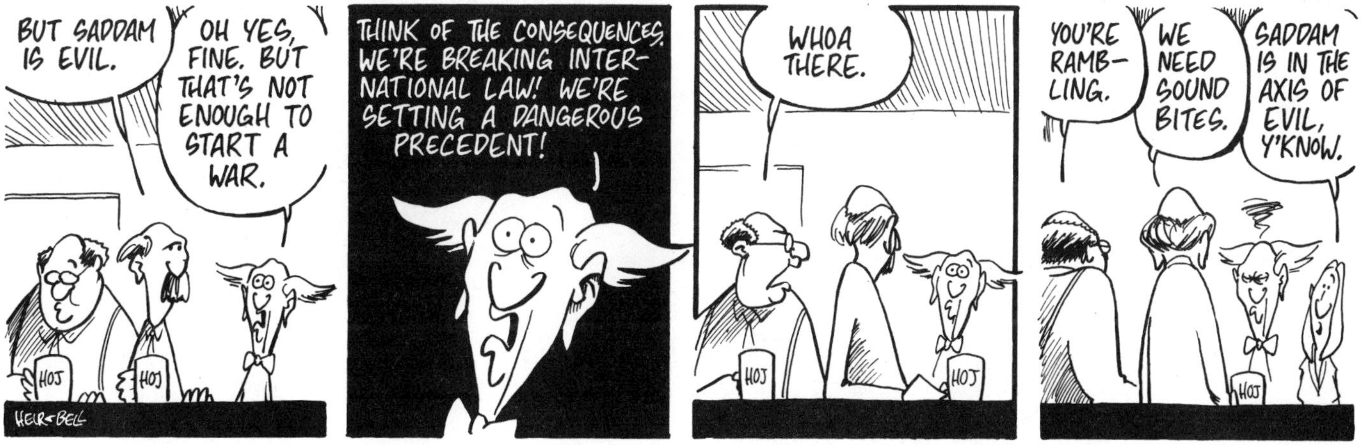
BUT SADDAM IS EVIL.
OH YES, FINE. BUT THAT'S NOT ENOUGH TO START A WAR.
HOJ
HOJ
THINK OF THE CONSEQUENCES. WE'RE BREAKING INTERNATIONAL LAW! WE'RE SETTING A DANGEROUS PRECEDENT!
WHOA THERE.
HOJ
HOJ
YOU'RE RAMBLING.
WE NEED SOUND BITES.
SADDAM IS IN THE AXIS OF EVIL, Y'KNOW.
HOJ

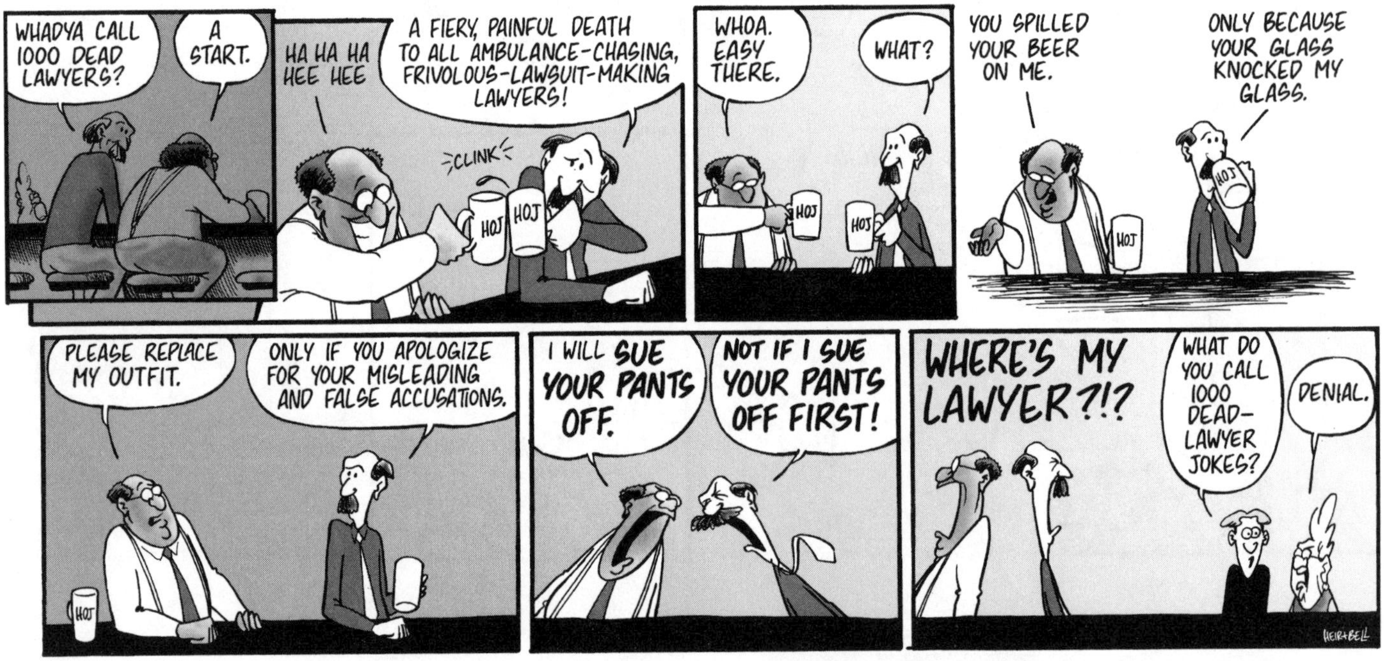
WHADYA CALL 1000 DEAD LAWYERS?
A START.
HA HA HA HEE HEE
A FIERY, PAINFUL DEATH TO ALL AMBULANCE-CHASING, FRIVOLOUS-LAWSUIT-MAKING LAWYERS!
CLINK
HOJ
HOJ
WHOA. EASY THERE.
WHAT?
YOU SPILLED YOUR BEER ON ME.
ONLY BECAUSE YOUR GLASS KNOCKED MY GLASS.
PLEASE REPLACE MY OUTFIT.
ONLY IF YOU APOLOGIZE FOR YOUR MISLEADING AND FALSE ACCUSATIONS.
I WILL SUE YOUR PANTS OFF.
NOT IF I SUE YOUR PANTS OFF FIRST!
WHERE'S MY LAWYER?!?
WHAT DO YOU CALL 1000 DEAD-LAWYER JOKES?
DENIAL.

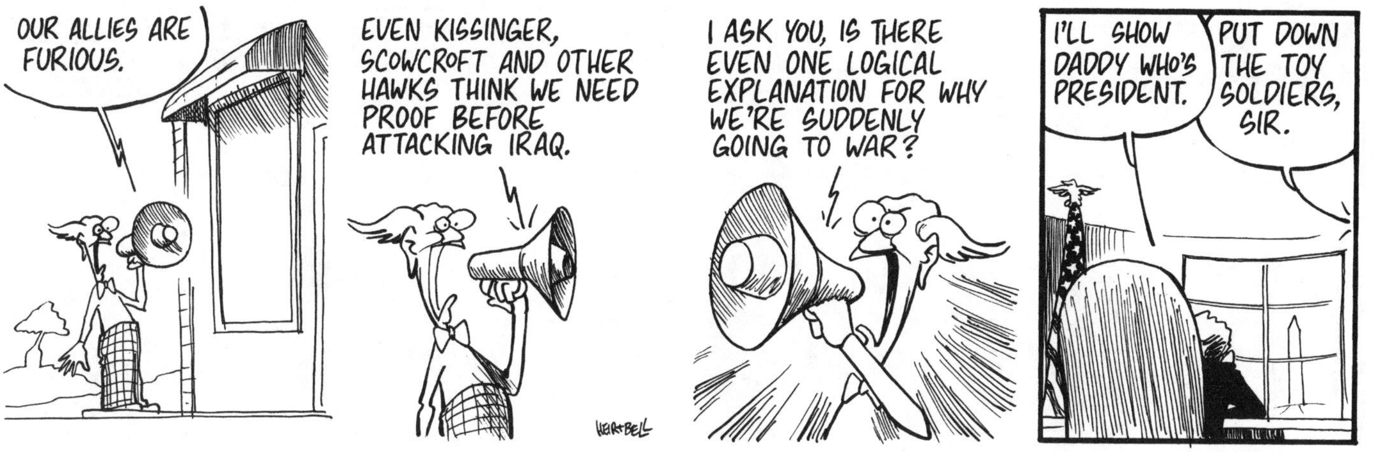
OUR ALLIES ARE FURIOUS.
EVEN KISSINGER, SCOWCROFT AND OTHER HAWKS THINK WE NEED PROOF BEFORE ATTACKING IRAQ.
HEIR+BELL
I ASK YOU, IS THERE EVEN ONE LOGICAL EXPLANATION FOR WHY WE'RE SUDDENLY GOING TO WAR?
I'LL SHOW DADDY WHO'S PRESIDENT.
PUT DOWN THE TOY SOLDIERS, SIR.

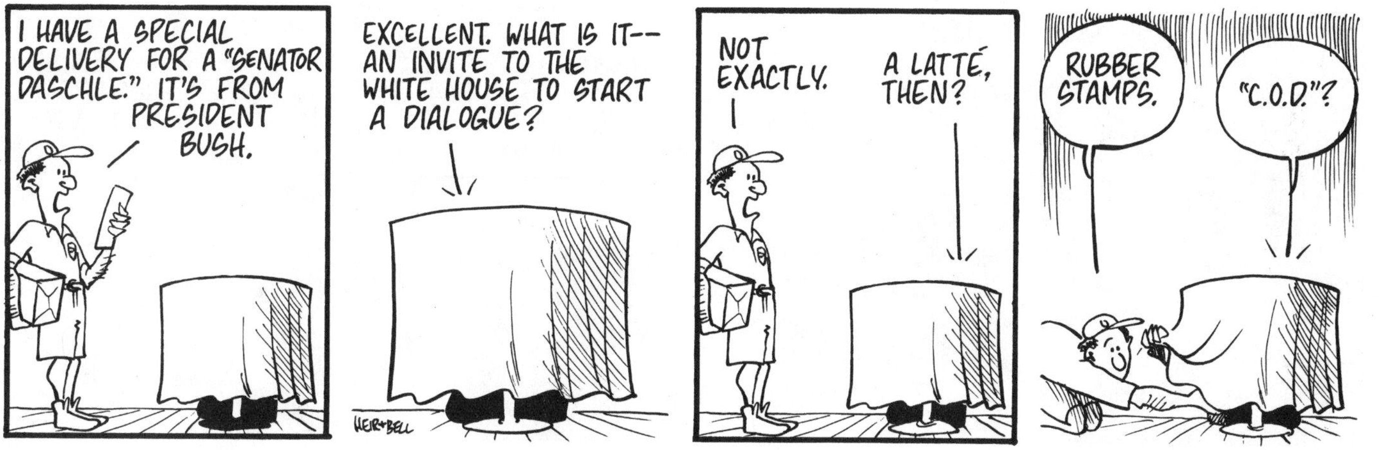
I HAVE A SPECIAL DELIVERY FOR A "SENATOR DASCHLE." IT'S FROM PRESIDENT BUSH.
EXCELLENT. WHAT IS IT-- AN INVITE TO THE WHITE HOUSE TO START A DIALOGUE?
HEIR+BELL
NOT EXACTLY.
A LATTÉ, THEN?
RUBBER STAMPS.
"C.O.D."?

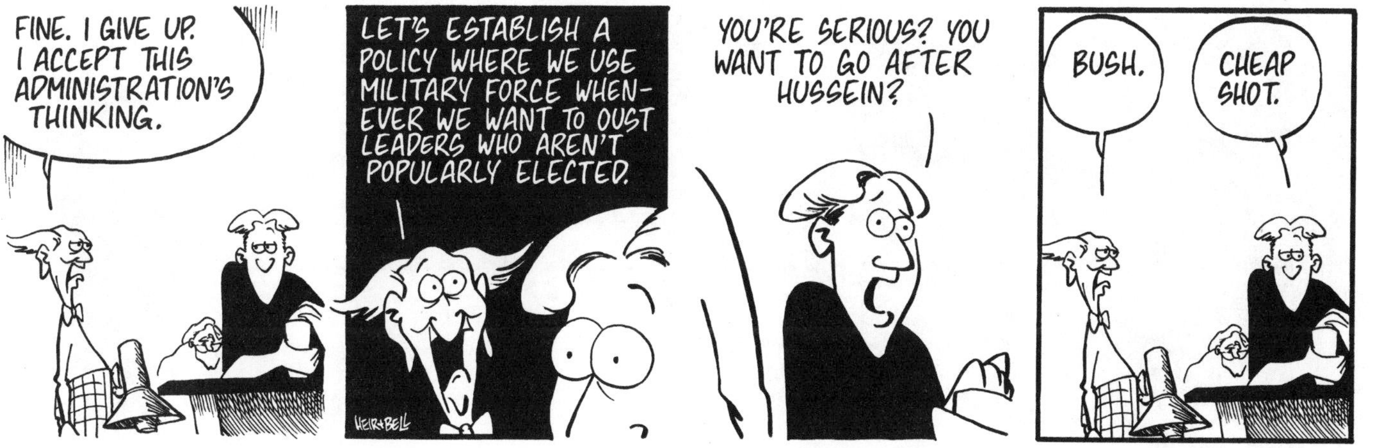
FINE. I GIVE UP. I ACCEPT THIS ADMINISTRATION'S THINKING.
LET'S ESTABLISH A POLICY WHERE WE USE MILITARY FORCE WHENEVER WE WANT TO OUST LEADERS WHO AREN'T POPULARLY ELECTED.
HEIR+BELL
YOU'RE SERIOUS? YOU WANT TO GO AFTER HUSSEIN?
BUSH.
CHEAP SHOT.

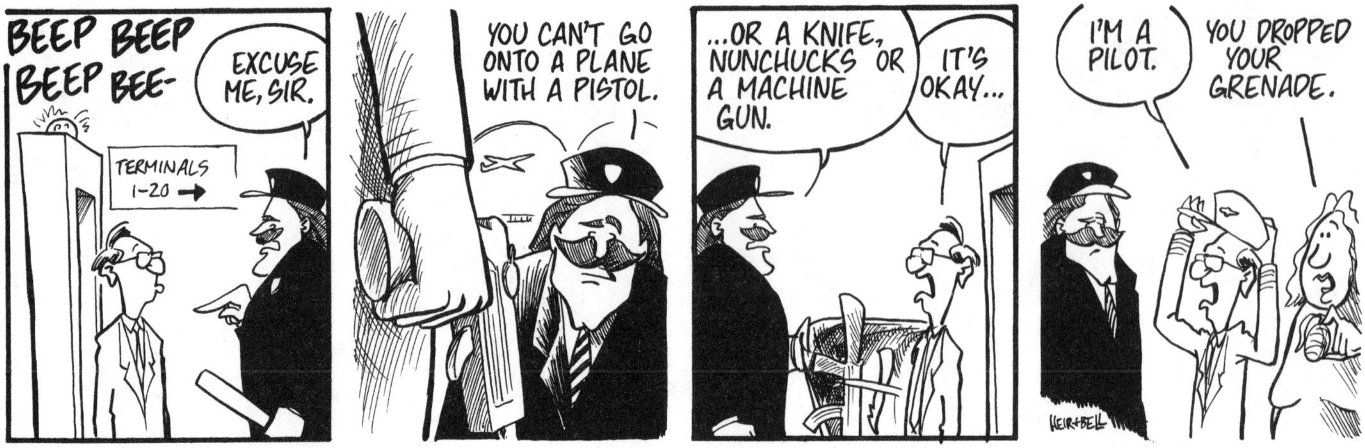
BEEP BEEP BEEP BEE-
EXCUSE ME, SIR.
TERMINALS 1-20 →
YOU CAN'T GO ONTO A PLANE WITH A PISTOL.
...OR A KNIFE, NUNCHUCKS OR A MACHINE GUN.
IT'S OKAY...
I'M A PILOT.
YOU DROPPED YOUR GRENADE.
HEIR+BELL

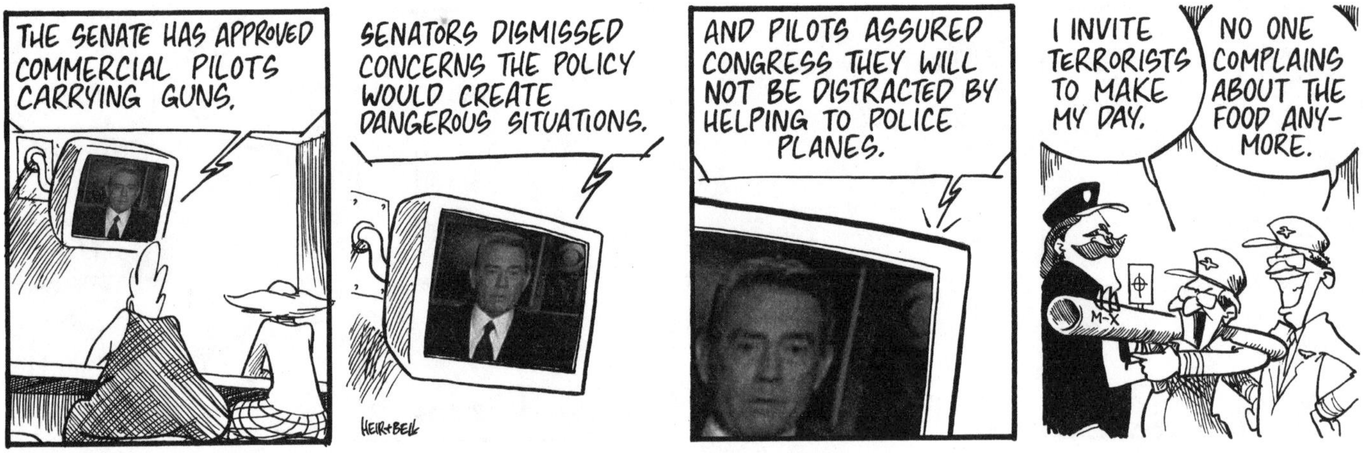
THE SENATE HAS APPROVED COMMERCIAL PILOTS CARRYING GUNS.
SENATORS DISMISSED CONCERNS THE POLICY WOULD CREATE DANGEROUS SITUATIONS.
HEIR+BELL
AND PILOTS ASSURED CONGRESS THEY WILL NOT BE DISTRACTED BY HELPING TO POLICE PLANES.
I INVITE TERRORISTS TO MAKE MY DAY.
NO ONE COMPLAINS ABOUT THE FOOD ANY-MORE.
M-X

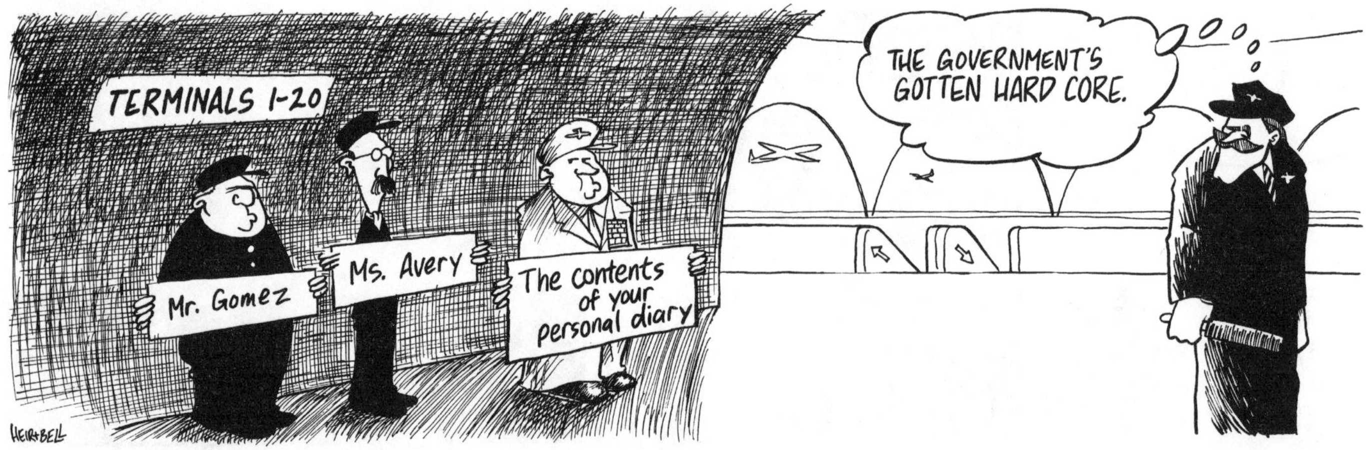
TERMINALS 1-20
Mr. Gomez
Ms. Avery
The contents of your personal diary
THE GOVERNMENT'S GOTTEN HARD CORE.
HEIR+BELL

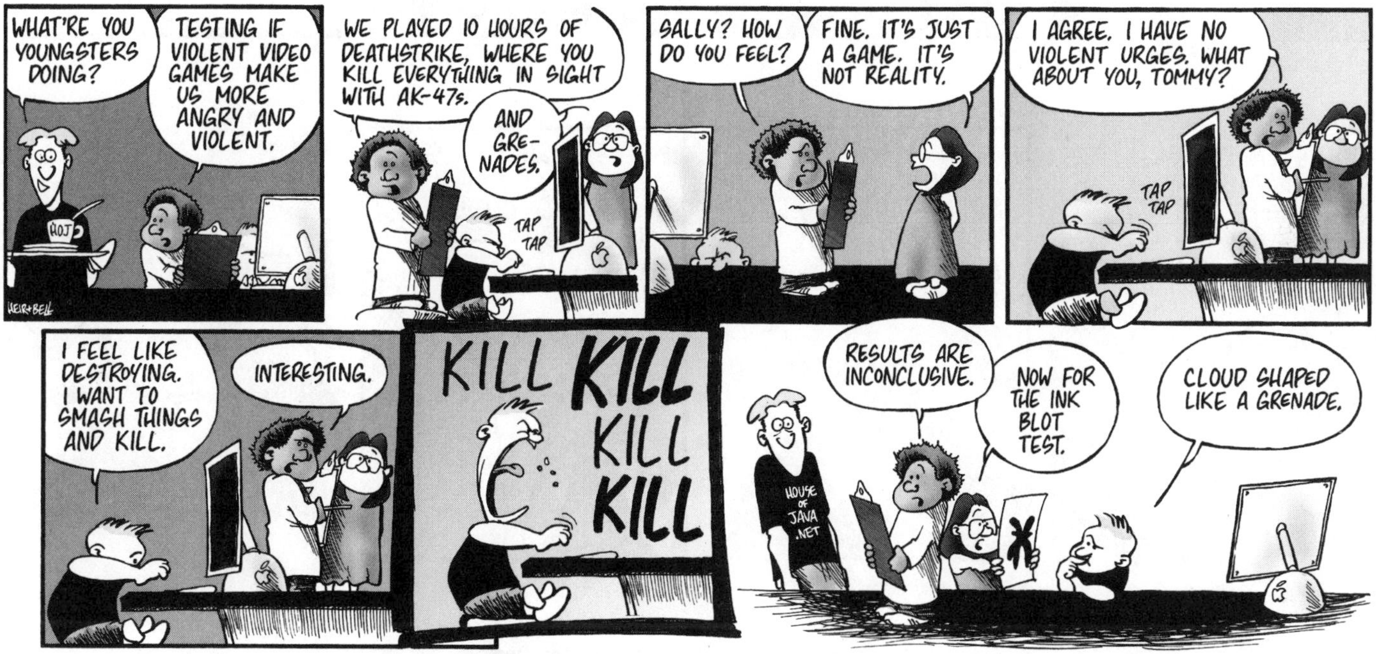
WHAT'RE YOU YOUNGSTERS DOING?
TESTING IF VIOLENT VIDEO GAMES MAKE US MORE ANGRY AND VIOLENT.
HOJ
HEIR+BELL
WE PLAYED 10 HOURS OF DEATHSTRIKE, WHERE YOU KILL EVERYTHING IN SIGHT WITH AK-47s.
AND GRE-NADES.
TAP TAP
SALLY? HOW DO YOU FEEL?
FINE. IT'S JUST A GAME. IT'S NOT REALITY.
I AGREE. I HAVE NO VIOLENT URGES. WHAT ABOUT YOU, TOMMY?
TAP TAP
I FEEL LIKE DESTROYING. I WANT TO SMASH THINGS AND KILL.
INTERESTING.
KILL KILL KILL KILL
RESULTS ARE INCONCLUSIVE.
NOW FOR THE INK BLOT TEST.
CLOUD SHAPED LIKE A GRENADE.
HOUSE OF JAVA .NET

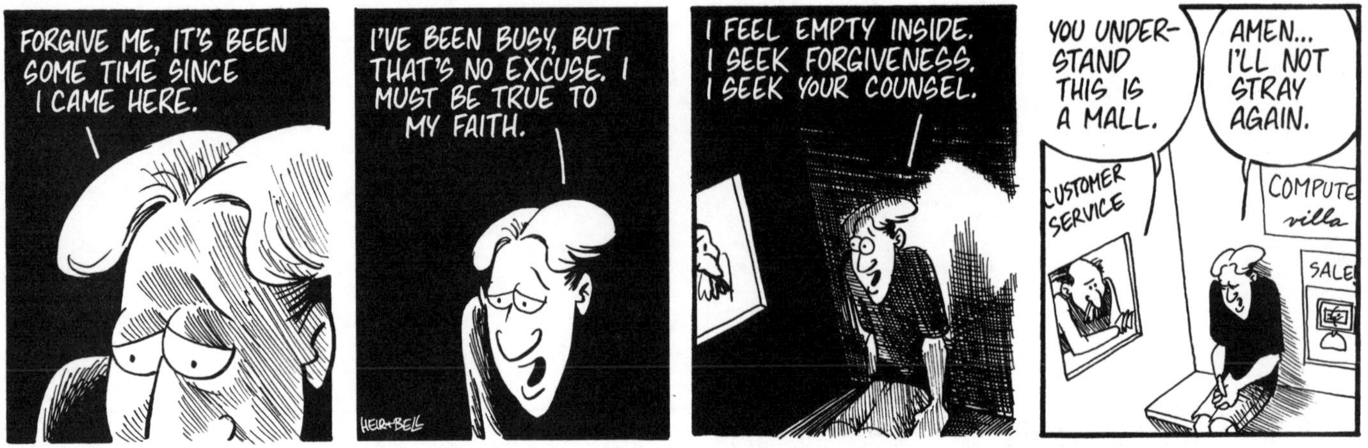
FORGIVE ME, IT'S BEEN SOME TIME SINCE I CAME HERE.
I'VE BEEN BUSY, BUT THAT'S NO EXCUSE. I MUST BE TRUE TO MY FAITH.
HEIR+BELL
I FEEL EMPTY INSIDE. I SEEK FORGIVENESS. I SEEK YOUR COUNSEL.
YOU UNDERSTAND THIS IS A MALL.
AMEN... I'LL NOT STRAY AGAIN.
CUSTOMER SERVICE
COMPUTE villa
SALE

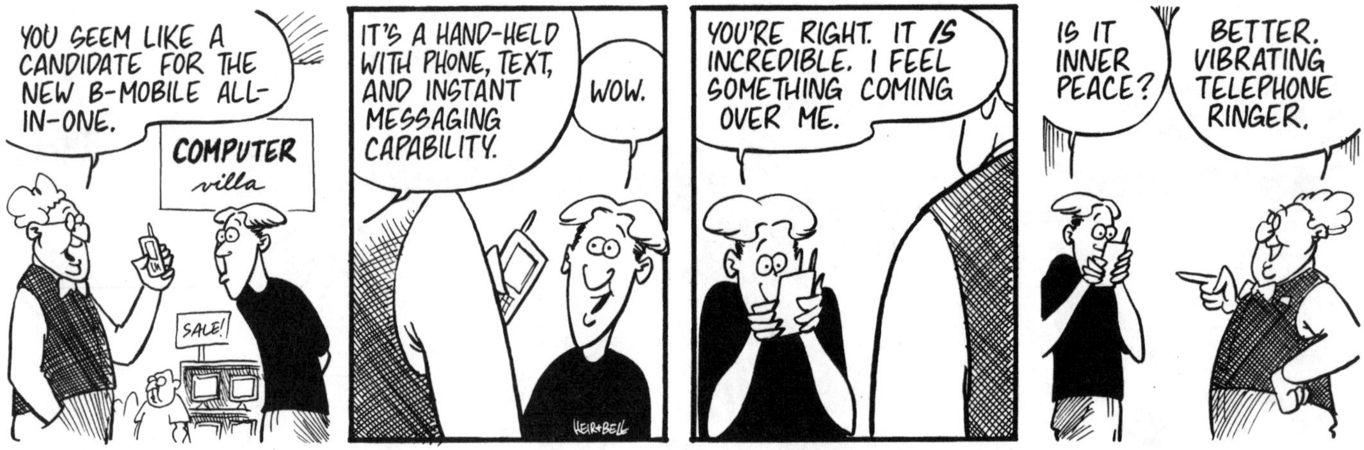
YOU SEEM LIKE A CANDIDATE FOR THE NEW B-MOBILE ALL-IN-ONE.
COMPUTER villa
SALE!
IT'S A HAND-HELD WITH PHONE, TEXT, AND INSTANT MESSAGING CAPABILITY.
WOW.
HEIR+BELL
YOU'RE RIGHT. IT *IS* INCREDIBLE. I FEEL SOMETHING COMING OVER ME.
IS IT INNER PEACE?
BETTER. VIBRATING TELEPHONE RINGER.

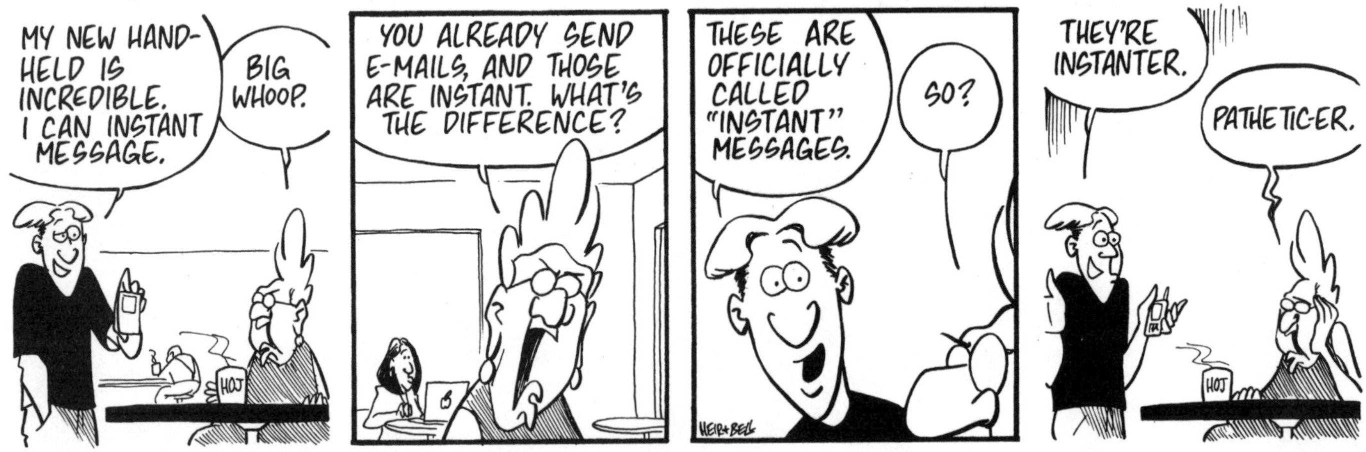
MY NEW HAND-HELD IS INCREDIBLE. I CAN INSTANT MESSAGE.
BIG WHOOP.
HOJ
YOU ALREADY SEND E-MAILS, AND THOSE ARE INSTANT. WHAT'S THE DIFFERENCE?
THESE ARE OFFICIALLY CALLED "INSTANT" MESSAGES.
SO?
HEIR+BELL
THEY'RE INSTANTER.
PATHETIC-ER.
HOJ

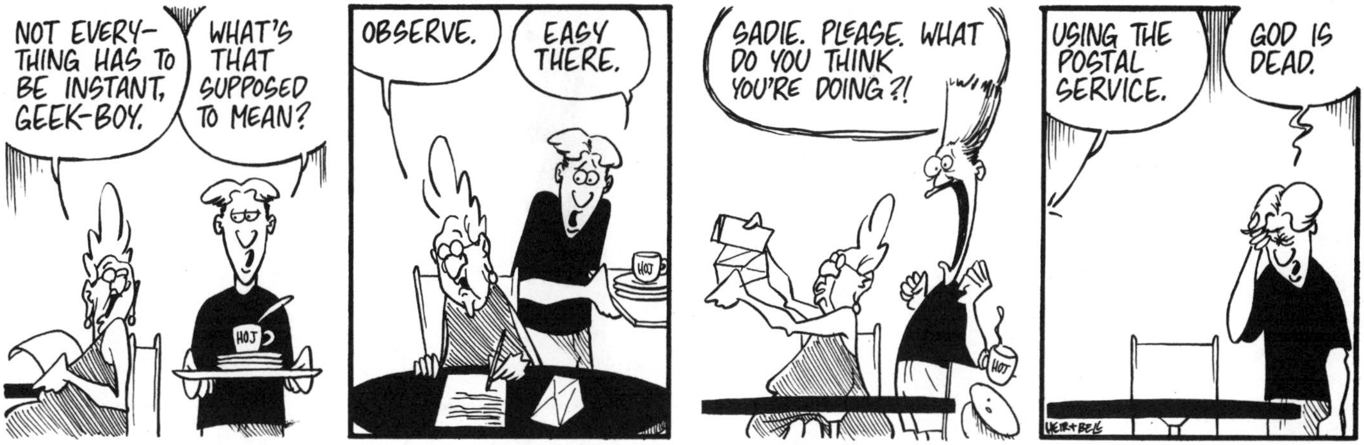
NOT EVERYTHING HAS TO BE INSTANT, GEEK-BOY.
WHAT'S THAT SUPPOSED TO MEAN?
OBSERVE.
EASY THERE.
SADIE. PLEASE. WHAT DO YOU THINK YOU'RE DOING?!
USING THE POSTAL SERVICE.
GOD IS DEAD.

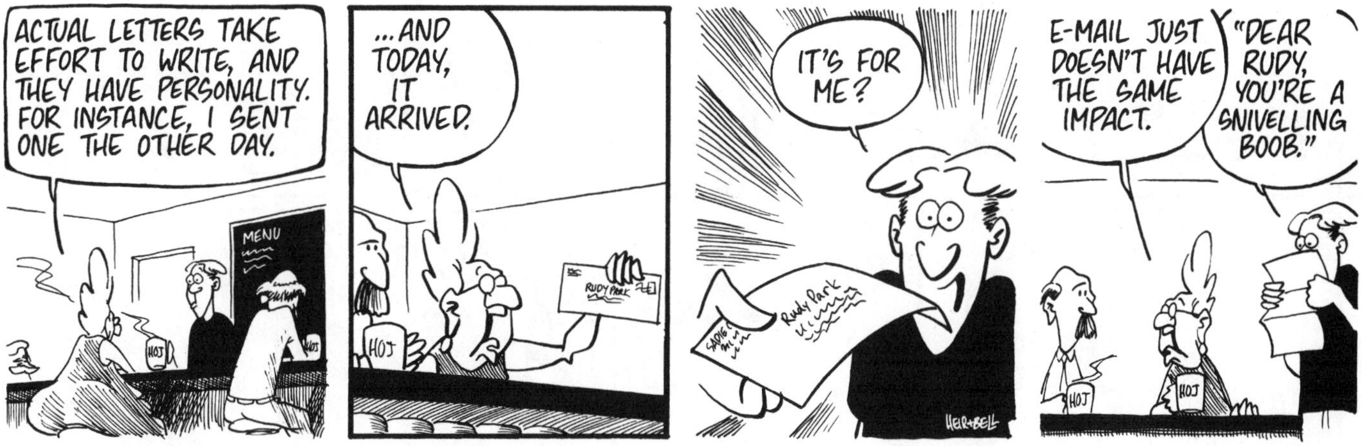
ACTUAL LETTERS TAKE EFFORT TO WRITE, AND THEY HAVE PERSONALITY. FOR INSTANCE, I SENT ONE THE OTHER DAY.
...AND TODAY, IT ARRIVED.
IT'S FOR ME?
E-MAIL JUST DOESN'T HAVE THE SAME IMPACT.
"DEAR RUDY, YOU'RE A SNIVELLING BOOB."

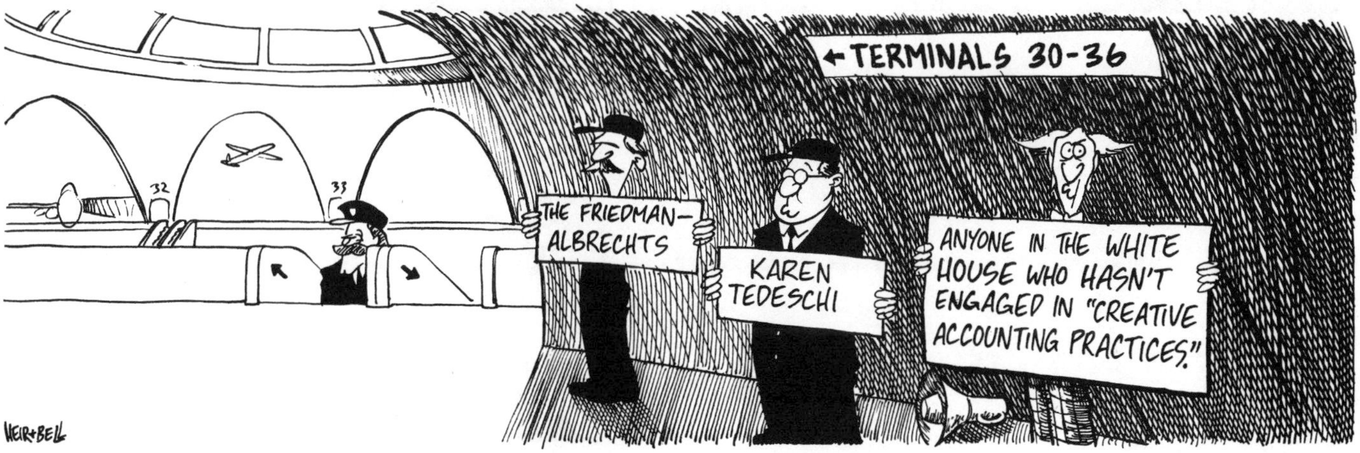
← TERMINALS 30-36
THE FRIEDMAN-ALBRECHTS
KAREN TEDESCHI
ANYONE IN THE WHITE HOUSE WHO HASN'T ENGAGED IN "CREATIVE ACCOUNTING PRACTICES."

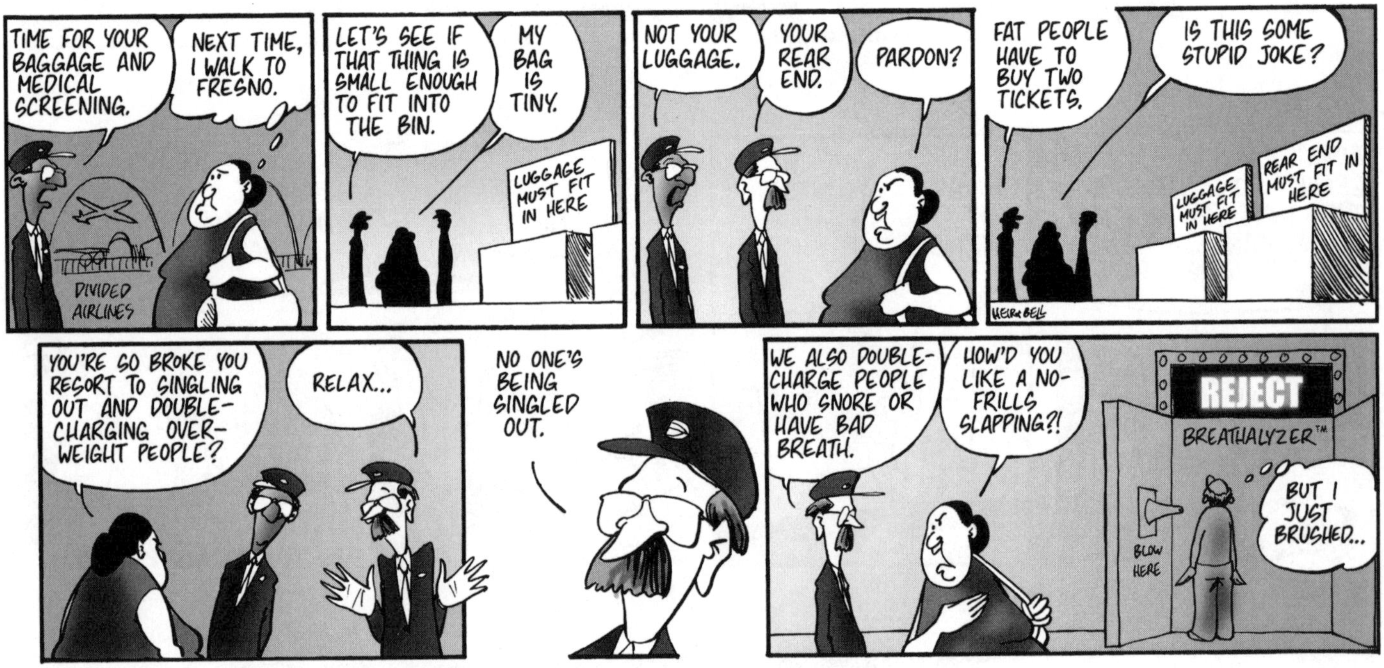
TIME FOR YOUR BAGGAGE AND MEDICAL SCREENING.
NEXT TIME, I WALK TO FRESNO.
DIVIDED AIRLINES
LET'S SEE IF THAT THING IS SMALL ENOUGH TO FIT INTO THE BIN.
MY BAG IS TINY.
LUGGAGE MUST FIT IN HERE
NOT YOUR LUGGAGE.
YOUR REAR END.
PARDON?
FAT PEOPLE HAVE TO BUY TWO TICKETS.
IS THIS SOME STUPID JOKE?
LUGGAGE MUST FIT IN HERE
REAR END MUST FIT IN HERE
YOU'RE SO BROKE YOU RESORT TO SINGLING OUT AND DOUBLE-CHARGING OVER-WEIGHT PEOPLE?
RELAX...
NO ONE'S BEING SINGLED OUT.
WE ALSO DOUBLE-CHARGE PEOPLE WHO SNORE OR HAVE BAD BREATH.
HOW'D YOU LIKE A NO-FRILLS SLAPPING?!
REJECT
BREATHALYZER™
BLOW HERE
BUT I JUST BRUSHED...

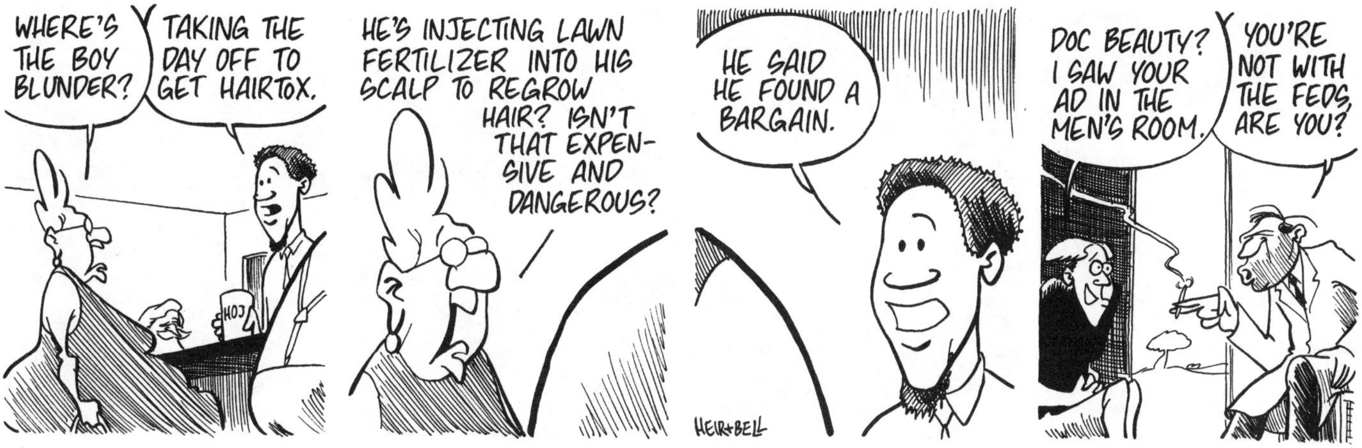
WHERE'S THE BOY BLUNDER?
TAKING THE DAY OFF TO GET HAIRTOX.
HOJ
HE'S INJECTING LAWN FERTILIZER INTO HIS SCALP TO REGROW
HAIR? ISN'T THAT EXPENSIVE AND DANGEROUS?
HE SAID HE FOUND A BARGAIN.
HEIR+BELL
DOC BEAUTY? I SAW YOUR AD IN THE MEN'S ROOM.
YOU'RE NOT WITH THE FEDS, ARE YOU?

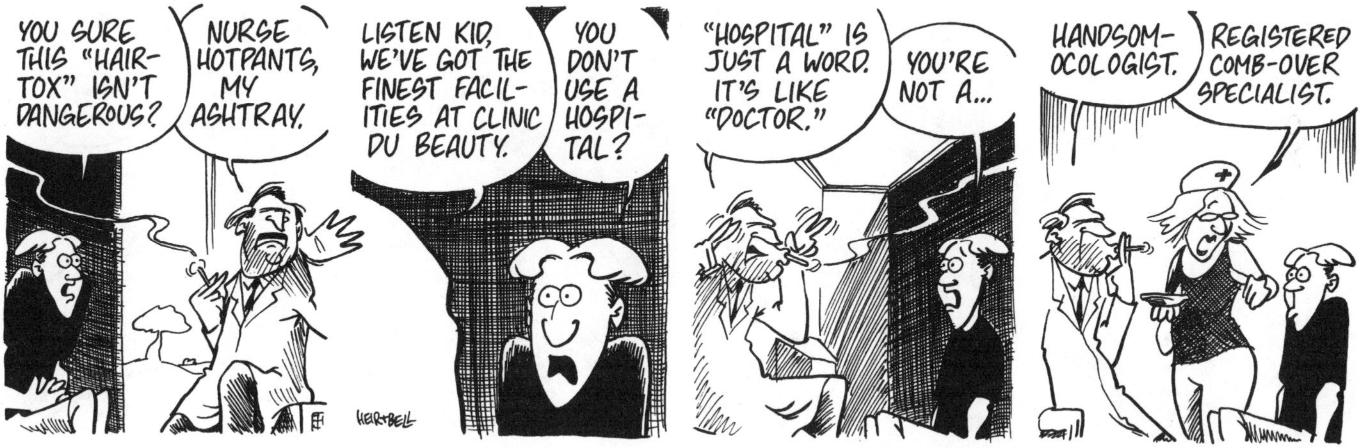
YOU SURE THIS "HAIR-TOX" ISN'T DANGEROUS?
NURSE HOTPANTS, MY ASHTRAY.
LISTEN KID, WE'VE GOT THE FINEST FACIL-ITIES AT CLINIC DU BEAUTY.
YOU DON'T USE A HOSPI-TAL?
HEIR+BELL
"HOSPITAL" IS JUST A WORD. IT'S LIKE "DOCTOR."
YOU'RE NOT A...
HANDSOM-OCOLOGIST.
REGISTERED COMB-OVER SPECIALIST.

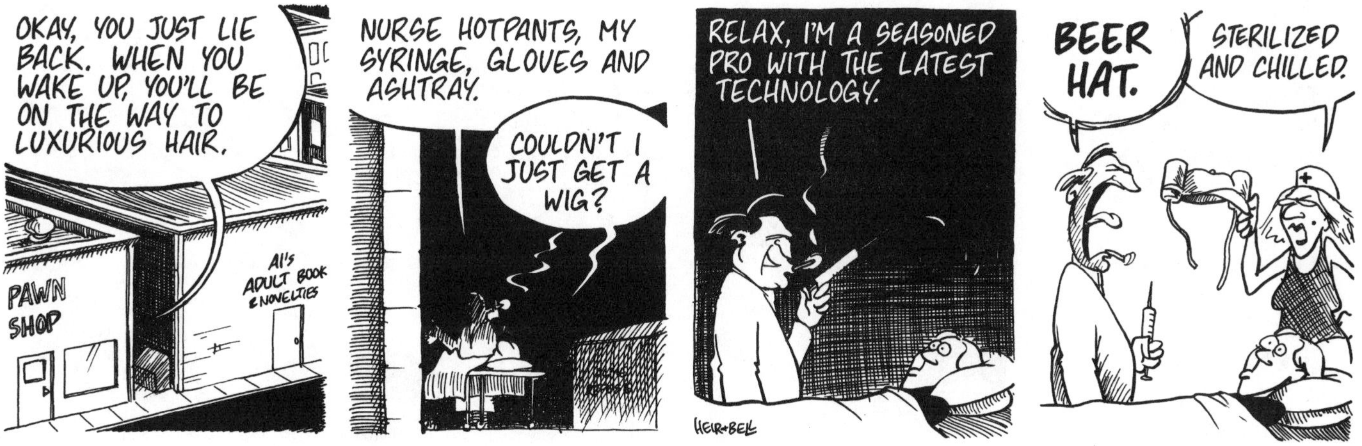
OKAY, YOU JUST LIE BACK. WHEN YOU WAKE UP, YOU'LL BE ON THE WAY TO LUXURIOUS HAIR.
PAWN SHOP
AL'S ADULT BOOK & NOVELTIES
NURSE HOTPANTS, MY SYRINGE, GLOVES AND ASHTRAY.
COULDN'T I JUST GET A WIG?
RELAX, I'M A SEASONED PRO WITH THE LATEST TECHNOLOGY.
HEIR+BELL
BEER HAT.
STERILIZED AND CHILLED.

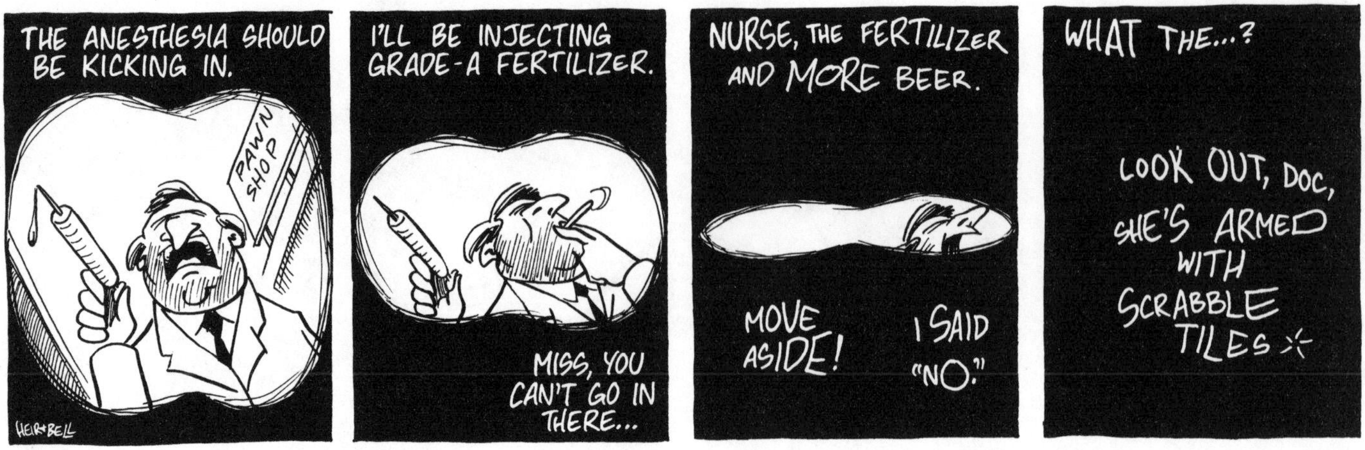
THE ANESTHESIA SHOULD BE KICKING IN.
PAWN SHOP
HEIR+BELL
I'LL BE INJECTING GRADE-A FERTILIZER.
MISS, YOU CAN'T GO IN THERE...
NURSE, THE FERTILIZER AND MORE BEER.
MOVE ASIDE!
I SAID "NO."
WHAT THE...?
LOOK OUT, DOC, SHE'S ARMED WITH SCRABBLE TILES

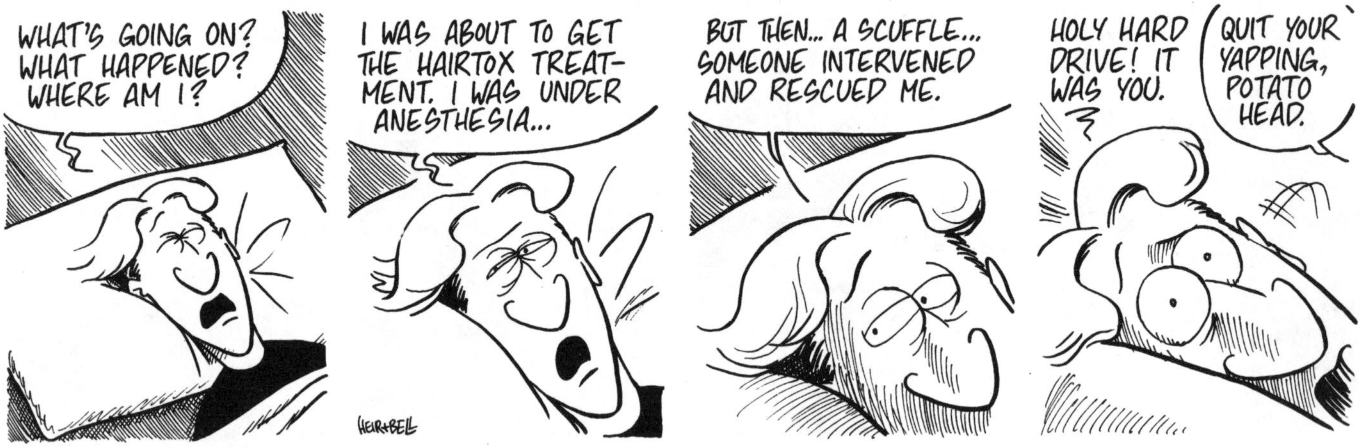
WHAT'S GOING ON? WHAT HAPPENED? WHERE AM I?
I WAS ABOUT TO GET THE HAIRTOX TREATMENT. I WAS UNDER ANESTHESIA...
HEIR+BELL
BUT THEN... A SCUFFLE... SOMEONE INTERVENED AND RESCUED ME.
HOLY HARD DRIVE! IT WAS YOU.
QUIT YOUR YAPPING, POTATO HEAD.

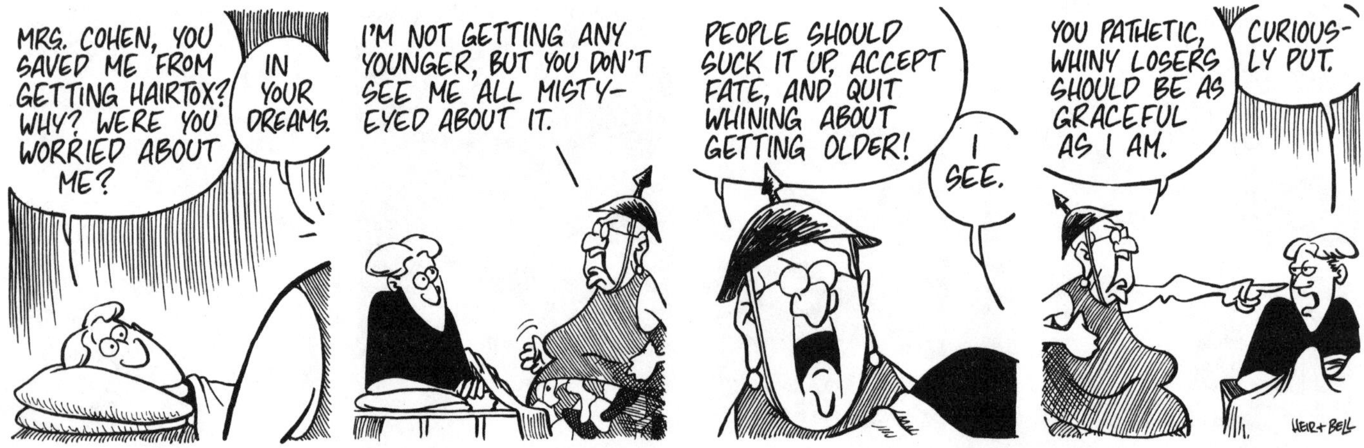
MRS. COHEN, YOU SAVED ME FROM GETTING HAIRTOX? WHY? WERE YOU WORRIED ABOUT ME?
IN YOUR DREAMS.
I'M NOT GETTING ANY YOUNGER, BUT YOU DON'T SEE ME ALL MISTY-EYED ABOUT IT.
PEOPLE SHOULD SUCK IT UP, ACCEPT FATE, AND QUIT WHINING ABOUT GETTING OLDER!
I SEE.
YOU PATHETIC, WHINY LOSERS SHOULD BE AS GRACEFUL AS I AM.
CURIOUSLY PUT.
HEIR+BELL

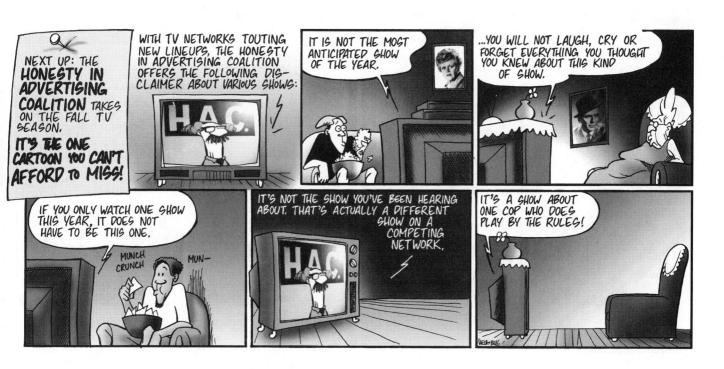

NEXT UP: THE **HONESTY IN ADVERTISING COALITION** TAKES ON THE FALL TV SEASON.

IT'S THE ONE CARTOON YOU CAN'T AFFORD TO MISS!

WITH TV NETWORKS TOUTING NEW LINEUPS, THE HONESTY IN ADVERTISING COALITION OFFERS THE FOLLOWING DISCLAIMER ABOUT VARIOUS SHOWS:

H.A.C.

IT IS NOT THE MOST ANTICIPATED SHOW OF THE YEAR.

...YOU WILL NOT LAUGH, CRY OR FORGET EVERYTHING YOU THOUGHT YOU KNEW ABOUT THIS KIND OF SHOW.

IF YOU ONLY WATCH ONE SHOW THIS YEAR, IT DOES NOT HAVE TO BE THIS ONE.

MUNCH CRUNCH   MUN—

IT'S NOT THE SHOW YOU'VE BEEN HEARING ABOUT. THAT'S ACTUALLY A DIFFERENT SHOW ON A COMPETING NETWORK.

H.A.C.

IT'S A SHOW ABOUT ONE COP WHO DOES PLAY BY THE RULES!

63

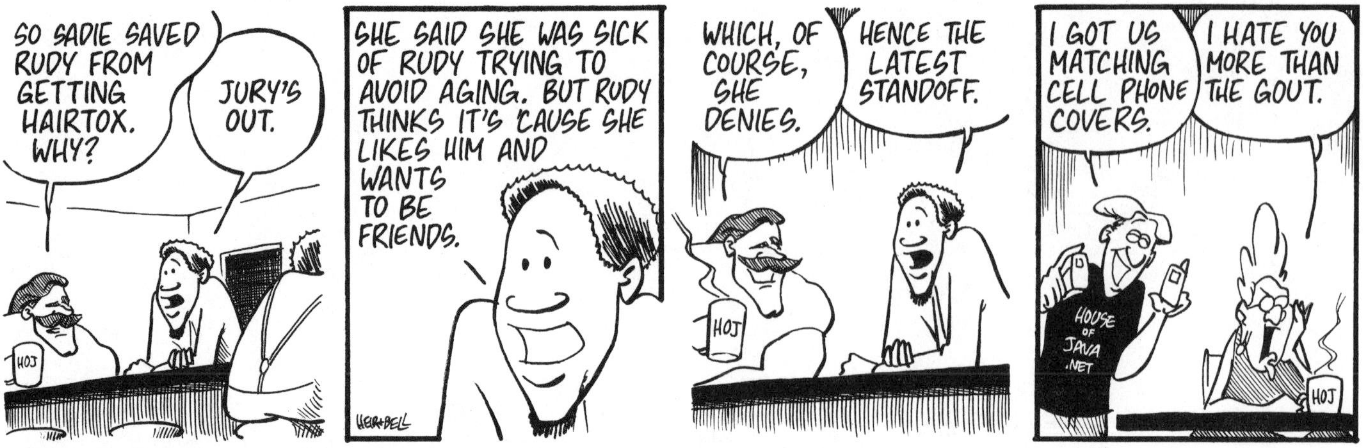
SO SADIE SAVED RUDY FROM GETTING HAIRTOX. WHY?
JURY'S OUT.
SHE SAID SHE WAS SICK OF RUDY TRYING TO AVOID AGING. BUT RUDY THINKS IT'S 'CAUSE SHE LIKES HIM AND WANTS TO BE FRIENDS.
WHICH, OF COURSE, SHE DENIES.
HENCE THE LATEST STANDOFF.
I GOT US MATCHING CELL PHONE COVERS.
I HATE YOU MORE THAN THE GOUT.
HOJ
HOUSE OF JAVA .NET
HEIR+BELL

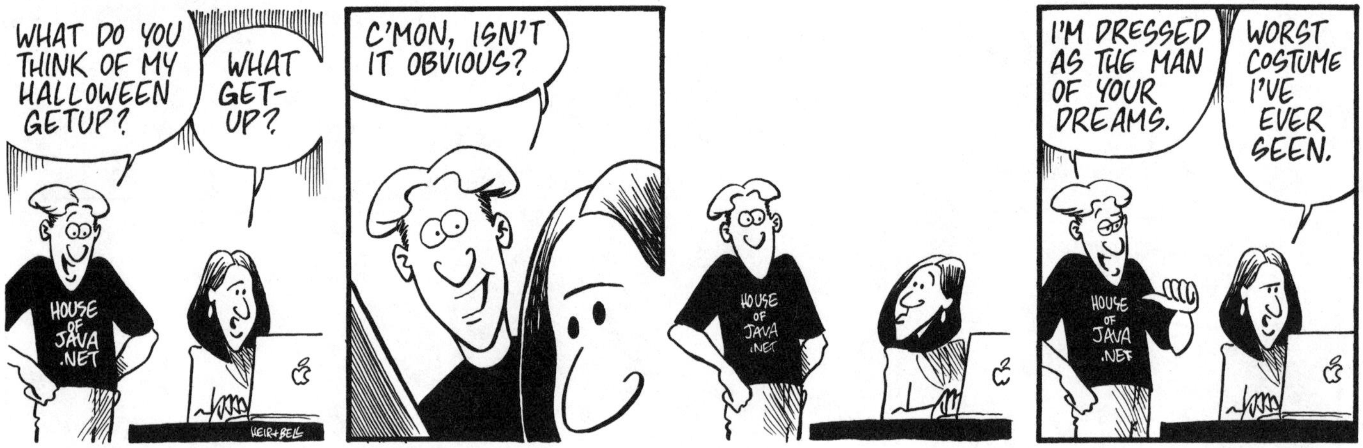
WHAT DO YOU THINK OF MY HALLOWEEN GETUP?
WHAT GET-UP?
C'MON, ISN'T IT OBVIOUS?
I'M DRESSED AS THE MAN OF YOUR DREAMS.
WORST COSTUME I'VE EVER SEEN.
HOUSE OF JAVA .NET
HEIR+BELL

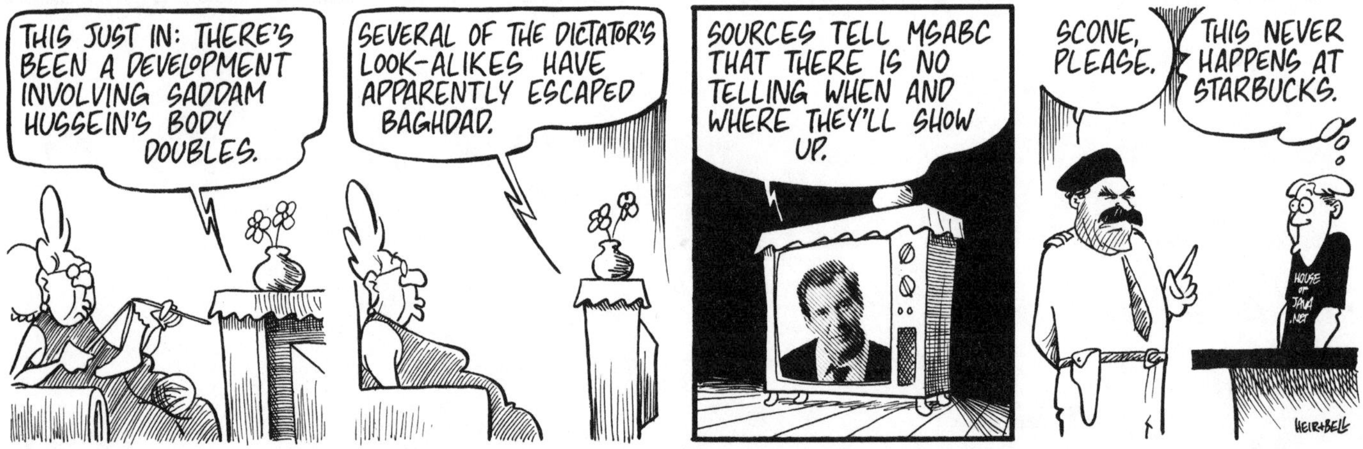
THIS JUST IN: THERE'S BEEN A DEVELOPMENT INVOLVING SADDAM HUSSEIN'S BODY DOUBLES.
SEVERAL OF THE DICTATOR'S LOOK-ALIKES HAVE APPARENTLY ESCAPED BAGHDAD.
SOURCES TELL MSABC THAT THERE IS NO TELLING WHEN AND WHERE THEY'LL SHOW UP.
SCONE, PLEASE.
THIS NEVER HAPPENS AT STARBUCKS.
HOUSE OF JAVA .NET
HEIR+BELL

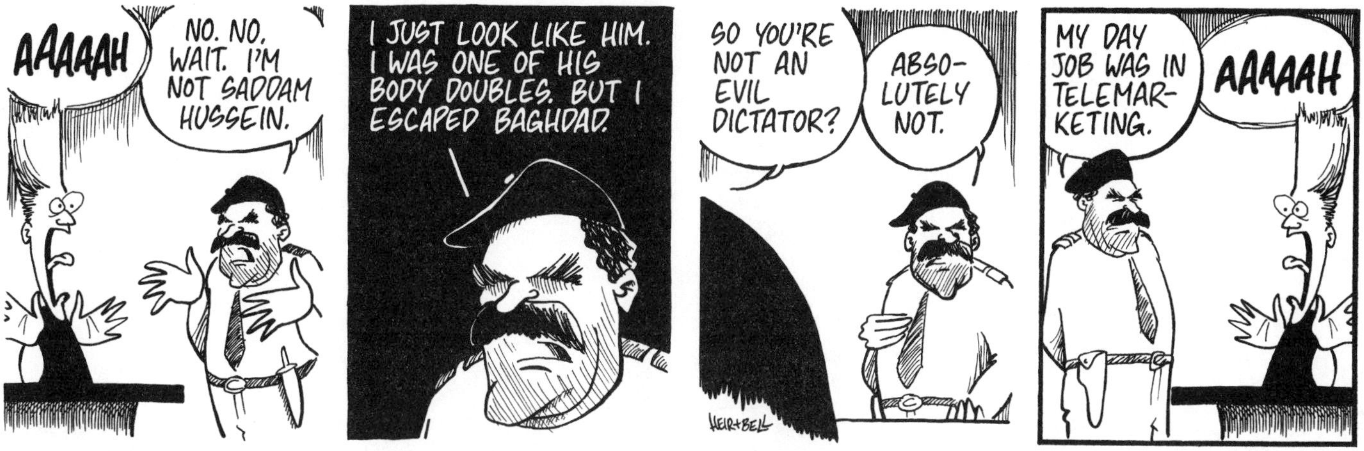
AAAAAH
NO. NO. WAIT. I'M NOT SADDAM HUSSEIN.
I JUST LOOK LIKE HIM. I WAS ONE OF HIS BODY DOUBLES. BUT I ESCAPED BAGHDAD.
SO YOU'RE NOT AN EVIL DICTATOR?
ABSOLUTELY NOT.
HEIR+BELL
MY DAY JOB WAS IN TELEMARKETING.
AAAAAH

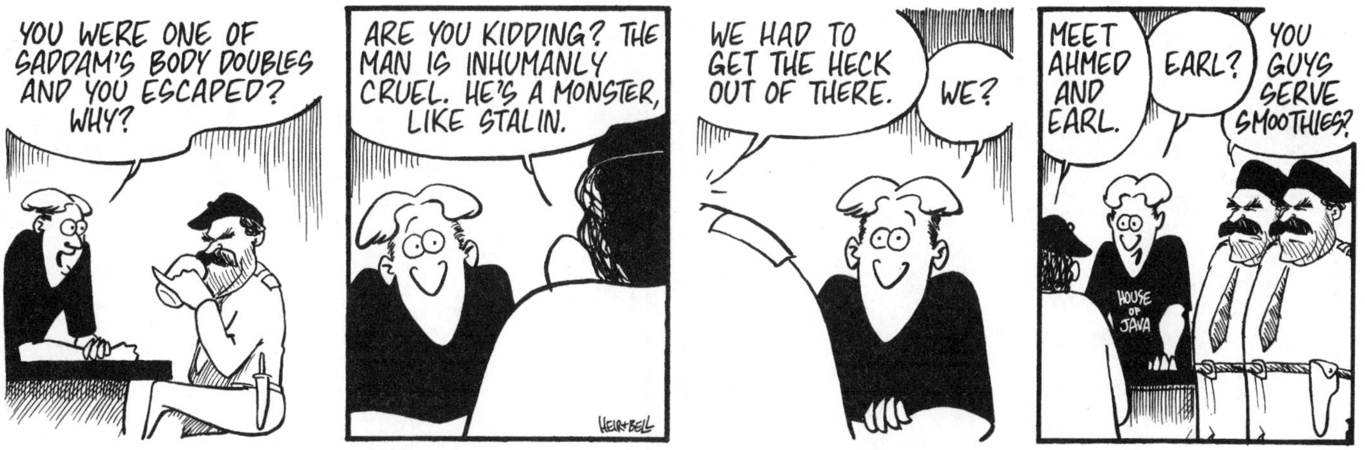
YOU WERE ONE OF SADDAM'S BODY DOUBLES AND YOU ESCAPED? WHY?
ARE YOU KIDDING? THE MAN IS INHUMANLY CRUEL. HE'S A MONSTER, LIKE STALIN.
HEIR+BELL
WE HAD TO GET THE HECK OUT OF THERE.
WE?
MEET AHMED AND EARL.
EARL?
YOU GUYS SERVE SMOOTHIES?
HOUSE OF JAVA

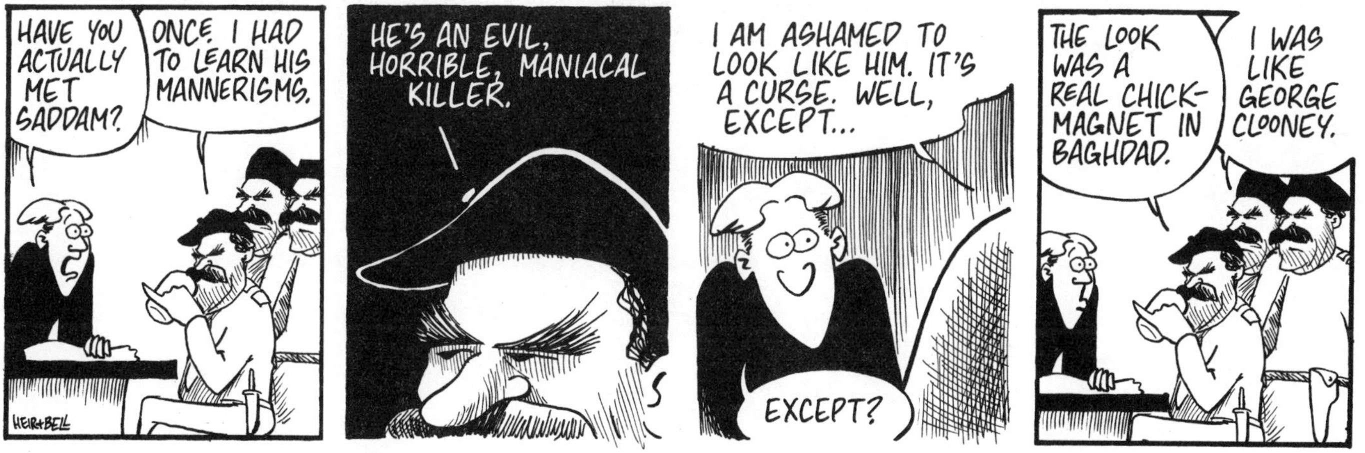
HAVE YOU ACTUALLY MET SADDAM?
ONCE. I HAD TO LEARN HIS MANNERISMS.
HEIR+BELL
HE'S AN EVIL, HORRIBLE, MANIACAL KILLER.
I AM ASHAMED TO LOOK LIKE HIM. IT'S A CURSE. WELL, EXCEPT...
EXCEPT?
THE LOOK WAS A REAL CHICK-MAGNET IN BAGHDAD.
I WAS LIKE GEORGE CLOONEY.

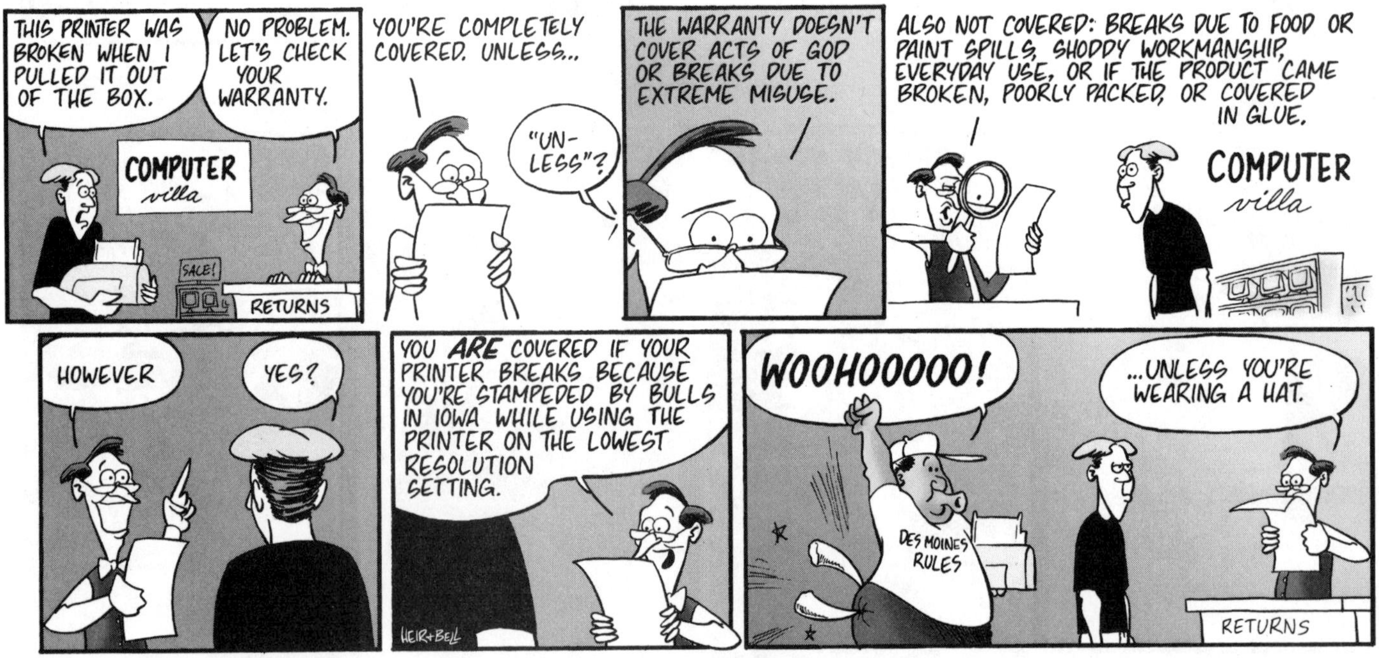
THIS PRINTER WAS BROKEN WHEN I PULLED IT OUT OF THE BOX.
NO PROBLEM. LET'S CHECK YOUR WARRANTY.
COMPUTER villa
SALE!
RETURNS
YOU'RE COMPLETELY COVERED. UNLESS...
"UN-LESS"?
THE WARRANTY DOESN'T COVER ACTS OF GOD OR BREAKS DUE TO EXTREME MISUSE.
ALSO NOT COVERED: BREAKS DUE TO FOOD OR PAINT SPILLS, SHODDY WORKMANSHIP, EVERYDAY USE, OR IF THE PRODUCT CAME BROKEN, POORLY PACKED, OR COVERED IN GLUE.
COMPUTER villa
HOWEVER
YES?
YOU ARE COVERED IF YOUR PRINTER BREAKS BECAUSE YOU'RE STAMPEDED BY BULLS IN IOWA WHILE USING THE PRINTER ON THE LOWEST RESOLUTION SETTING.
HEIR+BELL
WOOHOOOOO!
...UNLESS YOU'RE WEARING A HAT.
DES MOINES RULES
RETURNS

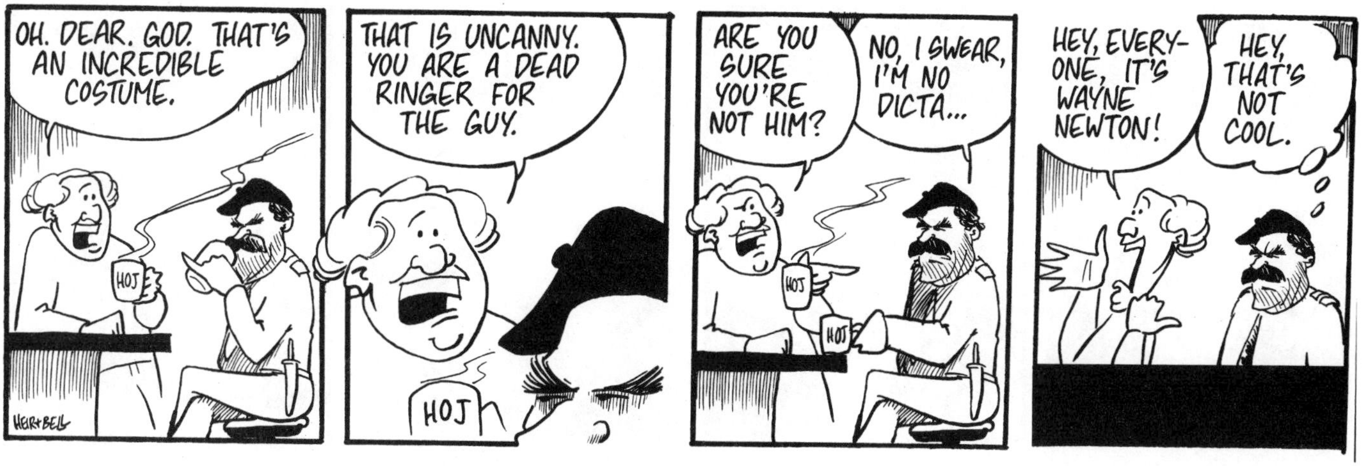
OH. DEAR. GOD. THAT'S AN INCREDIBLE COSTUME.
HEIR+BELL
HOJ
THAT IS UNCANNY. YOU ARE A DEAD RINGER FOR THE GUY.
HOJ
ARE YOU SURE YOU'RE NOT HIM?
NO, I SWEAR, I'M NO DICTA...
HOJ
HOJ
HEY, EVERY-ONE, IT'S WAYNE NEWTON!
HEY, THAT'S NOT COOL.

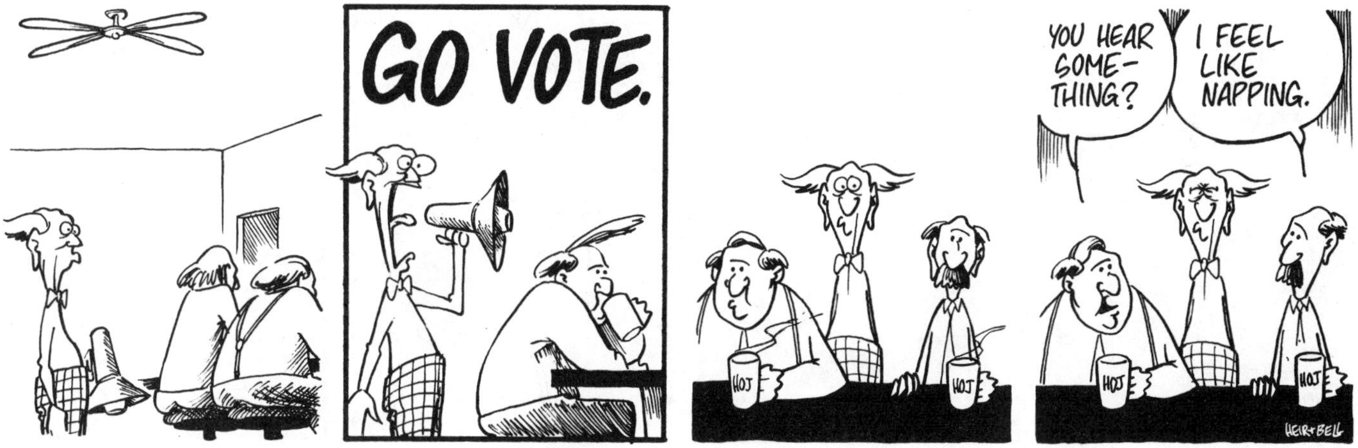
GO VOTE.
HOJ
HOJ
YOU HEAR SOME-THING?
I FEEL LIKE NAPPING.
HOJ
HOJ
HEIR+BELL

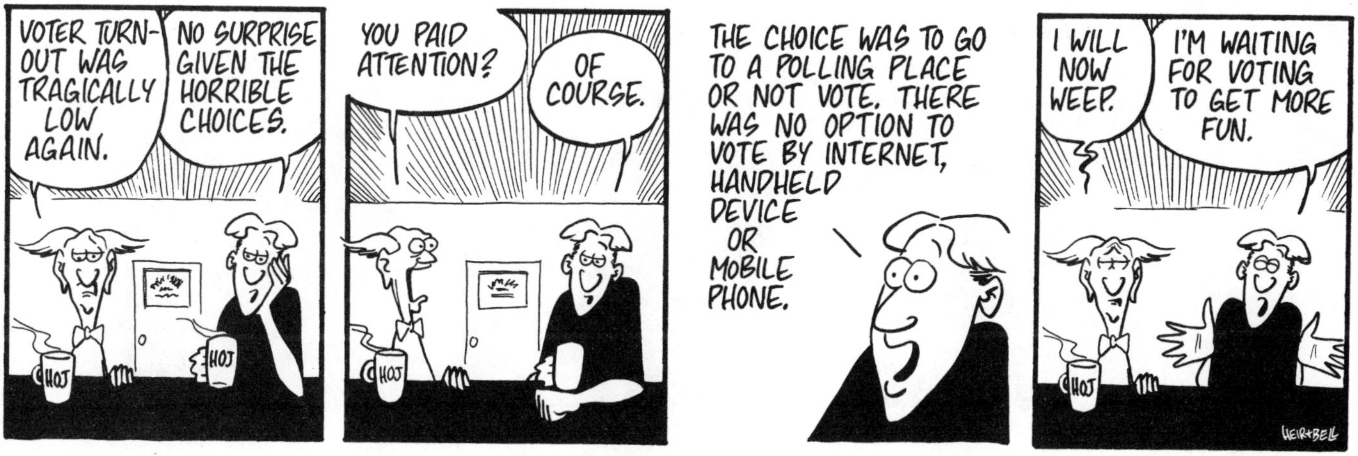
VOTER TURN-OUT WAS TRAGICALLY LOW AGAIN.
NO SURPRISE GIVEN THE HORRIBLE CHOICES.
HOJ
HOJ
YOU PAID ATTENTION?
OF COURSE.
HOJ
THE CHOICE WAS TO GO TO A POLLING PLACE OR NOT VOTE. THERE WAS NO OPTION TO VOTE BY INTERNET, HANDHELD DEVICE OR MOBILE PHONE.
I WILL NOW WEEP.
I'M WAITING FOR VOTING TO GET MORE FUN.
HOJ
HEIR+BELL

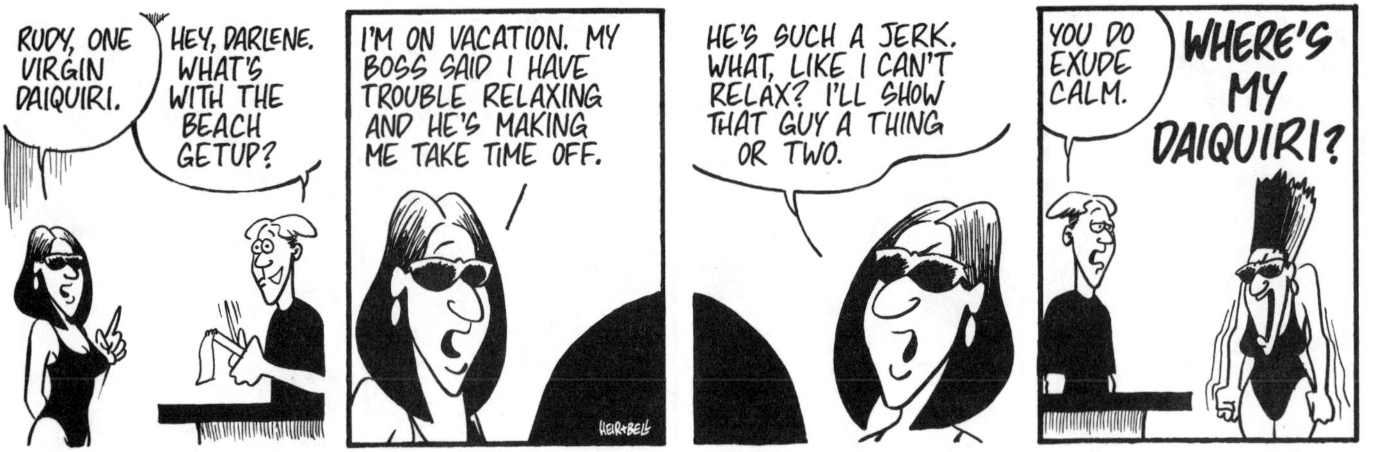
RUDY, ONE VIRGIN DAIQUIRI.
HEY, DARLENE. WHAT'S WITH THE BEACH GETUP?
I'M ON VACATION. MY BOSS SAID I HAVE TROUBLE RELAXING AND HE'S MAKING ME TAKE TIME OFF.
HEIR+BELL
HE'S SUCH A JERK. WHAT, LIKE I CAN'T RELAX? I'LL SHOW THAT GUY A THING OR TWO.
YOU DO EXUDE CALM.
WHERE'S MY DAIQUIRI?

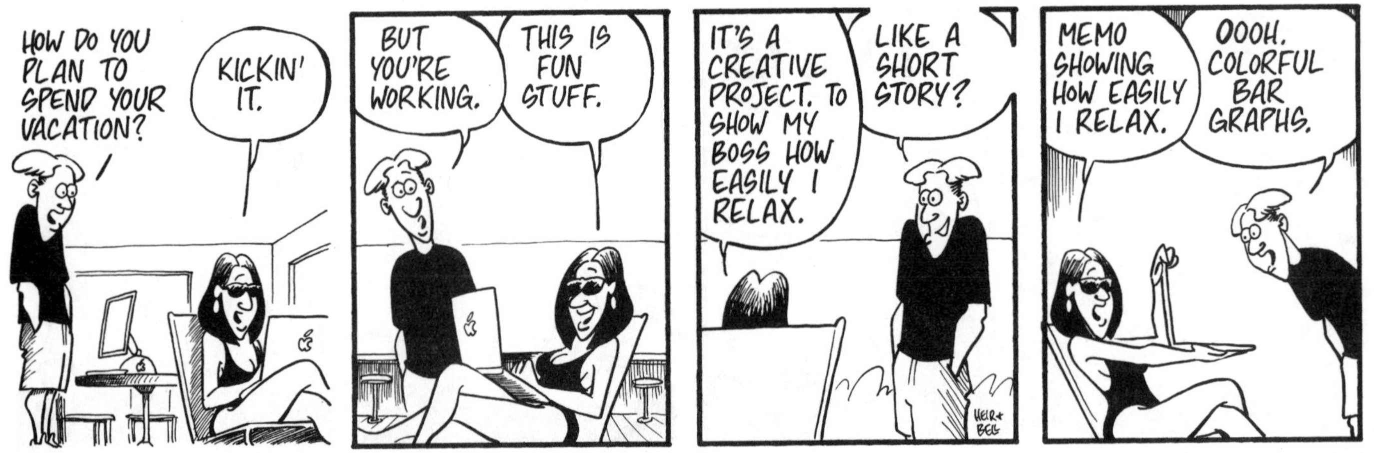
HOW DO YOU PLAN TO SPEND YOUR VACATION?
KICKIN' IT.
BUT YOU'RE WORKING.
THIS IS FUN STUFF.
IT'S A CREATIVE PROJECT. TO SHOW MY BOSS HOW EASILY I RELAX.
LIKE A SHORT STORY?
HEIR+BELL
MEMO SHOWING HOW EASILY I RELAX.
OOOH. COLORFUL BAR GRAPHS.

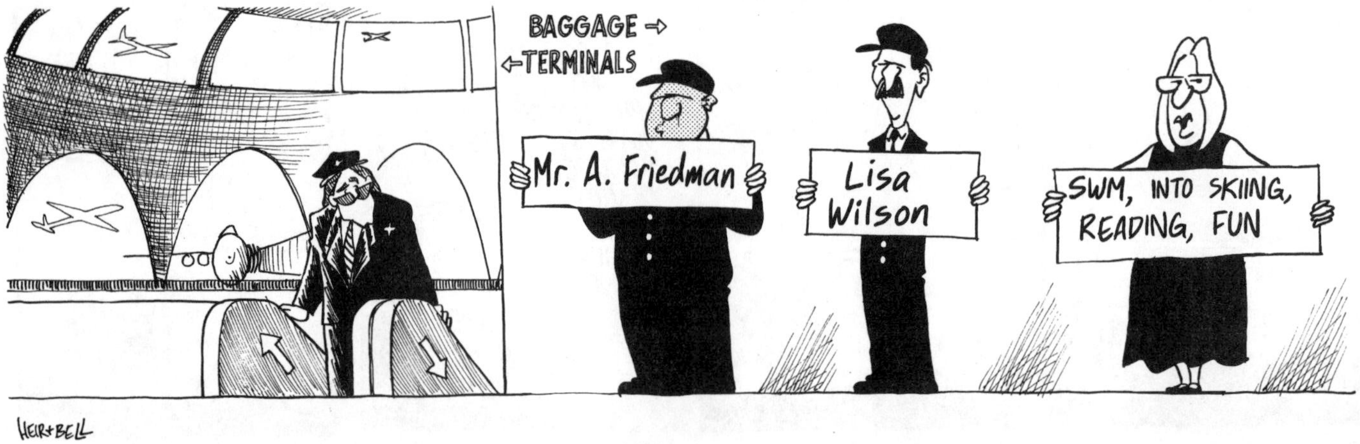
BAGGAGE →
← TERMINALS
Mr. A. Friedman
Lisa Wilson
SWM, INTO SKIING, READING, FUN
HEIR+BELL

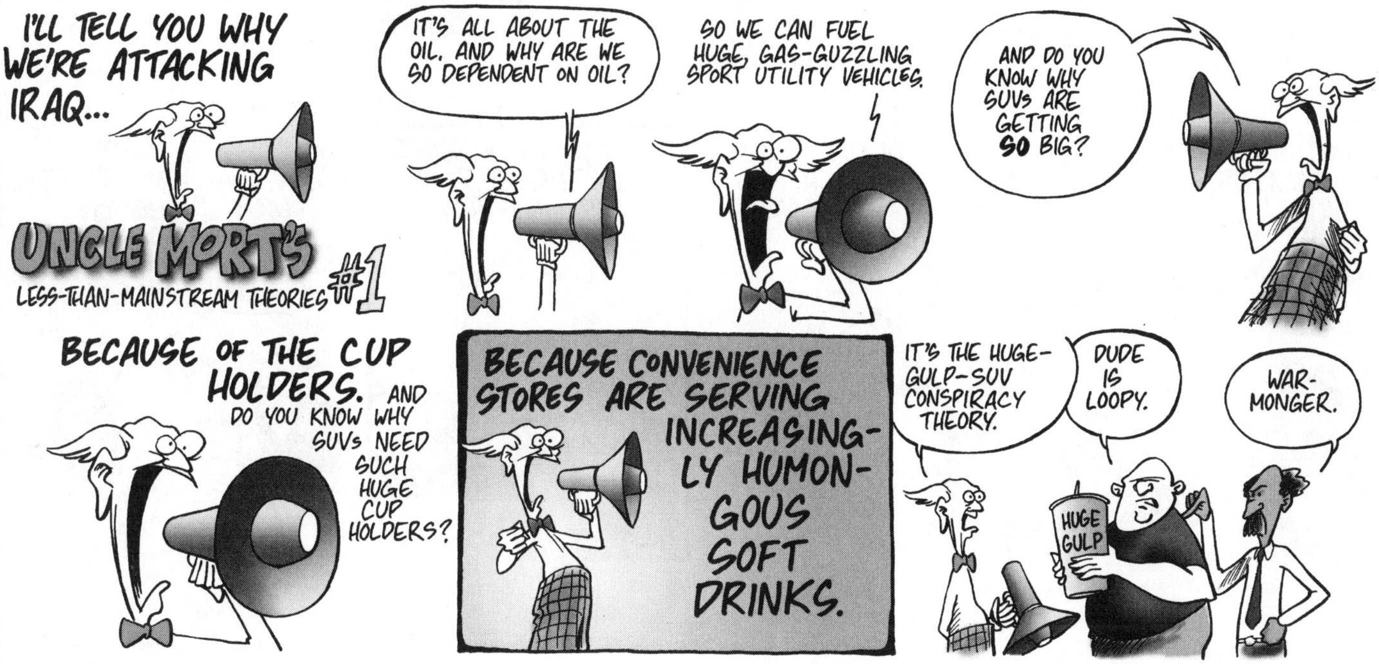
I'LL TELL YOU WHY WE'RE ATTACKING IRAQ...
UNCLE MORT'S
LESS-THAN-MAINSTREAM THEORIES #1
IT'S ALL ABOUT THE OIL. AND WHY ARE WE SO DEPENDENT ON OIL?
SO WE CAN FUEL HUGE, GAS-GUZZLING SPORT UTILITY VEHICLES.
AND DO YOU KNOW WHY SUVs ARE GETTING SO BIG?
BECAUSE OF THE CUP HOLDERS.
AND DO YOU KNOW WHY SUVs NEED SUCH HUGE CUP HOLDERS?
BECAUSE CONVENIENCE STORES ARE SERVING INCREASINGLY HUMONGOUS SOFT DRINKS.
IT'S THE HUGE-GULP-SUV CONSPIRACY THEORY.
DUDE IS LOOPY.
WAR-MONGER.
HUGE GULP

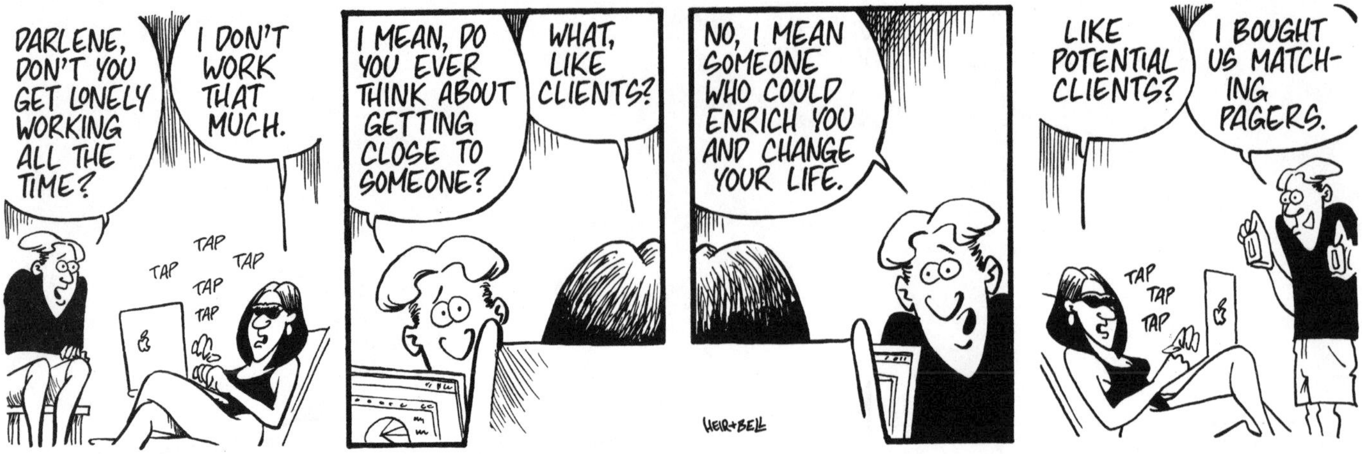
DARLENE, DON'T YOU GET LONELY WORKING ALL THE TIME?
I DON'T WORK THAT MUCH.
TAP TAP TAP TAP TAP
I MEAN, DO YOU EVER THINK ABOUT GETTING CLOSE TO SOMEONE?
WHAT, LIKE CLIENTS?
NO, I MEAN SOMEONE WHO COULD ENRICH YOU AND CHANGE YOUR LIFE.
HEIR+BELL
LIKE POTENTIAL CLIENTS?
I BOUGHT US MATCHING PAGERS.
TAP TAP TAP

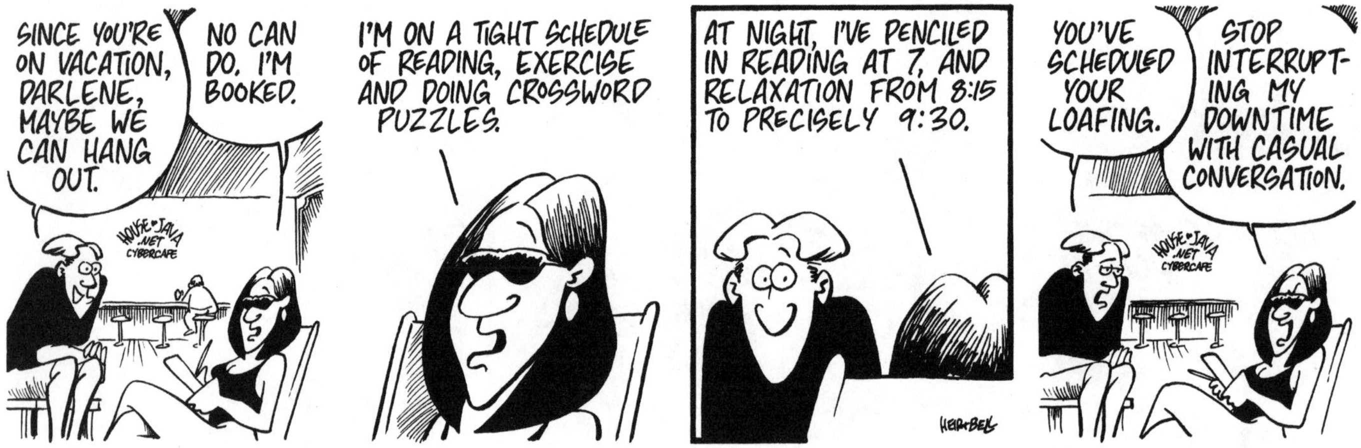
SINCE YOU'RE ON VACATION, DARLENE, MAYBE WE CAN HANG OUT.
NO CAN DO. I'M BOOKED.
HOUSE JAVA .NET CYBERCAFE
I'M ON A TIGHT SCHEDULE OF READING, EXERCISE AND DOING CROSSWORD PUZZLES.
AT NIGHT, I'VE PENCILED IN READING AT 7, AND RELAXATION FROM 8:15 TO PRECISELY 9:30.
HEIR+BELL
YOU'VE SCHEDULED YOUR LOAFING.
STOP INTERRUPTING MY DOWNTIME WITH CASUAL CONVERSATION.
HOUSE JAVA .NET CYBERCAFE

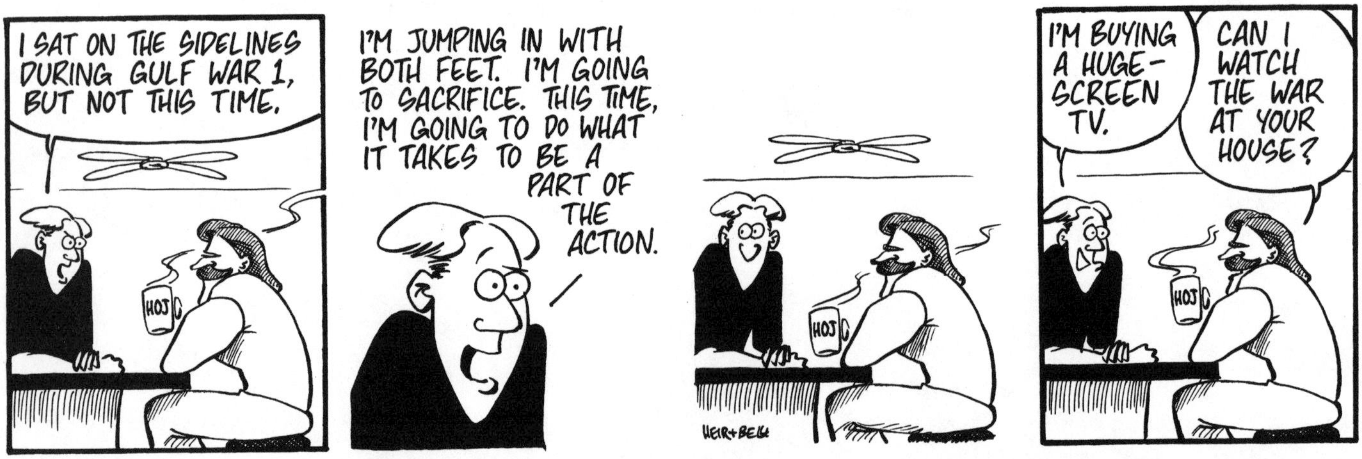
I SAT ON THE SIDELINES DURING GULF WAR 1, BUT NOT THIS TIME.
HOJ
I'M JUMPING IN WITH BOTH FEET. I'M GOING TO SACRIFICE. THIS TIME, I'M GOING TO DO WHAT IT TAKES TO BE A PART OF THE ACTION.
HOJ
HEIR+BELL
I'M BUYING A HUGE-SCREEN TV.
CAN I WATCH THE WAR AT YOUR HOUSE?
HOJ

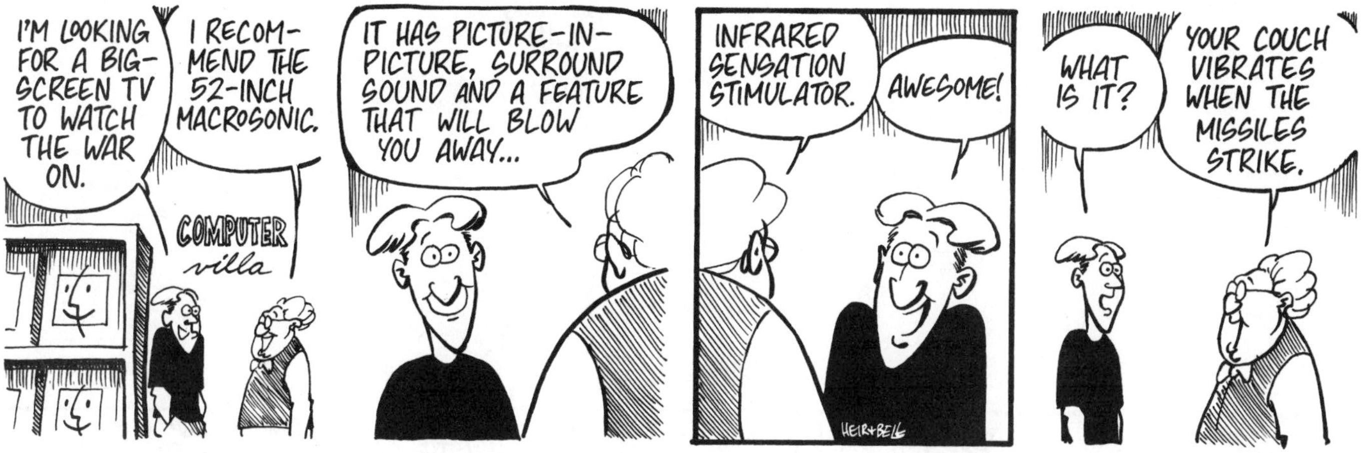
I'M LOOKING FOR A BIG-SCREEN TV TO WATCH THE WAR ON.
I RECOMMEND THE 52-INCH MACROSONIC.
COMPUTER villa
IT HAS PICTURE-IN-PICTURE, SURROUND SOUND AND A FEATURE THAT WILL BLOW YOU AWAY...
INFRARED SENSATION STIMULATOR.
AWESOME!
HEIR+BELL
WHAT IS IT?
YOUR COUCH VIBRATES WHEN THE MISSILES STRIKE.

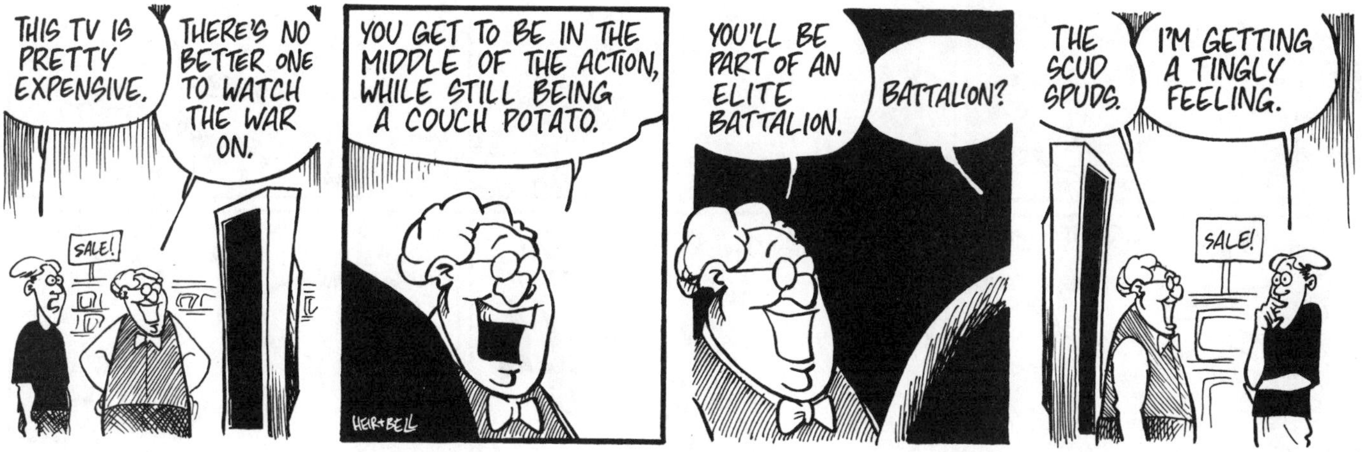
THIS TV IS PRETTY EXPENSIVE.
THERE'S NO BETTER ONE TO WATCH THE WAR ON.
SALE!
YOU GET TO BE IN THE MIDDLE OF THE ACTION, WHILE STILL BEING A COUCH POTATO.
HEIR+BELL
YOU'LL BE PART OF AN ELITE BATTALION.
BATTALION?
THE SCUD SPUDS.
I'M GETTING A TINGLY FEELING.
SALE!

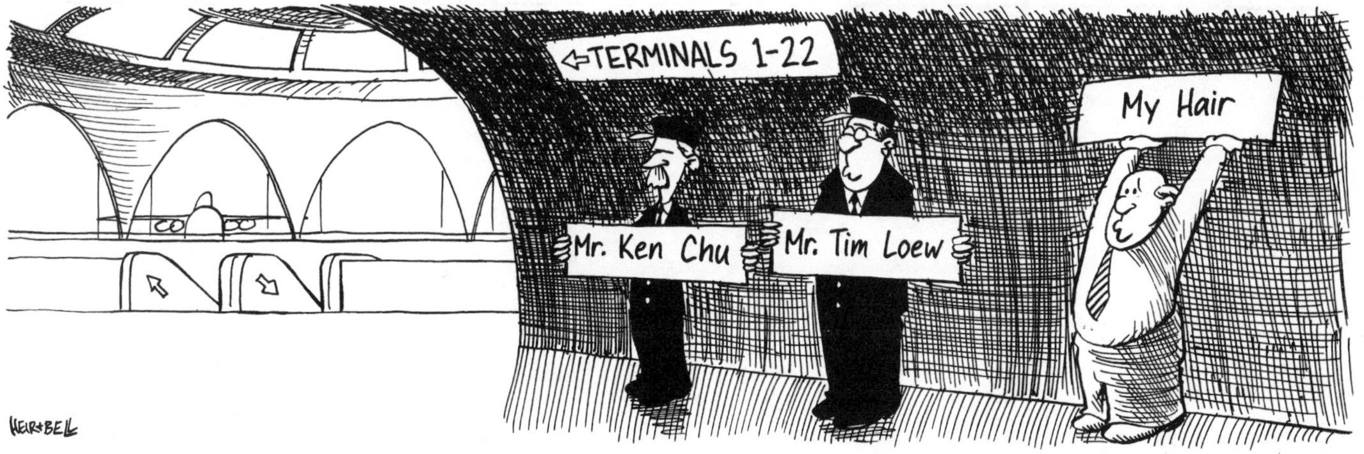
TERMINALS 1-22
My Hair
Mr. Ken Chu
Mr. Tim Loew
HEIR+BELL

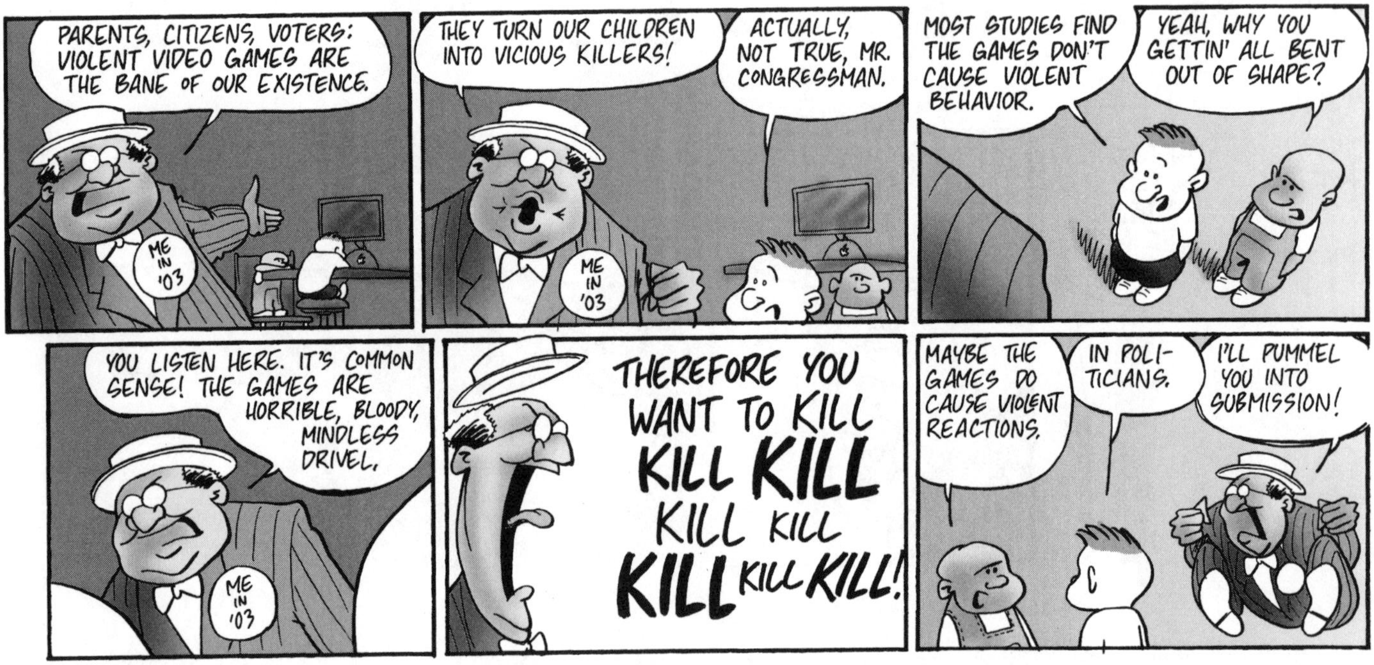
PARENTS, CITIZENS, VOTERS: VIOLENT VIDEO GAMES ARE THE BANE OF OUR EXISTENCE.
ME IN '03
THEY TURN OUR CHILDREN INTO VICIOUS KILLERS!
ACTUALLY, NOT TRUE, MR. CONGRESSMAN.
ME IN '03
MOST STUDIES FIND THE GAMES DON'T CAUSE VIOLENT BEHAVIOR.
YEAH, WHY YOU GETTIN' ALL BENT OUT OF SHAPE?
YOU LISTEN HERE. IT'S COMMON SENSE! THE GAMES ARE HORRIBLE, BLOODY, MINDLESS DRIVEL.
ME IN '03
THEREFORE YOU WANT TO KILL KILL KILL KILL KILL KILL KILL KILL!
MAYBE THE GAMES DO CAUSE VIOLENT REACTIONS.
IN POLITICIANS.
I'LL PUMMEL YOU INTO SUBMISSION!

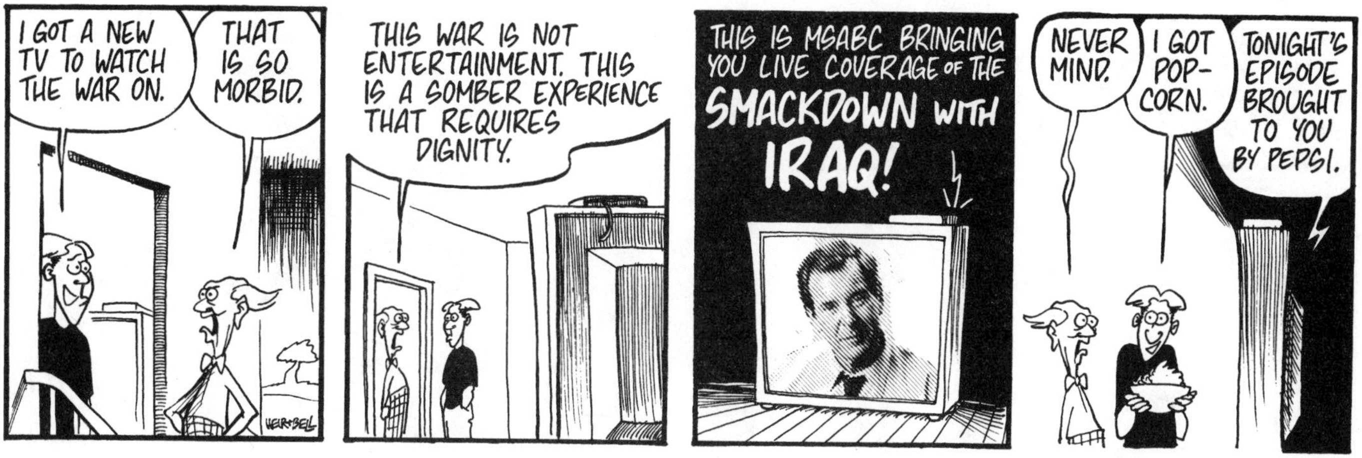
I GOT A NEW TV TO WATCH THE WAR ON.
THAT IS SO MORBID.
HEIR+BELL
THIS WAR IS NOT ENTERTAINMENT. THIS IS A SOMBER EXPERIENCE THAT REQUIRES DIGNITY.
THIS IS MSABC BRINGING YOU LIVE COVERAGE OF THE SMACKDOWN WITH IRAQ!
NEVER MIND.
I GOT POP-CORN.
TONIGHT'S EPISODE BROUGHT TO YOU BY PEPSI.

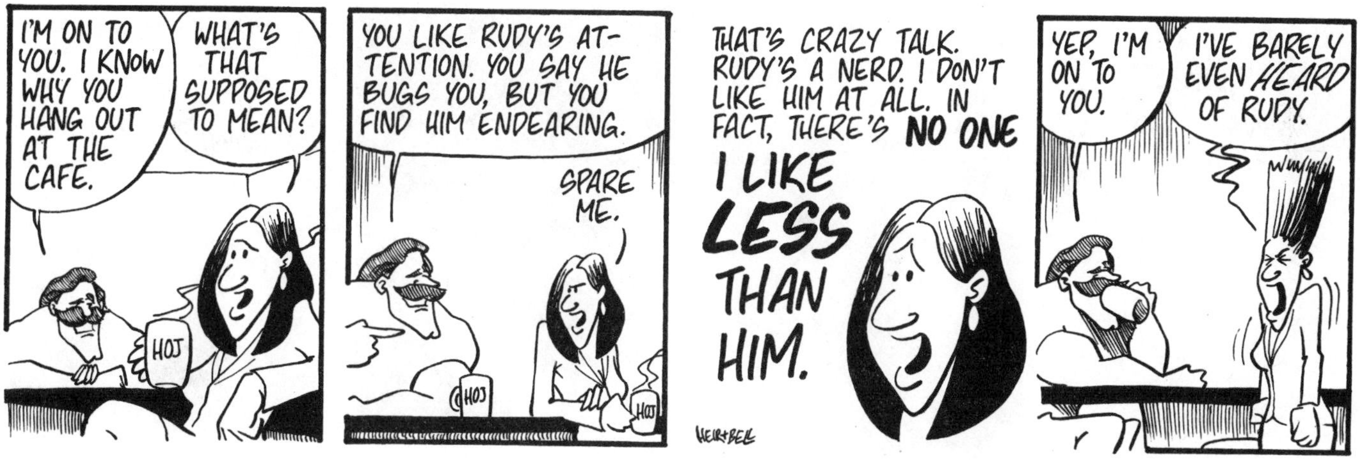
I'M ON TO YOU. I KNOW WHY YOU HANG OUT AT THE CAFE.
WHAT'S THAT SUPPOSED TO MEAN?
HOJ
YOU LIKE RUDY'S AT-TENTION. YOU SAY HE BUGS YOU, BUT YOU FIND HIM ENDEARING.
SPARE ME.
HOJ
HOJ
THAT'S CRAZY TALK. RUDY'S A NERD. I DON'T LIKE HIM AT ALL. IN FACT, THERE'S NO ONE I LIKE LESS THAN HIM.
HEIR+BELL
YEP, I'M ON TO YOU.
I'VE BARELY EVEN *HEARD* OF RUDY.

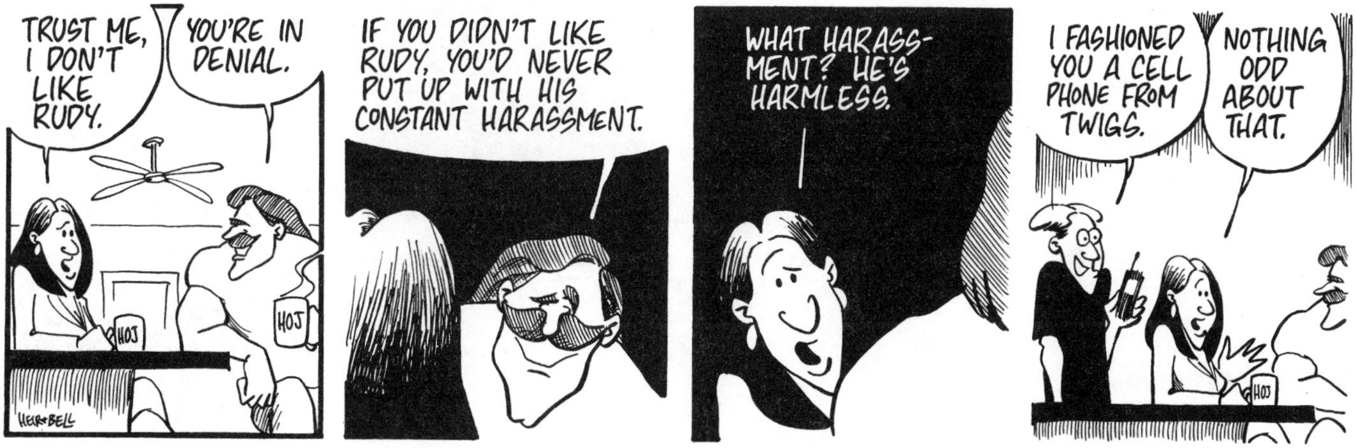
TRUST ME, I DON'T LIKE RUDY.
YOU'RE IN DENIAL.
HOJ
HOJ
HEIR+BELL
IF YOU DIDN'T LIKE RUDY, YOU'D NEVER PUT UP WITH HIS CONSTANT HARASSMENT.
WHAT HARASS-MENT? HE'S HARMLESS.
I FASHIONED YOU A CELL PHONE FROM TWIGS.
NOTHING ODD ABOUT THAT.
HOJ

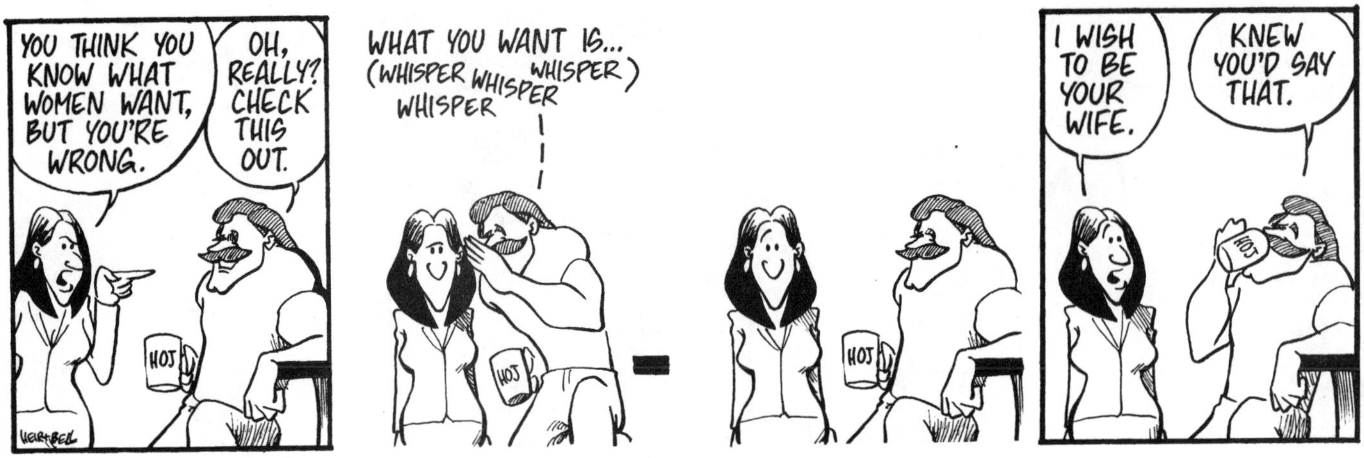
YOU THINK YOU KNOW WHAT WOMEN WANT, BUT YOU'RE WRONG.
OH, REALLY? CHECK THIS OUT.
HOJ
HEIR+BELL
WHAT YOU WANT IS... (WHISPER WHISPER WHISPER WHISPER)
HOJ
HOJ
I WISH TO BE YOUR WIFE.
KNEW YOU'D SAY THAT.
HOJ

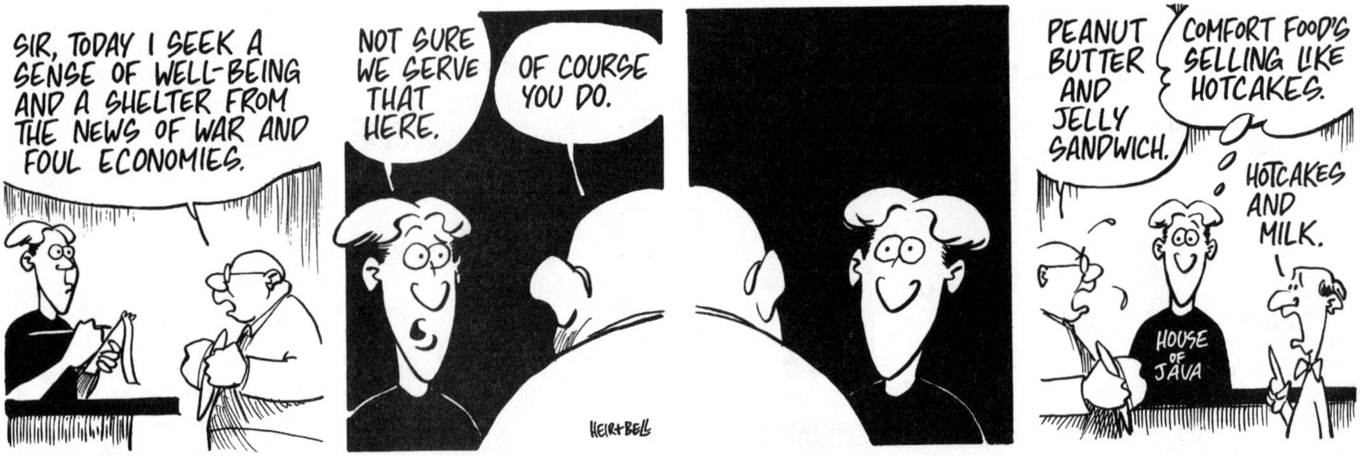
SIR, TODAY I SEEK A SENSE OF WELL-BEING AND A SHELTER FROM THE NEWS OF WAR AND FOUL ECONOMIES.
NOT SURE WE SERVE THAT HERE.
OF COURSE YOU DO.
HEIR+BELL
PEANUT BUTTER AND JELLY SANDWICH.
COMFORT FOOD'S SELLING LIKE HOTCAKES.
HOTCAKES AND MILK.
HOUSE OF JAVA

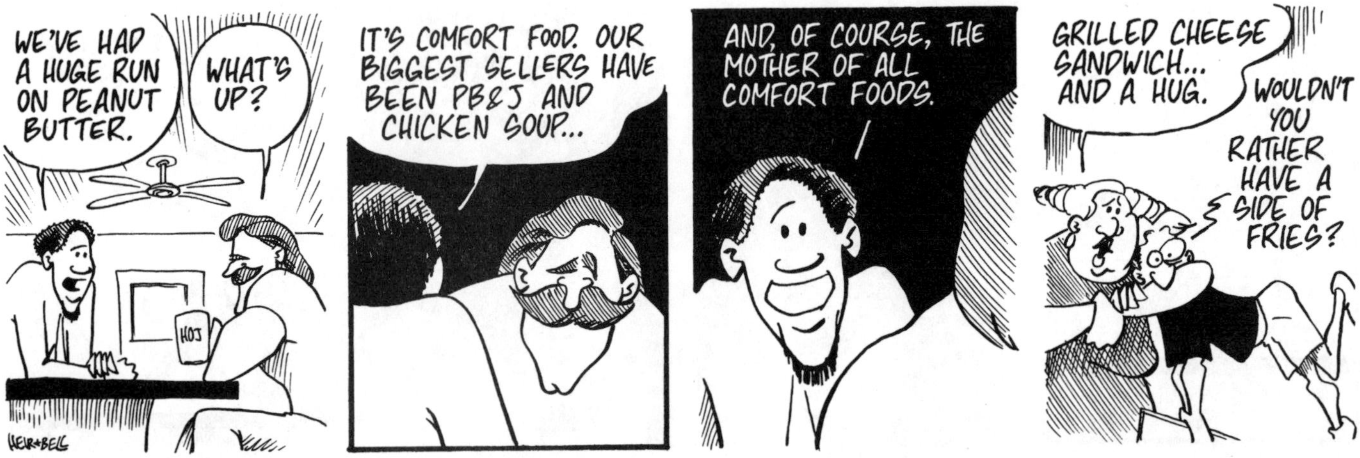
WE'VE HAD A HUGE RUN ON PEANUT BUTTER.
WHAT'S UP?
HOJ
HEIR+BELL
IT'S COMFORT FOOD. OUR BIGGEST SELLERS HAVE BEEN PB&J AND CHICKEN SOUP...
AND, OF COURSE, THE MOTHER OF ALL COMFORT FOODS.
GRILLED CHEESE SANDWICH... AND A HUG.
WOULDN'T YOU RATHER HAVE A SIDE OF FRIES?

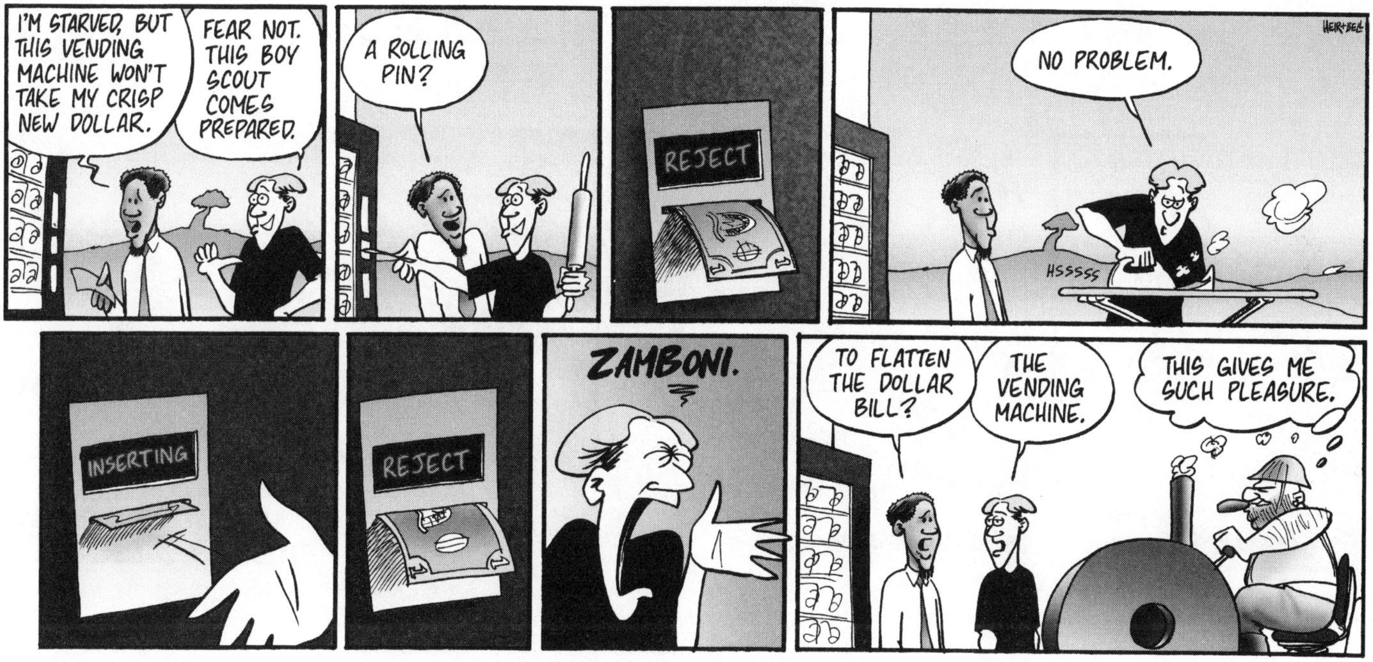
I'M STARVED, BUT THIS VENDING MACHINE WON'T TAKE MY CRISP NEW DOLLAR.
FEAR NOT. THIS BOY SCOUT COMES PREPARED.
A ROLLING PIN?
REJECT
NO PROBLEM.
HSSSSS
INSERTING
REJECT
ZAMBONI.
TO FLATTEN THE DOLLAR BILL?
THE VENDING MACHINE.
THIS GIVES ME SUCH PLEASURE.

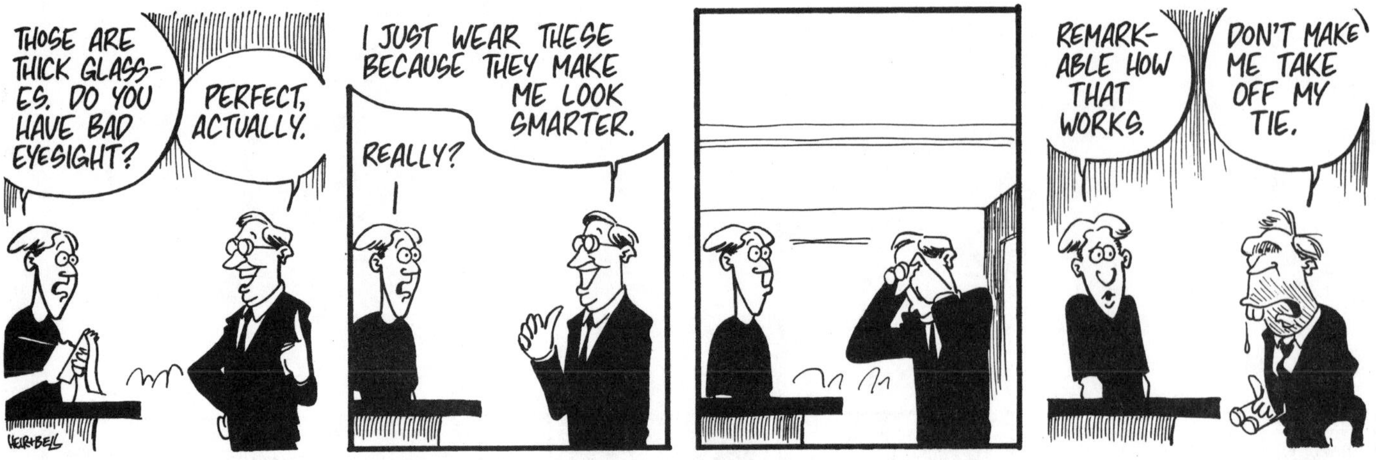
THOSE ARE THICK GLASSES. DO YOU HAVE BAD EYESIGHT?
PERFECT, ACTUALLY.
I JUST WEAR THESE BECAUSE THEY MAKE ME LOOK SMARTER.
REALLY?
REMARKABLE HOW THAT WORKS.
DON'T MAKE ME TAKE OFF MY TIE.

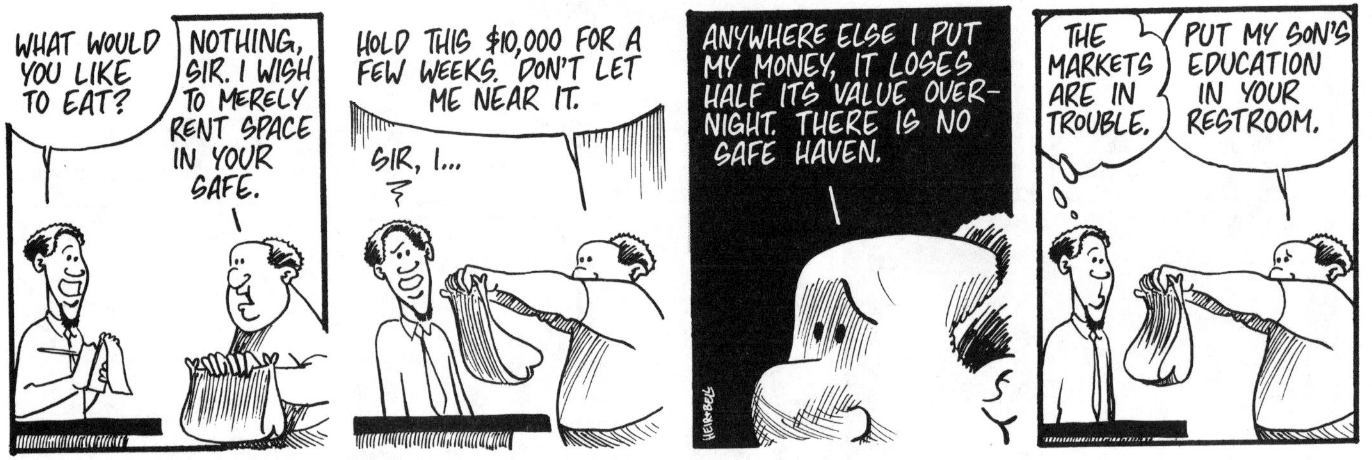
WHAT WOULD YOU LIKE TO EAT?
NOTHING, SIR. I WISH TO MERELY RENT SPACE IN YOUR SAFE.
HOLD THIS $10,000 FOR A FEW WEEKS. DON'T LET ME NEAR IT.
SIR, I...
ANYWHERE ELSE I PUT MY MONEY, IT LOSES HALF ITS VALUE OVERNIGHT. THERE IS NO SAFE HAVEN.
THE MARKETS ARE IN TROUBLE.
PUT MY SON'S EDUCATION IN YOUR RESTROOM.

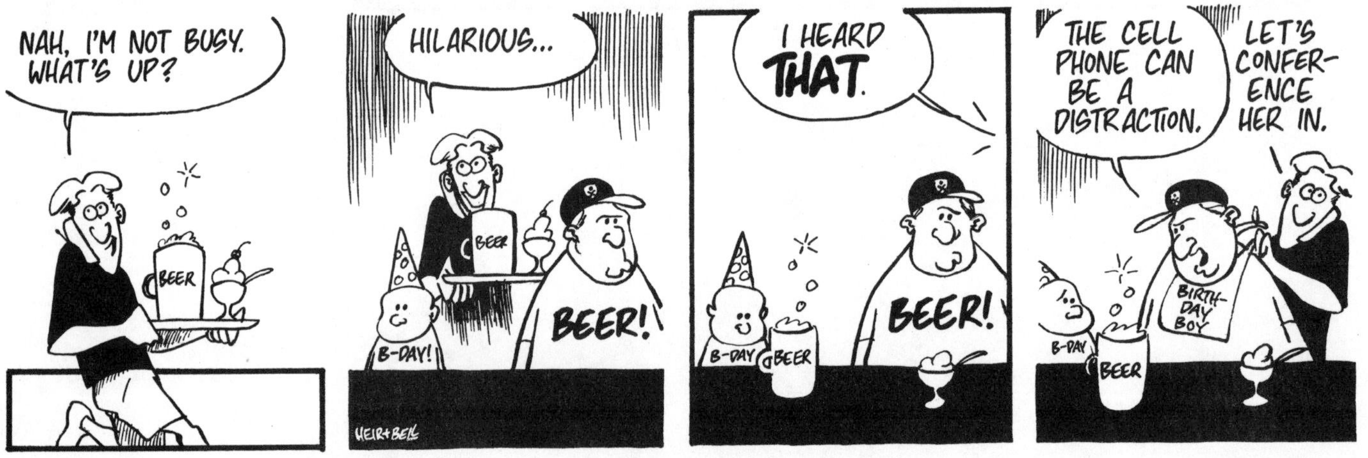
NAH, I'M NOT BUSY. WHAT'S UP?
BEER
HILARIOUS...
BEER
B-DAY!
BEER!
I HEARD THAT.
B-DAY
BEER
BEER!
THE CELL PHONE CAN BE A DISTRACTION.
LET'S CONFERENCE HER IN.
BIRTHDAY BOY
B-DAY
BEER

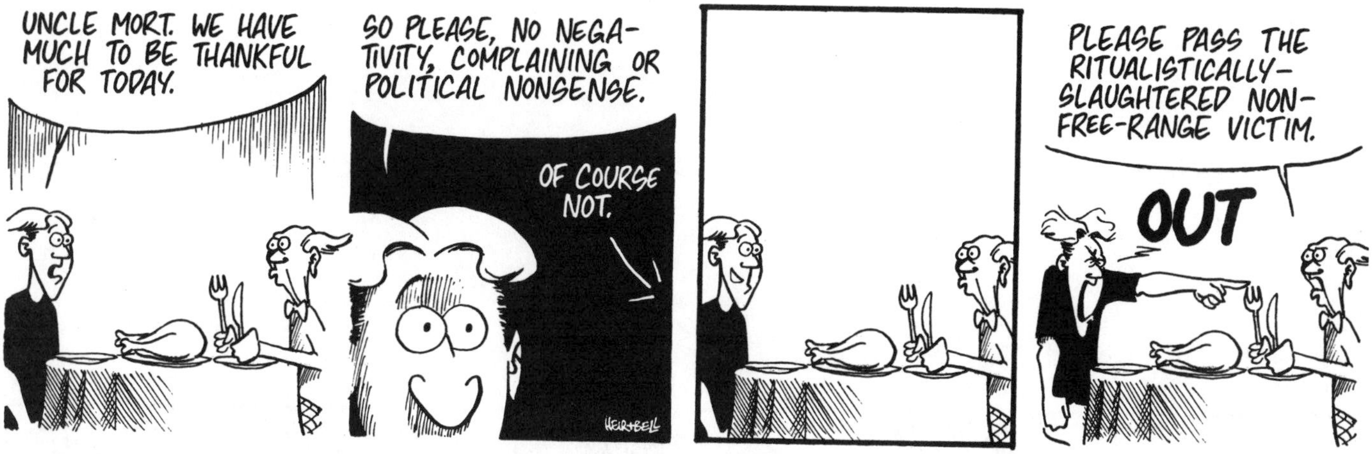
UNCLE MORT. WE HAVE MUCH TO BE THANKFUL FOR TODAY.
SO PLEASE, NO NEGATIVITY, COMPLAINING OR POLITICAL NONSENSE.
OF COURSE NOT.
PLEASE PASS THE RITUALISTICALLY-SLAUGHTERED NON-FREE-RANGE VICTIM.
OUT
HEIR+BELL

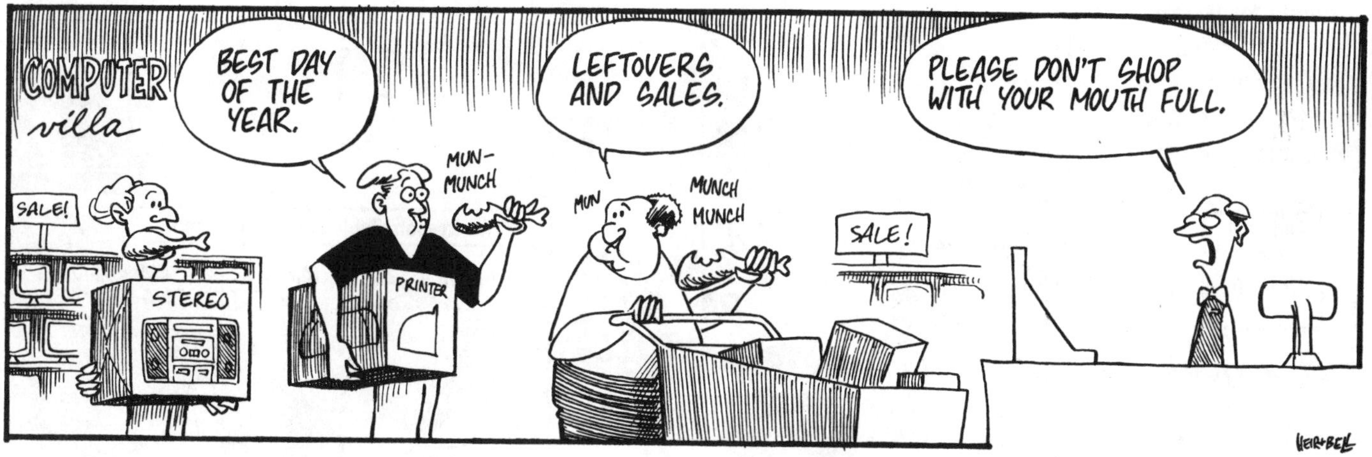
COMPUTER villa
SALE!
BEST DAY OF THE YEAR.
MUN-MUNCH
LEFTOVERS AND SALES.
MUN
MUNCH MUNCH
SALE!
PLEASE DON'T SHOP WITH YOUR MOUTH FULL.
STEREO
PRINTER
HEIR+BELL

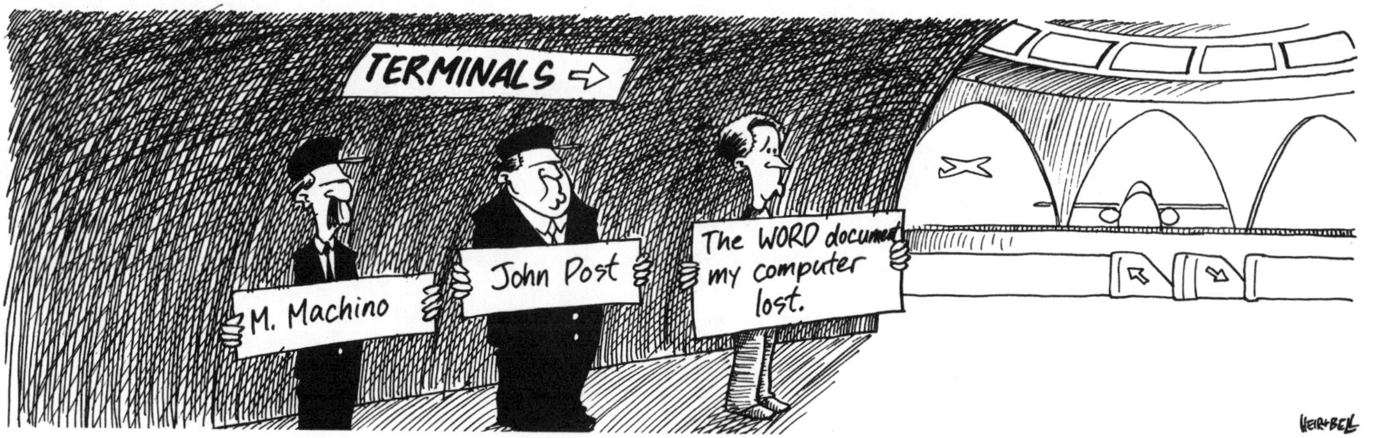
TERMINALS
M. Machino
John Post
The WORD document my computer lost.
HEIR+BELL

Sometimes there can be no common ground. Sometimes issues tear us asunder, leaving no room for fruitful debate. Such a time grips our nation...

...FOR THE LAST TIME, YOU ARE A WEAK-MINDED SIMPLETON.

WELL, YOUR POSITION STARTLES ME.

I CAN NO LONGER CALL YOU FRIEND.

THINK OF THE CHILDREN.

And what is this pressing issue?

THE BEST WAY TO PREPARE FOR THANKSGIVING IS TO EAT ALL DAY TO EXPAND YOUR STOMACH.

IT'S BEST NOT TO EAT ALL DAY SO YOU'LL BE RAVENOUS!

Two irreconcilable positions indeed!

HEATHEN.

BARBARIAN.

WASN'T THANKSGIVING THREE DAYS AGO?

THEY ARGUED THROUGH IT.

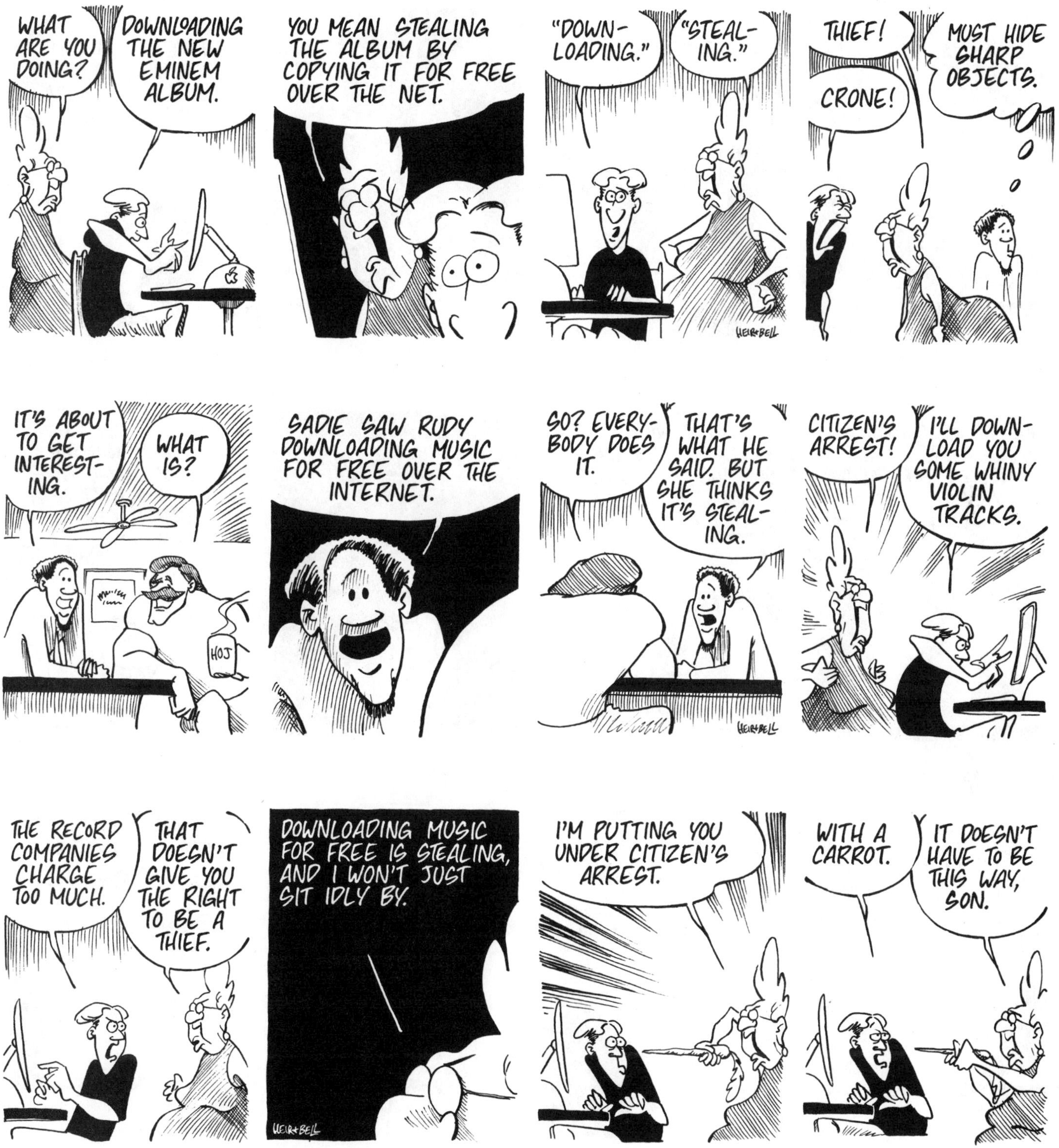
WHAT ARE YOU DOING?
DOWNLOADING THE NEW EMINEM ALBUM.
YOU MEAN STEALING THE ALBUM BY COPYING IT FOR FREE OVER THE NET.
"DOWN-LOADING."
"STEAL-ING."
THIEF!
CRONE!
MUST HIDE SHARP OBJECTS.
HEIR+BELL
IT'S ABOUT TO GET INTEREST-ING.
WHAT IS?
HOJ
SADIE SAW RUDY DOWNLOADING MUSIC FOR FREE OVER THE INTERNET.
SO? EVERY-BODY DOES IT.
THAT'S WHAT HE SAID. BUT SHE THINKS IT'S STEAL-ING.
CITIZEN'S ARREST!
I'LL DOWN-LOAD YOU SOME WHINY VIOLIN TRACKS.
HEIR+BELL
THE RECORD COMPANIES CHARGE TOO MUCH.
THAT DOESN'T GIVE YOU THE RIGHT TO BE A THIEF.
DOWNLOADING MUSIC FOR FREE IS STEALING, AND I WON'T JUST SIT IDLY BY.
HEIR+BELL
I'M PUTTING YOU UNDER CITIZEN'S ARREST.
WITH A CARROT.
IT DOESN'T HAVE TO BE THIS WAY, SON.

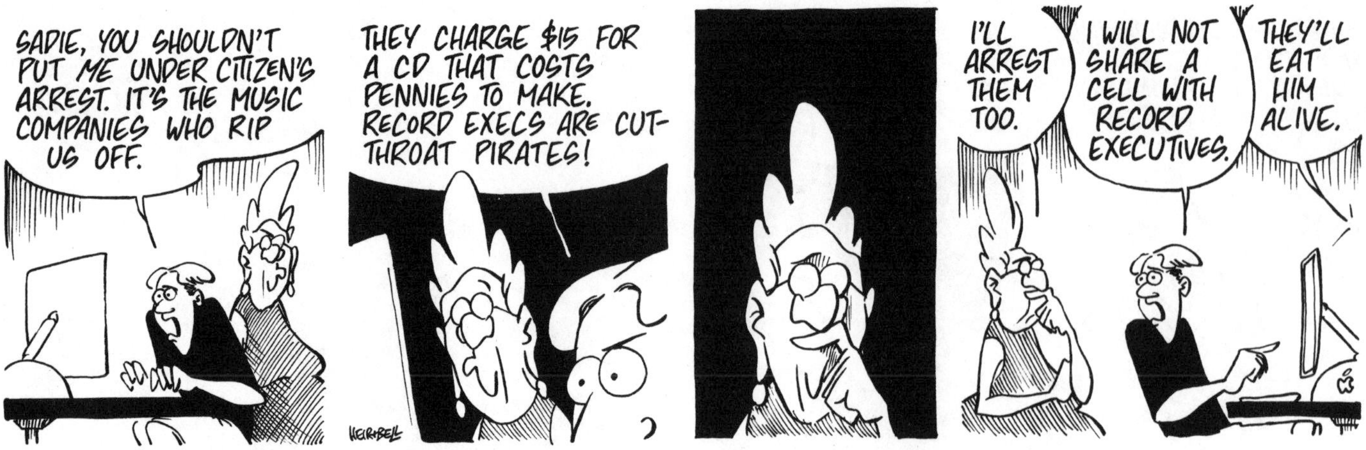
SADIE, YOU SHOULDN'T PUT ME UNDER CITIZEN'S ARREST. IT'S THE MUSIC COMPANIES WHO RIP US OFF.
THEY CHARGE $15 FOR A CD THAT COSTS PENNIES TO MAKE. RECORD EXECS ARE CUT-THROAT PIRATES!
I'LL ARREST THEM TOO.
I WILL NOT SHARE A CELL WITH RECORD EXECUTIVES.
THEY'LL EAT HIM ALIVE.

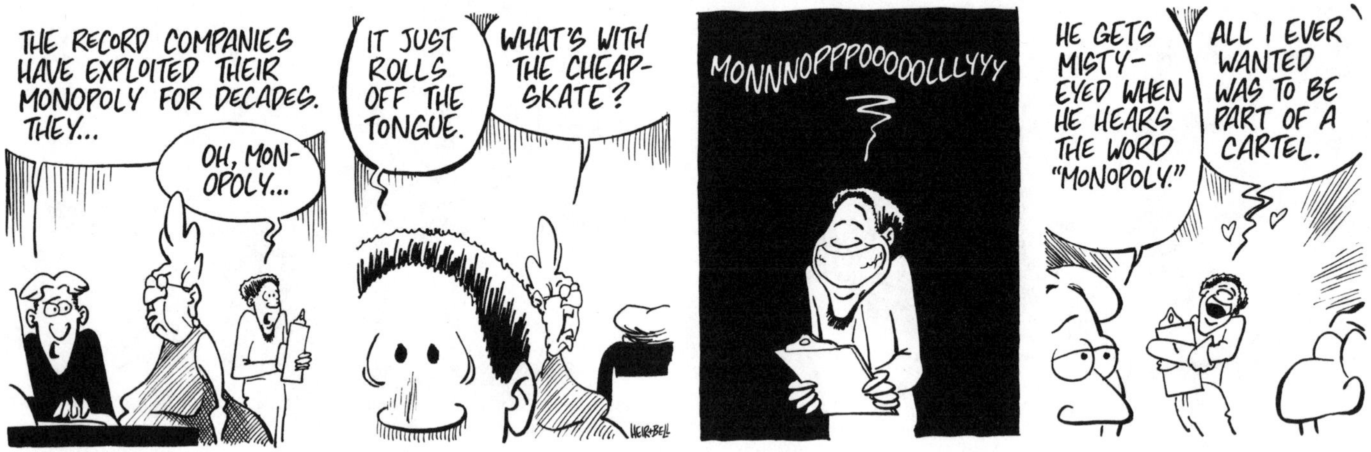
THE RECORD COMPANIES HAVE EXPLOITED THEIR MONOPOLY FOR DECADES. THEY...
OH, MON-OPOLY...
IT JUST ROLLS OFF THE TONGUE.
WHAT'S WITH THE CHEAP-SKATE?
MONNNOPPPOOOOOLLLYYY
HE GETS MISTY-EYED WHEN HE HEARS THE WORD "MONOPOLY."
ALL I EVER WANTED WAS TO BE PART OF A CARTEL.

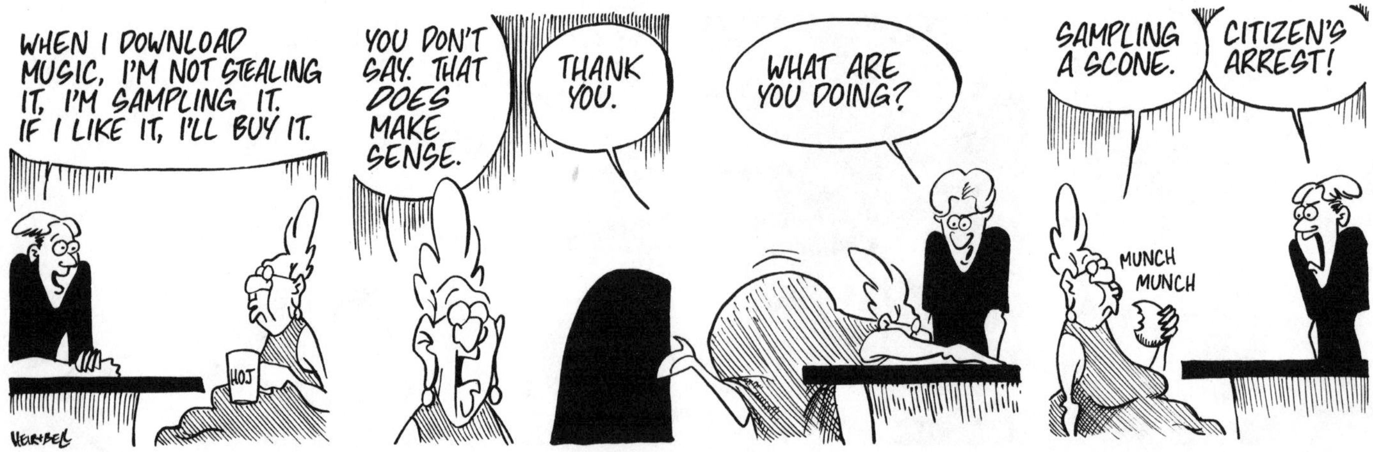
WHEN I DOWNLOAD MUSIC, I'M NOT STEALING IT, I'M SAMPLING IT. IF I LIKE IT, I'LL BUY IT.
YOU DON'T SAY. THAT DOES MAKE SENSE.
THANK YOU.
WHAT ARE YOU DOING?
MUNCH MUNCH
SAMPLING A SCONE.
CITIZEN'S ARREST!

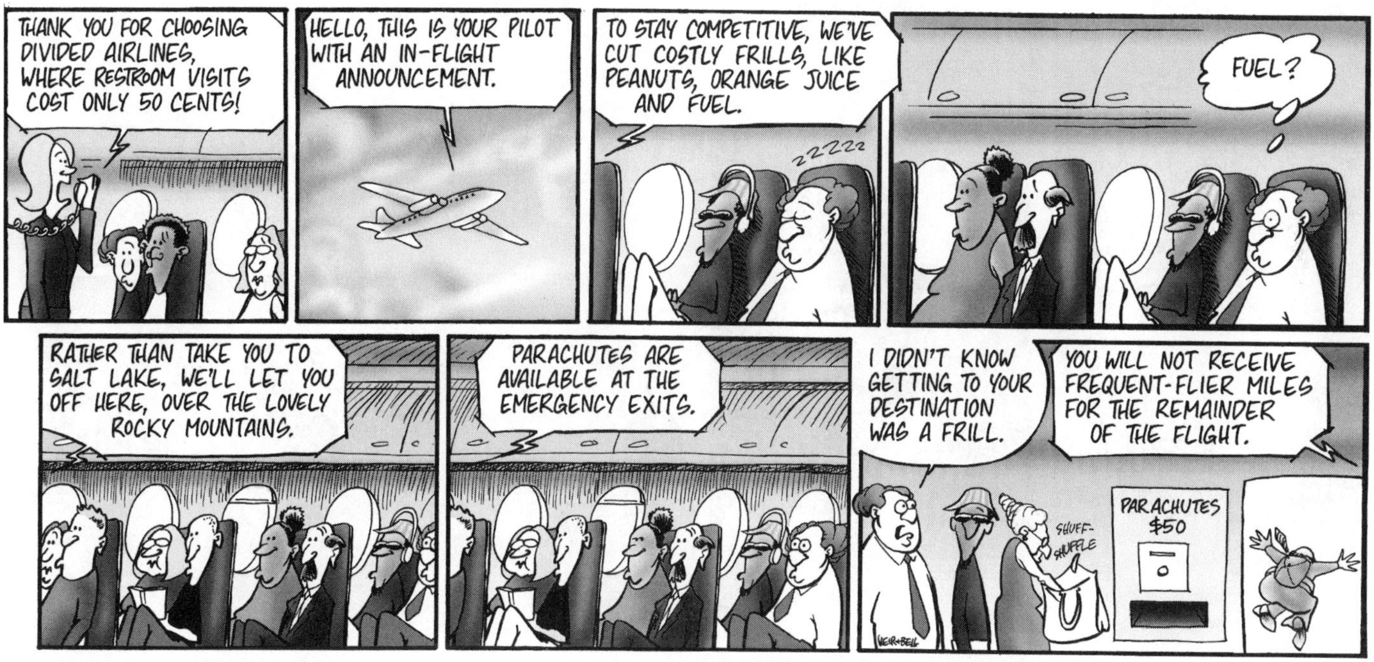
THANK YOU FOR CHOOSING DIVIDED AIRLINES, WHERE RESTROOM VISITS COST ONLY 50 CENTS!
HELLO, THIS IS YOUR PILOT WITH AN IN-FLIGHT ANNOUNCEMENT.
TO STAY COMPETITIVE, WE'VE CUT COSTLY FRILLS, LIKE PEANUTS, ORANGE JUICE AND FUEL.
ZZZZZ
FUEL?
RATHER THAN TAKE YOU TO SALT LAKE, WE'LL LET YOU OFF HERE, OVER THE LOVELY ROCKY MOUNTAINS.
PARACHUTES ARE AVAILABLE AT THE EMERGENCY EXITS.
I DIDN'T KNOW GETTING TO YOUR DESTINATION WAS A FRILL.
YOU WILL NOT RECEIVE FREQUENT-FLIER MILES FOR THE REMAINDER OF THE FLIGHT.
SHUFF-SHUFFLE
PARACHUTES $50
WEIR+BELL

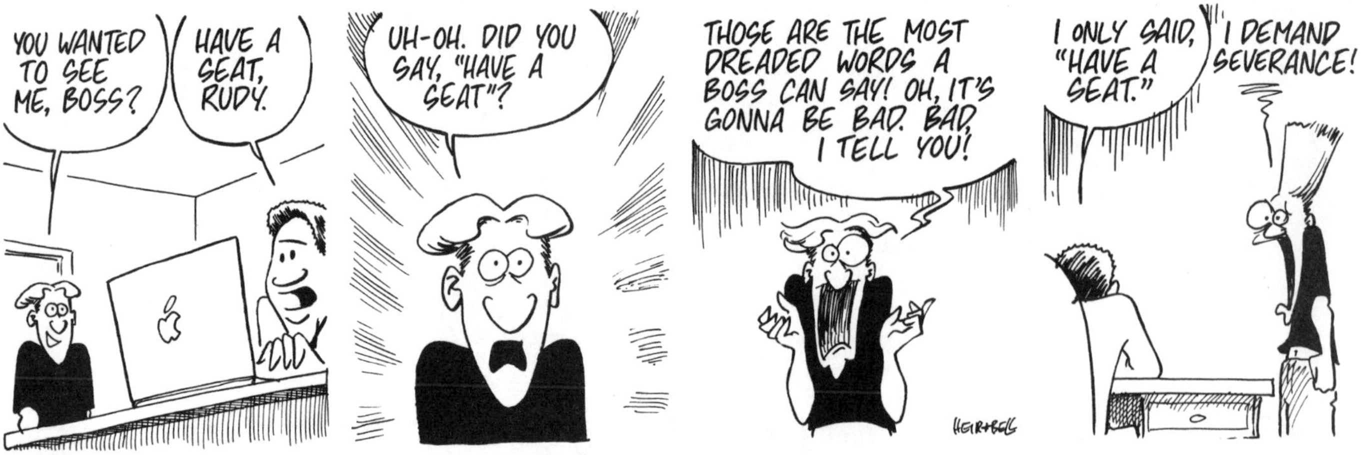
YOU WANTED TO SEE ME, BOSS?
HAVE A SEAT, RUDY.
UH-OH. DID YOU SAY, "HAVE A SEAT"?
THOSE ARE THE MOST DREADED WORDS A BOSS CAN SAY! OH, IT'S GONNA BE BAD. BAD, I TELL YOU!
I ONLY SAID, "HAVE A SEAT."
I DEMAND SEVERANCE!

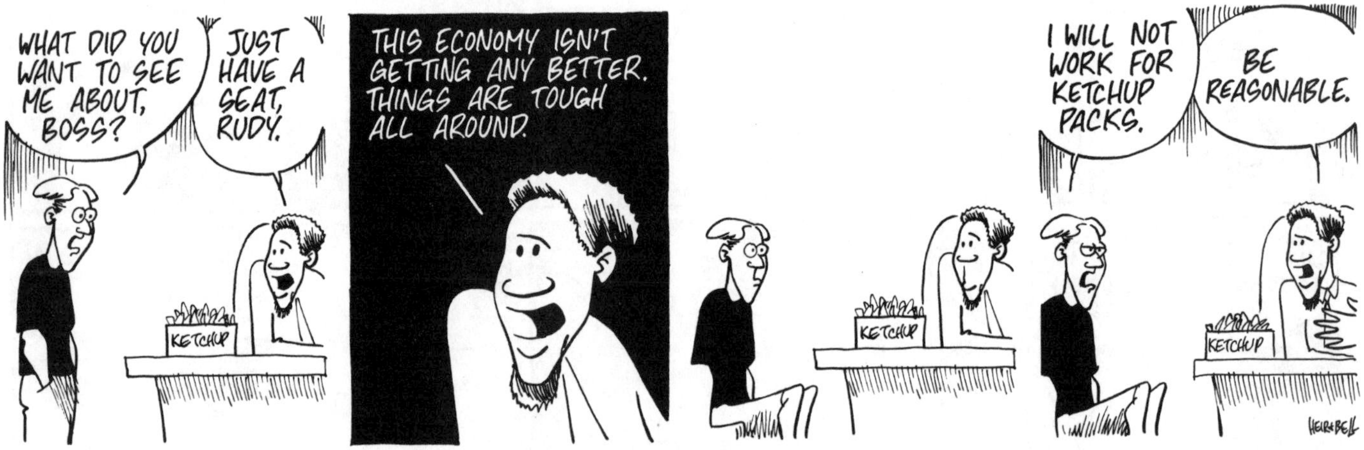
WHAT DID YOU WANT TO SEE ME ABOUT, BOSS?
JUST HAVE A SEAT, RUDY.
KETCHUP
THIS ECONOMY ISN'T GETTING ANY BETTER. THINGS ARE TOUGH ALL AROUND.
KETCHUP
I WILL NOT WORK FOR KETCHUP PACKS.
BE REASONABLE.
KETCHUP

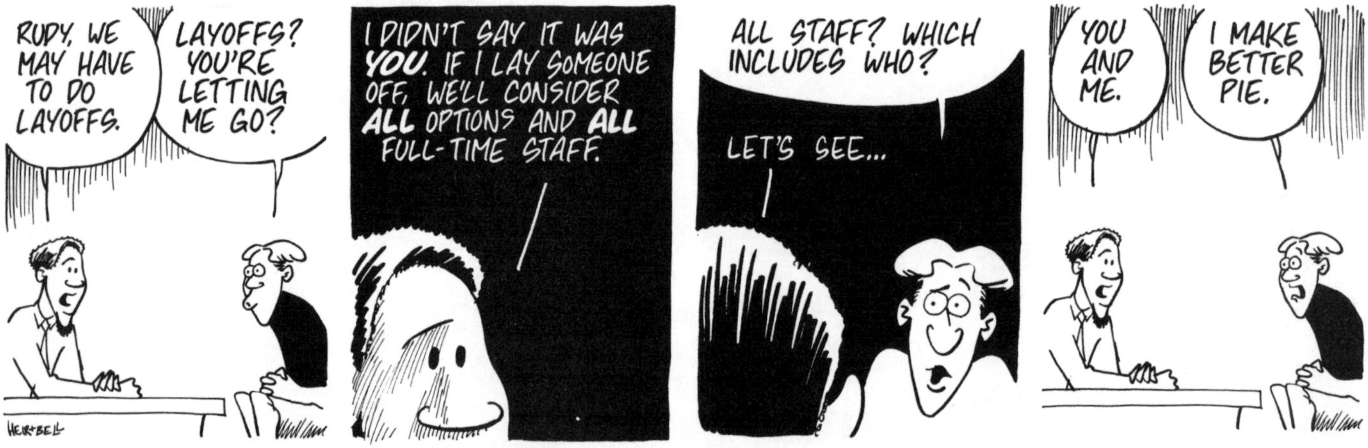
RUDY, WE MAY HAVE TO DO LAYOFFS.
LAYOFFS? YOU'RE LETTING ME GO?
I DIDN'T SAY IT WAS **YOU**. IF I LAY SOMEONE OFF, WE'LL CONSIDER **ALL** OPTIONS AND **ALL** FULL-TIME STAFF.
ALL STAFF? WHICH INCLUDES WHO?
LET'S SEE...
YOU AND ME.
I MAKE BETTER PIE.

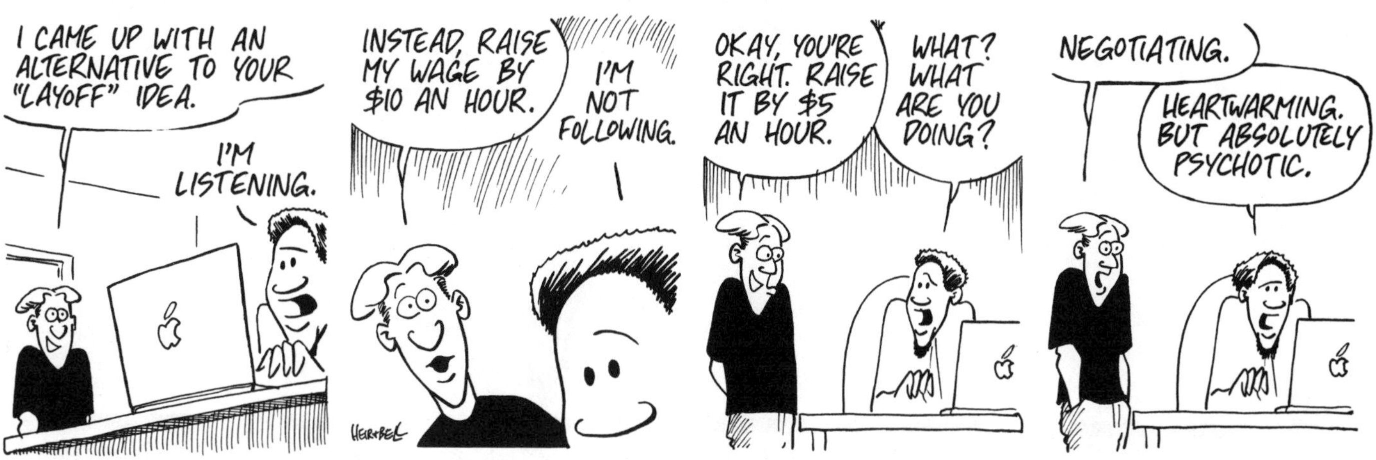
I CAME UP WITH AN ALTERNATIVE TO YOUR "LAYOFF" IDEA.
I'M LISTENING.
INSTEAD, RAISE MY WAGE BY $10 AN HOUR.
I'M NOT FOLLOWING.
OKAY, YOU'RE RIGHT. RAISE IT BY $5 AN HOUR.
WHAT? WHAT ARE YOU DOING?
NEGOTIATING.
HEARTWARMING. BUT ABSOLUTELY PSYCHOTIC.

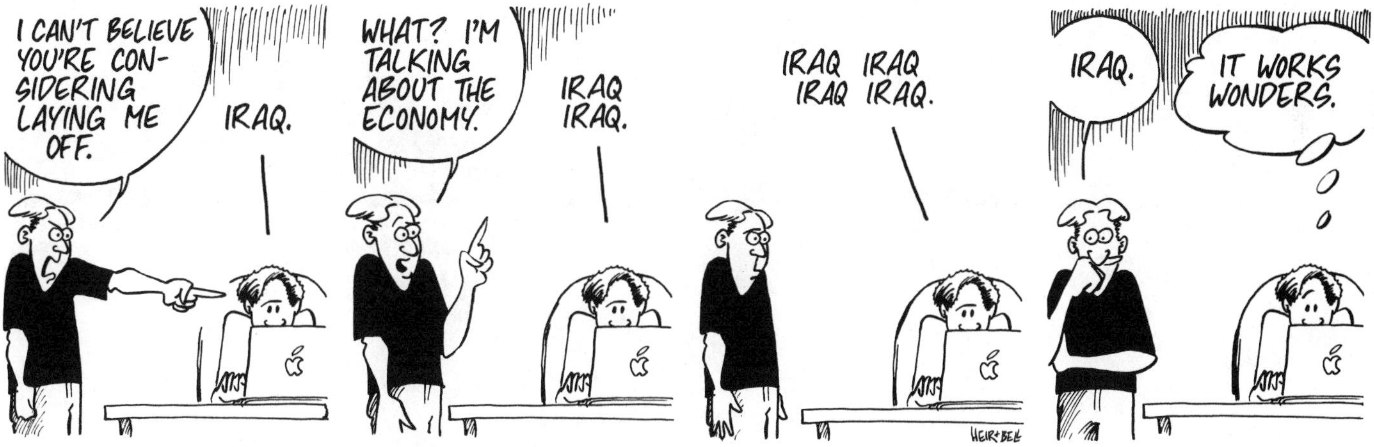
I CAN'T BELIEVE YOU'RE CONSIDERING LAYING ME OFF.
IRAQ.
WHAT? I'M TALKING ABOUT THE ECONOMY.
IRAQ IRAQ.
IRAQ IRAQ IRAQ IRAQ.
IRAQ.
IT WORKS WONDERS.

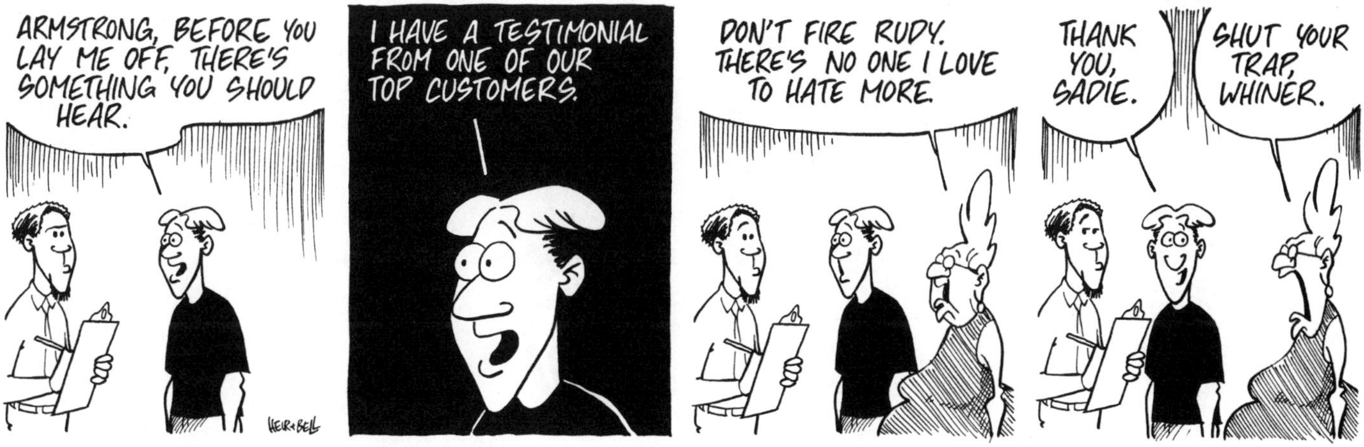
ARMSTRONG, BEFORE YOU LAY ME OFF, THERE'S SOMETHING YOU SHOULD HEAR.
I HAVE A TESTIMONIAL FROM ONE OF OUR TOP CUSTOMERS.
DON'T FIRE RUDY. THERE'S NO ONE I LOVE TO HATE MORE.
THANK YOU, SADIE.
SHUT YOUR TRAP, WHINER.

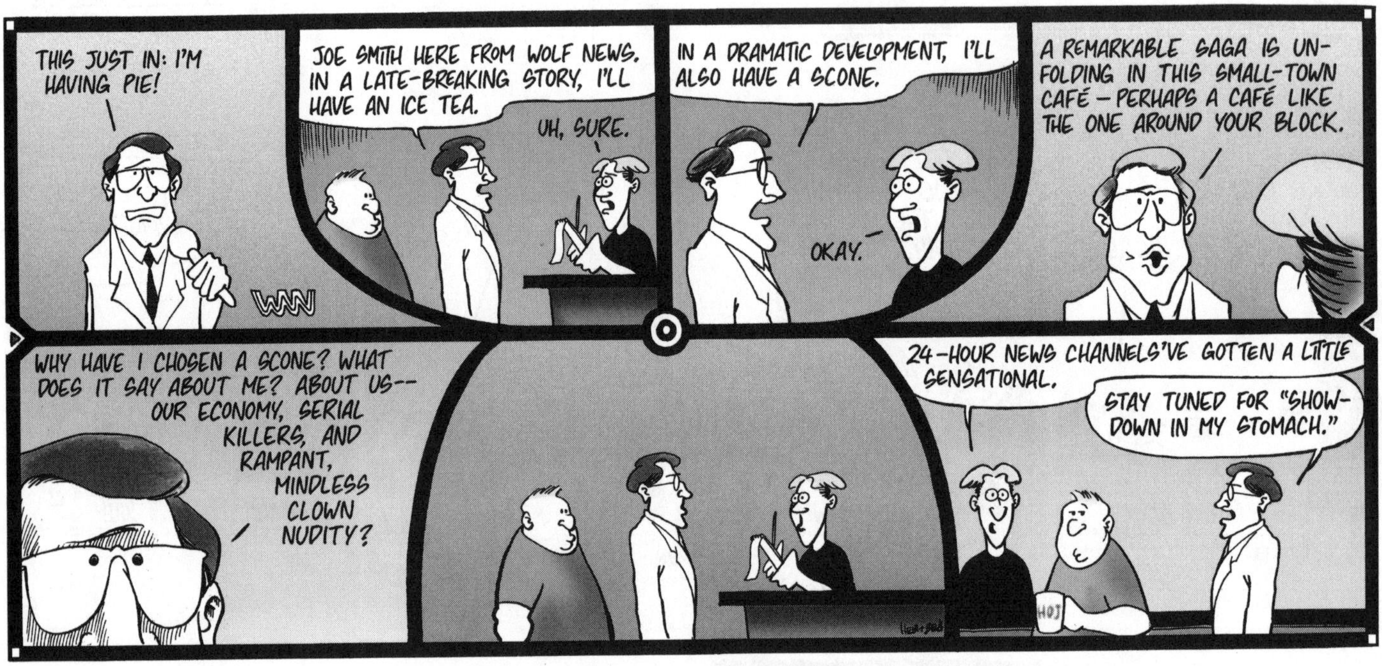
THIS JUST IN: I'M HAVING PIE!
JOE SMITH HERE FROM WOLF NEWS. IN A LATE-BREAKING STORY, I'LL HAVE AN ICE TEA.
UH, SURE.
IN A DRAMATIC DEVELOPMENT, I'LL ALSO HAVE A SCONE.
OKAY.
A REMARKABLE SAGA IS UNFOLDING IN THIS SMALL-TOWN CAFÉ — PERHAPS A CAFÉ LIKE THE ONE AROUND YOUR BLOCK.
WHY HAVE I CHOSEN A SCONE? WHAT DOES IT SAY ABOUT ME? ABOUT US-- OUR ECONOMY, SERIAL KILLERS, AND RAMPANT, MINDLESS CLOWN NUDITY?
24-HOUR NEWS CHANNELS'VE GOTTEN A LITTLE SENSATIONAL.
STAY TUNED FOR "SHOWDOWN IN MY STOMACH."

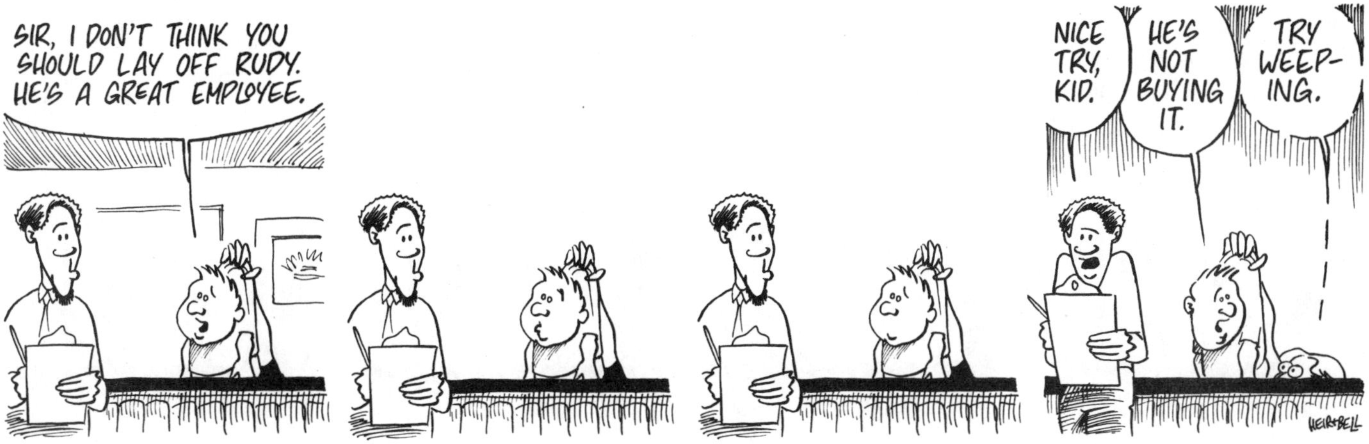
SIR, I DON'T THINK YOU SHOULD LAY OFF RUDY. HE'S A GREAT EMPLOYEE.
NICE TRY, KID.
HE'S NOT BUYING IT.
TRY WEEP-ING.
HEIR+BELL

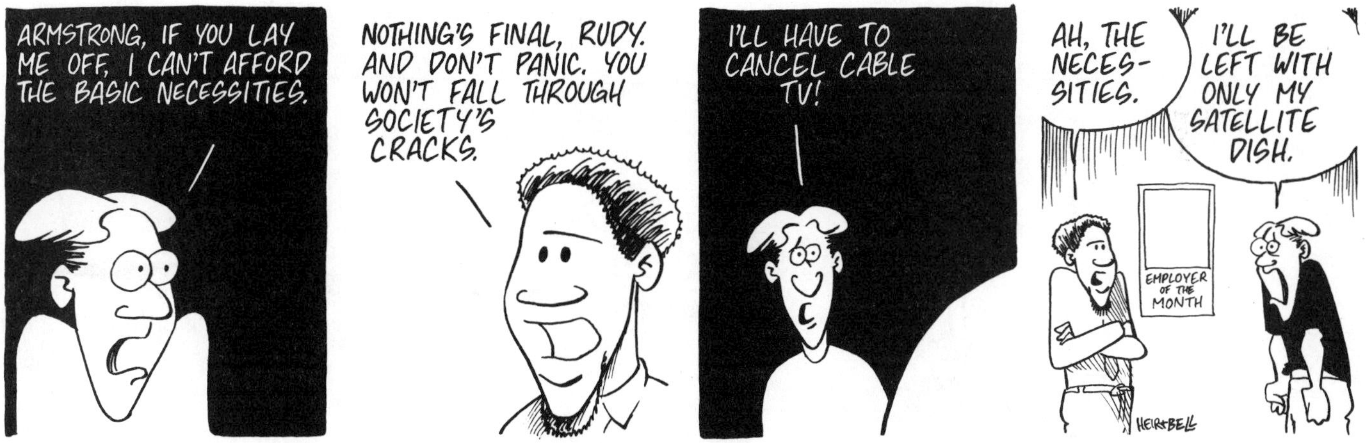
ARMSTRONG, IF YOU LAY ME OFF, I CAN'T AFFORD THE BASIC NECESSITIES.
NOTHING'S FINAL, RUDY. AND DON'T PANIC. YOU WON'T FALL THROUGH SOCIETY'S CRACKS.
I'LL HAVE TO CANCEL CABLE TV!
AH, THE NECES-SITIES.
I'LL BE LEFT WITH ONLY MY SATELLITE DISH.
EMPLOYER OF THE MONTH
HEIR+BELL

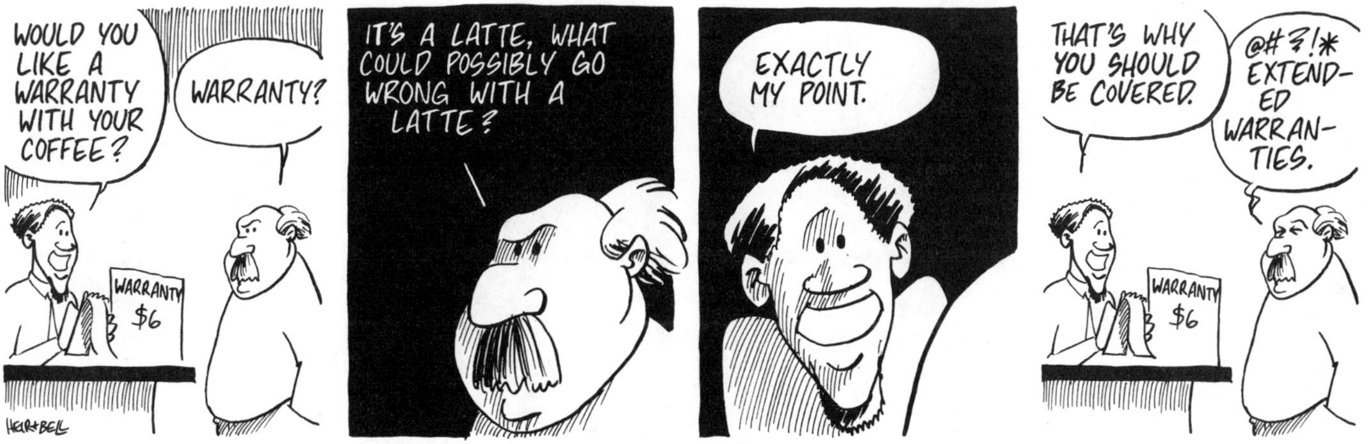
WOULD YOU LIKE A WARRANTY WITH YOUR COFFEE?
WARRANTY?
WARRANTY $6
IT'S A LATTE, WHAT COULD POSSIBLY GO WRONG WITH A LATTE?
EXACTLY MY POINT.
THAT'S WHY YOU SHOULD BE COVERED.
@#?!* EXTEND-ED WARRAN-TIES.
WARRANTY $6
HEIR+BELL

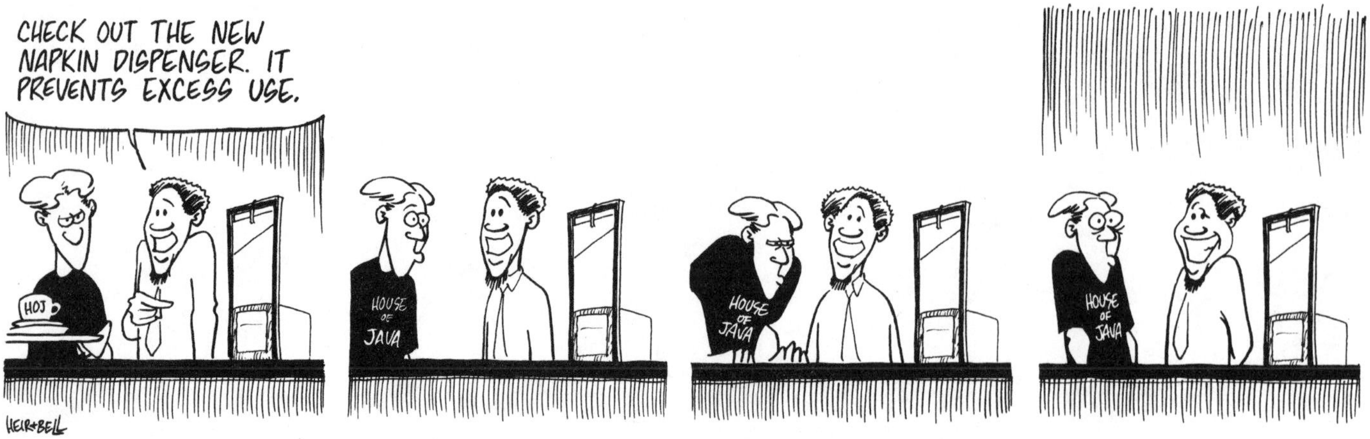
CHECK OUT THE NEW NAPKIN DISPENSER. IT PREVENTS EXCESS USE.
HOJ
HOUSE OF JAVA
HEIR+BELL

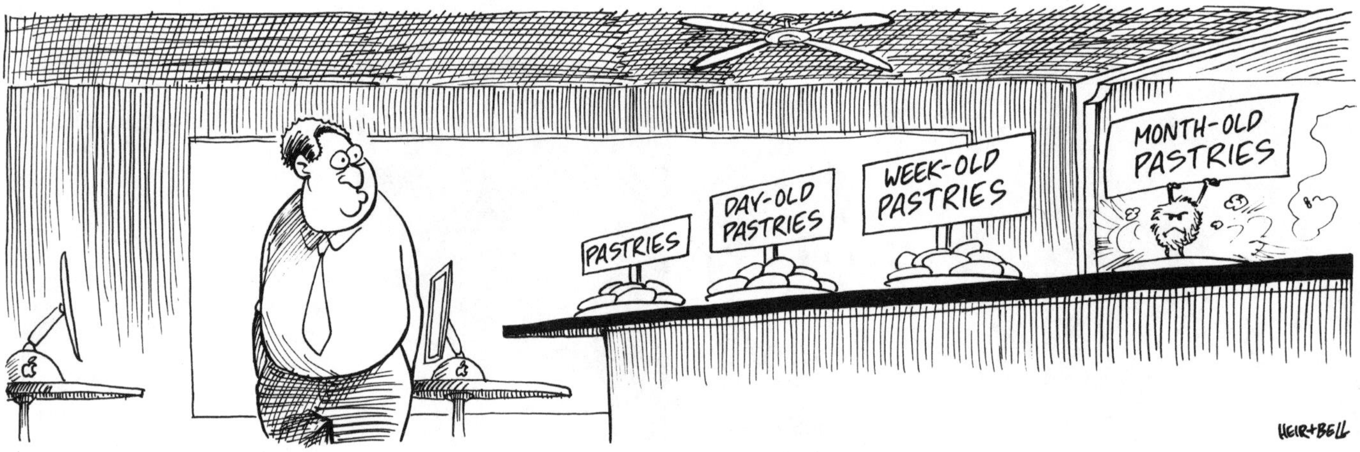
PASTRIES
DAY-OLD PASTRIES
WEEK-OLD PASTRIES
MONTH-OLD PASTRIES
HEIR+BELL

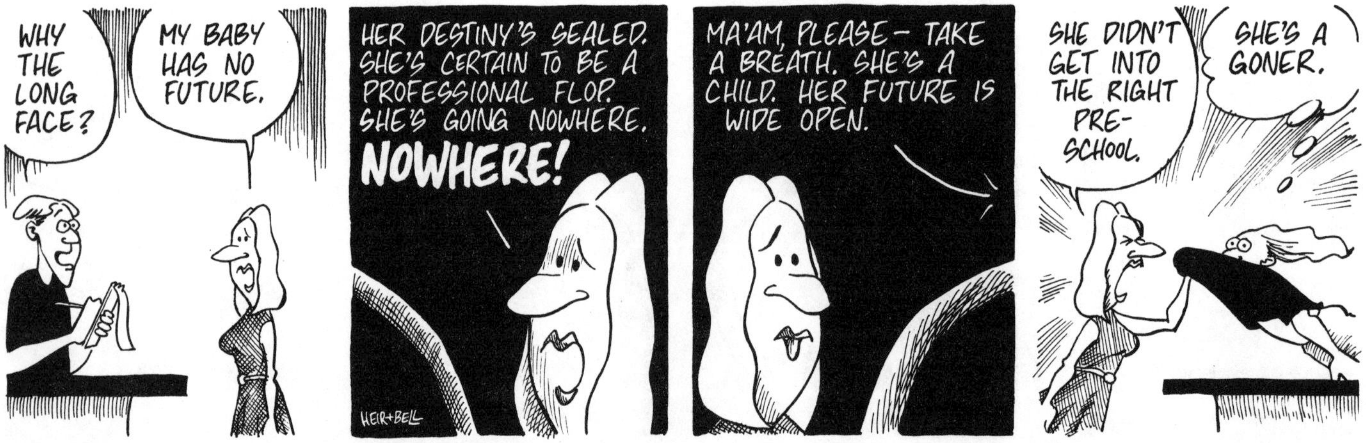
WHY THE LONG FACE?
MY BABY HAS NO FUTURE.
HER DESTINY'S SEALED. SHE'S CERTAIN TO BE A PROFESSIONAL FLOP. SHE'S GOING NOWHERE.
NOWHERE!
HEIR+BELL
MA'AM, PLEASE – TAKE A BREATH. SHE'S A CHILD. HER FUTURE IS WIDE OPEN.
SHE DIDN'T GET INTO THE RIGHT PRE-SCHOOL.
SHE'S A GONER.

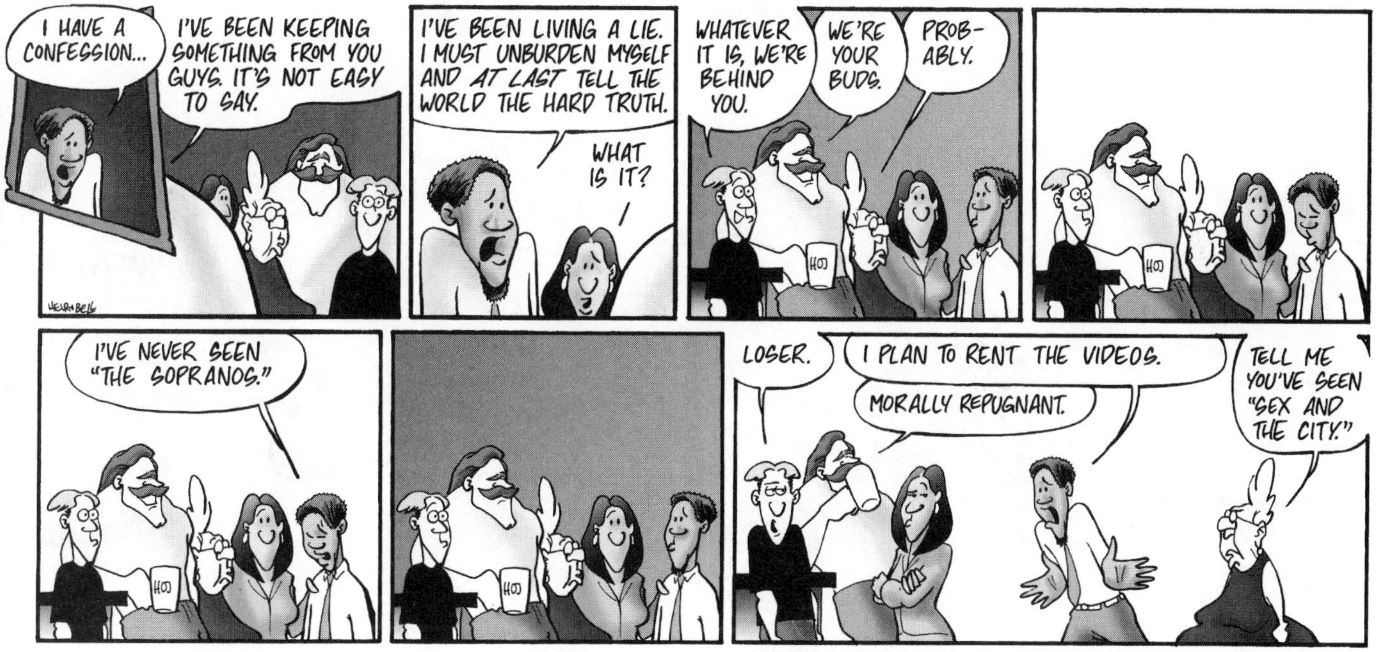
I HAVE A CONFESSION...
I'VE BEEN KEEPING SOMETHING FROM YOU GUYS. IT'S NOT EASY TO SAY.
I'VE BEEN LIVING A LIE. I MUST UNBURDEN MYSELF AND AT LAST TELL THE WORLD THE HARD TRUTH.
WHAT IS IT?
WHATEVER IT IS, WE'RE BEHIND YOU.
WE'RE YOUR BUDS.
PROB-ABLY.
I'VE NEVER SEEN "THE SOPRANOS."
LOSER.
I PLAN TO RENT THE VIDEOS.
MORALLY REPUGNANT.
TELL ME YOU'VE SEEN "SEX AND THE CITY."

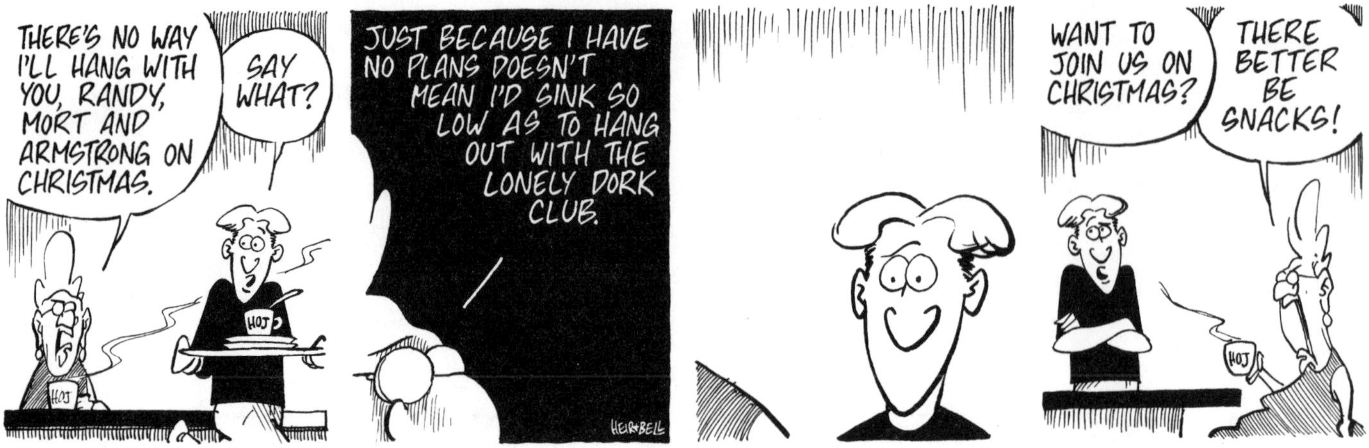
THERE'S NO WAY I'LL HANG WITH YOU, RANDY, MORT AND ARMSTRONG ON CHRISTMAS.
SAY WHAT?
HOJ
HOJ
JUST BECAUSE I HAVE NO PLANS DOESN'T MEAN I'D SINK SO LOW AS TO HANG OUT WITH THE LONELY DORK CLUB.
HEIR+BELL
WANT TO JOIN US ON CHRISTMAS?
THERE BETTER BE SNACKS!
HOJ

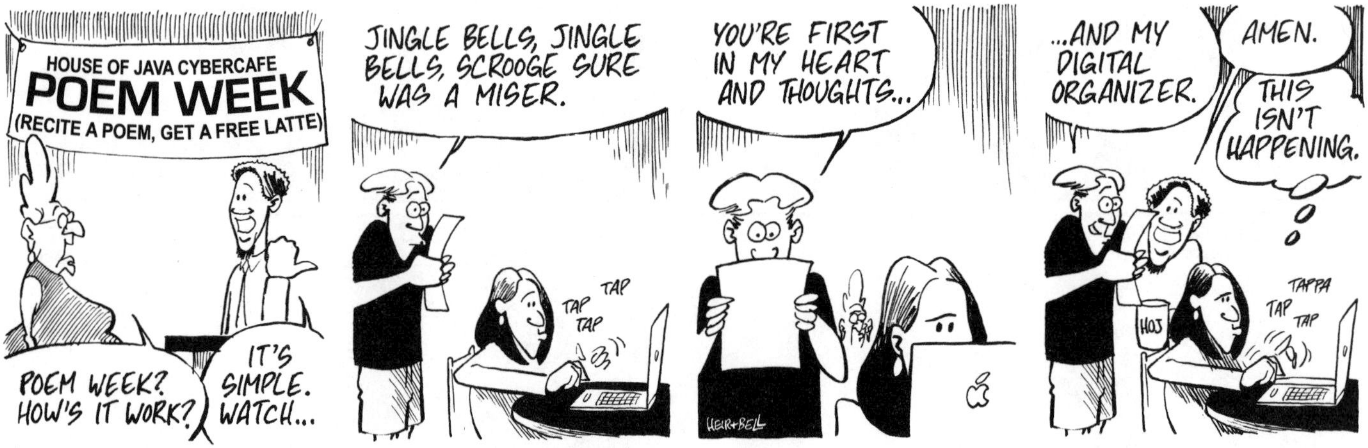
HOUSE OF JAVA CYBERCAFE
POEM WEEK
(RECITE A POEM, GET A FREE LATTE)
POEM WEEK? HOW'S IT WORK?
IT'S SIMPLE. WATCH...
JINGLE BELLS, JINGLE BELLS, SCROOGE SURE WAS A MISER.
TAP TAP
TAP
YOU'RE FIRST IN MY HEART AND THOUGHTS...
HEIR+BELL
...AND MY DIGITAL ORGANIZER.
AMEN.
THIS ISN'T HAPPENING.
TAPPA
TAP
TAP
HOJ

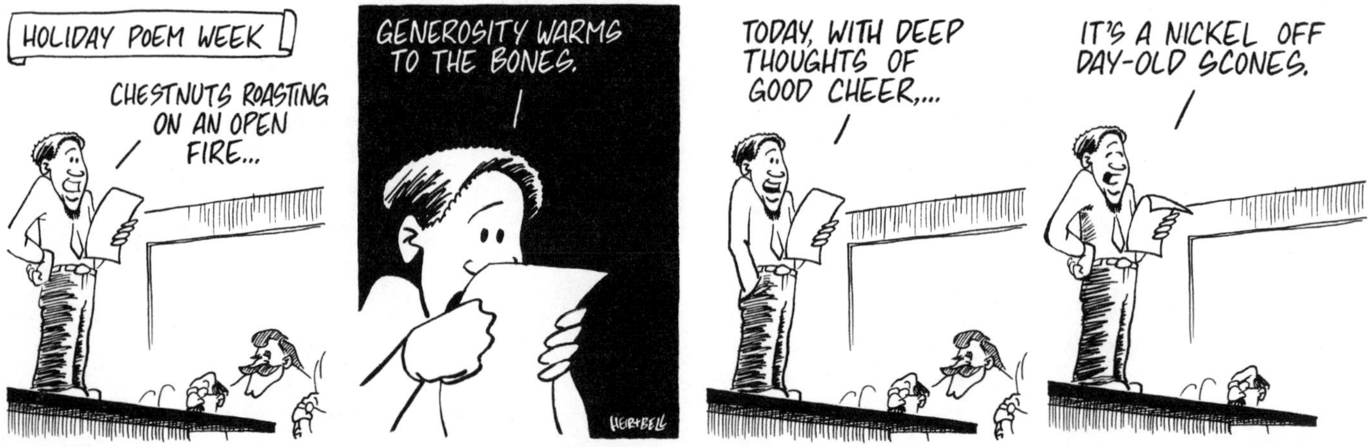
HOLIDAY POEM WEEK
CHESTNUTS ROASTING ON AN OPEN FIRE...
GENEROSITY WARMS TO THE BONES.
HEIR+BELL
TODAY, WITH DEEP THOUGHTS OF GOOD CHEER,...
IT'S A NICKEL OFF DAY-OLD SCONES.

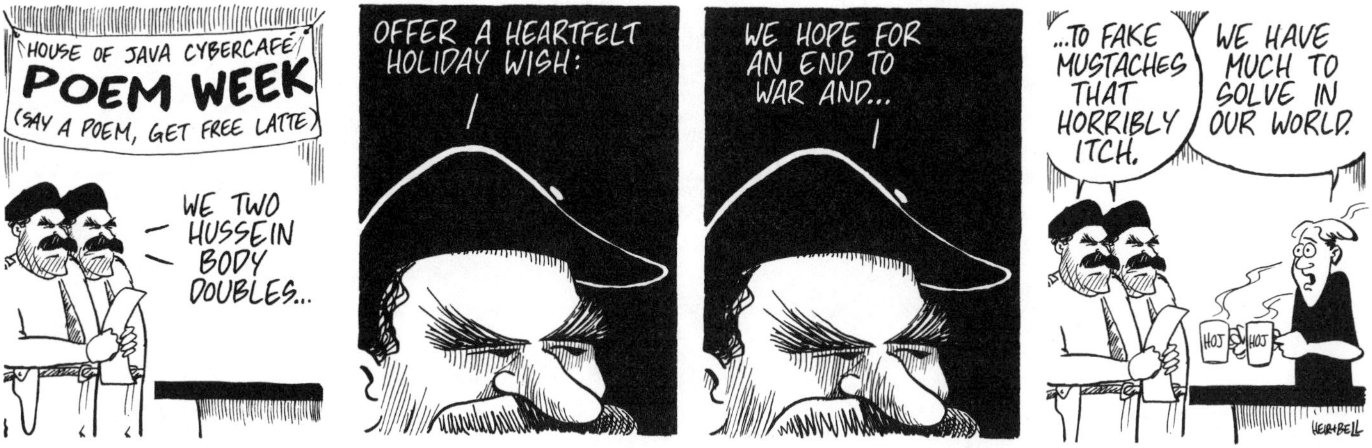
HOUSE OF JAVA CYBERCAFE
POEM WEEK
(SAY A POEM, GET FREE LATTE)
WE TWO HUSSEIN BODY DOUBLES...
OFFER A HEARTFELT HOLIDAY WISH:
WE HOPE FOR AN END TO WAR AND...
...TO FAKE MUSTACHES THAT HORRIBLY ITCH.
WE HAVE MUCH TO SOLVE IN OUR WORLD.
HOJ
HOJ
HEIR+BELL

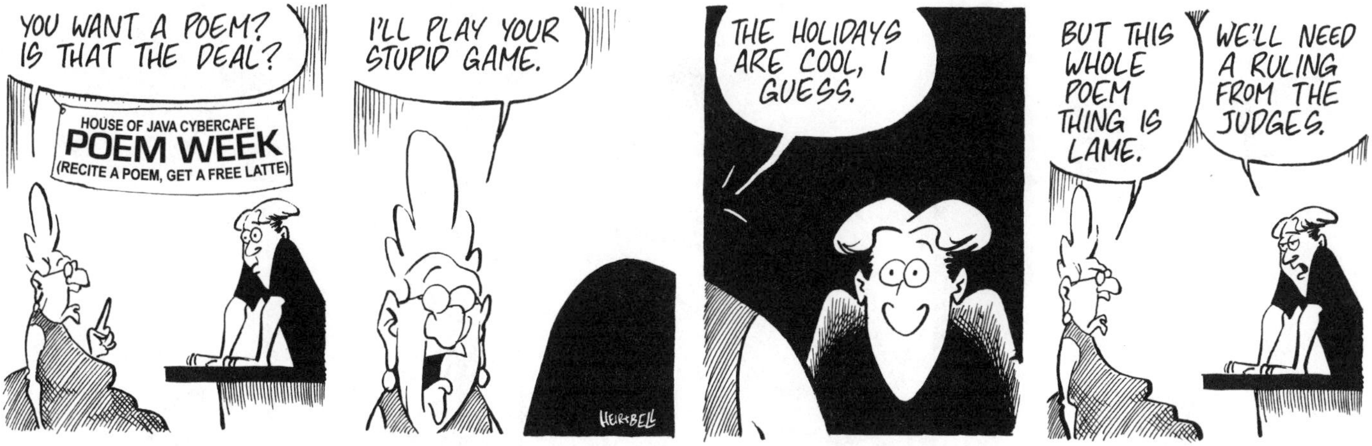
YOU WANT A POEM? IS THAT THE DEAL?
HOUSE OF JAVA CYBERCAFE
POEM WEEK
(RECITE A POEM, GET A FREE LATTE)
I'LL PLAY YOUR STUPID GAME.
THE HOLIDAYS ARE COOL, I GUESS.
BUT THIS WHOLE POEM THING IS LAME.
WE'LL NEED A RULING FROM THE JUDGES.
HEIR+BELL

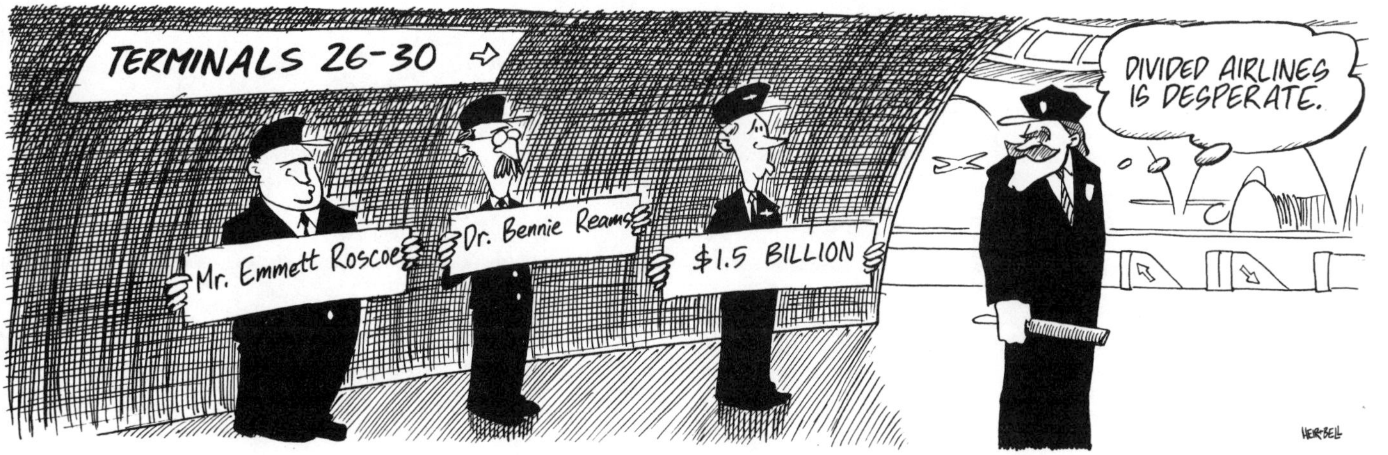
TERMINALS 26-30
DIVIDED AIRLINES IS DESPERATE.
Mr. Emmett Roscoe
Dr. Bennie Reams
$1.5 BILLION
HEIR+BELL

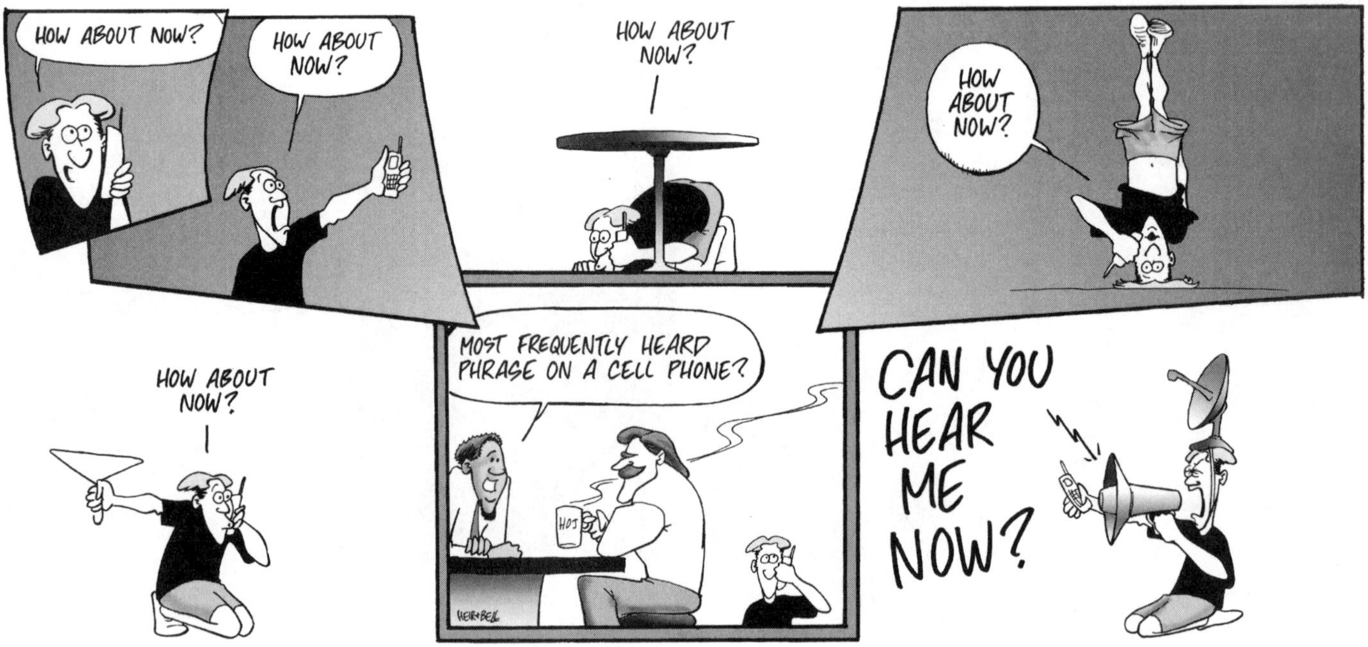
HOW ABOUT NOW?
HOW ABOUT NOW?
HOW ABOUT NOW?
HOW ABOUT NOW?
HOW ABOUT NOW?
MOST FREQUENTLY HEARD PHRASE ON A CELL PHONE?
HOJ
CAN YOU HEAR ME NOW?
HEIR+BELL

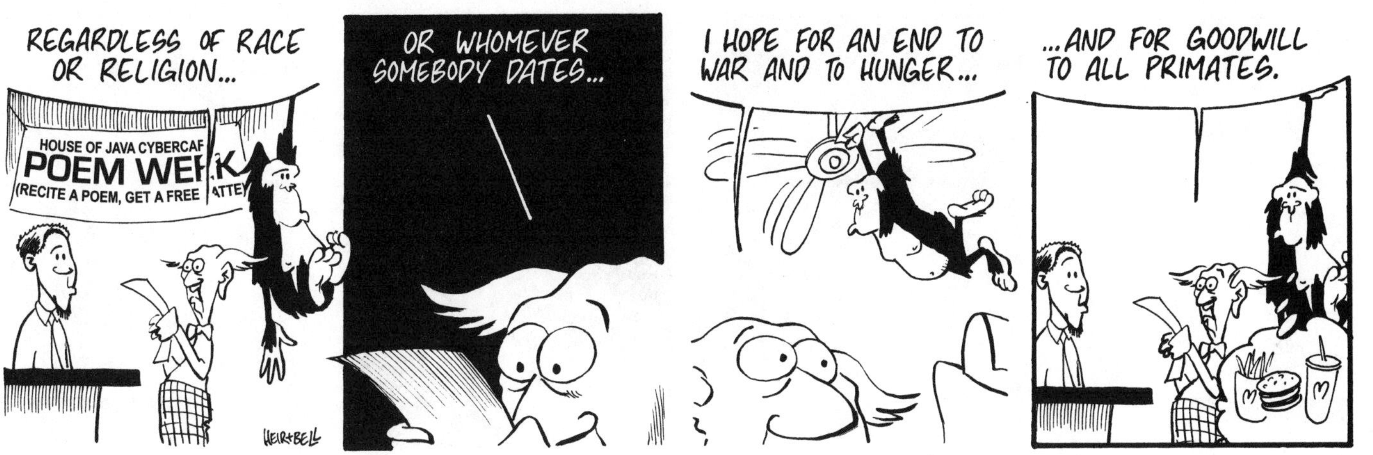
REGARDLESS OF RACE OR RELIGION...
HOUSE OF JAVA CYBERCAFE
(RECITE A POEM, GET A FREE
OR WHOMEVER SOMEBODY DATES...
I HOPE FOR AN END TO WAR AND TO HUNGER...
...AND FOR GOODWILL TO ALL PRIMATES.
HEIR+BELL

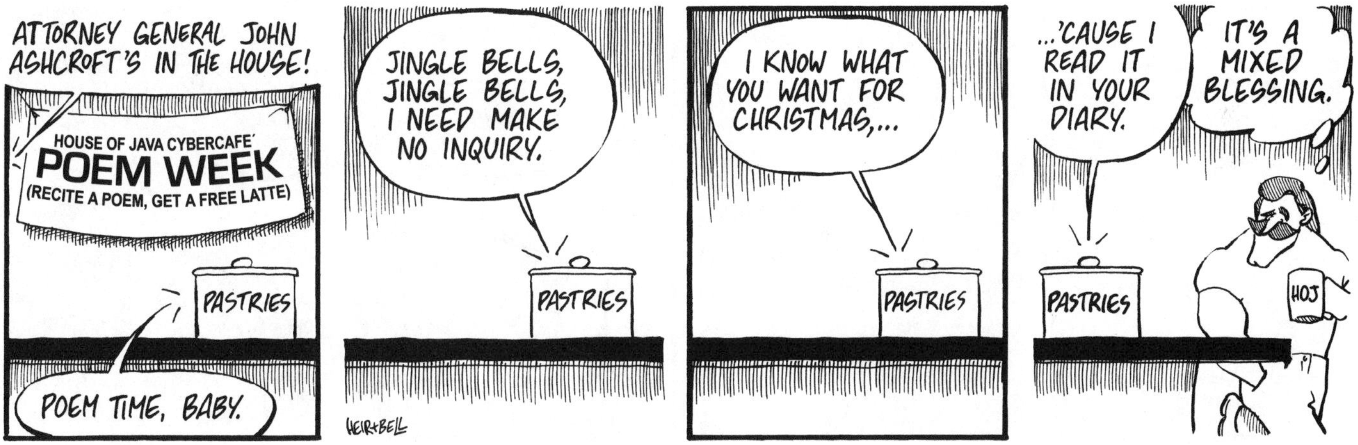
ATTORNEY GENERAL JOHN ASHCROFT'S IN THE HOUSE!
HOUSE OF JAVA CYBERCAFE
POEM WEEK
(RECITE A POEM, GET A FREE LATTE)
PASTRIES
POEM TIME, BABY.
JINGLE BELLS, JINGLE BELLS, I NEED MAKE NO INQUIRY.
PASTRIES
I KNOW WHAT YOU WANT FOR CHRISTMAS,...
PASTRIES
...'CAUSE I READ IT IN YOUR DIARY.
IT'S A MIXED BLESSING.
PASTRIES
HOJ
HEIR+BELL

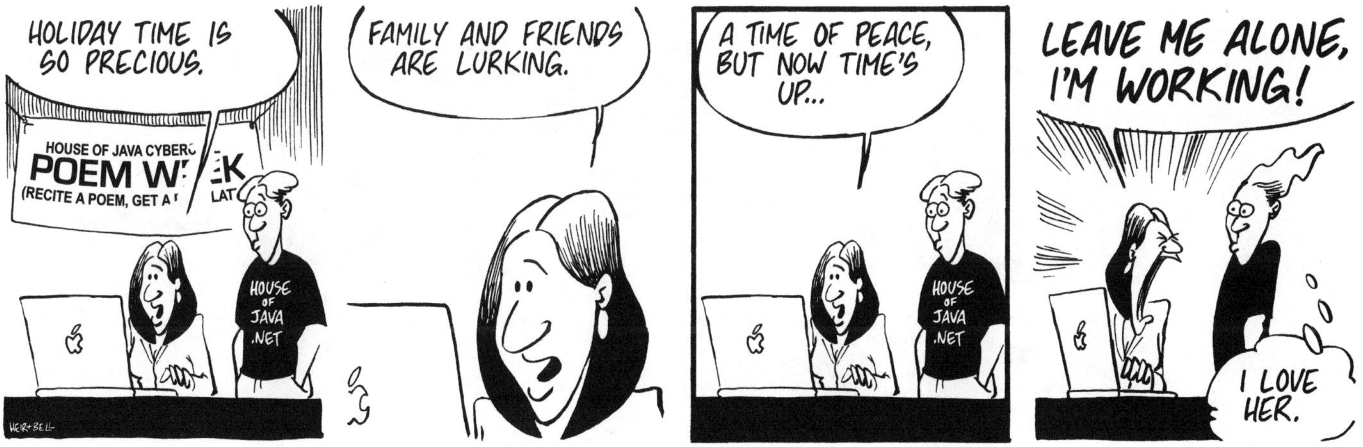
HOLIDAY TIME IS SO PRECIOUS.
HOUSE OF JAVA
.NET
FAMILY AND FRIENDS ARE LURKING.
A TIME OF PEACE, BUT NOW TIME'S UP...
HOUSE OF JAVA .NET
LEAVE ME ALONE, I'M WORKING!
I LOVE HER.
HEIR+BELL

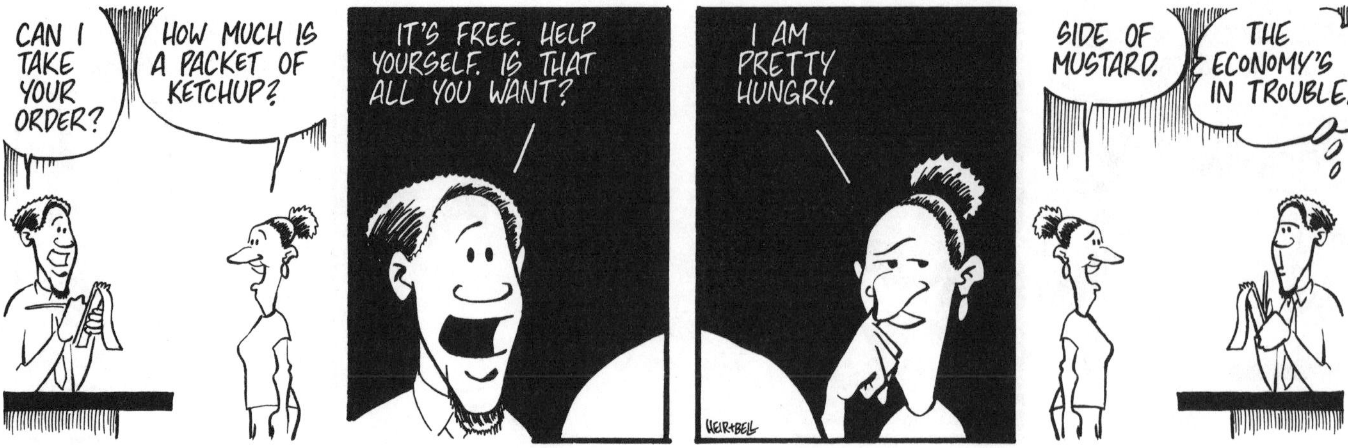
CAN I TAKE YOUR ORDER?
HOW MUCH IS A PACKET OF KETCHUP?
IT'S FREE. HELP YOURSELF. IS THAT ALL YOU WANT?
I AM PRETTY HUNGRY.
SIDE OF MUSTARD.
THE ECONOMY'S IN TROUBLE.

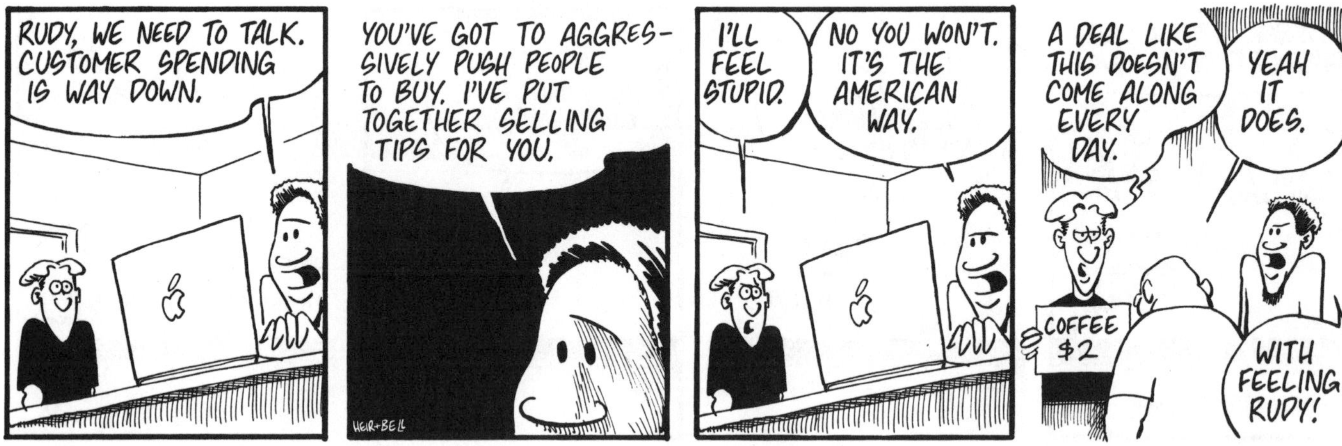
RUDY, WE NEED TO TALK. CUSTOMER SPENDING IS WAY DOWN.
YOU'VE GOT TO AGGRES- SIVELY PUSH PEOPLE TO BUY. I'VE PUT TOGETHER SELLING TIPS FOR YOU.
I'LL FEEL STUPID.
NO YOU WON'T. IT'S THE AMERICAN WAY.
A DEAL LIKE THIS DOESN'T COME ALONG EVERY DAY.
YEAH IT DOES.
COFFEE $2
WITH FEELING, RUDY!

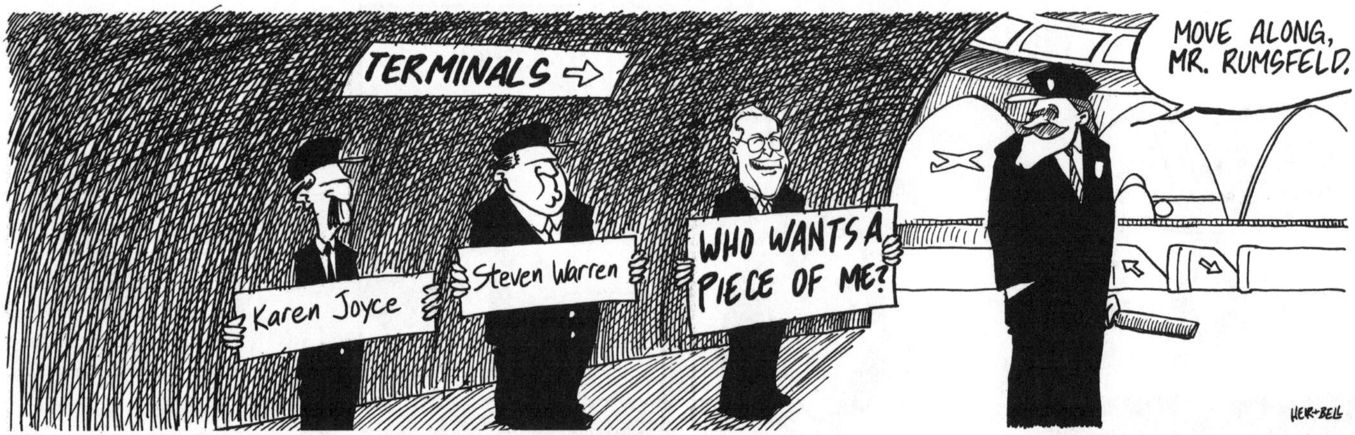
TERMINALS
Karen Joyce
Steven Warren
WHO WANTS A PIECE OF ME?
MOVE ALONG, MR. RUMSFELD.

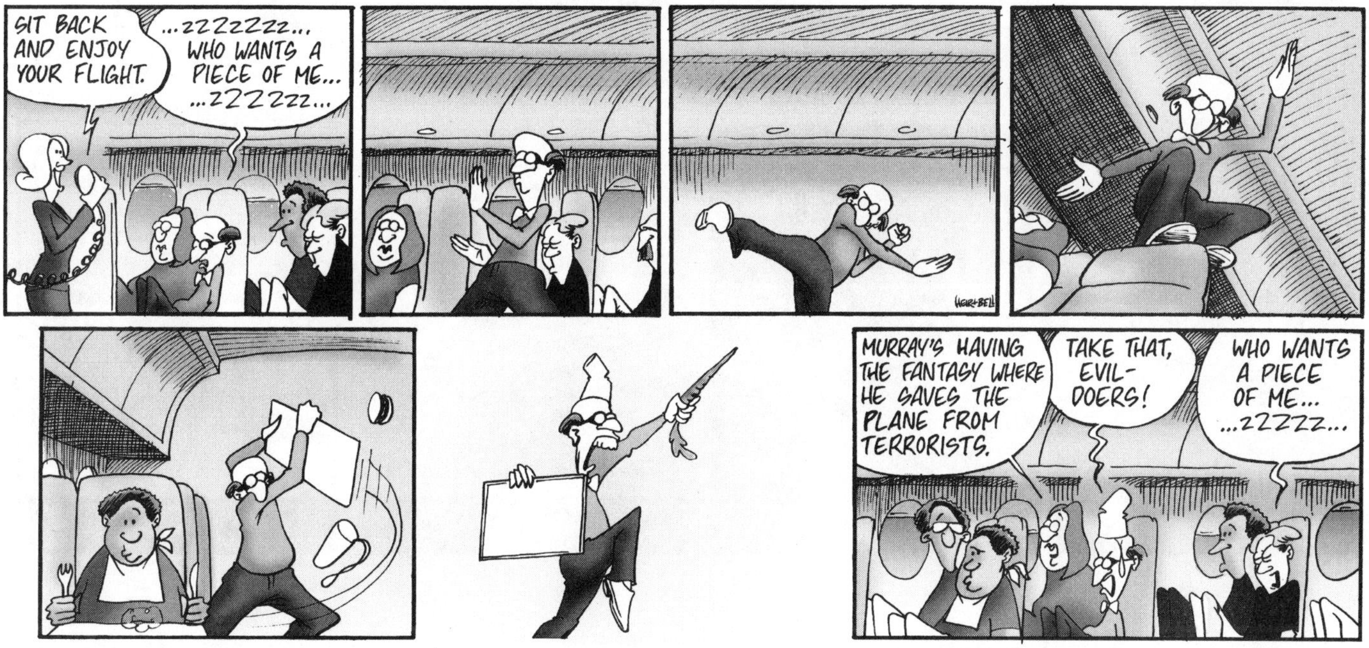
SIT BACK AND ENJOY YOUR FLIGHT.
...zzzzzzz... WHO WANTS A PIECE OF ME... ...zzzzzz...
MURRAY'S HAVING THE FANTASY WHERE HE SAVES THE PLANE FROM TERRORISTS.
TAKE THAT, EVIL-DOERS!
WHO WANTS A PIECE OF ME... ...zzzzz...

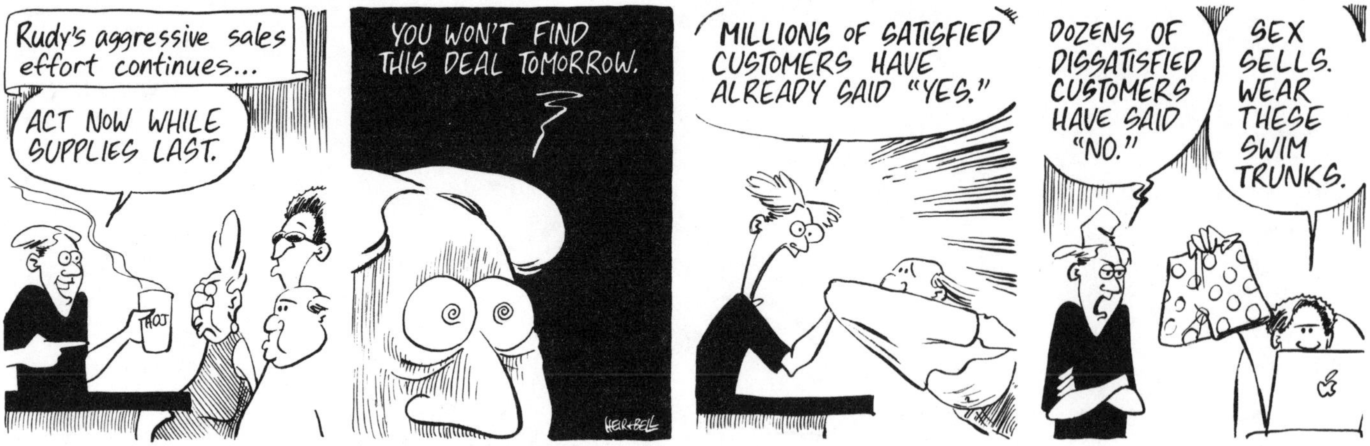
Rudy's aggressive sales effort continues...
ACT NOW WHILE SUPPLIES LAST.
YOU WON'T FIND THIS DEAL TOMORROW.
HEIR+BELL
MILLIONS OF SATISFIED CUSTOMERS HAVE ALREADY SAID "YES."
DOZENS OF DISSATISFIED CUSTOMERS HAVE SAID "NO."
SEX SELLS. WEAR THESE SWIM TRUNKS.

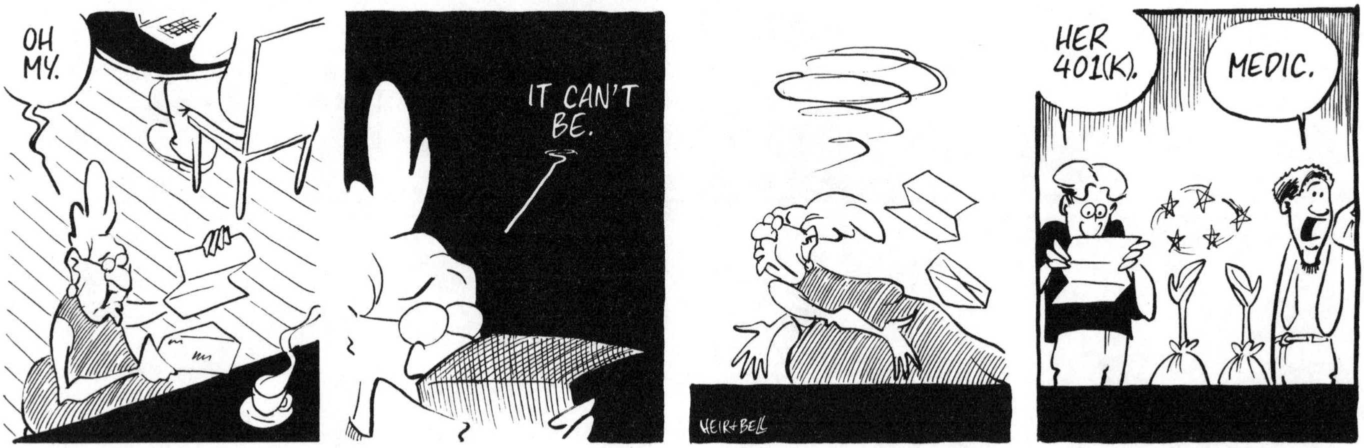
OH MY.
IT CAN'T BE.
HEIR+BELL
HER 401(K).
MEDIC.

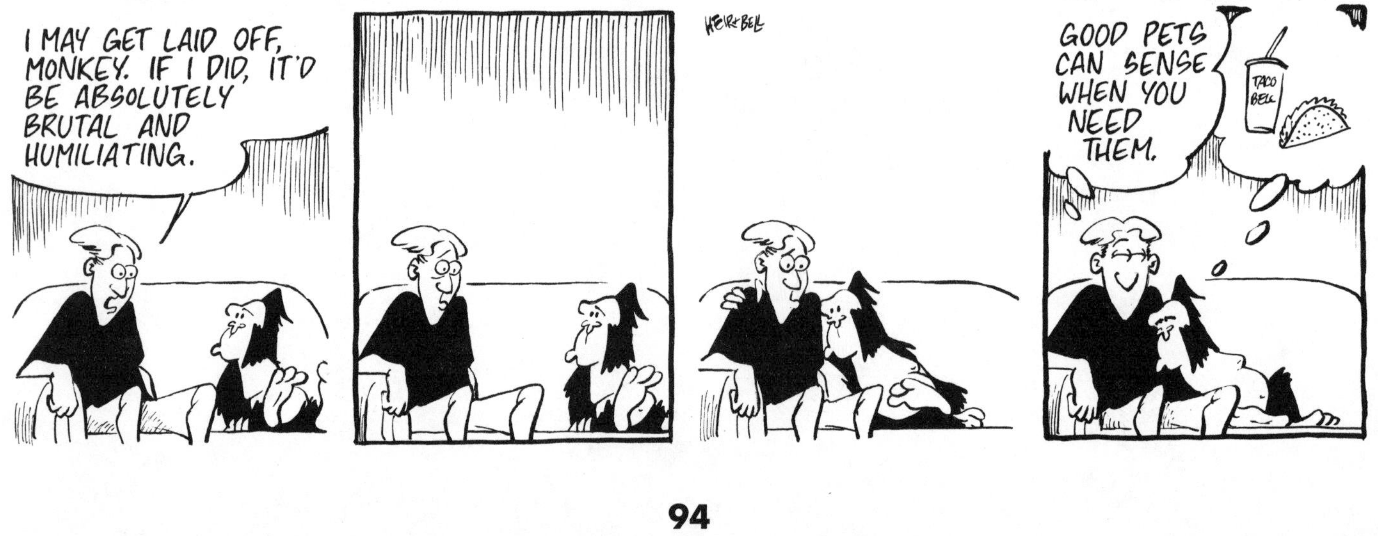
I MAY GET LAID OFF, MONKEY. IF I DID, IT'D BE ABSOLUTELY BRUTAL AND HUMILIATING.
HEIR+BELL
GOOD PETS CAN SENSE WHEN YOU NEED THEM.
TACO BELL

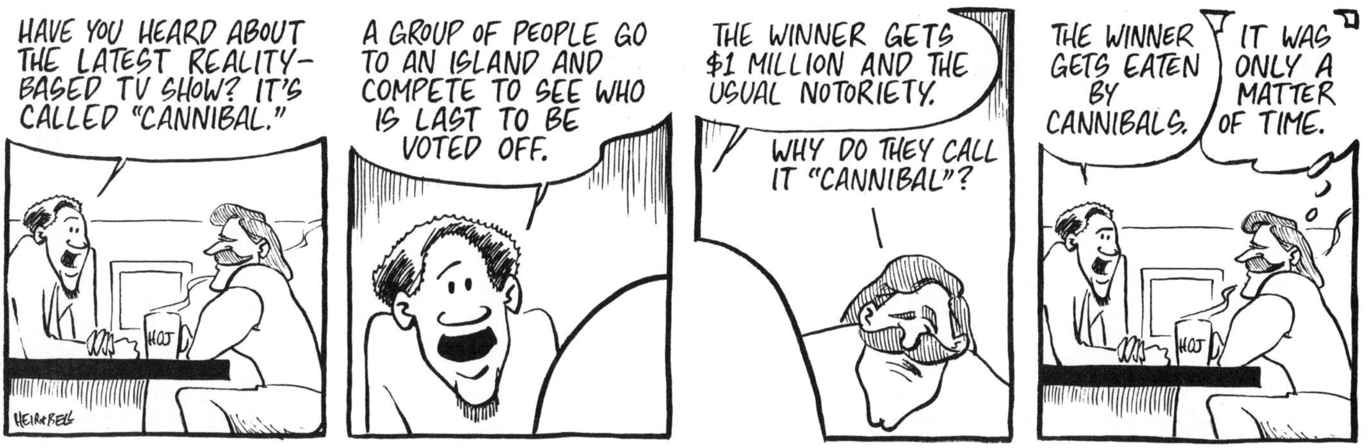
HAVE YOU HEARD ABOUT THE LATEST REALITY-BASED TV SHOW? IT'S CALLED "CANNIBAL."
A GROUP OF PEOPLE GO TO AN ISLAND AND COMPETE TO SEE WHO IS LAST TO BE VOTED OFF.
THE WINNER GETS $1 MILLION AND THE USUAL NOTORIETY.
WHY DO THEY CALL IT "CANNIBAL"?
THE WINNER GETS EATEN BY CANNIBALS.
IT WAS ONLY A MATTER OF TIME.
HOJ
HEIR+BELL

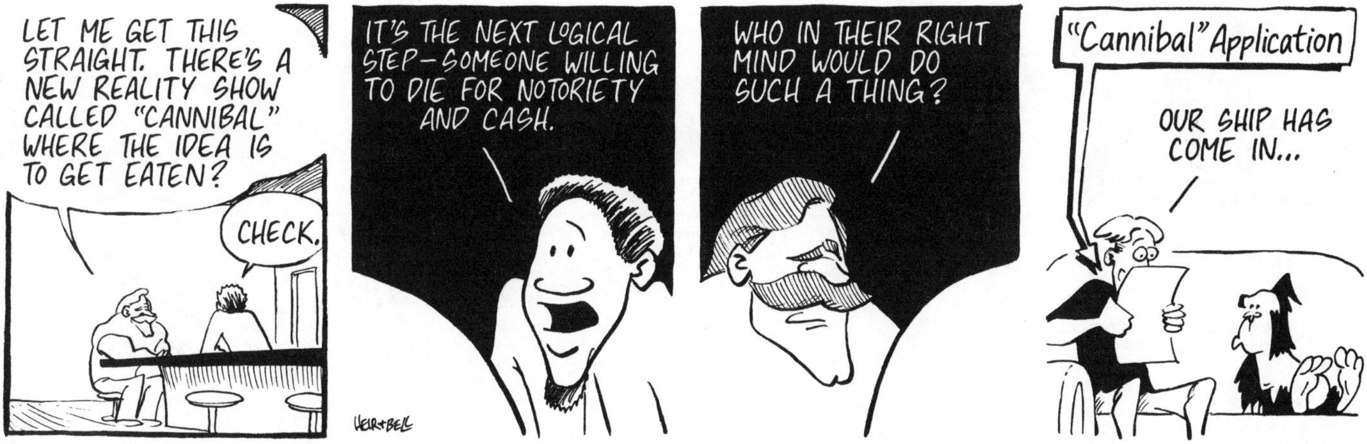
LET ME GET THIS STRAIGHT. THERE'S A NEW REALITY SHOW CALLED "CANNIBAL" WHERE THE IDEA IS TO GET EATEN?
CHECK.
IT'S THE NEXT LOGICAL STEP—SOMEONE WILLING TO DIE FOR NOTORIETY AND CASH.
WHO IN THEIR RIGHT MIND WOULD DO SUCH A THING?
"Cannibal" Application
OUR SHIP HAS COME IN...
HEIR+BELL

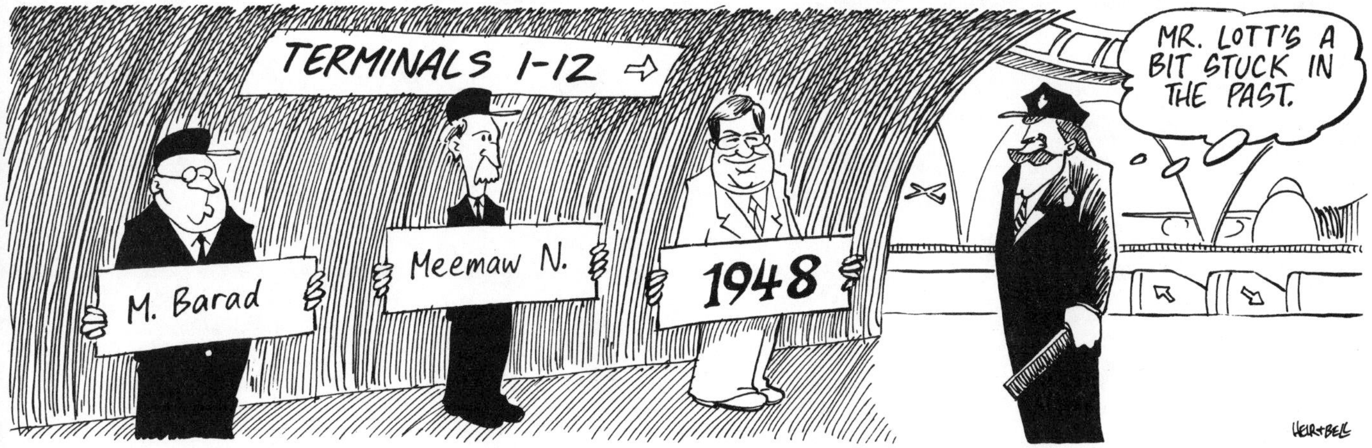
TERMINALS 1-12 ⇨
MR. LOTT'S A BIT STUCK IN THE PAST.
M. Barad
Meemaw N.
1948
HEIR+BELL

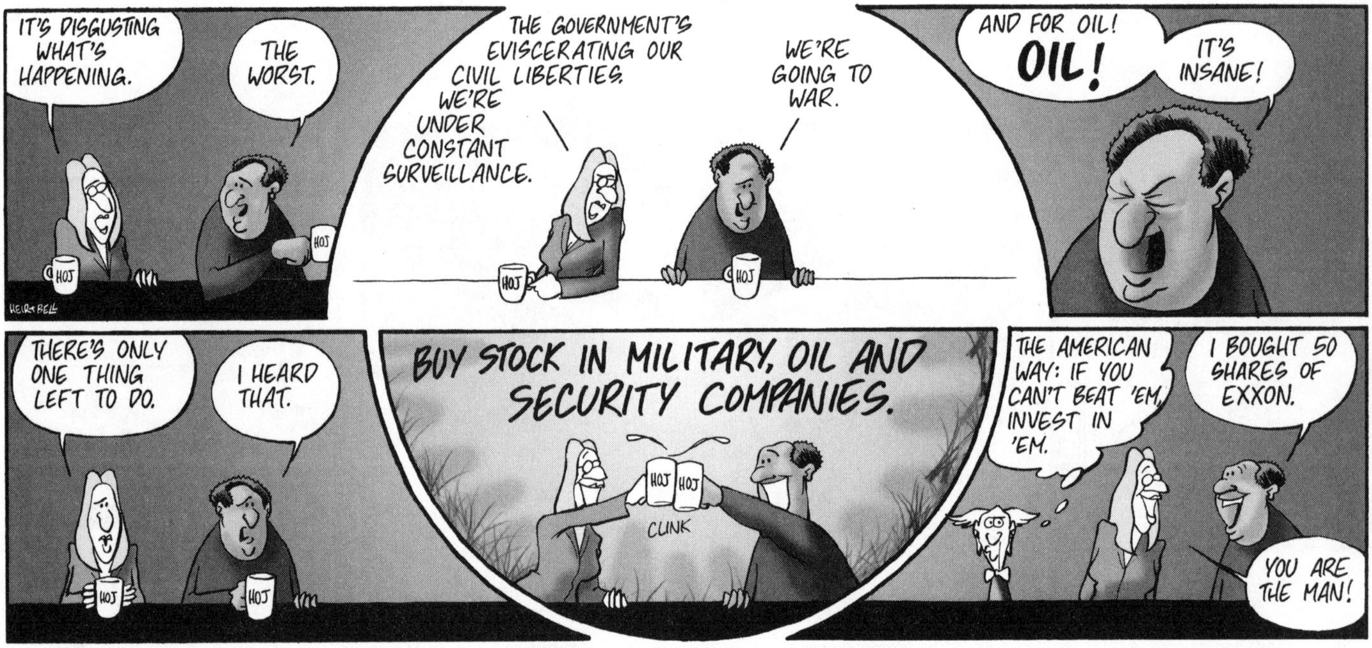
IT'S DISGUSTING WHAT'S HAPPENING.
THE WORST.
THE GOVERNMENT'S EVISCERATING OUR CIVIL LIBERTIES.
WE'RE UNDER CONSTANT SURVEILLANCE.
WE'RE GOING TO WAR.
AND FOR OIL! OIL!
IT'S INSANE!
THERE'S ONLY ONE THING LEFT TO DO.
I HEARD THAT.
BUY STOCK IN MILITARY, OIL AND SECURITY COMPANIES.
CLINK
THE AMERICAN WAY: IF YOU CAN'T BEAT 'EM, INVEST IN 'EM.
I BOUGHT 50 SHARES OF EXXON.
YOU ARE THE MAN!

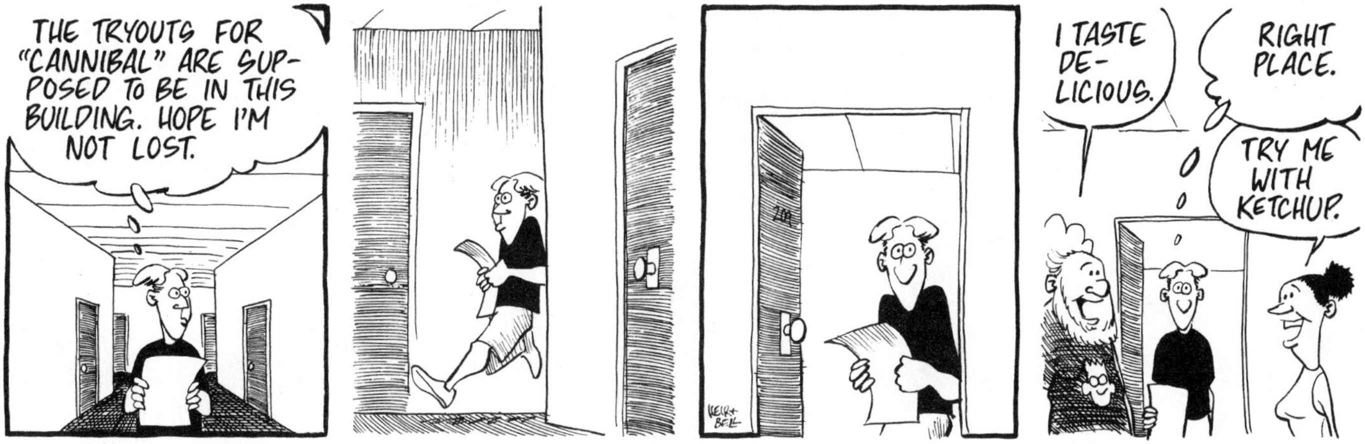
THE TRYOUTS FOR "CANNIBAL" ARE SUPPOSED TO BE IN THIS BUILDING. HOPE I'M NOT LOST.
HEIR+BELL
I TASTE DE-LICIOUS.
RIGHT PLACE.
TRY ME WITH KETCHUP.

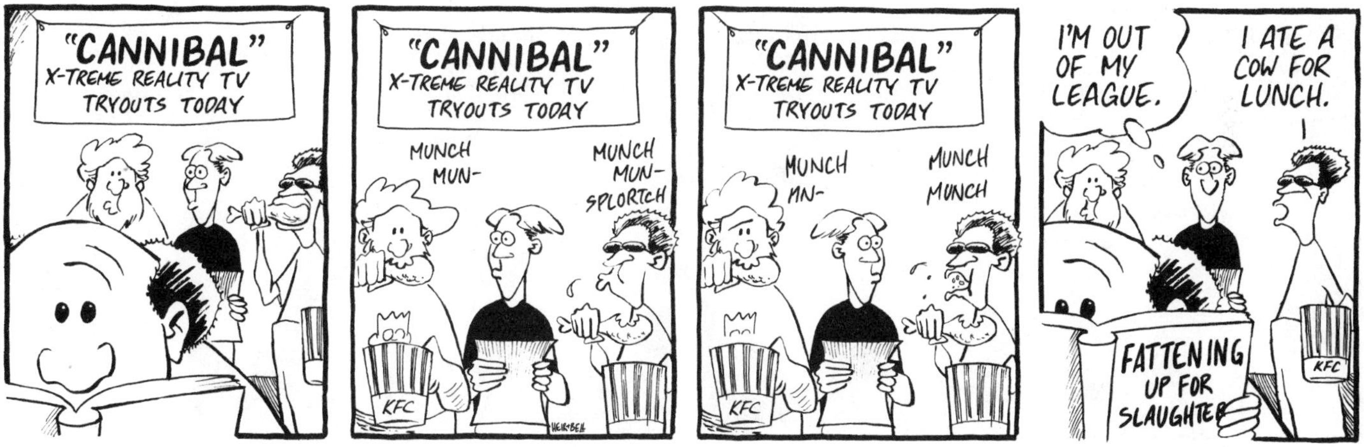
"CANNIBAL" X-TREME REALITY TV TRYOUTS TODAY
"CANNIBAL" X-TREME REALITY TV TRYOUTS TODAY
MUNCH MUN-
MUNCH MUN-SPLORTCH
KFC
HEIR+BELL
"CANNIBAL" X-TREME REALITY TV TRYOUTS TODAY
MUNCH MN-
MUNCH MUNCH
KFC
I'M OUT OF MY LEAGUE.
I ATE A COW FOR LUNCH.
FATTENING UP FOR SLAUGHTE
KFC

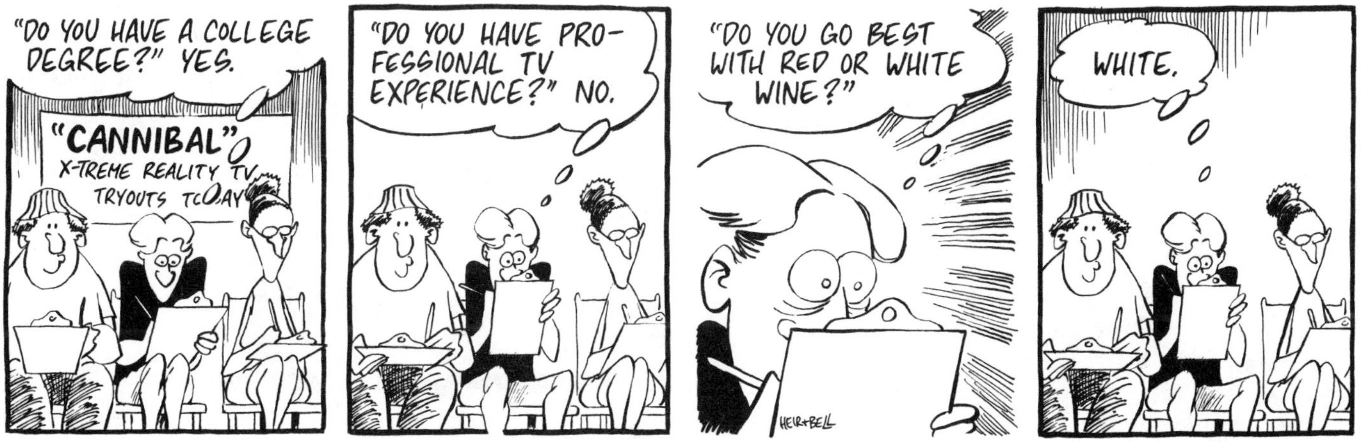
"DO YOU HAVE A COLLEGE DEGREE?" YES.
"CANNIBAL" X-TREME REALITY TV TRYOUTS TODAY
"DO YOU HAVE PROFESSIONAL TV EXPERIENCE?" NO.
"DO YOU GO BEST WITH RED OR WHITE WINE?"
HEIR+BELL
WHITE.

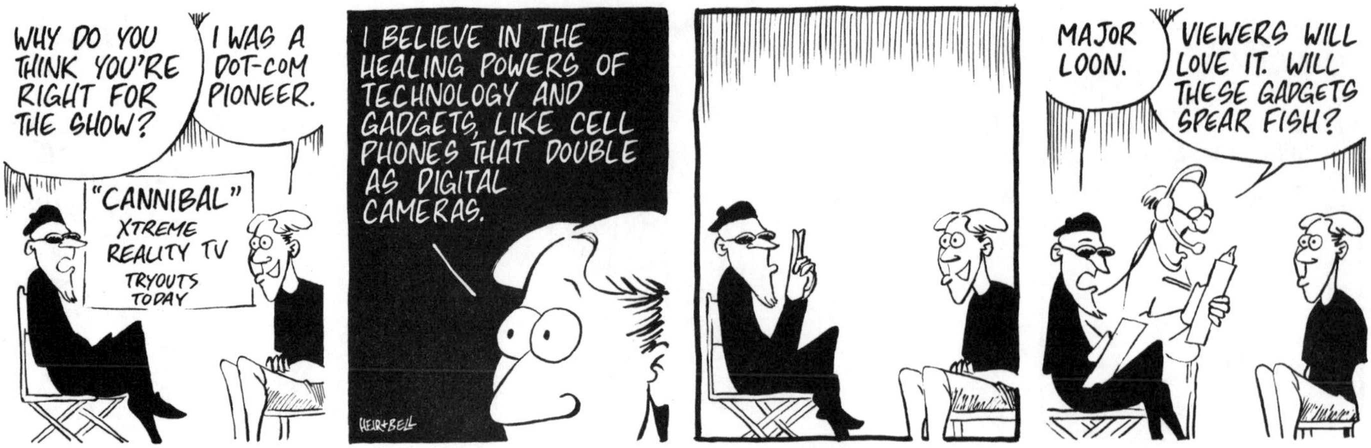
WHY DO YOU THINK YOU'RE RIGHT FOR THE SHOW?
I WAS A DOT-COM PIONEER.
"CANNIBAL" XTREME REALITY TV TRYOUTS TODAY
I BELIEVE IN THE HEALING POWERS OF TECHNOLOGY AND GADGETS, LIKE CELL PHONES THAT DOUBLE AS DIGITAL CAMERAS.
HEIR+BELL
MAJOR LOON.
VIEWERS WILL LOVE IT. WILL THESE GADGETS SPEAR FISH?

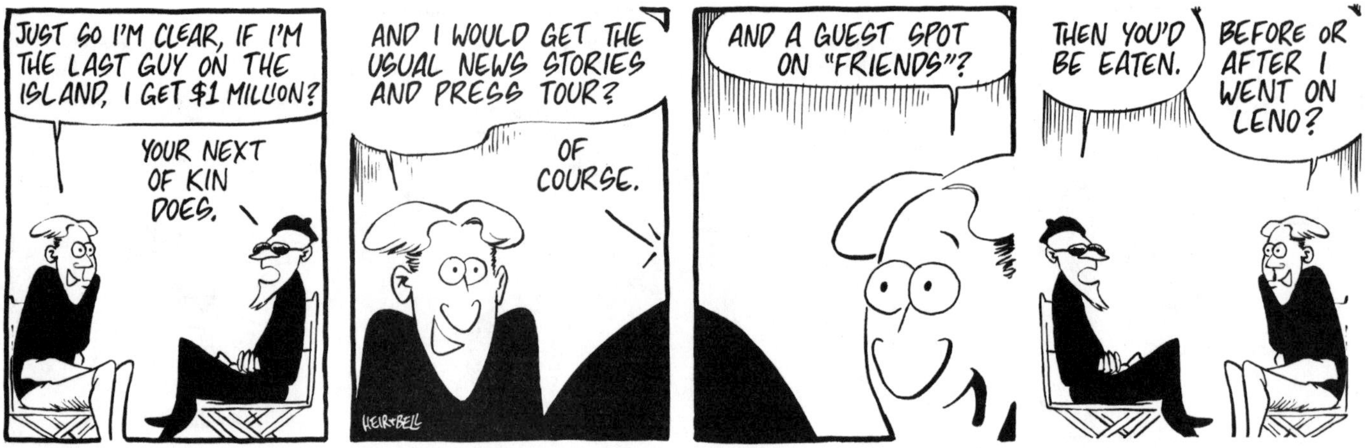
JUST SO I'M CLEAR, IF I'M THE LAST GUY ON THE ISLAND, I GET $1 MILLION?
YOUR NEXT OF KIN DOES.
AND I WOULD GET THE USUAL NEWS STORIES AND PRESS TOUR?
OF COURSE.
HEIR+BELL
AND A GUEST SPOT ON "FRIENDS"?
THEN YOU'D BE EATEN.
BEFORE OR AFTER I WENT ON LENO?

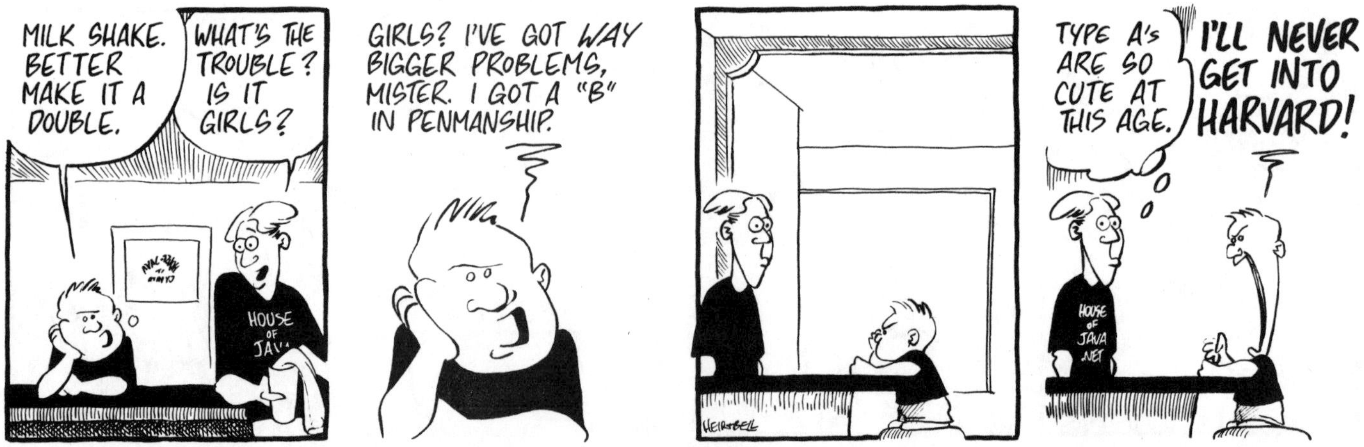
MILK SHAKE. BETTER MAKE IT A DOUBLE.
WHAT'S THE TROUBLE? IS IT GIRLS?
HOUSE OF JAVA
GIRLS? I'VE GOT WAY BIGGER PROBLEMS, MISTER. I GOT A "B" IN PENMANSHIP.
HEIR+BELL
TYPE A's ARE SO CUTE AT THIS AGE.
I'LL NEVER GET INTO HARVARD!
HOUSE OF JAVA .NET

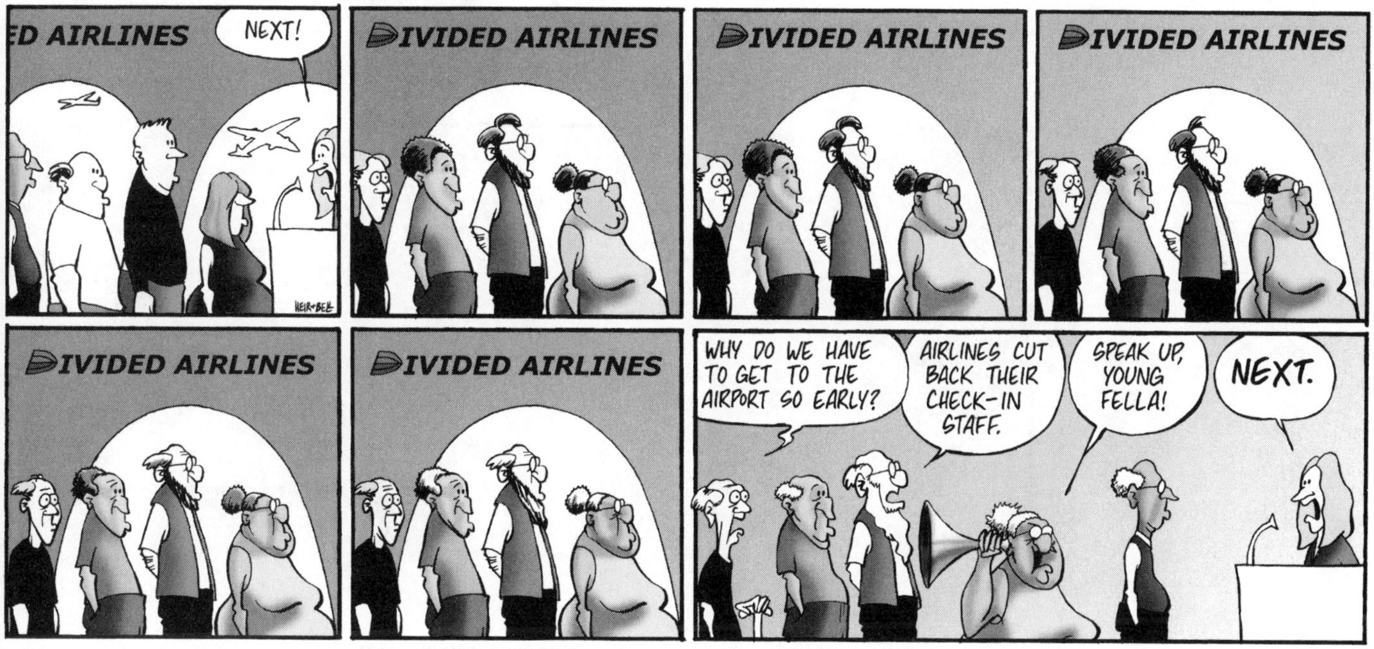
ED AIRLINES
NEXT!
DIVIDED AIRLINES
DIVIDED AIRLINES
DIVIDED AIRLINES
DIVIDED AIRLINES
DIVIDED AIRLINES
WHY DO WE HAVE TO GET TO THE AIRPORT SO EARLY?
AIRLINES CUT BACK THEIR CHECK-IN STAFF.
SPEAK UP, YOUNG FELLA!
NEXT.

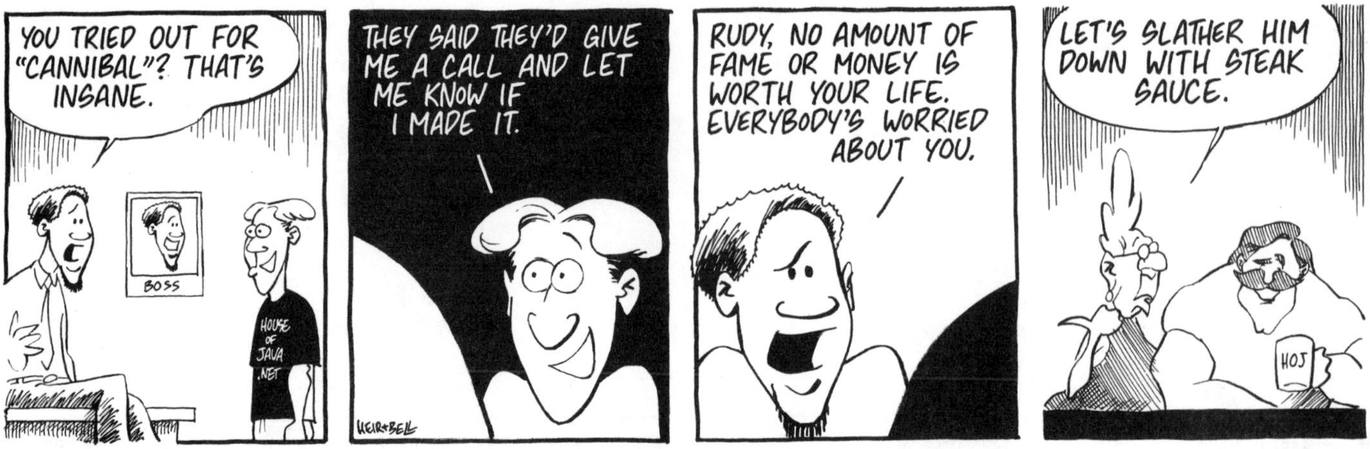
YOU TRIED OUT FOR "CANNIBAL"? THAT'S INSANE.
BOSS
HOUSE OF JAVA .NET
THEY SAID THEY'D GIVE ME A CALL AND LET ME KNOW IF I MADE IT.
HEIR+BELL
RUDY, NO AMOUNT OF FAME OR MONEY IS WORTH YOUR LIFE. EVERYBODY'S WORRIED ABOUT YOU.
LET'S SLATHER HIM DOWN WITH STEAK SAUCE.
HOJ

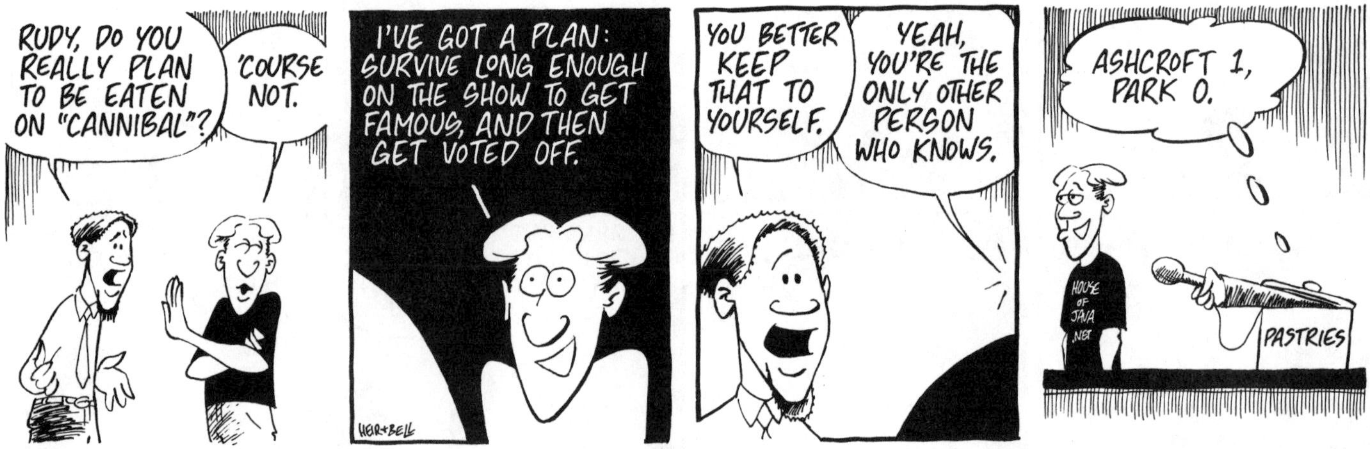
RUDY, DO YOU REALLY PLAN TO BE EATEN ON "CANNIBAL"?
'COURSE NOT.
I'VE GOT A PLAN: SURVIVE LONG ENOUGH ON THE SHOW TO GET FAMOUS, AND THEN GET VOTED OFF.
HEIR+BELL
YOU BETTER KEEP THAT TO YOURSELF.
YEAH, YOU'RE THE ONLY OTHER PERSON WHO KNOWS.
ASHCROFT 1, PARK 0.
HOUSE OF JAVA .NET
PASTRIES

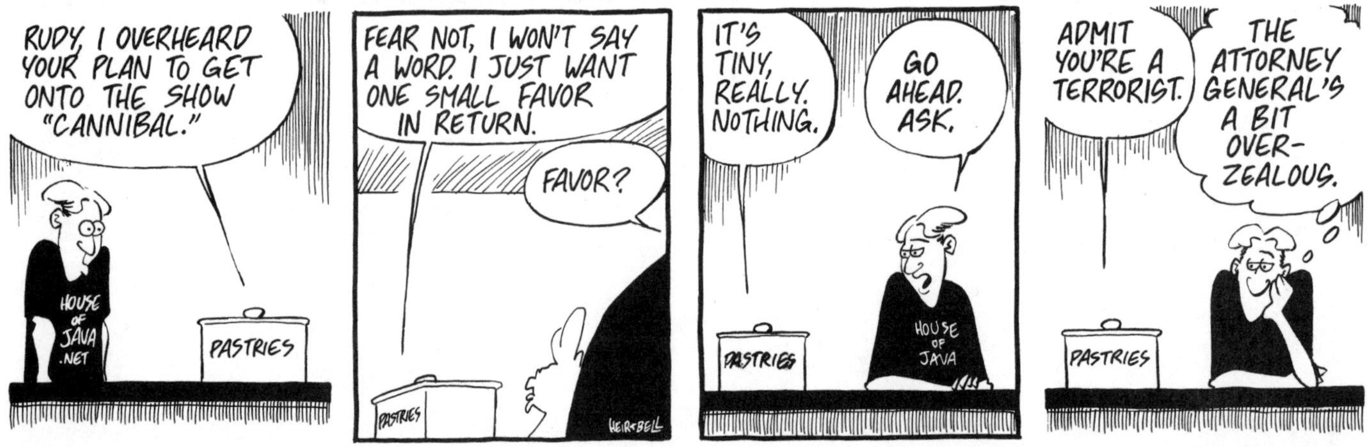
RUDY, I OVERHEARD YOUR PLAN TO GET ONTO THE SHOW "CANNIBAL."
HOUSE OF JAVA .NET
PASTRIES
FEAR NOT, I WON'T SAY A WORD. I JUST WANT ONE SMALL FAVOR IN RETURN.
FAVOR?
PASTRIES
HEIR+BELL
IT'S TINY, REALLY. NOTHING.
GO AHEAD. ASK.
PASTRIES
HOUSE OF JAVA
ADMIT YOU'RE A TERRORIST.
THE ATTORNEY GENERAL'S A BIT OVER-ZEALOUS.
PASTRIES

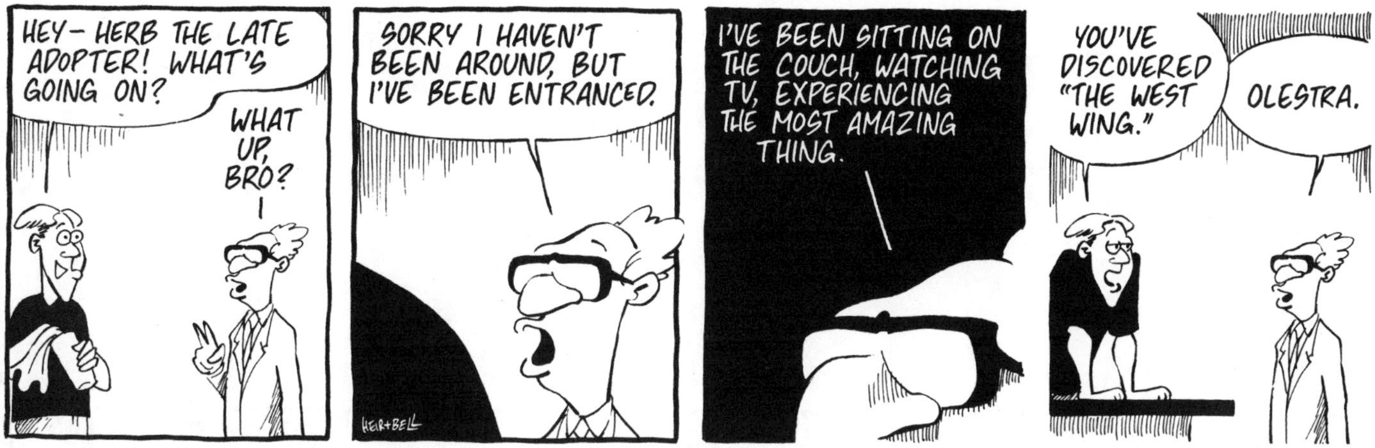
HEY– HERB THE LATE ADOPTER! WHAT'S GOING ON?
WHAT UP, BRO?
SORRY I HAVEN'T BEEN AROUND, BUT I'VE BEEN ENTRANCED.
I'VE BEEN SITTING ON THE COUCH, WATCHING TV, EXPERIENCING THE MOST AMAZING THING.
YOU'VE DISCOVERED "THE WEST WING."
OLESTRA.

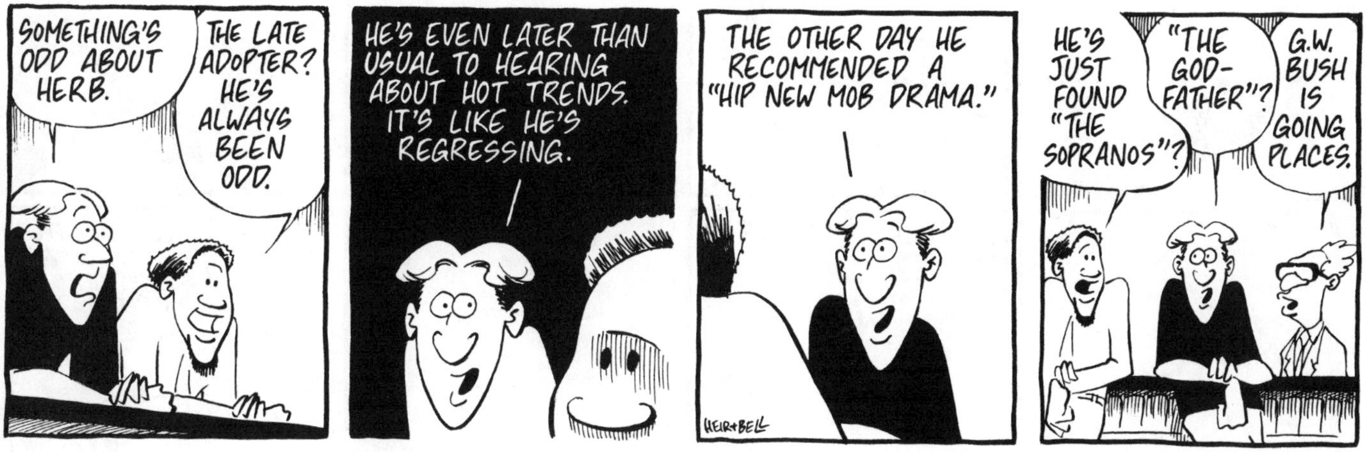
SOMETHING'S ODD ABOUT HERB.
THE LATE ADOPTER? HE'S ALWAYS BEEN ODD.
HE'S EVEN LATER THAN USUAL TO HEARING ABOUT HOT TRENDS. IT'S LIKE HE'S REGRESSING.
THE OTHER DAY HE RECOMMENDED A "HIP NEW MOB DRAMA."
HE'S JUST FOUND "THE SOPRANOS"?
"THE GOD-FATHER"?
G.W. BUSH IS GOING PLACES.

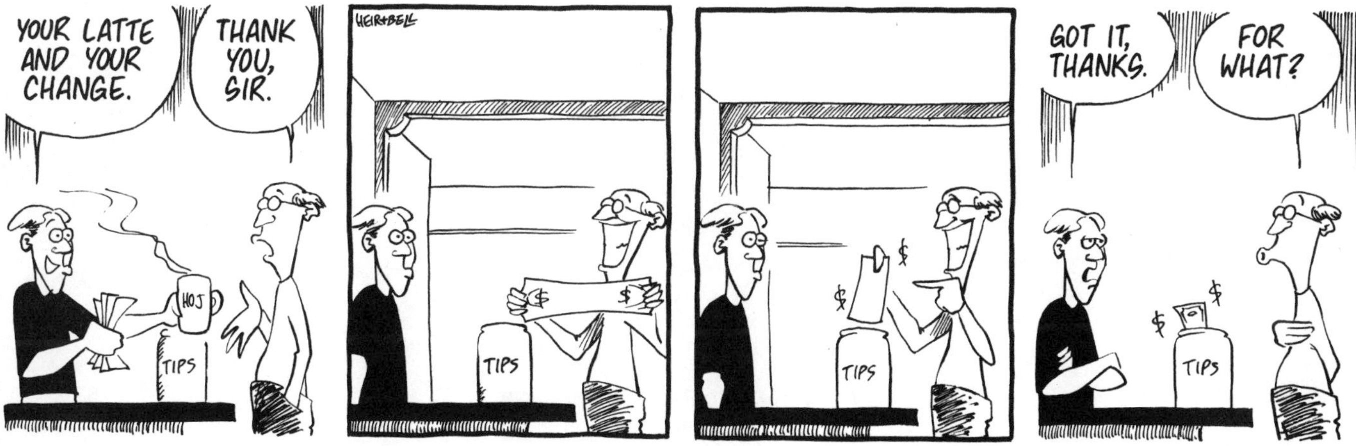
YOUR LATTE AND YOUR CHANGE.
THANK YOU, SIR.
TIPS
GOT IT, THANKS.
FOR WHAT?

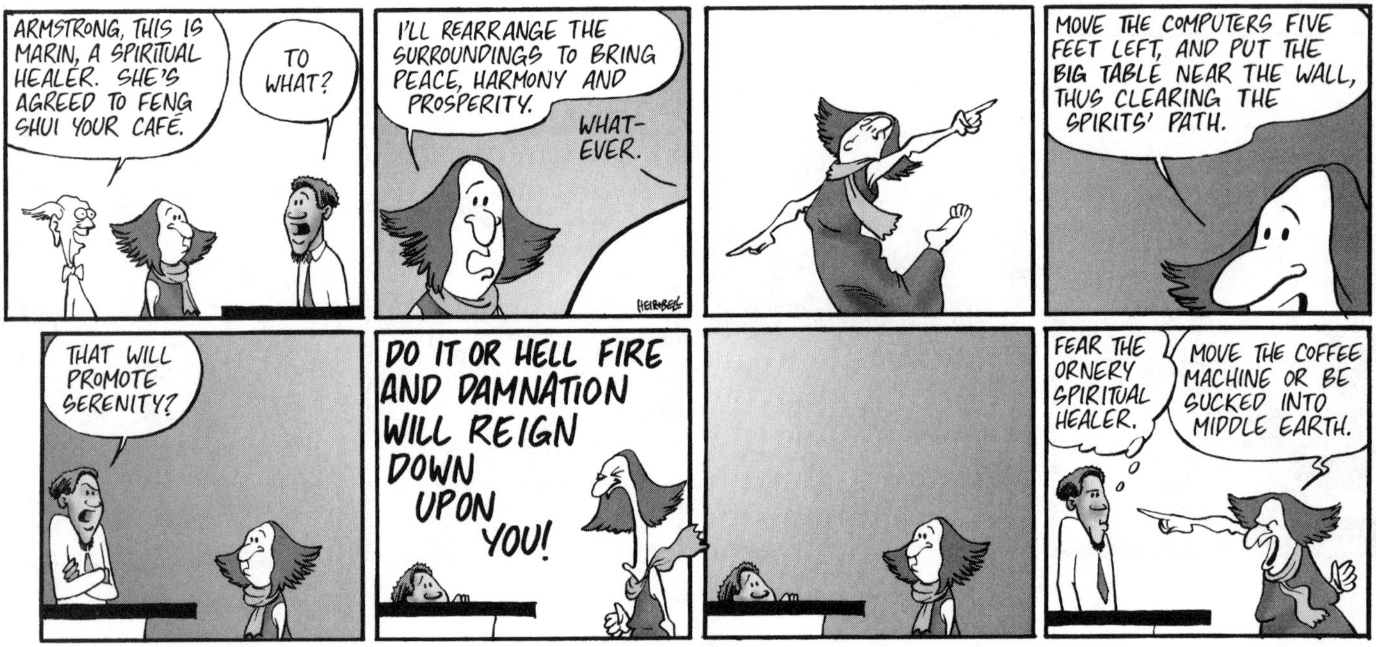
ARMSTRONG, THIS IS MARIN, A SPIRITUAL HEALER. SHE'S AGREED TO FENG SHUI YOUR CAFÉ.
TO WHAT?
I'LL REARRANGE THE SURROUNDINGS TO BRING PEACE, HARMONY AND PROSPERITY.
WHAT-EVER.
HEIRBELL
MOVE THE COMPUTERS FIVE FEET LEFT, AND PUT THE BIG TABLE NEAR THE WALL, THUS CLEARING THE SPIRITS' PATH.
THAT WILL PROMOTE SERENITY?
DO IT OR HELL FIRE AND DAMNATION WILL REIGN DOWN UPON YOU!
FEAR THE ORNERY SPIRITUAL HEALER.
MOVE THE COFFEE MACHINE OR BE SUCKED INTO MIDDLE EARTH.

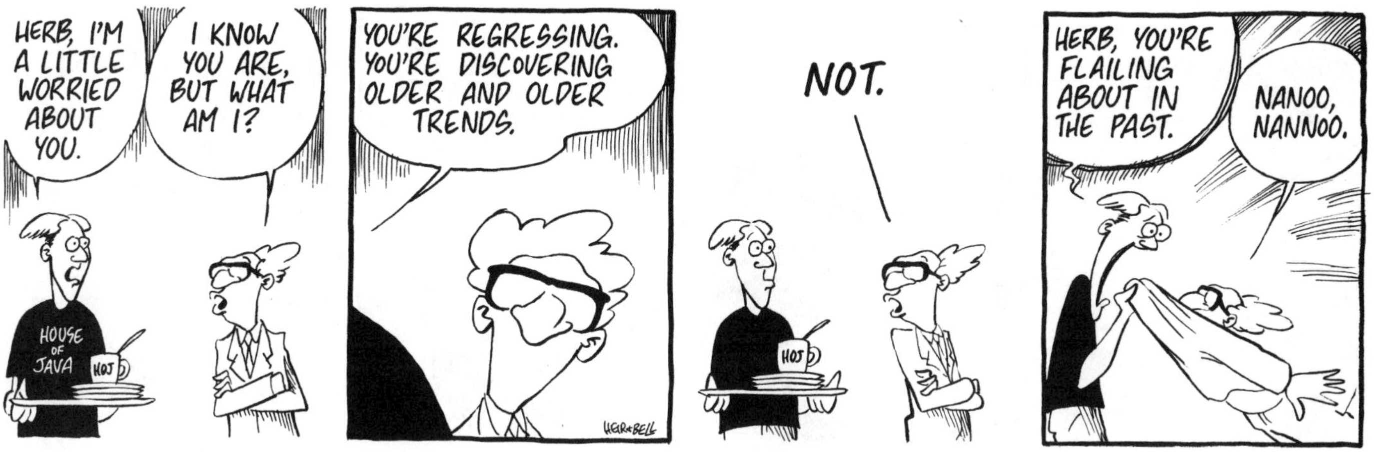
HERB, I'M A LITTLE WORRIED ABOUT YOU.
I KNOW YOU ARE, BUT WHAT AM I?
HOUSE OF JAVA
HOJ
YOU'RE REGRESSING. YOU'RE DISCOVERING OLDER AND OLDER TRENDS.
HEIR&BELL
NOT.
HOJ
HERB, YOU'RE FLAILING ABOUT IN THE PAST.
NANOO, NANNOO.

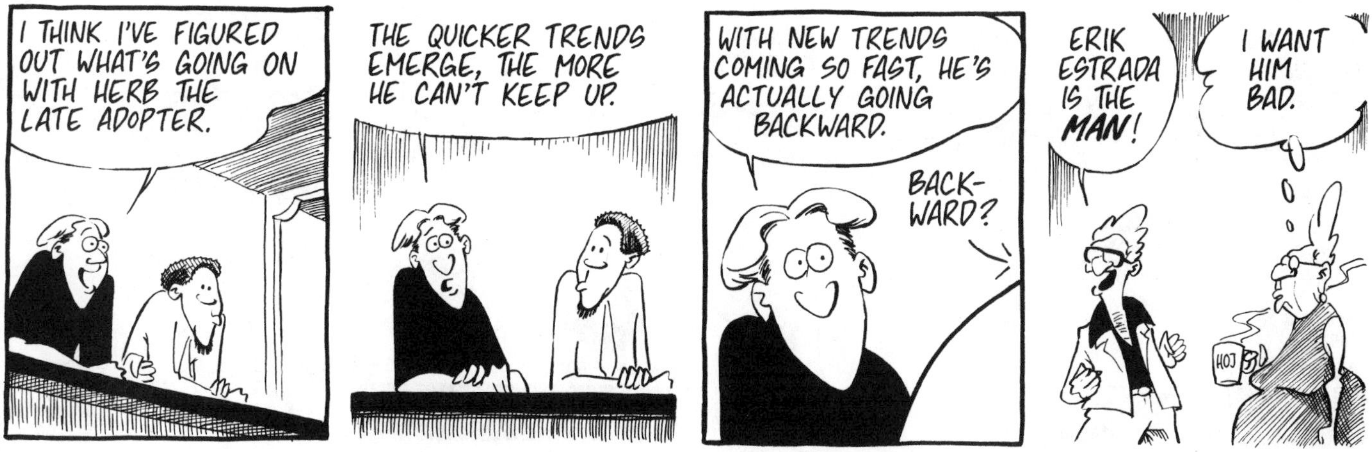
I THINK I'VE FIGURED OUT WHAT'S GOING ON WITH HERB THE LATE ADOPTER.
THE QUICKER TRENDS EMERGE, THE MORE HE CAN'T KEEP UP.
WITH NEW TRENDS COMING SO FAST, HE'S ACTUALLY GOING BACKWARD.
BACK-WARD?
ERIK ESTRADA IS THE **MAN**!
I WANT HIM BAD.
HOJ

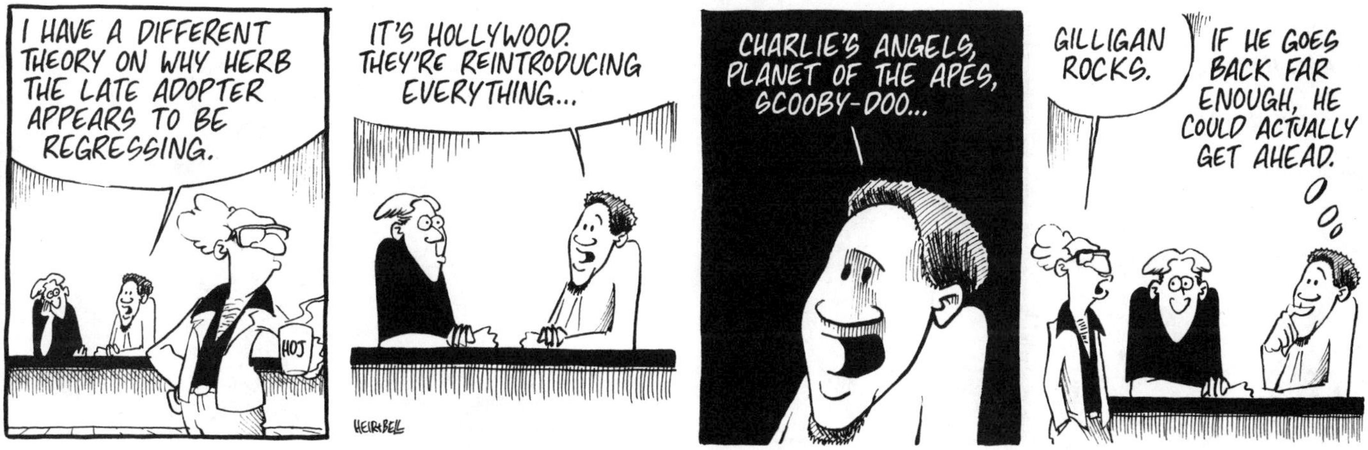
I HAVE A DIFFERENT THEORY ON WHY HERB THE LATE ADOPTER APPEARS TO BE REGRESSING.
HOJ
IT'S HOLLYWOOD. THEY'RE REINTRODUCING EVERYTHING...
HEIR&BELL
CHARLIE'S ANGELS, PLANET OF THE APES, SCOOBY-DOO...
GILLIGAN ROCKS.
IF HE GOES BACK FAR ENOUGH, HE COULD ACTUALLY GET AHEAD.

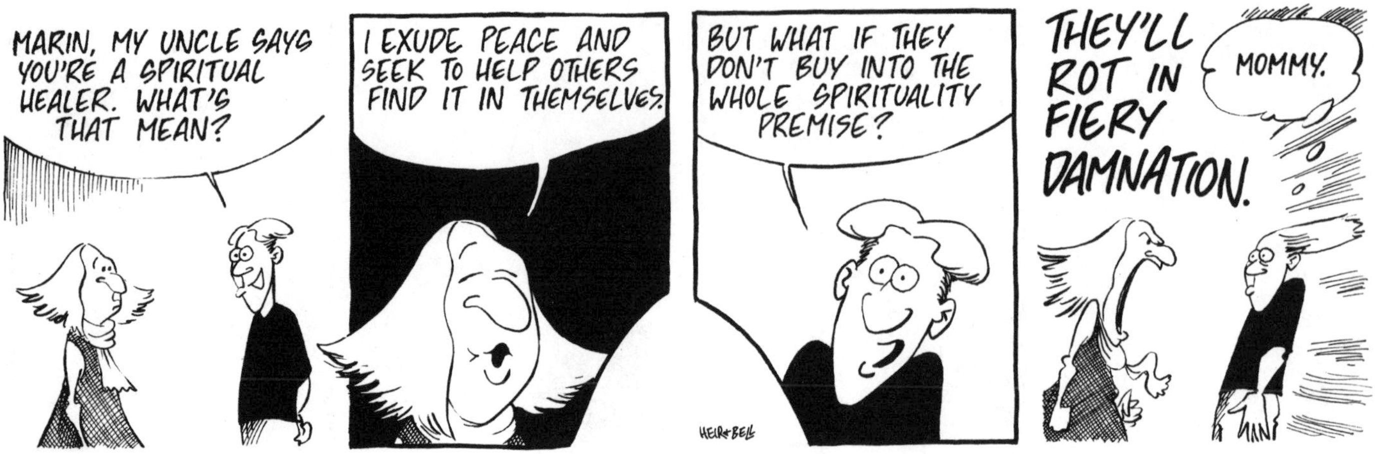
MARIN, MY UNCLE SAYS YOU'RE A SPIRITUAL HEALER. WHAT'S THAT MEAN?
I EXUDE PEACE AND SEEK TO HELP OTHERS FIND IT IN THEMSELVES.
BUT WHAT IF THEY DON'T BUY INTO THE WHOLE SPIRITUALITY PREMISE?
THEY'LL ROT IN FIERY DAMNATION.
MOMMY.
HEIR+BELL

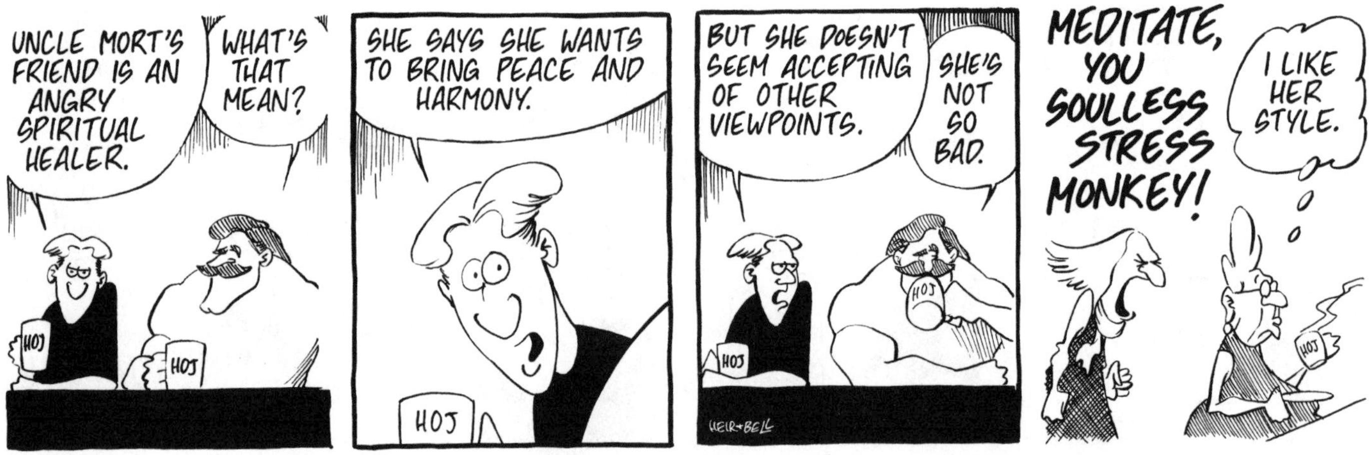
UNCLE MORT'S FRIEND IS AN ANGRY SPIRITUAL HEALER.
WHAT'S THAT MEAN?
HOJ
HOJ
SHE SAYS SHE WANTS TO BRING PEACE AND HARMONY.
HOJ
BUT SHE DOESN'T SEEM ACCEPTING OF OTHER VIEWPOINTS.
SHE'S NOT SO BAD.
HOJ
HOJ
HEIR+BELL
MEDITATE, YOU SOULLESS STRESS MONKEY!
I LIKE HER STYLE.
HOJ

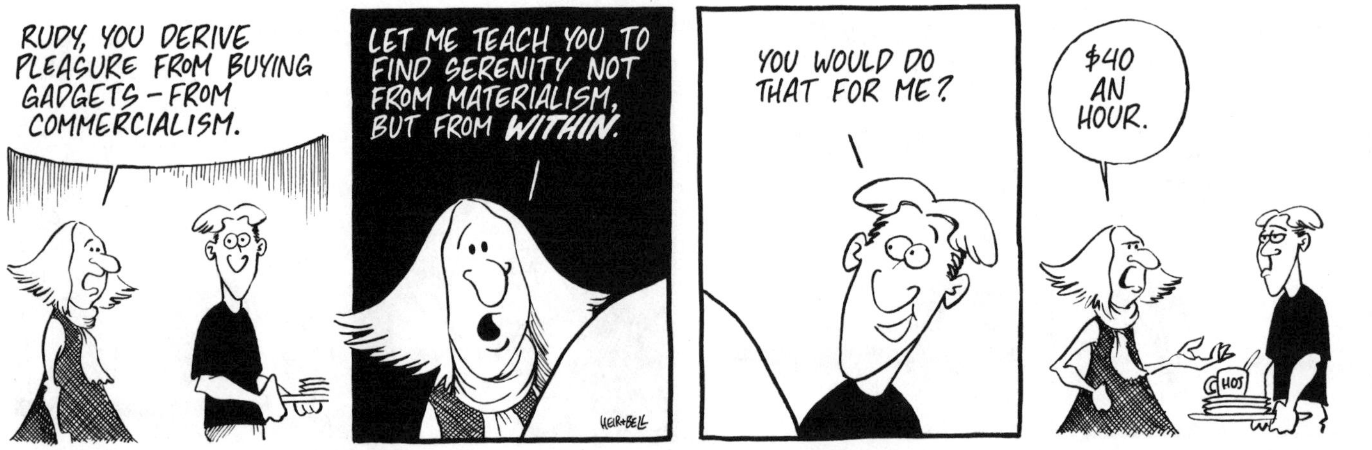
RUDY, YOU DERIVE PLEASURE FROM BUYING GADGETS—FROM COMMERCIALISM.
LET ME TEACH YOU TO FIND SERENITY NOT FROM MATERIALISM, BUT FROM WITHIN.
HEIR+BELL
YOU WOULD DO THAT FOR ME?
$40 AN HOUR.
HOJ

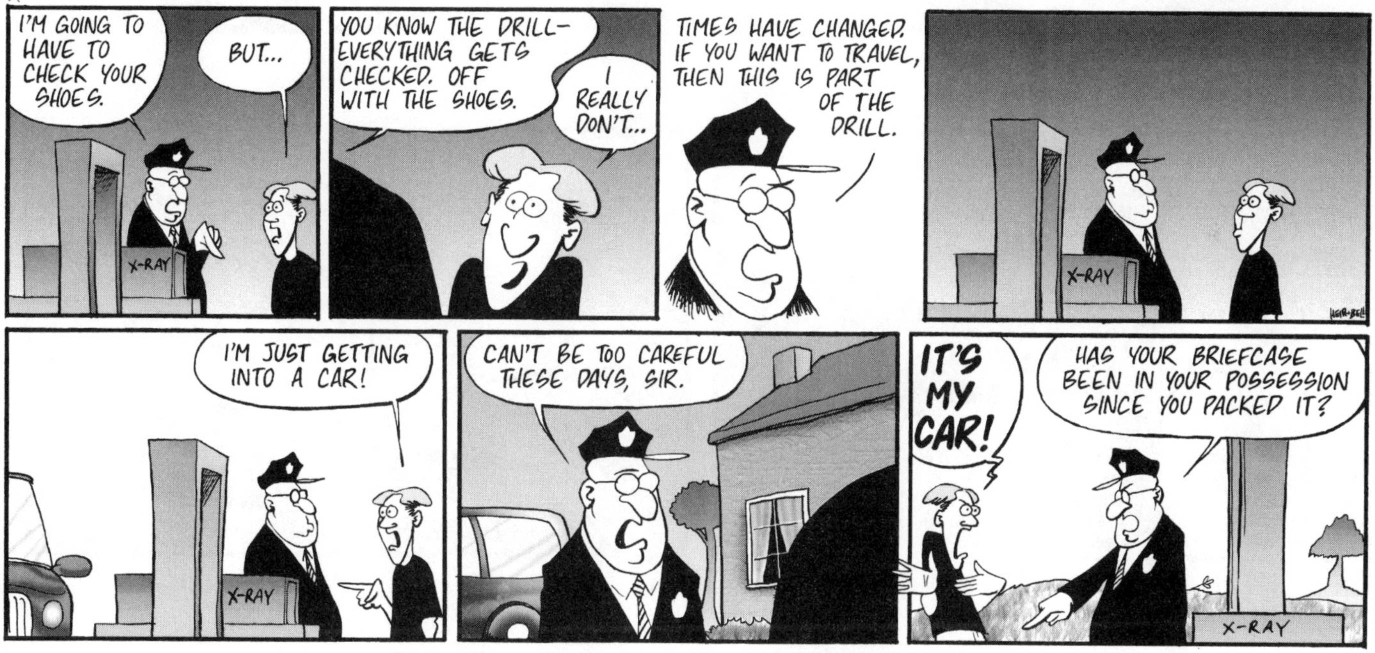
I'M GOING TO HAVE TO CHECK YOUR SHOES.
BUT...
YOU KNOW THE DRILL– EVERYTHING GETS CHECKED. OFF WITH THE SHOES.
I REALLY DON'T...
TIMES HAVE CHANGED. IF YOU WANT TO TRAVEL, THEN THIS IS PART OF THE DRILL.
X-RAY
X-RAY
I'M JUST GETTING INTO A CAR!
X-RAY
CAN'T BE TOO CAREFUL THESE DAYS, SIR.
IT'S MY CAR!
HAS YOUR BRIEFCASE BEEN IN YOUR POSSESSION SINCE YOU PACKED IT?
X-RAY

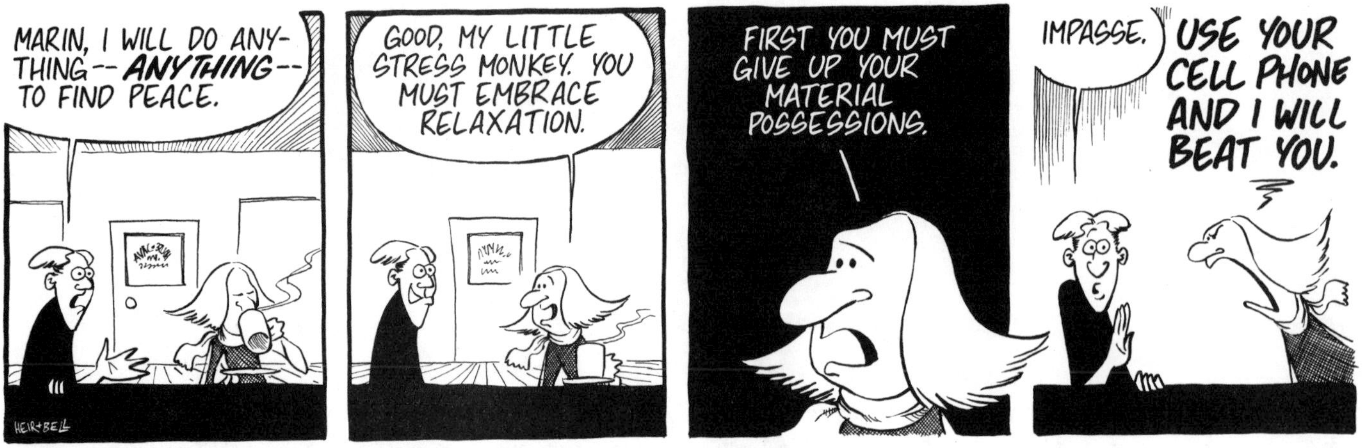
MARIN, I WILL DO ANYTHING-- ***ANYTHING***-- TO FIND PEACE.
GOOD, MY LITTLE STRESS MONKEY. YOU MUST EMBRACE RELAXATION.
FIRST YOU MUST GIVE UP YOUR MATERIAL POSSESSIONS.
IMPASSE.
USE YOUR CELL PHONE AND I WILL BEAT YOU.
HEIR+BELL

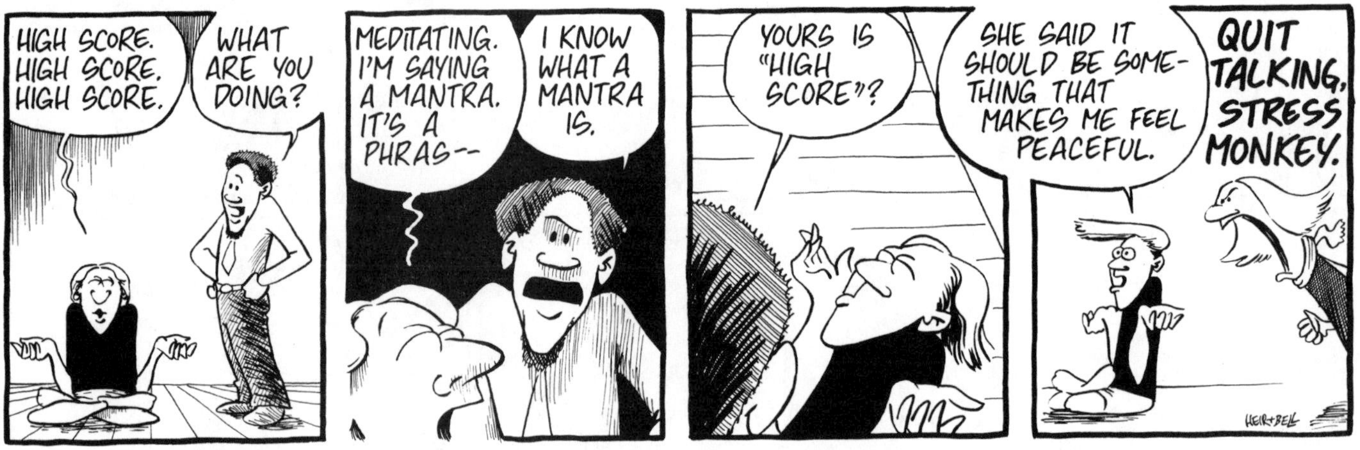
HIGH SCORE. HIGH SCORE. HIGH SCORE.
WHAT ARE YOU DOING?
MEDITATING. I'M SAYING A MANTRA. IT'S A PHRAS--
I KNOW WHAT A MANTRA IS.
YOURS IS "HIGH SCORE"?
SHE SAID IT SHOULD BE SOMETHING THAT MAKES ME FEEL PEACEFUL.
QUIT TALKING, STRESS MONKEY.
HEIR+BELL

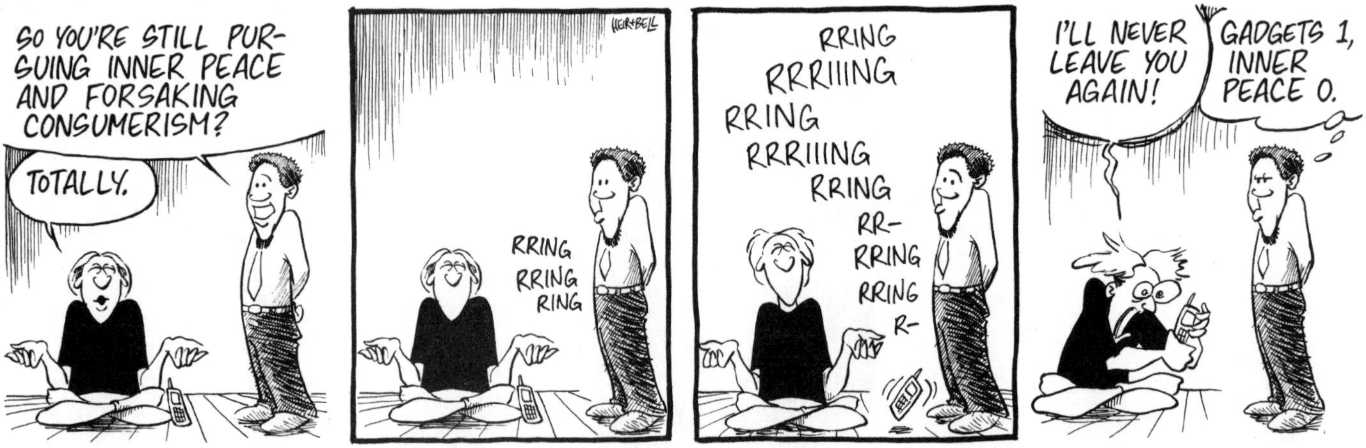
SO YOU'RE STILL PURSUING INNER PEACE AND FORSAKING CONSUMERISM?
TOTALLY.
HEIR+BELL
RRING RRING RING
RRING RRRIIING RRING RRRIIING RRING RR- RRING RRING R-
I'LL NEVER LEAVE YOU AGAIN!
GADGETS 1, INNER PEACE 0.

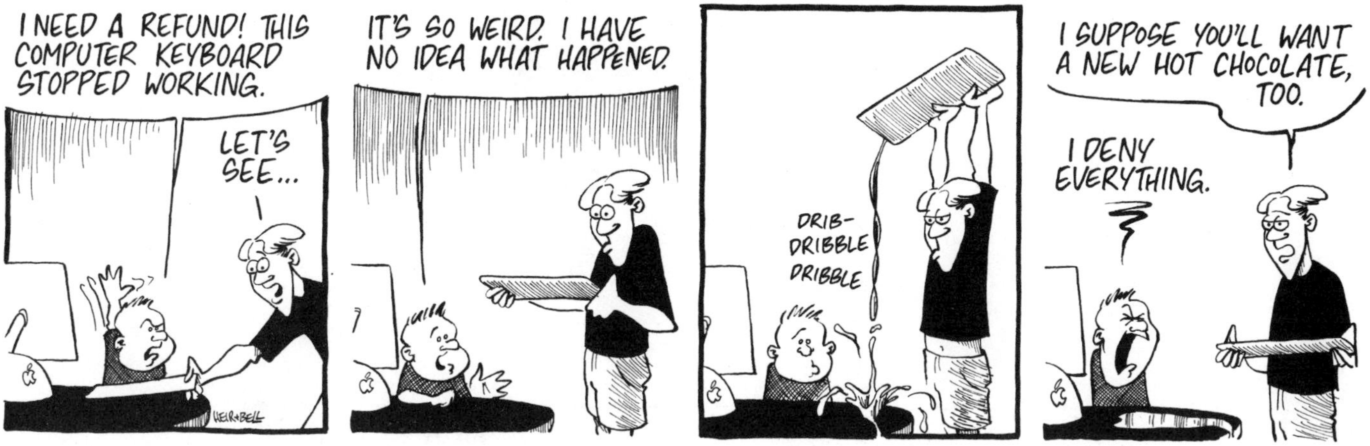
I NEED A REFUND! THIS COMPUTER KEYBOARD STOPPED WORKING.
LET'S SEE...
IT'S SO WEIRD. I HAVE NO IDEA WHAT HAPPENED.
DRIB-DRIBBLE DRIBBLE
I DENY EVERYTHING.
I SUPPOSE YOU'LL WANT A NEW HOT CHOCOLATE, TOO.
HEIR+BELL

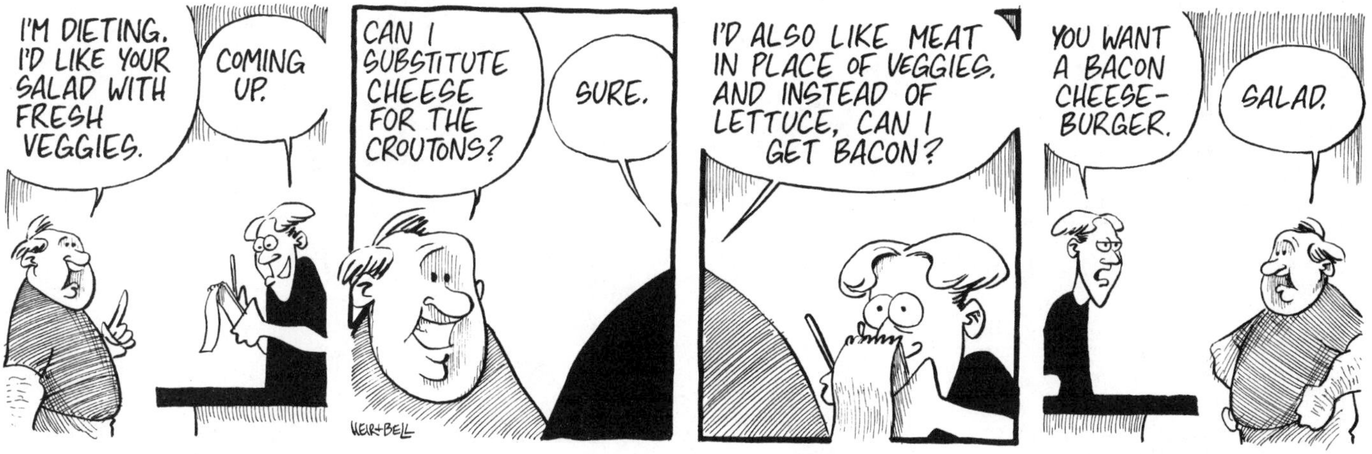
I'M DIETING. I'D LIKE YOUR SALAD WITH FRESH VEGGIES.
COMING UP.
CAN I SUBSTITUTE CHEESE FOR THE CROUTONS?
SURE.
I'D ALSO LIKE MEAT IN PLACE OF VEGGIES. AND INSTEAD OF LETTUCE, CAN I GET BACON?
YOU WANT A BACON CHEESE-BURGER.
SALAD.
HEIR+BELL

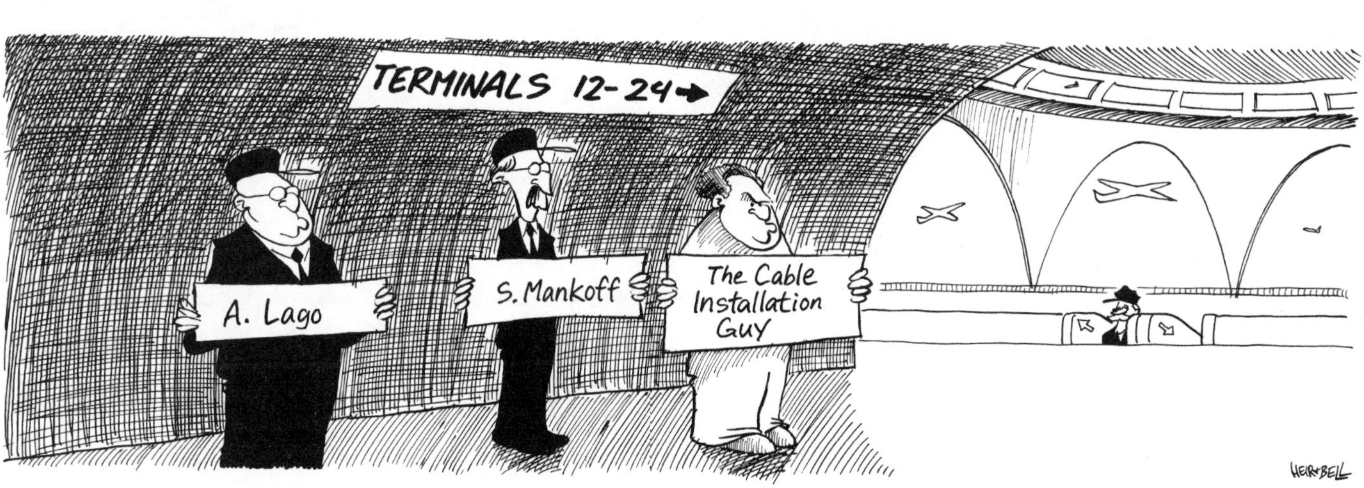
TERMINALS 12-24
A. Lago
S. Mankoff
The Cable Installation Guy
HEIR+BELL

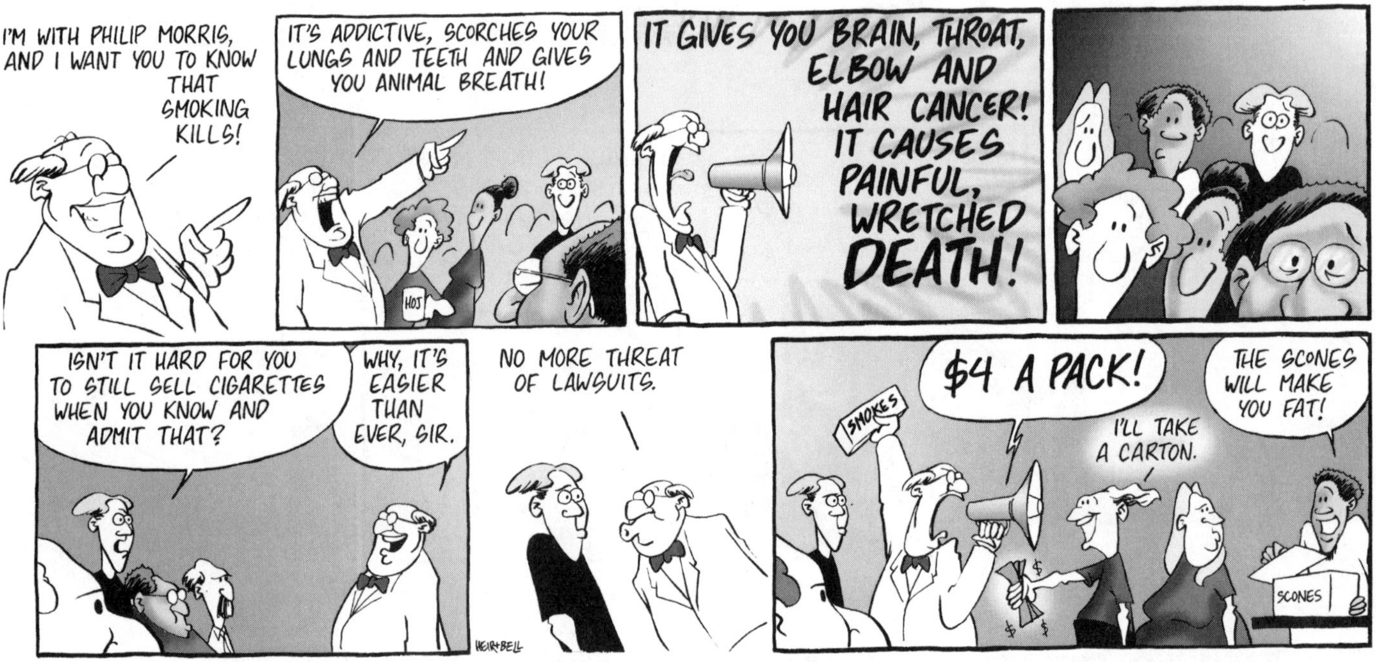
I'M WITH PHILIP MORRIS, AND I WANT YOU TO KNOW THAT SMOKING KILLS!
IT'S ADDICTIVE, SCORCHES YOUR LUNGS AND TEETH AND GIVES YOU ANIMAL BREATH!
HOJ
IT GIVES YOU BRAIN, THROAT, ELBOW AND HAIR CANCER! IT CAUSES PAINFUL, WRETCHED DEATH!
ISN'T IT HARD FOR YOU TO STILL SELL CIGARETTES WHEN YOU KNOW AND ADMIT THAT?
WHY, IT'S EASIER THAN EVER, SIR.
HEIR+BELL
NO MORE THREAT OF LAWSUITS.
SMOKES
$4 A PACK!
I'LL TAKE A CARTON.
THE SCONES WILL MAKE YOU FAT!
SCONES

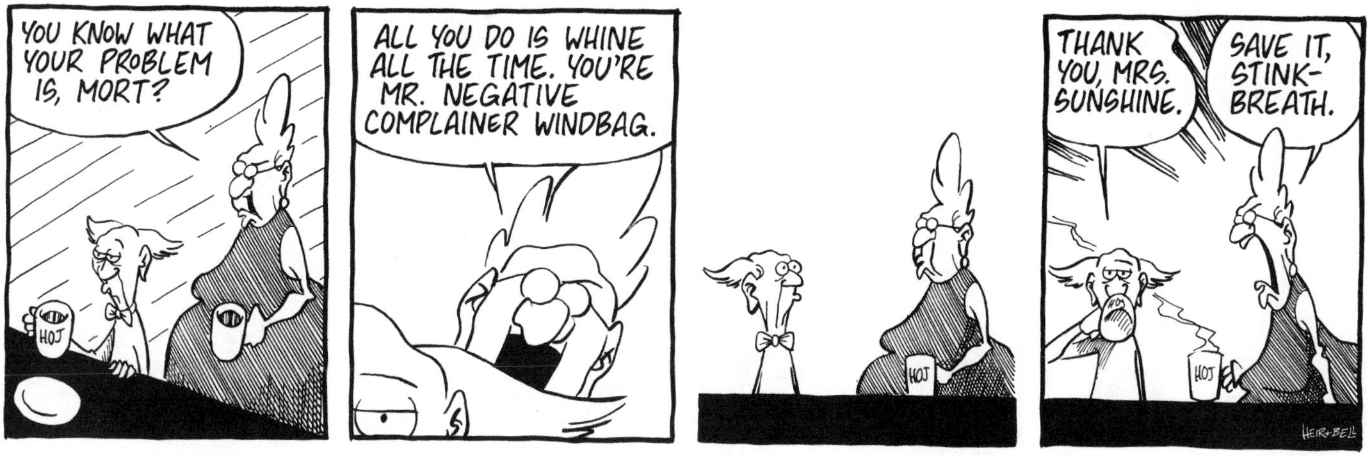
YOU KNOW WHAT YOUR PROBLEM IS, MORT?
HOJ
HOJ
ALL YOU DO IS WHINE ALL THE TIME. YOU'RE MR. NEGATIVE COMPLAINER WINDBAG.
HOJ
THANK YOU, MRS. SUNSHINE.
SAVE IT, STINK-BREATH.
HOJ
HEIR+BELL

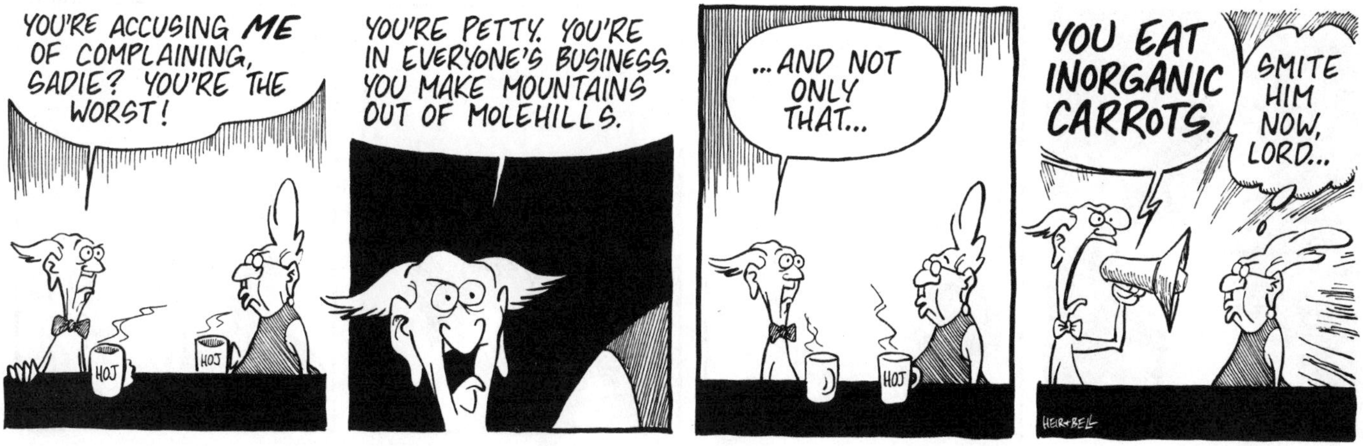
YOU'RE ACCUSING **ME** OF COMPLAINING, SADIE? YOU'RE THE WORST!
HOJ
HOJ
YOU'RE PETTY. YOU'RE IN EVERYONE'S BUSINESS. YOU MAKE MOUNTAINS OUT OF MOLEHILLS.
...AND NOT ONLY THAT...
HOJ
YOU EAT INORGANIC CARROTS.
SMITE HIM NOW, LORD...
HEIR+BELL

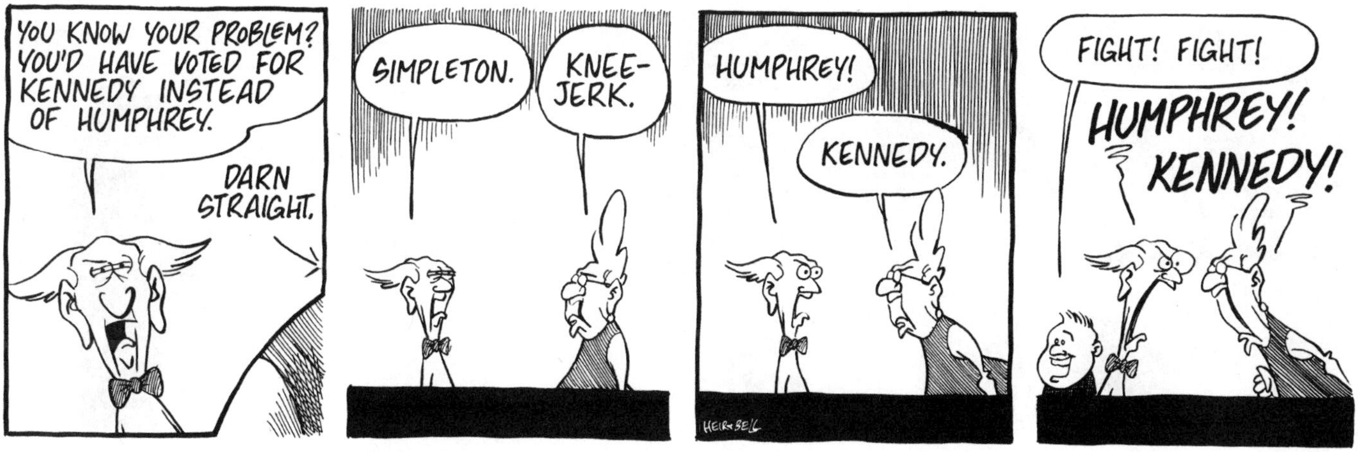
YOU KNOW YOUR PROBLEM? YOU'D HAVE VOTED FOR KENNEDY INSTEAD OF HUMPHREY.
DARN STRAIGHT.
SIMPLETON.
KNEE-JERK.
HUMPHREY!
KENNEDY.
HEIR+BELL
FIGHT! FIGHT!
HUMPHREY!
KENNEDY!

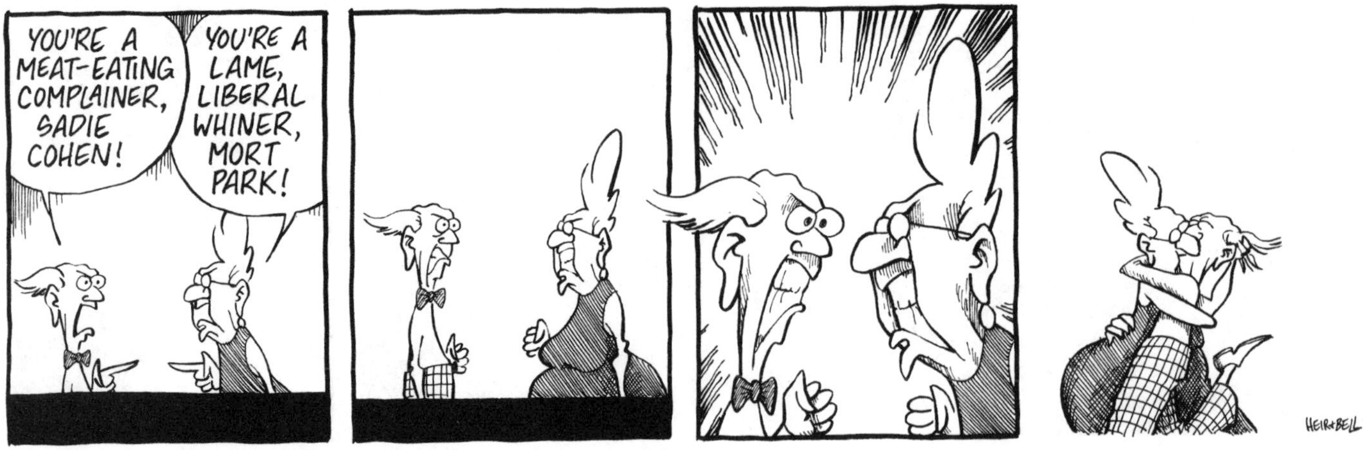
YOU'RE A MEAT-EATING COMPLAINER, SADIE COHEN!
YOU'RE A LAME, LIBERAL WHINER, MORT PARK!
HEIR+BELL

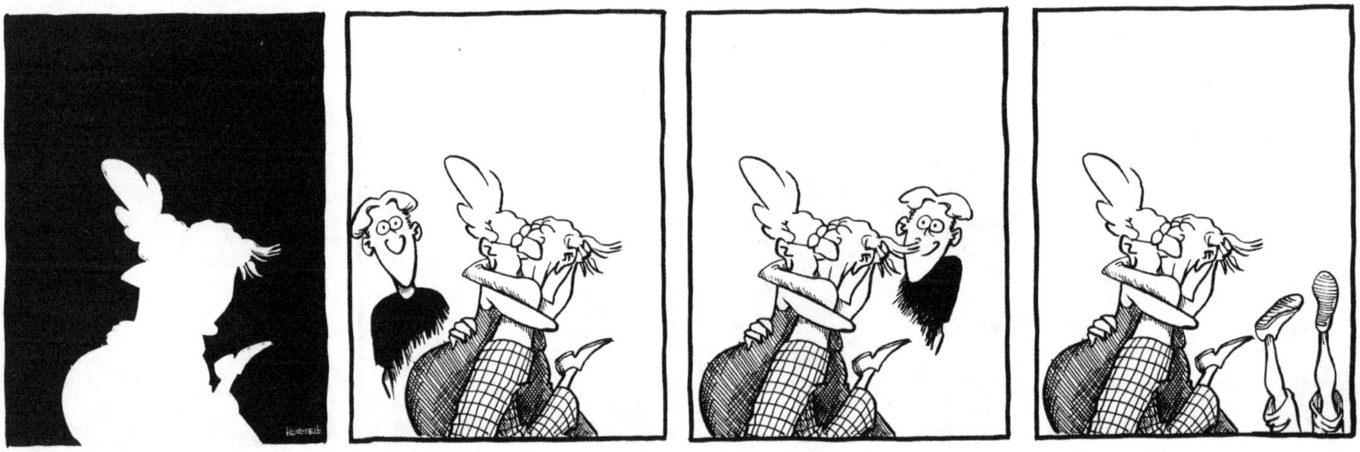

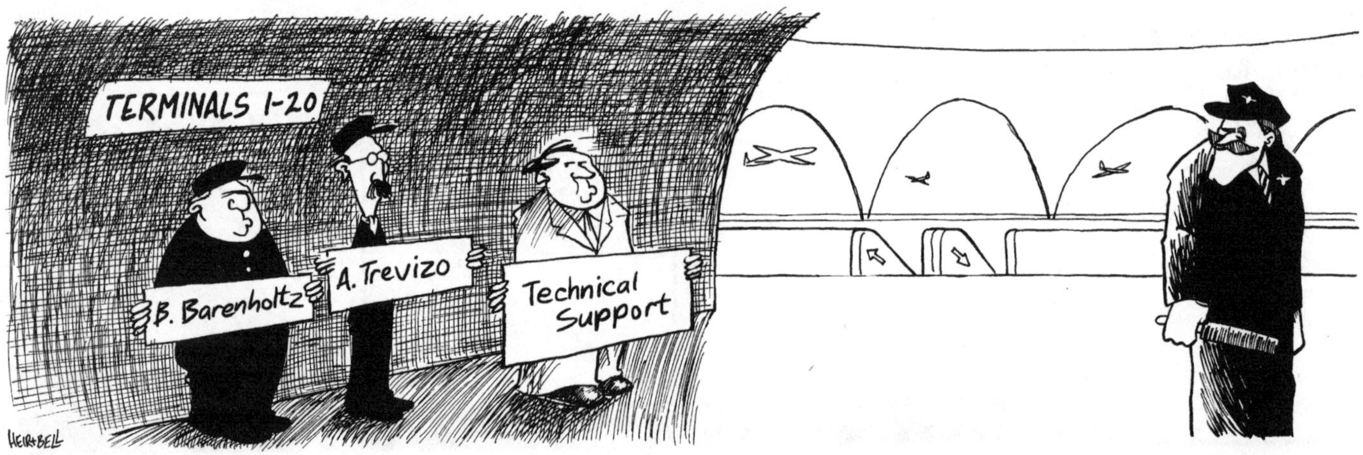
TERMINALS 1-20
B. Barenholtz
A. Trevizo
Technical Support
HEIR+BELL

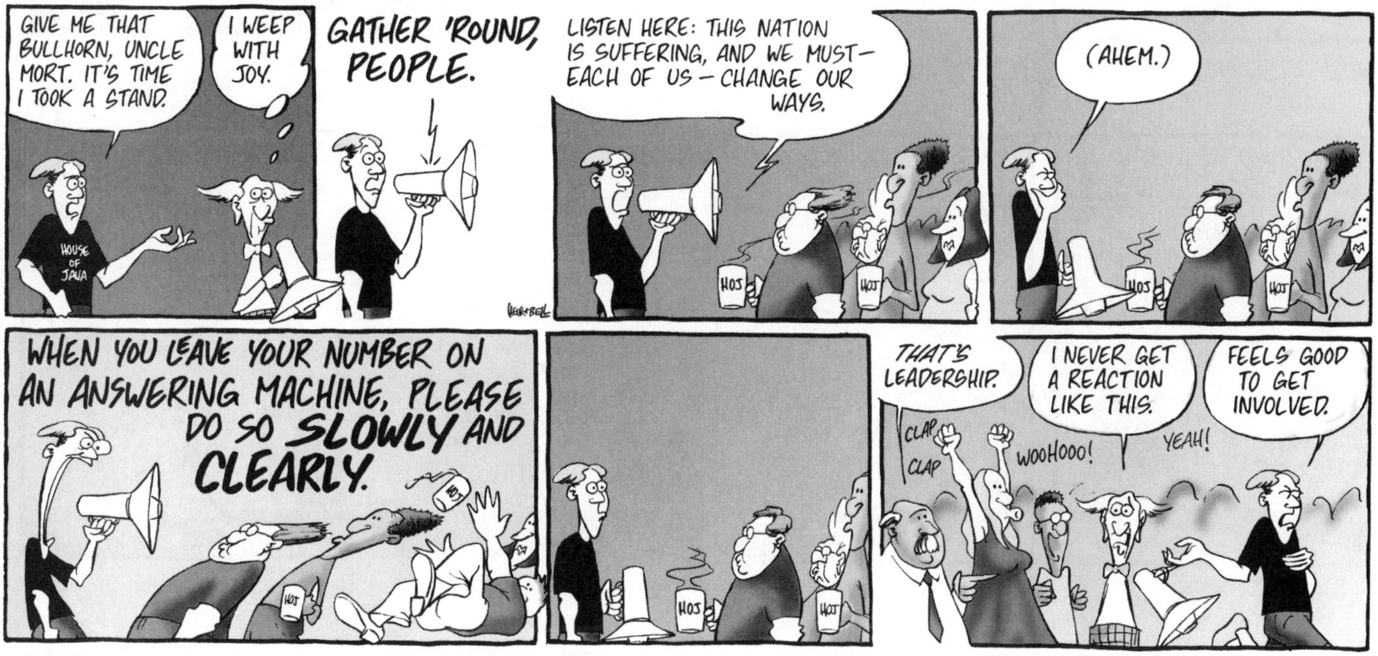
GIVE ME THAT BULLHORN, UNCLE MORT. IT'S TIME I TOOK A STAND.
I WEEP WITH JOY.
HOUSE OF JAVA
GATHER 'ROUND, PEOPLE.
LISTEN HERE: THIS NATION IS SUFFERING, AND WE MUST— EACH OF US — CHANGE OUR WAYS.
(AHEM.)
WHEN YOU LEAVE YOUR NUMBER ON AN ANSWERING MACHINE, PLEASE DO SO SLOWLY AND CLEARLY.
THAT'S LEADERSHIP.
I NEVER GET A REACTION LIKE THIS.
FEELS GOOD TO GET INVOLVED.
CLAP
CLAP
WOOHOOO!
YEAH!

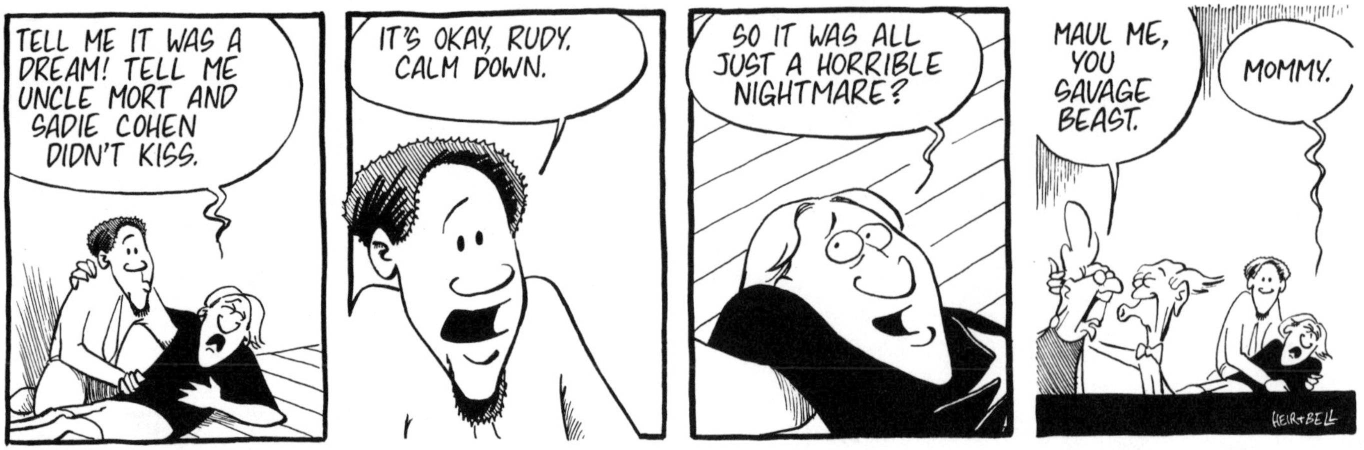
TELL ME IT WAS A DREAM! TELL ME UNCLE MORT AND SADIE COHEN DIDN'T KISS.
IT'S OKAY, RUDY. CALM DOWN.
SO IT WAS ALL JUST A HORRIBLE NIGHTMARE?
MAUL ME, YOU SAVAGE BEAST.
MOMMY.
HEIR+BELL

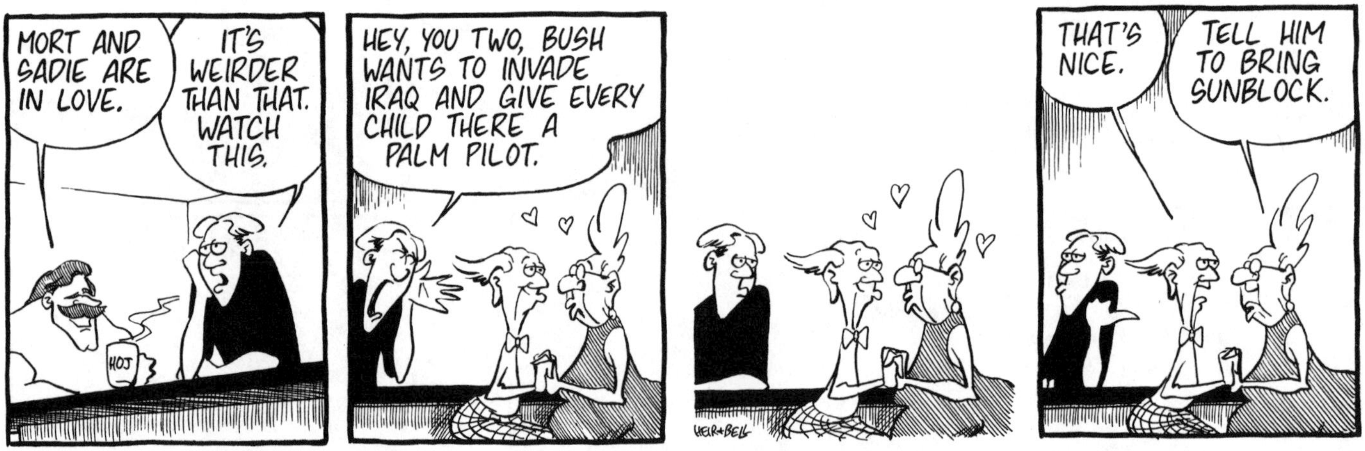
MORT AND SADIE ARE IN LOVE.
IT'S WEIRDER THAN THAT. WATCH THIS.
HOJ
HEY, YOU TWO, BUSH WANTS TO INVADE IRAQ AND GIVE EVERY CHILD THERE A PALM PILOT.
HEIR+BELL
THAT'S NICE.
TELL HIM TO BRING SUNBLOCK.

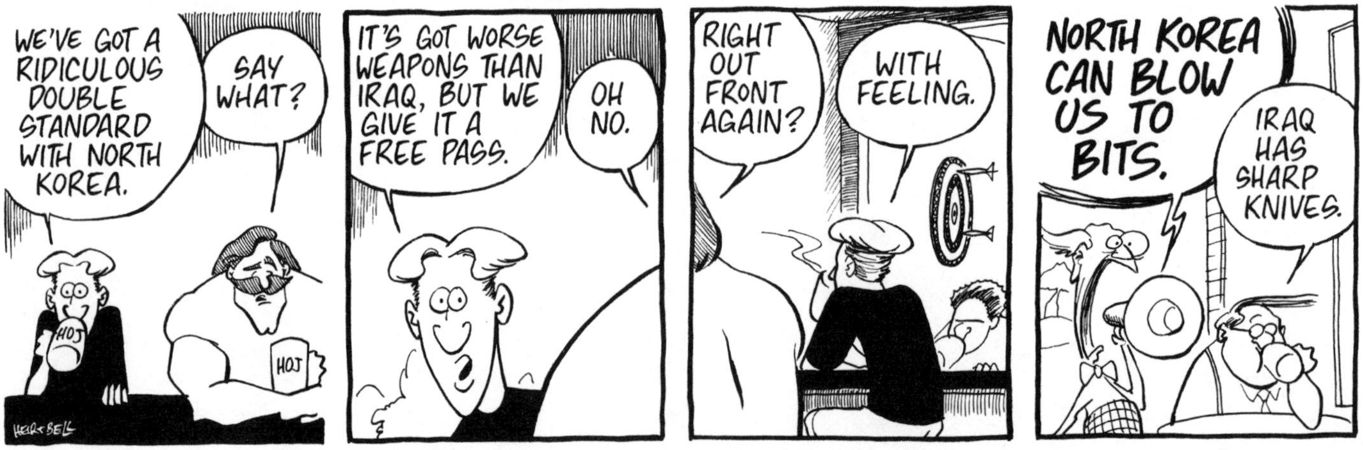
WE'VE GOT A RIDICULOUS DOUBLE STANDARD WITH NORTH KOREA.
SAY WHAT?
HOJ
HOJ
HEIR+BELL
IT'S GOT WORSE WEAPONS THAN IRAQ, BUT WE GIVE IT A FREE PASS.
OH NO.
RIGHT OUT FRONT AGAIN?
WITH FEELING.
NORTH KOREA CAN BLOW US TO BITS.
IRAQ HAS SHARP KNIVES.

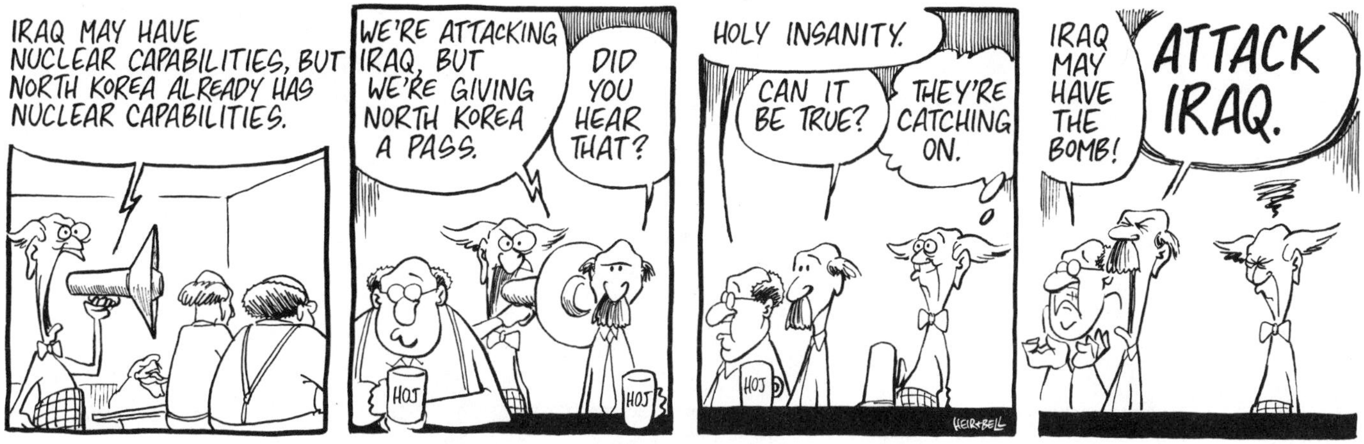
IRAQ MAY HAVE NUCLEAR CAPABILITIES, BUT NORTH KOREA ALREADY HAS NUCLEAR CAPABILITIES.
WE'RE ATTACKING IRAQ, BUT WE'RE GIVING NORTH KOREA A PASS.
DID YOU HEAR THAT?
HOJ
HOJ
HOLY INSANITY.
CAN IT BE TRUE?
THEY'RE CATCHING ON.
HOJ
HEIR+BELL
IRAQ MAY HAVE THE BOMB!
ATTACK IRAQ.

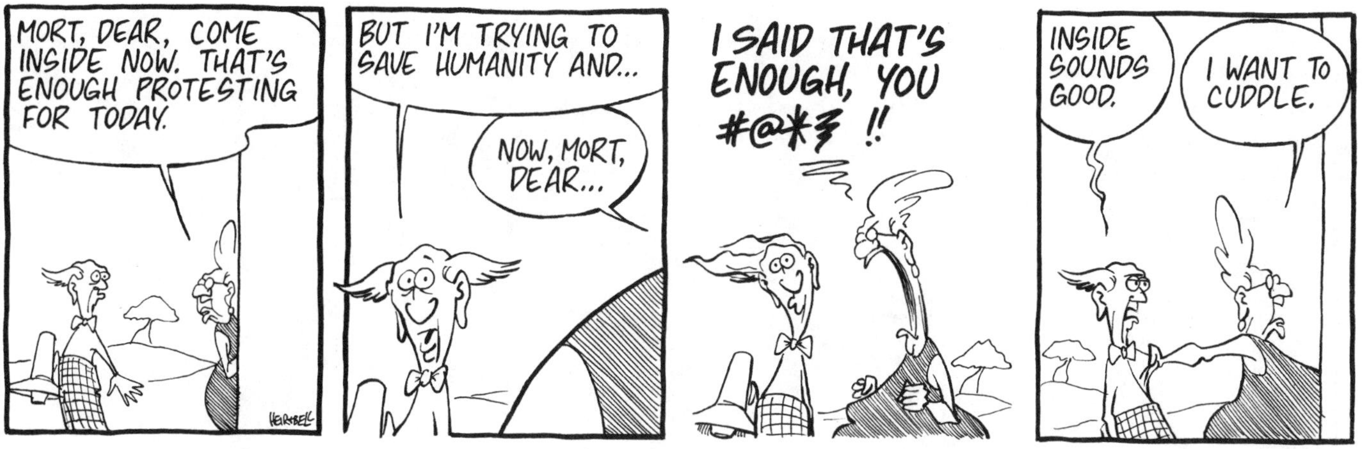
MORT, DEAR, COME INSIDE NOW. THAT'S ENOUGH PROTESTING FOR TODAY.
HEIR+BELL
BUT I'M TRYING TO SAVE HUMANITY AND...
NOW, MORT, DEAR...
I SAID THAT'S ENOUGH, YOU #@* !!
INSIDE SOUNDS GOOD.
I WANT TO CUDDLE.

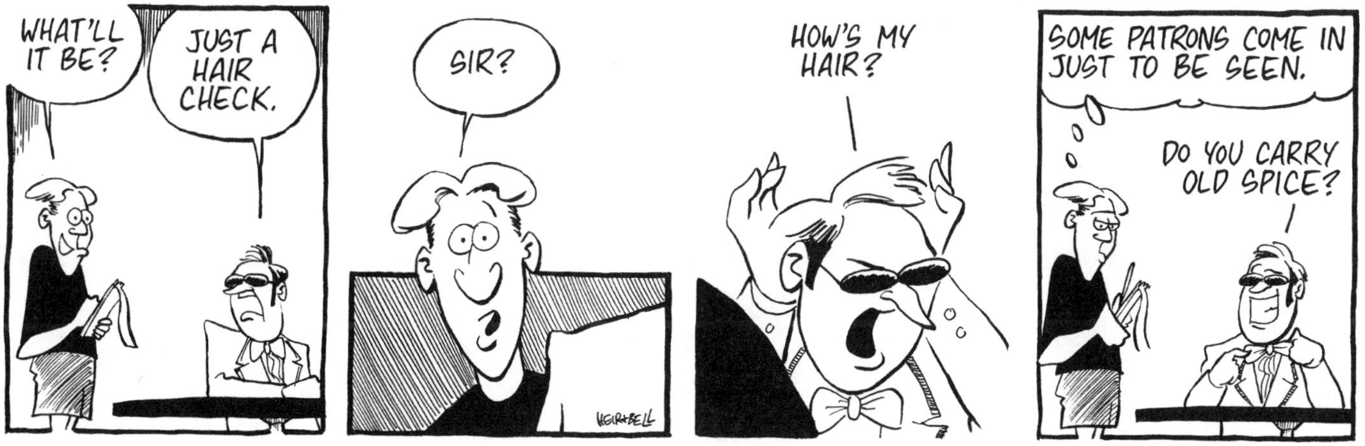
WHAT'LL IT BE?
JUST A HAIR CHECK.
SIR?
HEIR+BELL
HOW'S MY HAIR?
SOME PATRONS COME IN JUST TO BE SEEN.
DO YOU CARRY OLD SPICE?

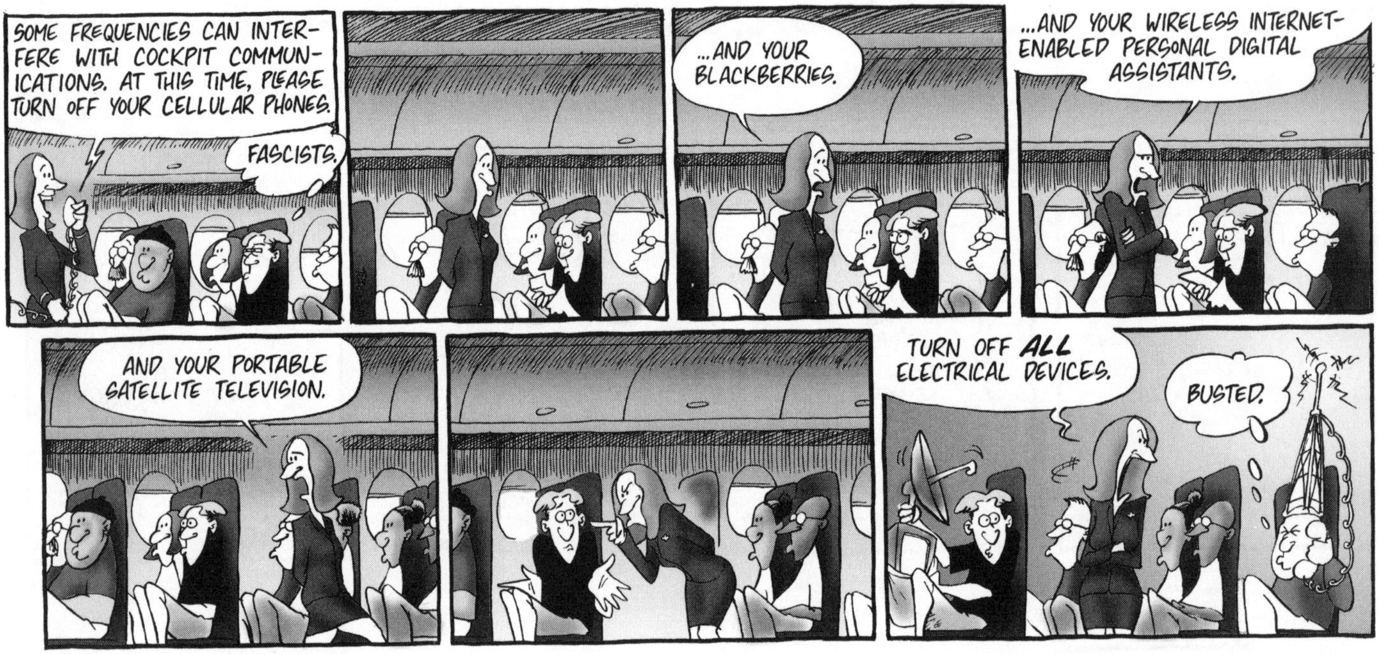
SOME FREQUENCIES CAN INTERFERE WITH COCKPIT COMMUNICATIONS. AT THIS TIME, PLEASE TURN OFF YOUR CELLULAR PHONES.
FASCISTS.
...AND YOUR BLACKBERRIES.
...AND YOUR WIRELESS INTERNET-ENABLED PERSONAL DIGITAL ASSISTANTS.
AND YOUR PORTABLE SATELLITE TELEVISION.
TURN OFF ALL ELECTRICAL DEVICES.
BUSTED.

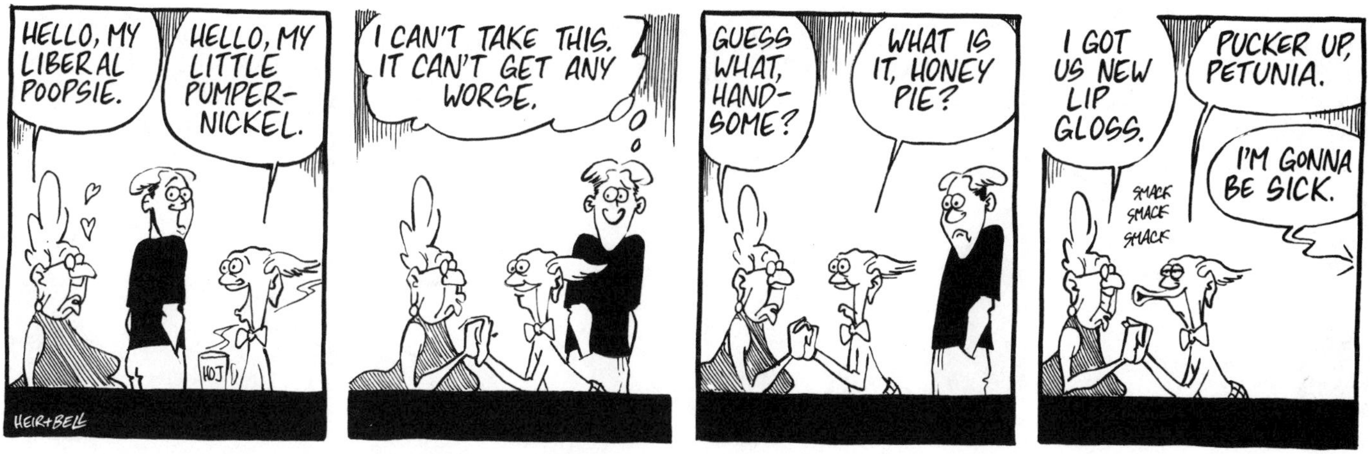
HELLO, MY LIBERAL POOPSIE.
HELLO, MY LITTLE PUMPER-NICKEL.
I CAN'T TAKE THIS. IT CAN'T GET ANY WORSE.
GUESS WHAT, HAND-SOME?
WHAT IS IT, HONEY PIE?
I GOT US NEW LIP GLOSS.
SMACK SMACK SMACK
PUCKER UP, PETUNIA.
I'M GONNA BE SICK.
HEIR+BELL

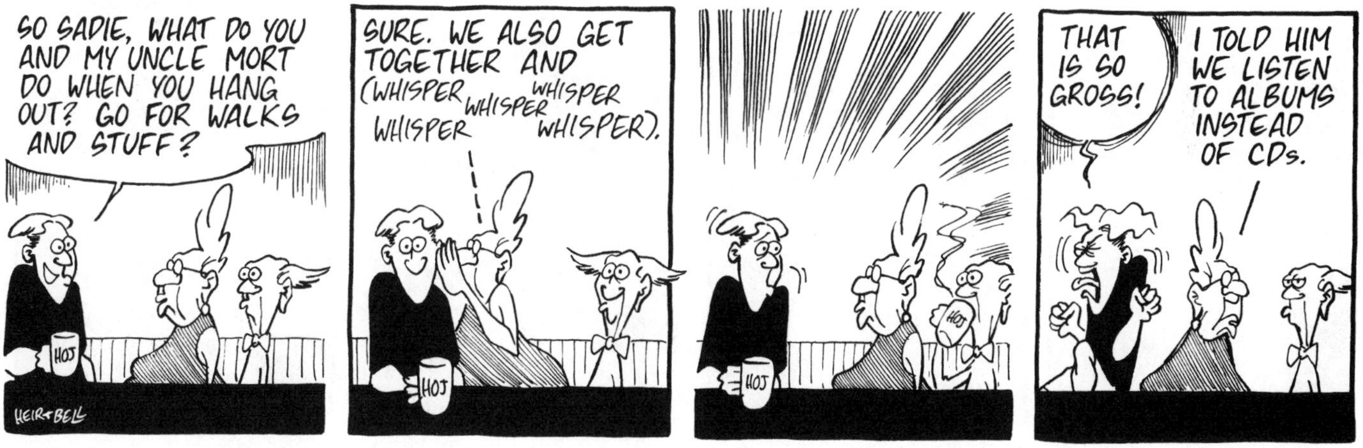
SO SADIE, WHAT DO YOU AND MY UNCLE MORT DO WHEN YOU HANG OUT? GO FOR WALKS AND STUFF?
SURE. WE ALSO GET TOGETHER AND (WHISPER WHISPER WHISPER WHISPER WHISPER).
THAT IS SO GROSS!
I TOLD HIM WE LISTEN TO ALBUMS INSTEAD OF CDs.
HEIR+BELL

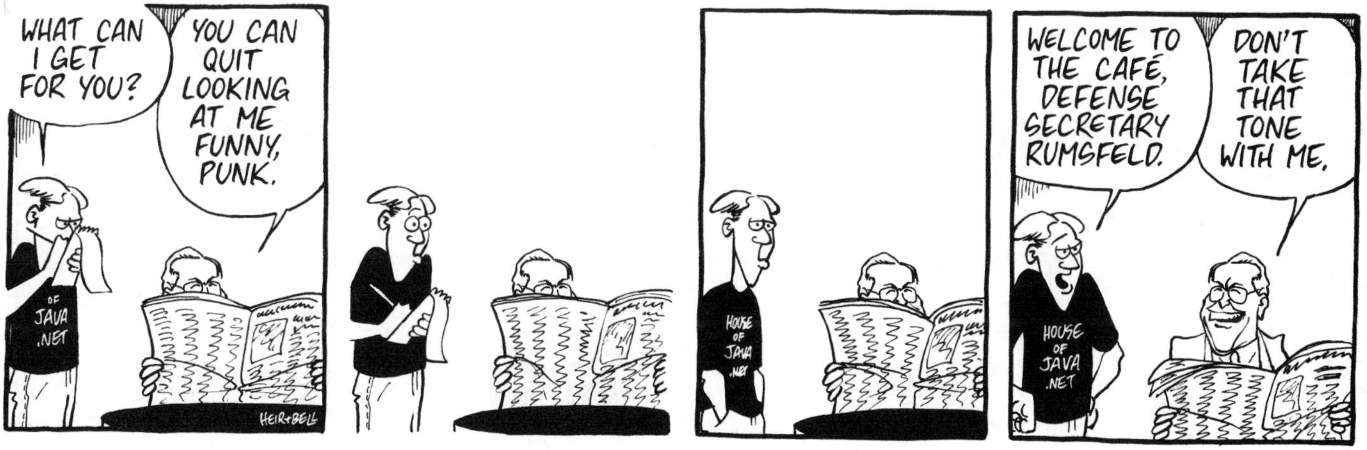
WHAT CAN I GET FOR YOU?
YOU CAN QUIT LOOKING AT ME FUNNY, PUNK.
WELCOME TO THE CAFÉ, DEFENSE SECRETARY RUMSFELD.
DON'T TAKE THAT TONE WITH ME.
HEIR+BELL

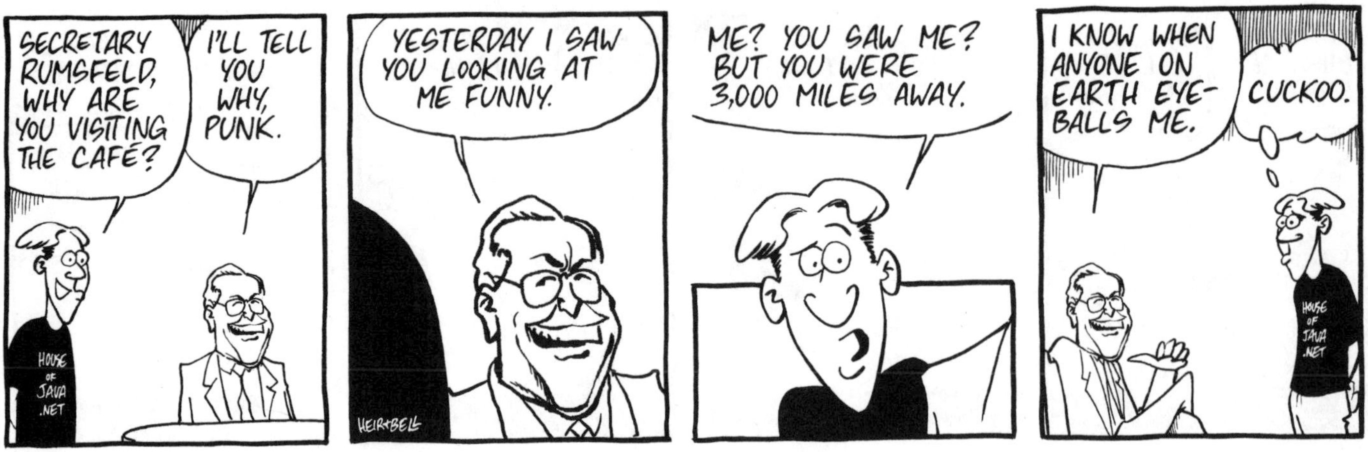
SECRETARY RUMSFELD, WHY ARE YOU VISITING THE CAFÉ?
I'LL TELL YOU WHY, PUNK.
YESTERDAY I SAW YOU LOOKING AT ME FUNNY.
ME? YOU SAW ME? BUT YOU WERE 3,000 MILES AWAY.
I KNOW WHEN ANYONE ON EARTH EYE-BALLS ME.
CUCKOO.

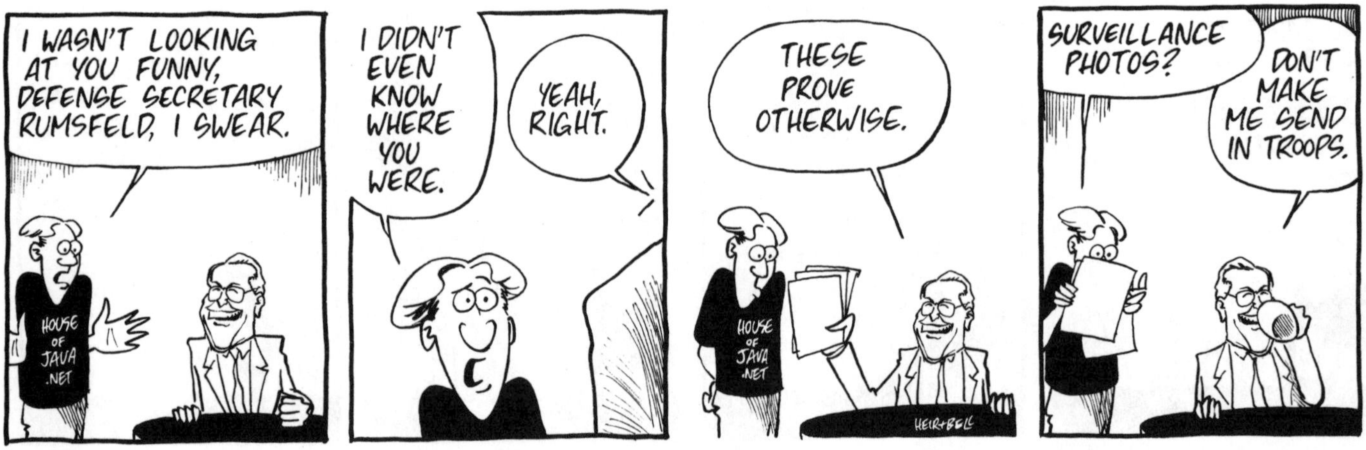
I WASN'T LOOKING AT YOU FUNNY, DEFENSE SECRETARY RUMSFELD, I SWEAR.
I DIDN'T EVEN KNOW WHERE YOU WERE.
YEAH, RIGHT.
THESE PROVE OTHERWISE.
SURVEILLANCE PHOTOS?
DON'T MAKE ME SEND IN TROOPS.

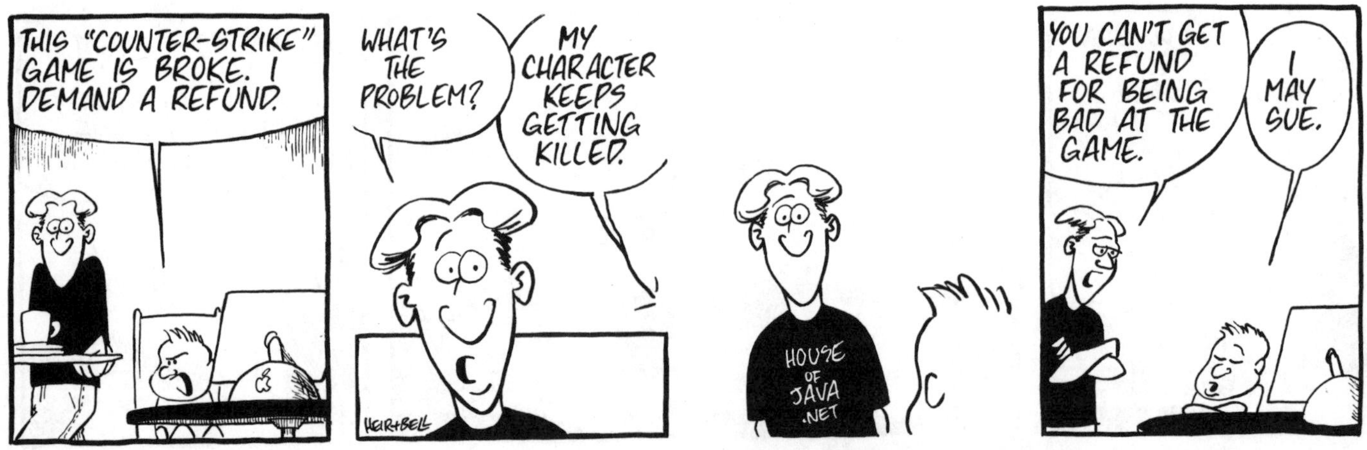
THIS "COUNTER-STRIKE" GAME IS BROKE. I DEMAND A REFUND.
WHAT'S THE PROBLEM?
MY CHARACTER KEEPS GETTING KILLED.
YOU CAN'T GET A REFUND FOR BEING BAD AT THE GAME.
I MAY SUE.

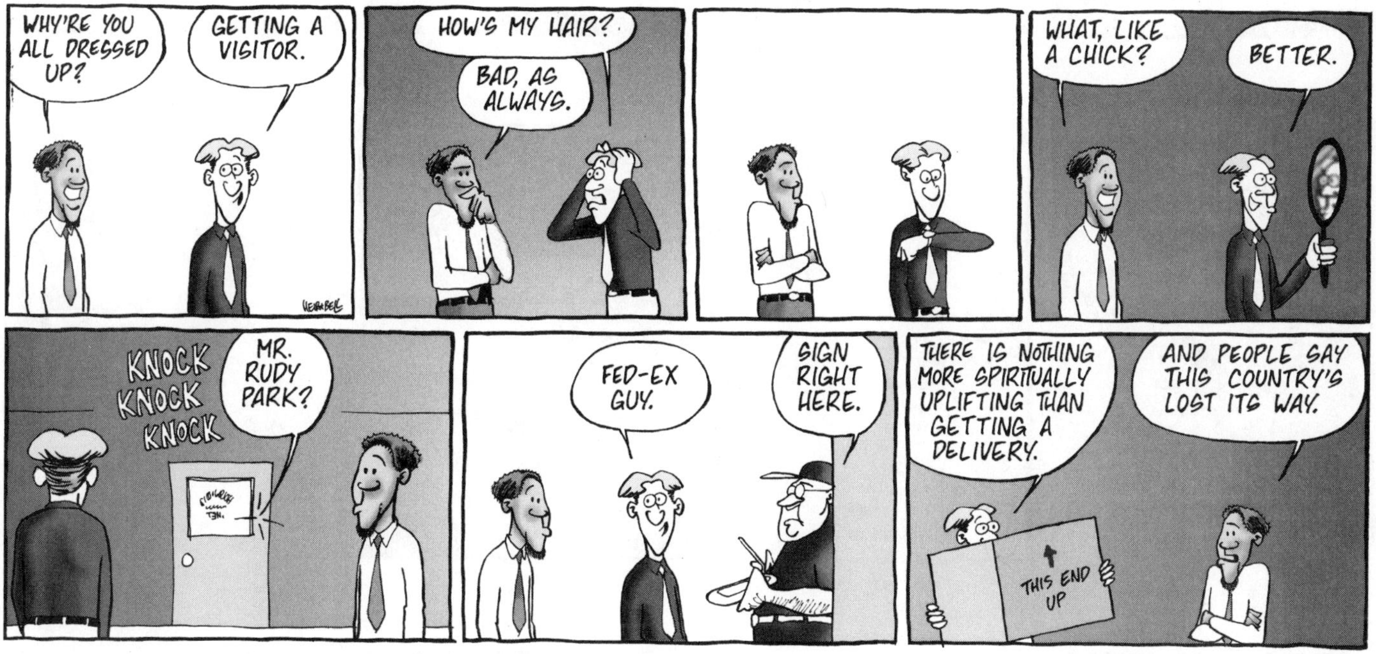
WHY'RE YOU ALL DRESSED UP?
GETTING A VISITOR.
HOW'S MY HAIR?
BAD, AS ALWAYS.
WHAT, LIKE A CHICK?
BETTER.
KNOCK KNOCK KNOCK
MR. RUDY PARK?
FED-EX GUY.
SIGN RIGHT HERE.
THERE IS NOTHING MORE SPIRITUALLY UPLIFTING THAN GETTING A DELIVERY.
AND PEOPLE SAY THIS COUNTRY'S LOST ITS WAY.
THIS END UP

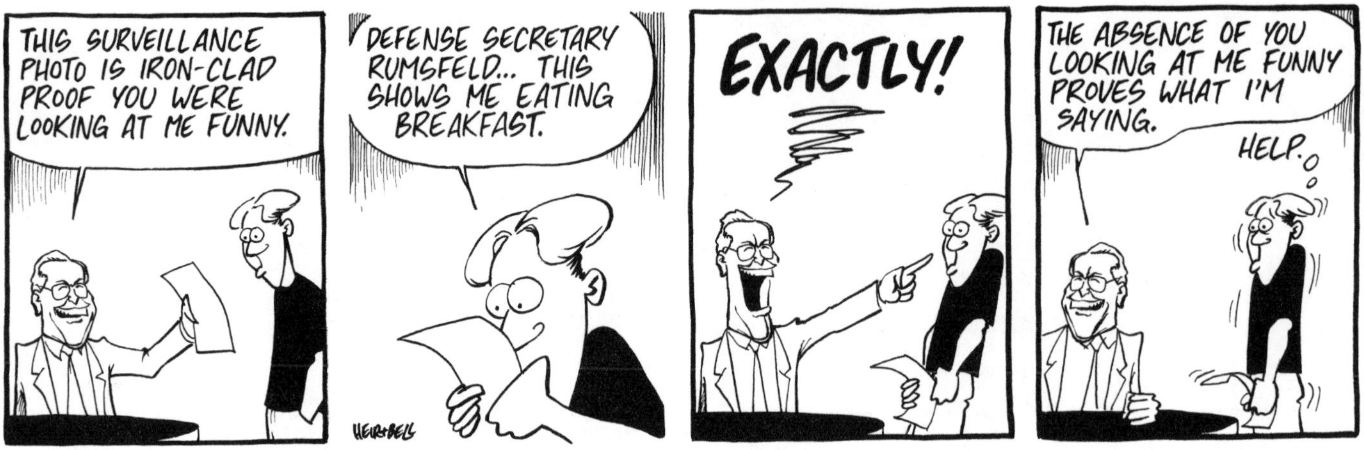
THIS SURVEILLANCE PHOTO IS IRON-CLAD PROOF YOU WERE LOOKING AT ME FUNNY.
DEFENSE SECRETARY RUMSFELD... THIS SHOWS ME EATING BREAKFAST.
EXACTLY!
THE ABSENCE OF YOU LOOKING AT ME FUNNY PROVES WHAT I'M SAYING.
HELP.

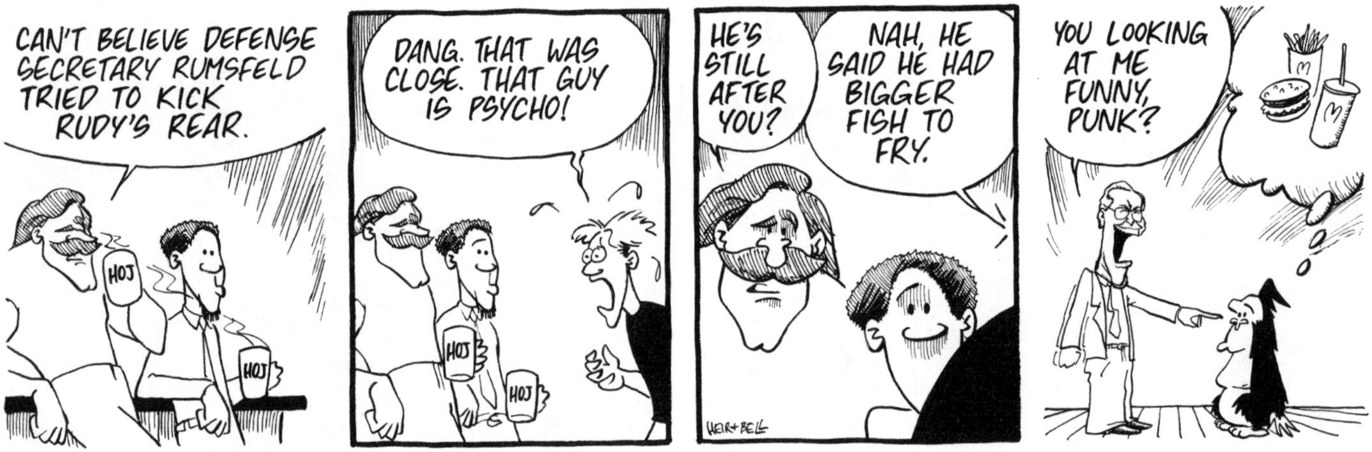
CAN'T BELIEVE DEFENSE SECRETARY RUMSFELD TRIED TO KICK RUDY'S REAR.
HOJ
HOJ
DANG. THAT WAS CLOSE. THAT GUY IS PSYCHO!
HOJ
HOJ
HE'S STILL AFTER YOU?
NAH, HE SAID HE HAD BIGGER FISH TO FRY.
YOU LOOKING AT ME FUNNY, PUNK?

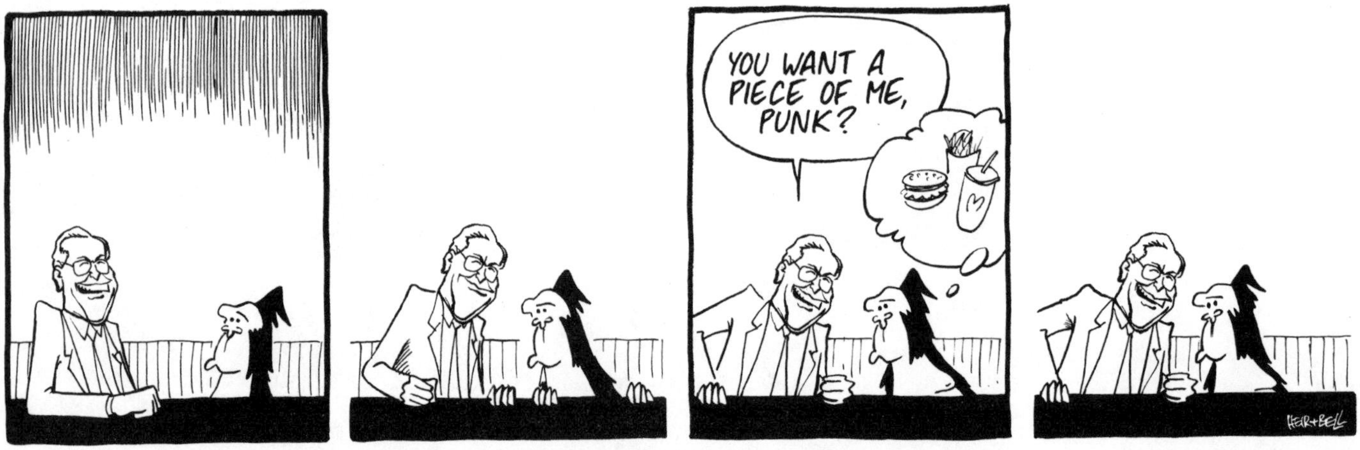
YOU WANT A PIECE OF ME, PUNK?

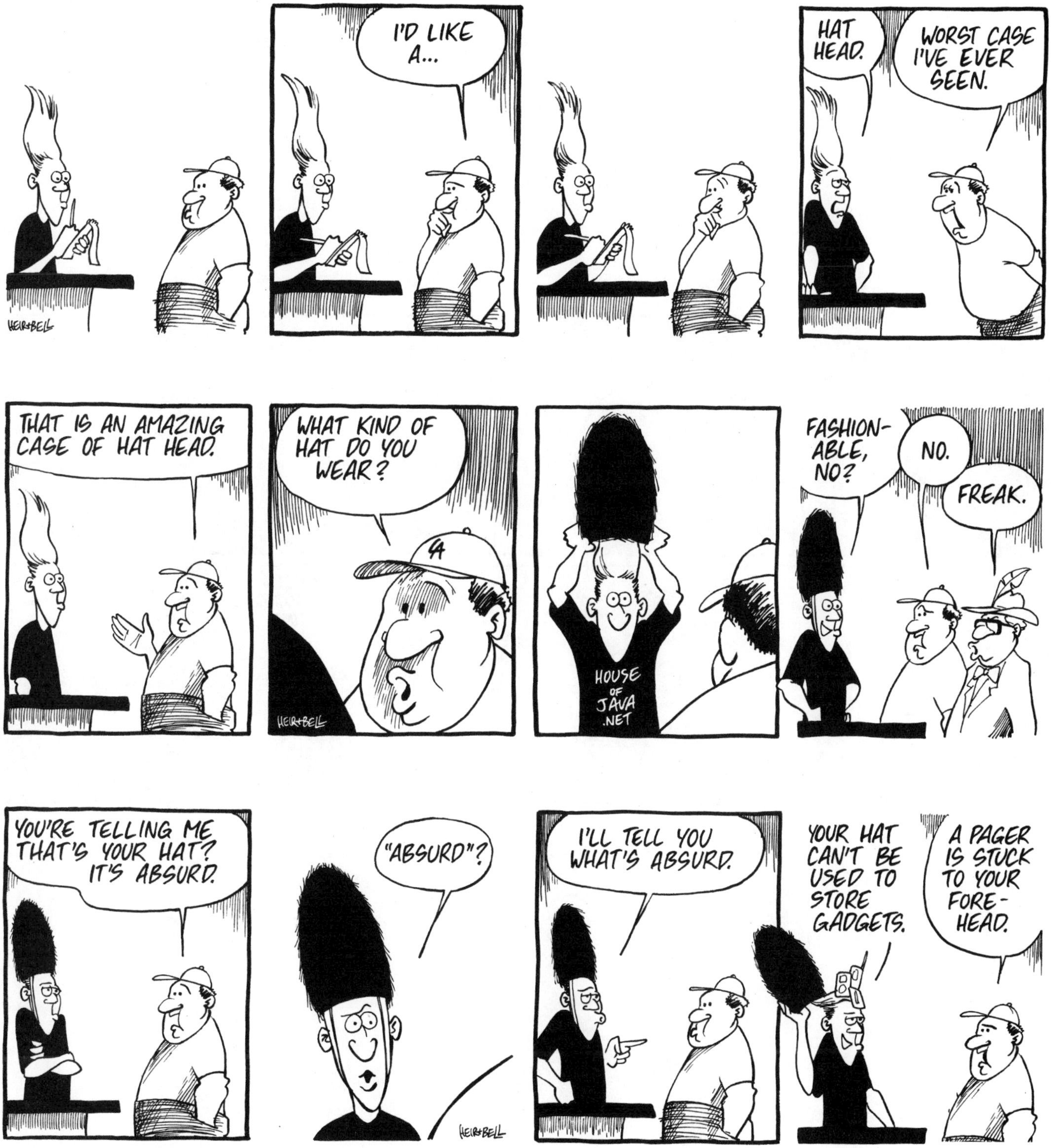
I'D LIKE A...
HAT HEAD.
WORST CASE I'VE EVER SEEN.
THAT IS AN AMAZING CASE OF HAT HEAD.
WHAT KIND OF HAT DO YOU WEAR?
HOUSE OF JAVA .NET
FASHION-ABLE, NO?
NO.
FREAK.
YOU'RE TELLING ME THAT'S YOUR HAT? IT'S ABSURD.
"ABSURD"?
I'LL TELL YOU WHAT'S ABSURD.
YOUR HAT CAN'T BE USED TO STORE GADGETS.
A PAGER IS STUCK TO YOUR FORE-HEAD.

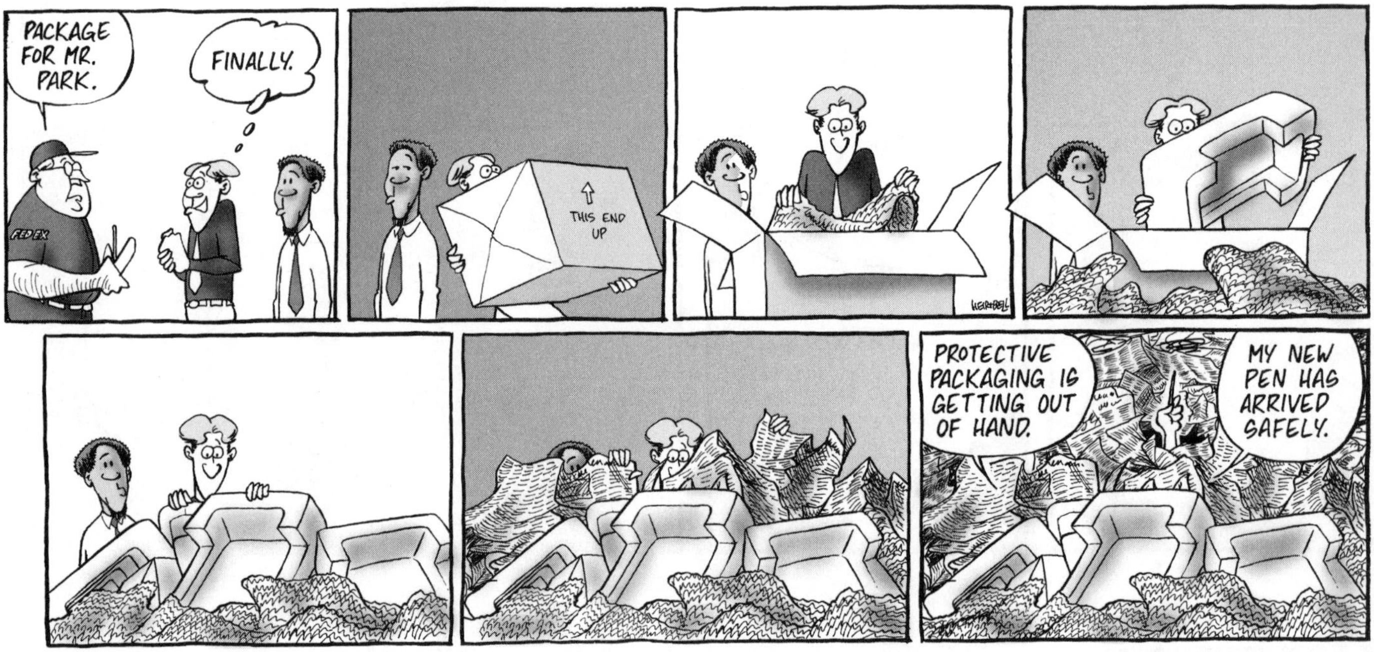
PACKAGE FOR MR. PARK.
FINALLY.
THIS END UP
PROTECTIVE PACKAGING IS GETTING OUT OF HAND.
MY NEW PEN HAS ARRIVED SAFELY.

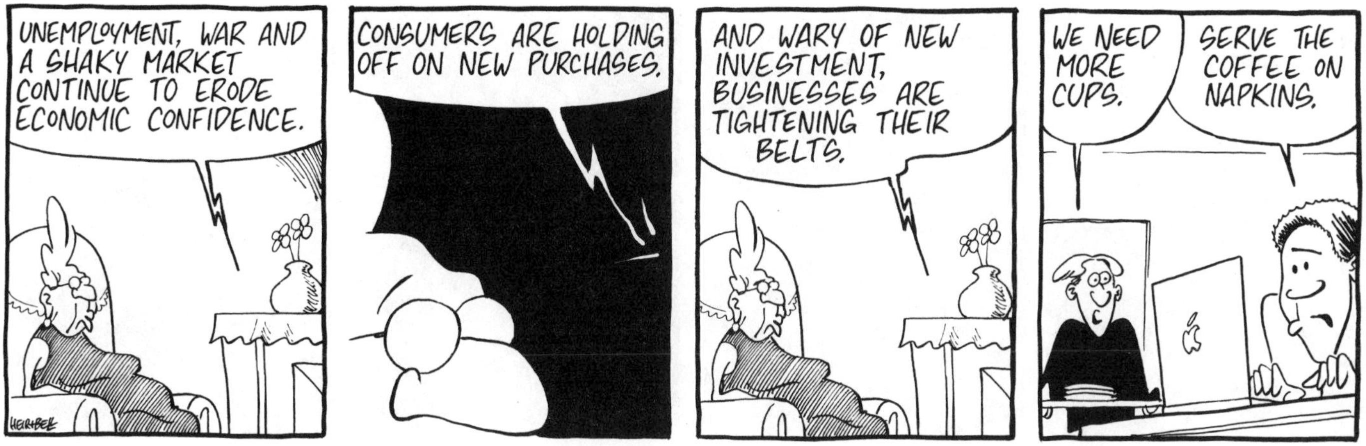
UNEMPLOYMENT, WAR AND A SHAKY MARKET CONTINUE TO ERODE ECONOMIC CONFIDENCE.
CONSUMERS ARE HOLDING OFF ON NEW PURCHASES.
AND WARY OF NEW INVESTMENT, BUSINESSES ARE TIGHTENING THEIR BELTS.
WE NEED MORE CUPS.
SERVE THE COFFEE ON NAPKINS.

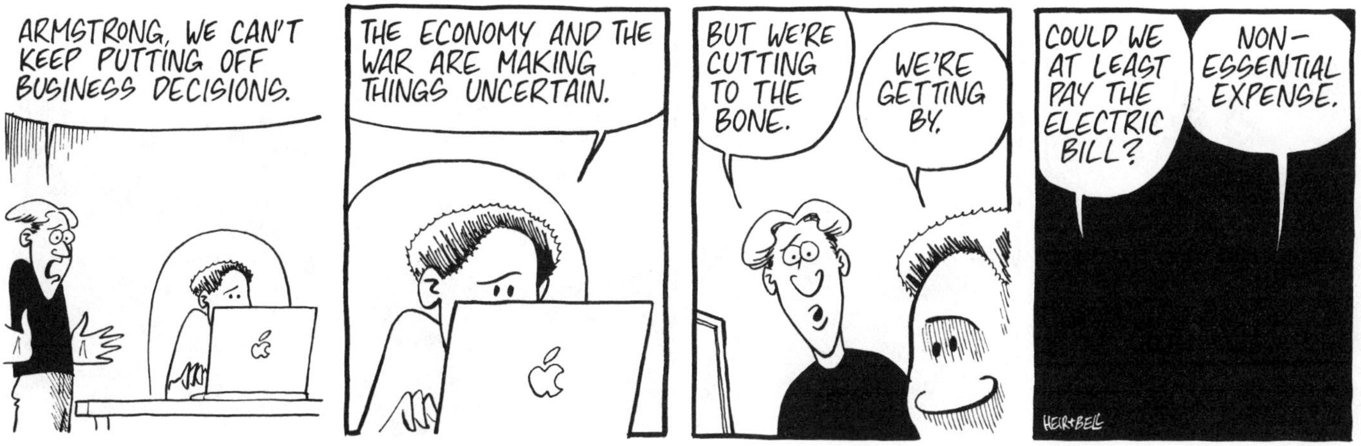
ARMSTRONG, WE CAN'T KEEP PUTTING OFF BUSINESS DECISIONS.
THE ECONOMY AND THE WAR ARE MAKING THINGS UNCERTAIN.
BUT WE'RE CUTTING TO THE BONE.
WE'RE GETTING BY.
COULD WE AT LEAST PAY THE ELECTRIC BILL?
NON-ESSENTIAL EXPENSE.

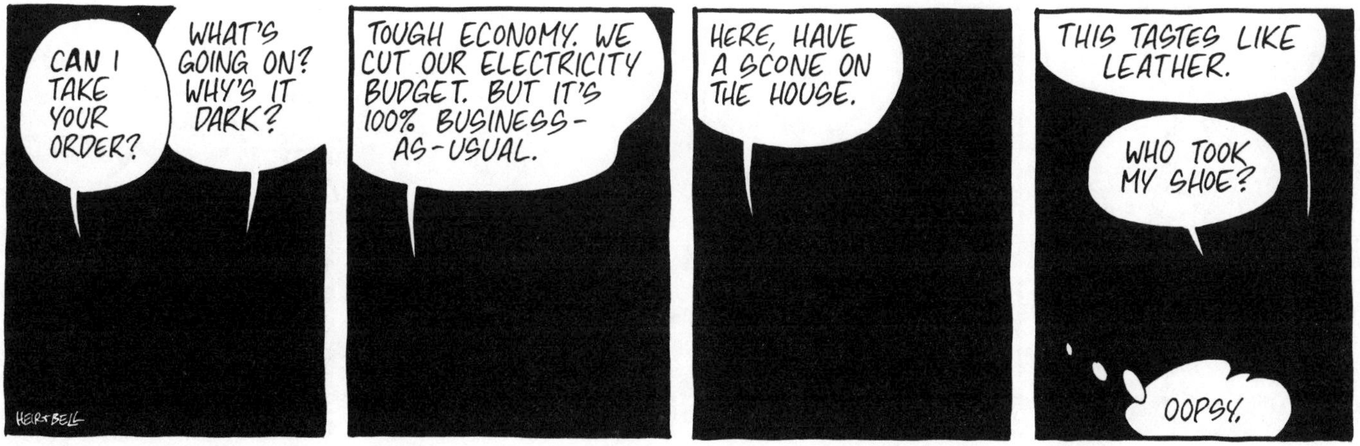
CAN I TAKE YOUR ORDER?
WHAT'S GOING ON? WHY'S IT DARK?
TOUGH ECONOMY. WE CUT OUR ELECTRICITY BUDGET. BUT IT'S 100% BUSINESS-AS-USUAL.
HERE, HAVE A SCONE ON THE HOUSE.
THIS TASTES LIKE LEATHER.
WHO TOOK MY SHOE?
OOPSY.

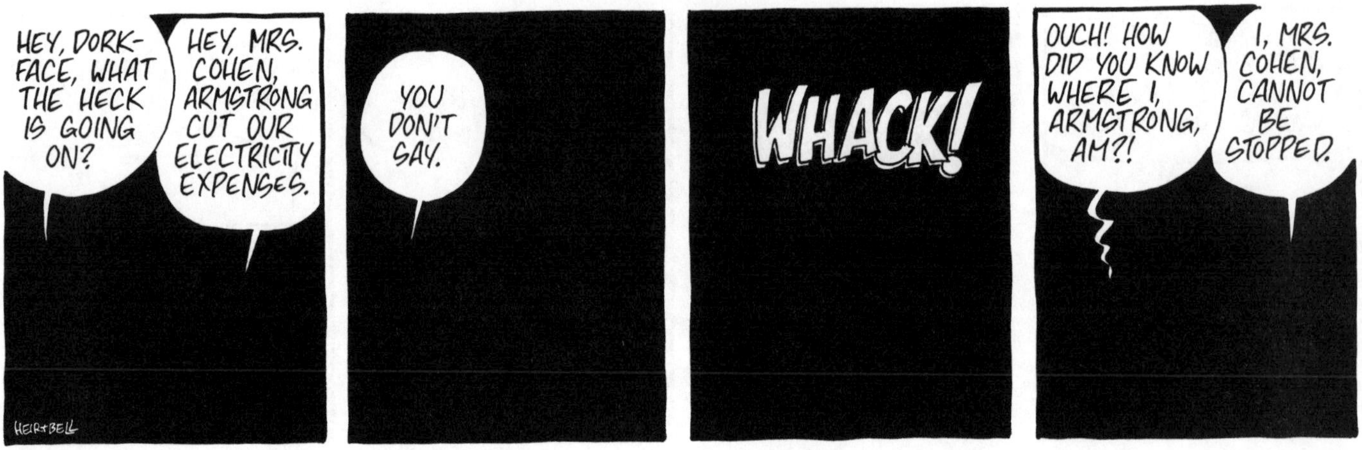
HEY, DORK-FACE, WHAT THE HECK IS GOING ON?
HEY, MRS. COHEN, ARMSTRONG CUT OUR ELECTRICITY EXPENSES.
HEIR+BELL
YOU DON'T SAY.
WHACK!
OUCH! HOW DID YOU KNOW WHERE I, ARMSTRONG, AM?!
I, MRS. COHEN, CANNOT BE STOPPED.

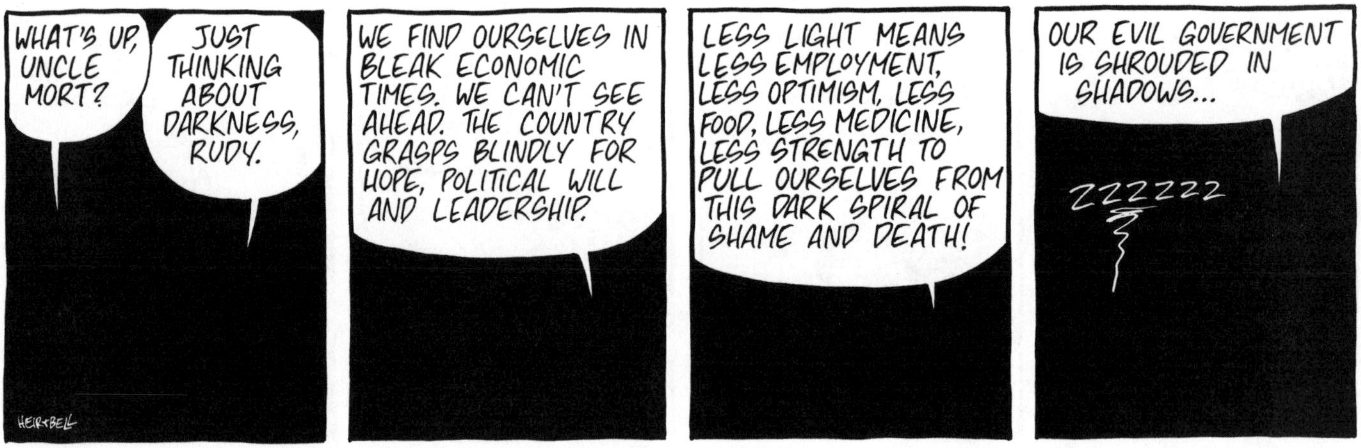
WHAT'S UP, UNCLE MORT?
JUST THINKING ABOUT DARKNESS, RUDY.
HEIR+BELL
WE FIND OURSELVES IN BLEAK ECONOMIC TIMES. WE CAN'T SEE AHEAD. THE COUNTRY GRASPS BLINDLY FOR HOPE, POLITICAL WILL AND LEADERSHIP.
LESS LIGHT MEANS LESS EMPLOYMENT, LESS OPTIMISM, LESS FOOD, LESS MEDICINE, LESS STRENGTH TO PULL OURSELVES FROM THIS DARK SPIRAL OF SHAME AND DEATH!
OUR EVIL GOVERNMENT IS SHROUDED IN SHADOWS...
ZZZZZZ

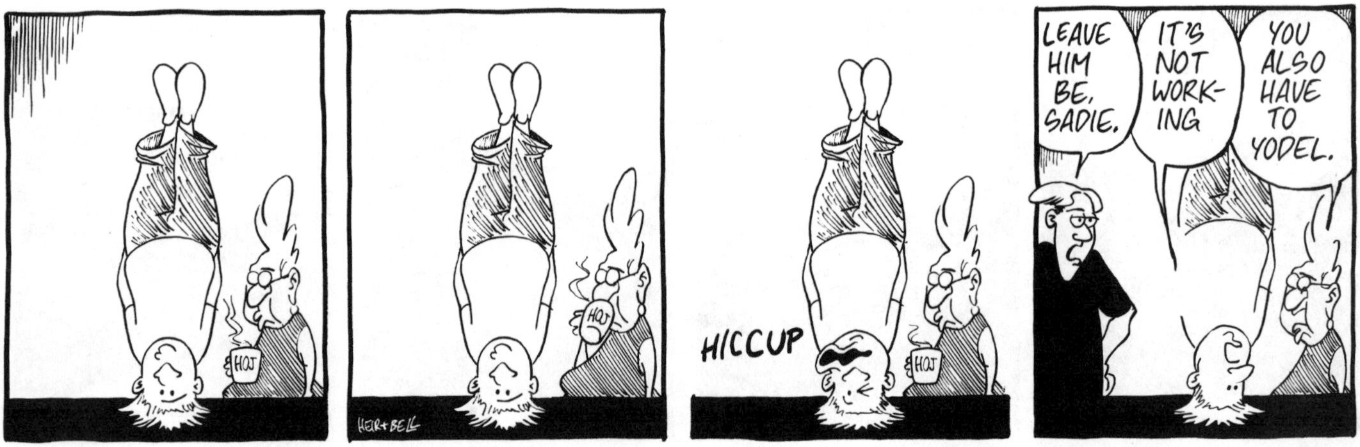
HOJ
HEIR+BELL
HICCUP
LEAVE HIM BE, SADIE.
IT'S NOT WORK-ING
YOU ALSO HAVE TO YODEL.

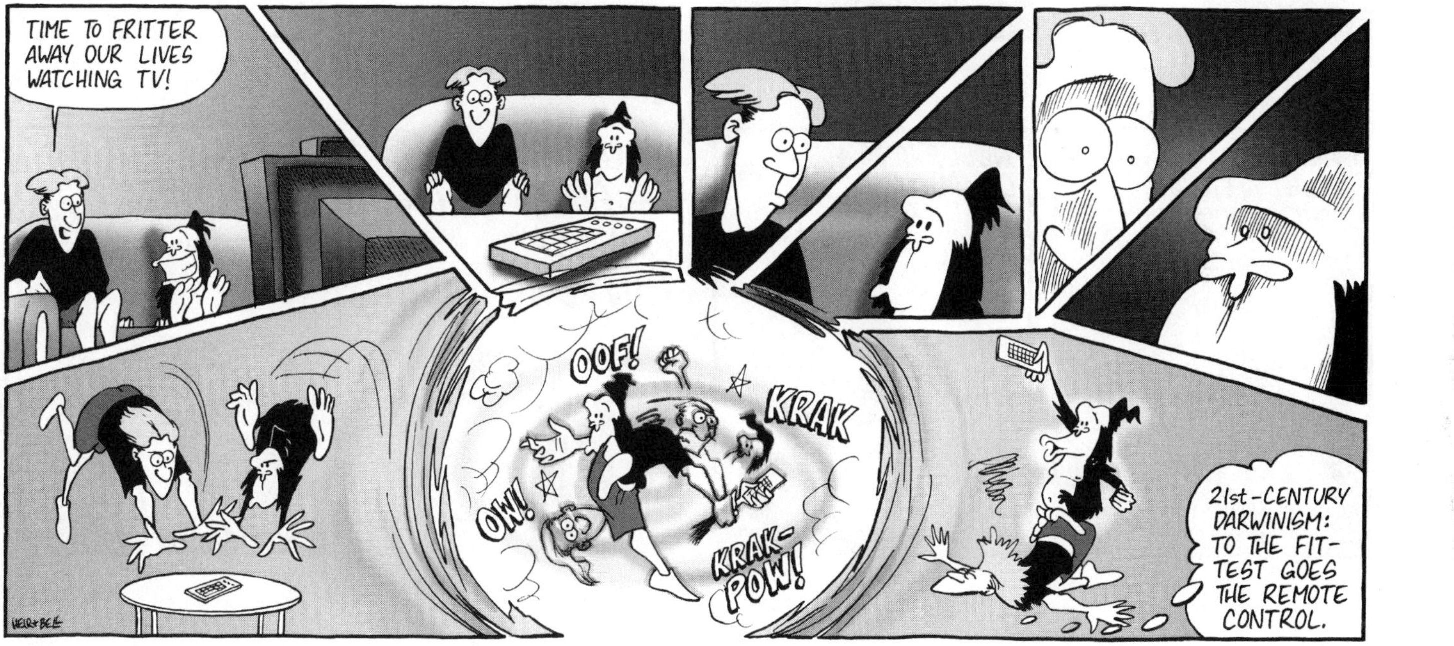
TIME TO FRITTER AWAY OUR LIVES WATCHING TV!
OOF!
KRAK
OW!
KRAK-POW!
21st-CENTURY DARWINISM: TO THE FIT-TEST GOES THE REMOTE CONTROL.
HEIR+BELL

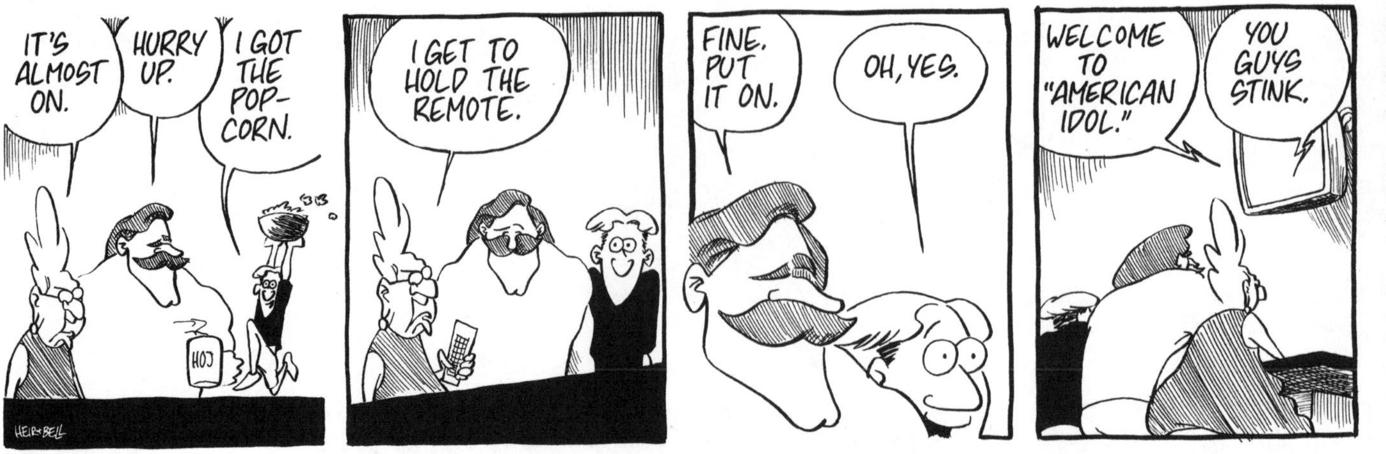
IT'S ALMOST ON.
HURRY UP.
I GOT THE POP-CORN.
I GET TO HOLD THE REMOTE.
FINE. PUT IT ON.
OH, YES.
WELCOME TO "AMERICAN IDOL."
YOU GUYS STINK.

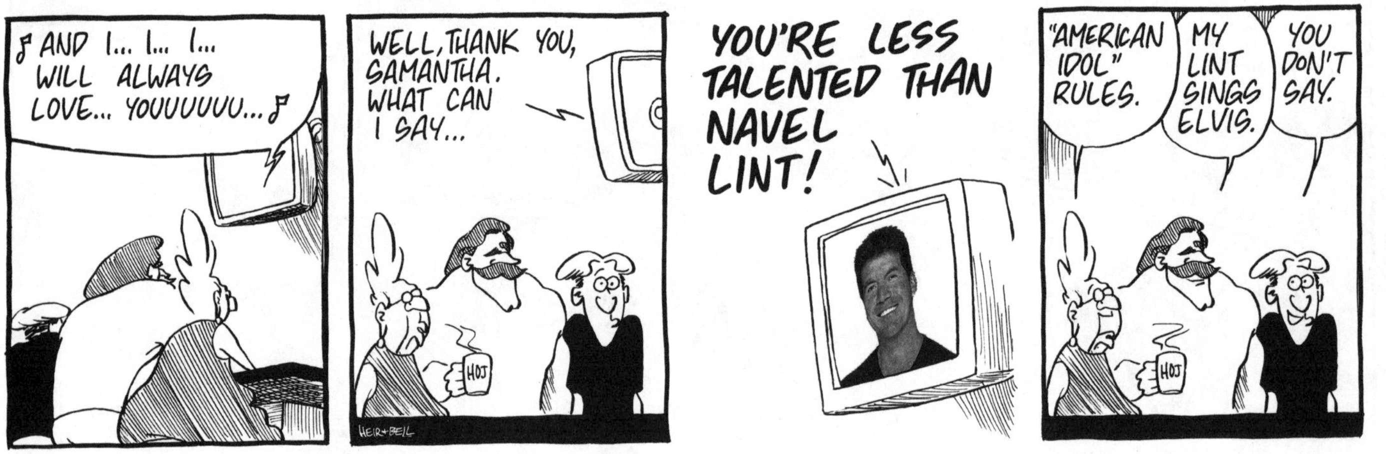
AND I... I... I... WILL ALWAYS LOVE... YOUUUUUU...
WELL, THANK YOU, SAMANTHA. WHAT CAN I SAY...
YOU'RE LESS TALENTED THAN NAVEL LINT!
"AMERICAN IDOL" RULES.
MY LINT SINGS ELVIS.
YOU DON'T SAY.

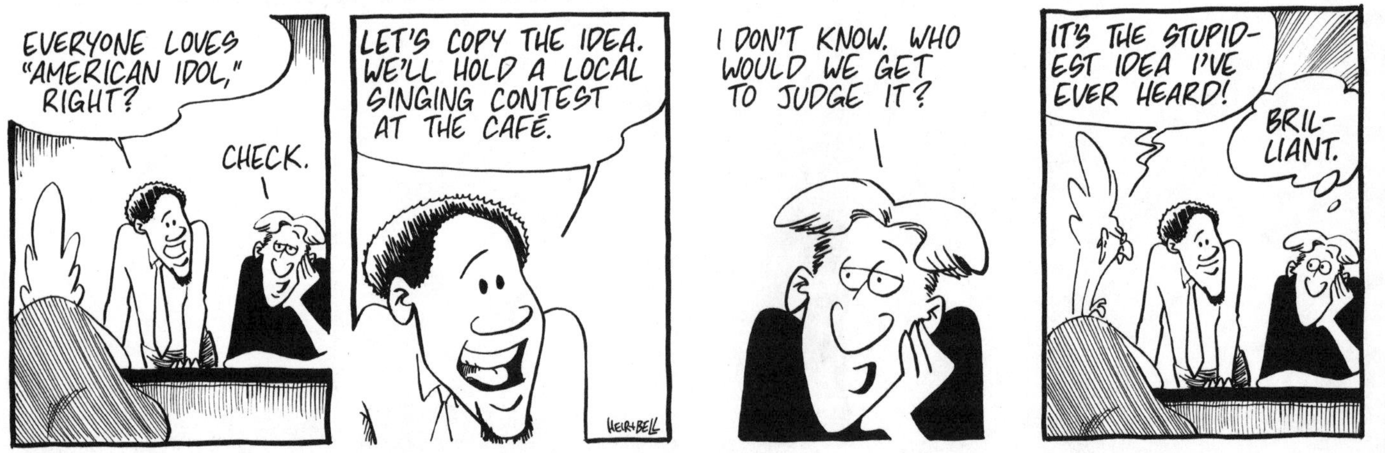
EVERYONE LOVES "AMERICAN IDOL," RIGHT?
CHECK.
LET'S COPY THE IDEA. WE'LL HOLD A LOCAL SINGING CONTEST AT THE CAFÉ.
I DON'T KNOW. WHO WOULD WE GET TO JUDGE IT?
IT'S THE STUPID-EST IDEA I'VE EVER HEARD!
BRIL-LIANT.

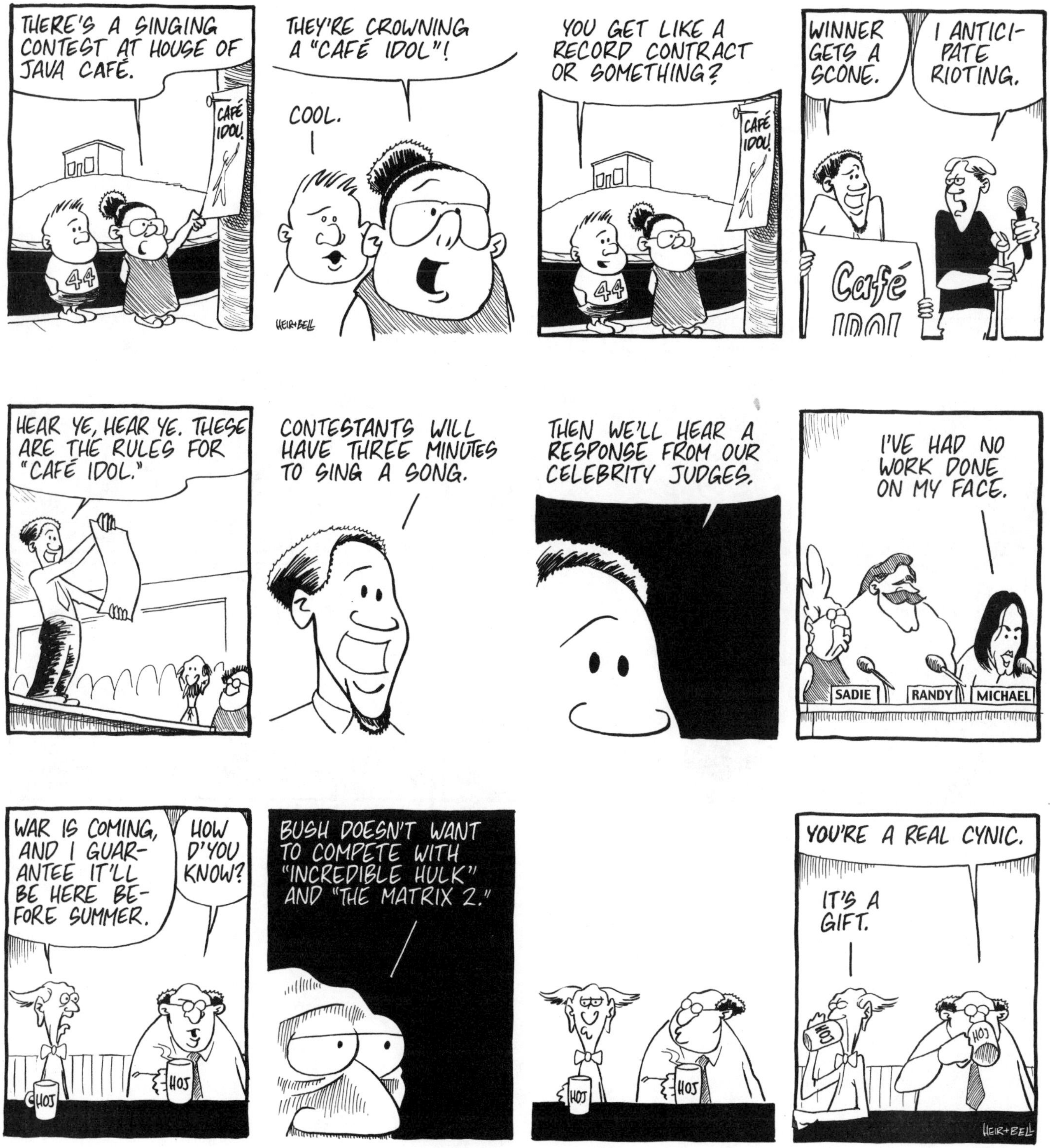
THERE'S A SINGING CONTEST AT HOUSE OF JAVA CAFÉ.
CAFÉ IDOL
THEY'RE CROWNING A "CAFÉ IDOL"!
COOL.
HEIR+BELL
YOU GET LIKE A RECORD CONTRACT OR SOMETHING?
CAFÉ IDOL
WINNER GETS A SCONE.
I ANTICIPATE RIOTING.
Café IDOL
HEAR YE, HEAR YE. THESE ARE THE RULES FOR "CAFÉ IDOL."
CONTESTANTS WILL HAVE THREE MINUTES TO SING A SONG.
THEN WE'LL HEAR A RESPONSE FROM OUR CELEBRITY JUDGES.
I'VE HAD NO WORK DONE ON MY FACE.
SADIE
RANDY
MICHAEL
WAR IS COMING, AND I GUARANTEE IT'LL BE HERE BEFORE SUMMER.
HOW D'YOU KNOW?
HOJ
HOJ
BUSH DOESN'T WANT TO COMPETE WITH "INCREDIBLE HULK" AND "THE MATRIX 2."
HOJ
HOJ
YOU'RE A REAL CYNIC.
IT'S A GIFT.
HOJ
HEIR+BELL

YOUR USUAL BURGER, MRS. MEEMAW?
TURKEY SANDWICH. I RESOLVED FOR NEW YEAR'S TO EAT HEALTHY!
"NEW YEAR'S"? THAT WAS THREE MONTHS AGO.
WHY, YOU'RE RIGHT, YOUNG FELLA. HOW SILLY OF ME.
HEIR+BELL
THEN IT'S TIME TO FACE THE UGLY TRUTH.
A SALAD THEN?
SPECIALS
LATTE+ 1 hour WEB $7.50
NO, THE TRUTH IS, YOU CAN'T START A DIET IN THE MIDDLE OF THE YEAR.
I SEE.
SO YOU'LL BEGIN IN JANUARY.
YES...
...THOUGH WHY START A DIET IN THE MIDDLE OF A DECADE?
BURGERS 'TIL 2010.
I'LL QUIT SMOKING AT THE MILLENNIUM.
HOUSE OF JAVA
HOJ

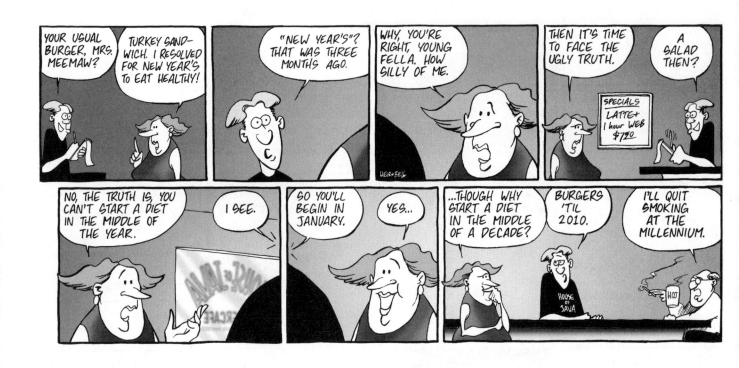

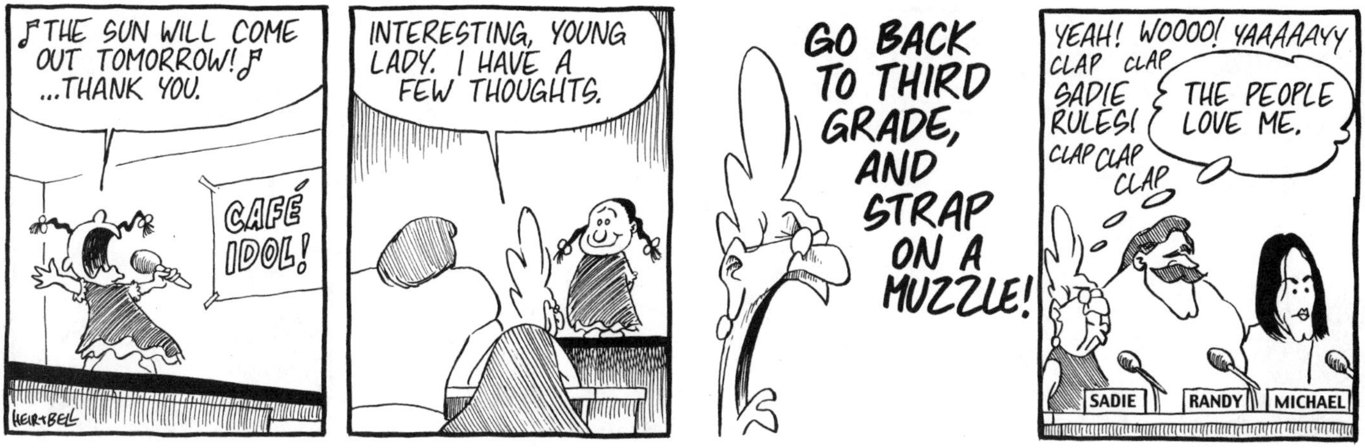
♪THE SUN WILL COME OUT TOMORROW!♪ ...THANK YOU.
CAFÉ IDOL!
HEIR+BELL
INTERESTING, YOUNG LADY. I HAVE A FEW THOUGHTS.
GO BACK TO THIRD GRADE, AND STRAP ON A MUZZLE!
YEAH! WOOOO! YAAAAAYY
CLAP CLAP
SADIE RULES!
CLAP CLAP CLAP
THE PEOPLE LOVE ME.
SADIE
RANDY
MICHAEL

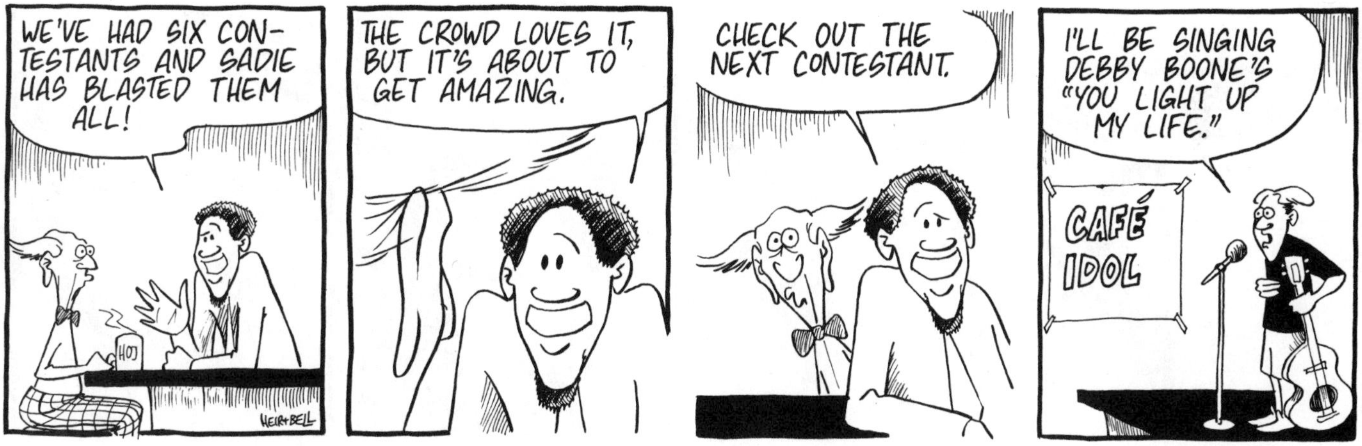
WE'VE HAD SIX CONTESTANTS AND SADIE HAS BLASTED THEM ALL!
HOT
HEIR+BELL
THE CROWD LOVES IT, BUT IT'S ABOUT TO GET AMAZING.
CHECK OUT THE NEXT CONTESTANT.
I'LL BE SINGING DEBBY BOONE'S "YOU LIGHT UP MY LIFE."
CAFÉ IDOL

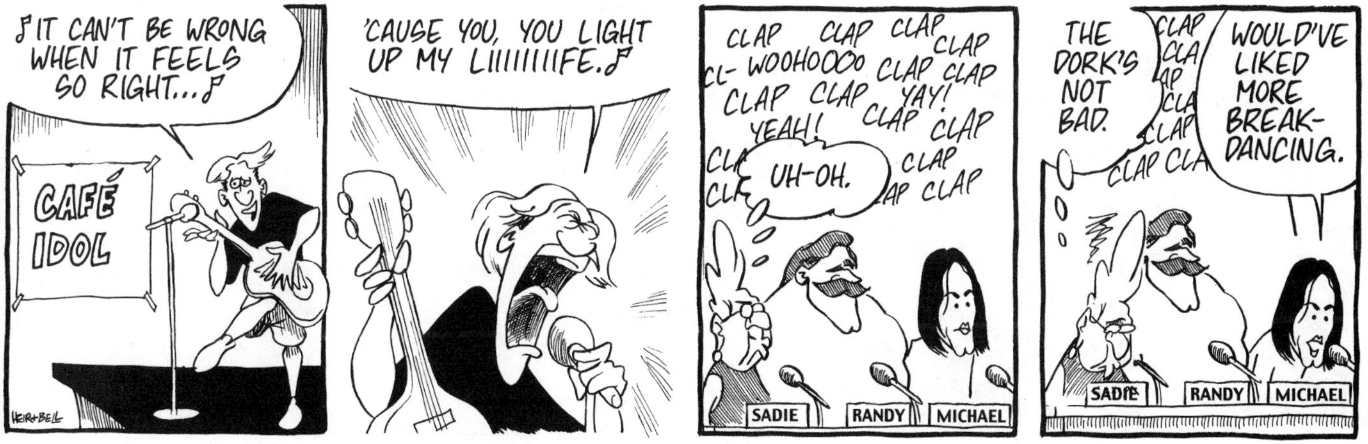
♪IT CAN'T BE WRONG WHEN IT FEELS SO RIGHT...♪
CAFÉ IDOL
HEIR+BELL
'CAUSE YOU, YOU LIGHT UP MY LIIIIIIIFE.♪
CLAP CLAP CLAP CLAP
WOOHOOOO CLAP CLAP
CLAP CLAP YAY!
YEAH! CLAP CLAP
CLAP CLAP
UH-OH.
SADIE
RANDY
MICHAEL
THE DORK'S NOT BAD.
CLAP CLA
WOULD'VE LIKED MORE BREAK-DANCING.
SADIE
RANDY
MICHAEL

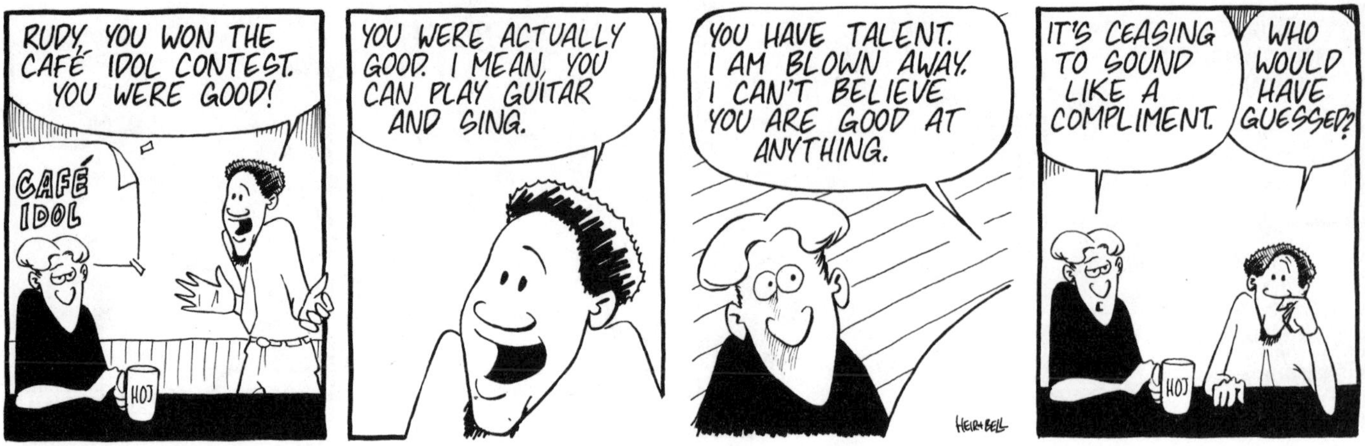
RUDY, YOU WON THE CAFÉ IDOL CONTEST. YOU WERE GOOD!
CAFÉ IDOL
HOJ
YOU WERE ACTUALLY GOOD. I MEAN, YOU CAN PLAY GUITAR AND SING.
YOU HAVE TALENT. I AM BLOWN AWAY. I CAN'T BELIEVE YOU ARE GOOD AT ANYTHING.
HEIR+BELL
IT'S CEASING TO SOUND LIKE A COMPLIMENT.
WHO WOULD HAVE GUESSED?
HOJ

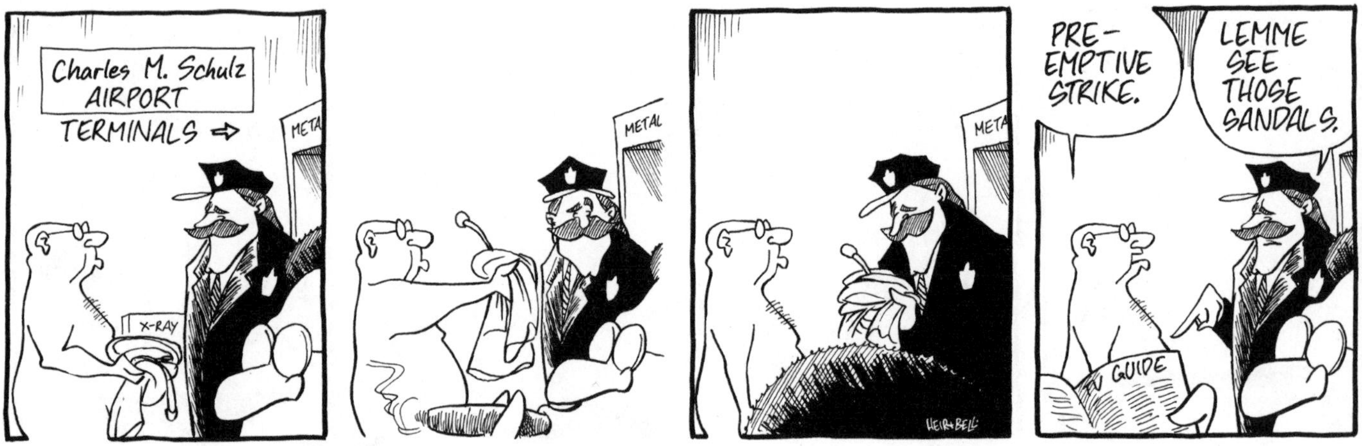
Charles M. Schulz AIRPORT
TERMINALS ⇨
META
X-RAY
METAL
META
HEIR+BELL
PRE-EMPTIVE STRIKE.
LEMME SEE THOSE SANDALS.
TV GUIDE

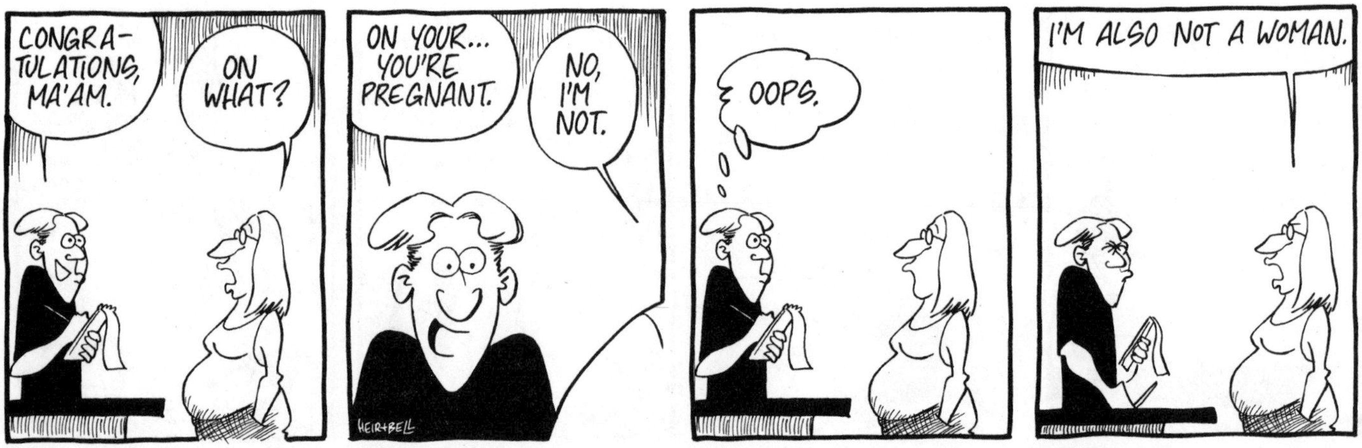
CONGRATULATIONS, MA'AM.
ON WHAT?
ON YOUR... YOU'RE PREGNANT.
NO, I'M NOT.
HEIR+BELL
OOPS.
I'M ALSO NOT A WOMAN.